SRA Art Connections

A comprehensive K–5 art program that integrates the four dimensions of art into every lesson.

Level K
Level 1
Level 2
Level 3
Level 4
Level 5

● **Art History and Culture**

Explore the great art, artists, and cultures of the world.

● **Aesthetic Perception**

Develop an understanding and appreciation for art.

● **Creative Expression in Art Production**

Encounter a broad range of art media in a variety of hands-on art activities that give students an avenue for self-expression and self-esteem.

● **Art Criticism**

Enrich critical thinking skills as students learn about the elements and principles of art through examining their own and others' artwork.

Plus *Art Connections* provides resources to **integrate the visu** into reading/language arts, math, science, social studies, and tech as well as the other arts—music, dance, and theater.

Meets national standards and state guidelines for art education.

A carefully crafted framework makes the big picture easy to see.

Art Connections, a new K–5 art program from SRA, is designed to prove that art is much more than oil paint on canvas. Through this comprehensive program, students can experience the entire spectrum of art education.

- **Student Editions** for every grade level with **Big Book** versions of the student books for K–2.

- **Teacher Editions** for each grade level.

Level 4 Student Edition

Level 4 Teacher Edition

Fine Art Resources

- Overhead Transparency Study Prints (36 per grade level)

- Large Prints (12 per grade level)

- Artist Profiles
  (1 book per grade level)

- Animals Through History Time Line

- Literature and Art Videos
  (6 per grade level)

- ARTSOURCE Audio/ Video Resource Package
  (1 per grade level)

- National Museum of Women in the Arts Collection

Lesson Enrichment Resources

- Vocabulary Book (English/Spanish, 36 activities per grade level)

- Assessment Book (English/Spanish, 36 assessments per grade level)

- Art Across the Curriculum Book (36 Reading/Language Arts, Math, Science, Social Studies, The Arts, and Technology activities per grade level)

- Student Artist Portfolio

- Art Manipulative Kit

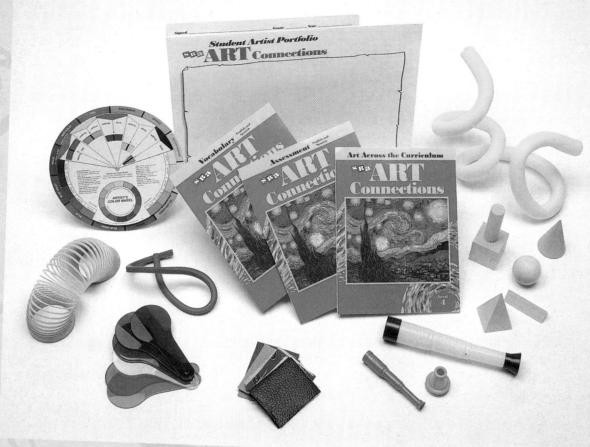

Multimedia Resources

- Literature and Art Video Collection (6 per grade level)

- Listening Cassettes in the Art Manipulative Kit (set of six selections)

- ARTSOURCE Audio/ Video Resource Package (1 per grade level)

- National Museum of Women in the Arts Collection CD-ROM and Videodisc

- Davidson's Multimedia Workshop CD-ROM

- National Geographic Picture Atlas of the World CD-ROM

- Internet Museum Resource Lists in the **Teacher Edition**

Mold a lifelong appreciation of art.

Each lesson in the **Student Edition** integrates objectives from the four art disciplines of aesthetic perception, creative expression, art history and culture, and art criticism.

Grade Levels
K–2 Student Editions

- **Big Book** versions of the student books provide the youngest students with an overview of the topics, so even nonreaders can participate in the learning.

- Thirty-six two-page lessons in each grade level give K–2 students enough information to challenge them, without overwhelming them with details.

K–2 Student Edition and Big Book

Unit 1 Lesson 3

Lines Can Show Feelings

Claude Monet. (French). *Poplars on the Epte.* 1891. Tate Gallery, London, England/Art Resource, New York.

This artist used vertical lines for the trees. What kind of line did he use to paint the shoreline? All the lines work together to give a feeling of stillness and quiet.

Seeing like an artist
Think of objects in your neighborhood that look like the lines in Monet's painting.

Unit 1

18

Level 2

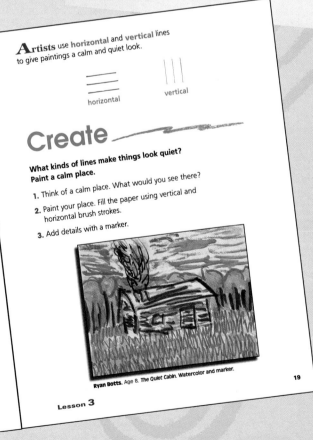

Artists use **horizontal** and **vertical** lines to give paintings a calm and quiet look.

horizontal   vertical

Create

What kinds of lines make things look quiet? Paint a calm place.

1. Think of a calm place. What would you see there?

2. Paint your place. Fill the paper using vertical and horizontal brush strokes.

3. Add details with a marker.

Ryan Botts. Age 8. *The Quiet Cabin.* Watercolor and marker.

Lesson 3

19

Grade Levels
3–5 Student Editions

- Four-page lessons provide more in-depth concept development and background information for older students who are ready for more challenging material.

- Two fine artworks in each lesson encourage students to compare art from around the world.

- **Elements and Principles of Art** such as line, shape, color, form, texture, balance, emphasis, and unity are the focus of *every* unit and lesson to help students understand and appreciate art on a more meaningful level.

- *Every* lesson starts with a form of **fine art** such as painting, sculpture, architecture, fabric art, printmaking, photography, or jewelry, so students see how artists put the elements and principles of art into play.

- **Student artwork** is featured in *every* lesson to help students see that they too can be artists and can integrate the elements and principles of art into the paintings and drawings they create.

- **Create** art activities featuring a wide array of media are incorporated into *every* lesson, so students get frequent hands-on practice building their artistic skills.

Unit 3 Lesson 1

The Color Wheel

Artists use the color wheel to organize colors and understand how they work together.

David Hockney. (English). *Large Interior Los Angeles.* 1988. Oil, ink on cut and pasted paper on canvas. Metropolitan Museum of Art, New York, New York. © David Hockney.

Both paintings on these pages use a wide range of color. David Hockney used a combination of bright primary colors with neutral colors in his painting. Stuart Davis used a mix of bright colors and unusual shapes. Notice how color is the most important element in both paintings.

Unit 3

Stuart Davis. (American). *Report from Rockport.* 1940. Oil on canvas. 24 × 30 inches. Metropolitan Museum of Art, NY, Edith and Milton Lowenthal Collection, Bequest of Edith Abrahamson Lowenthal, 1991.

Both artists use a variety of colors in their artwork.

- What colors did the artists use in their artworks?
- How did they separate colors in their artworks?
- Do the colors in each piece of art create the same feeling?
- If both artworks were done in only browns, blacks, and whites, would they communicate the same feelings and moods? Explain your answer.

SEEING LIKE AN ARTIST

Look around your classroom and notice how most objects have a dominant color.

Lesson 1

Level 4

77

The Color Spectrum

The colors in the color spectrum—red, orange, yellow, green, blue, and violet—appear in the same order in natural light. A rainbow is nature's color spectrum.

Red, yellow, and blue are the primary colors. You cannot mix any other colors to make them.

Secondary colors—orange, green, and violet—are created when two primary colors are mixed together. Primary and secondary colors are also called hues.

Intermediate colors are made by blending a primary color with a secondary color. Red-orange is an example of one of the six intermediate colors.

This color wheel is made up of three primary, three secondary, and six intermediate colors. Notice how the colors are organized so that you can easily understand how to mix a color.

Practice

Create a geometric design. Use crayon.

1. Use a black marker to draw one large geometric shape touching at least two edges of a sheet of paper. Draw a second geometric shape inside your first shape, and then a third shape inside your second shape. Inside each section create geometric patterns.

2. Fill your design with color. In the center shape use primary colors. In the middle shape use secondary colors. In the outside shape use intermediate colors.

Decide Does your design have primary colors at the center, secondary colors in the middle, and intermediate colors in the outside? What changes would you make?

78

Level 4

Unit 3

Amy Kus. Age 9. Mixed-media.

How did this student artist create a color wheel?

Create

What colors do you imagine you would see if you were a deep-sea diver in the Caribbean Sea? Create an undersea color-wheel drawing.

1. Imagine yourself swimming in the ocean. What creatures would you see?

2. Using pencil, draw a sea creature as large as your hand, adding details such as scales and teeth. Create an environment for your creature. Outline your drawing with black marker.

3. Divide your picture into 12 pie-shaped sections. Color each section as if it were part of a color wheel. Try to create as many of the colors as you can.

Describe What colors did you use in your drawing?

Analyze How did you create the intermediate colors in your drawing?

Interpret What would you choose as a title for your drawing?

Decide Were you successful in keeping your color wheel in sequenced order? Can you think of other themes that could be made into a color wheel?

Lesson 1

79

The learning curve is drawn with much more than a crayon, a marker, or a paintbrush.

As they move from lesson to lesson, students will discover that every line, brush stroke, and carefully drawn curve they see can lead to a better understanding of artists, their surroundings, and the times in which they lived.

● **Artist Profiles** in every unit allow students to meet a master artist, analyze the artist's work, and discuss the techniques and art concepts that were used to create that work.

● **ARTSOURCE lessons** at the end of every unit were developed by the Music Center of Los Angeles County to provide arts integration. These dynamic lessons show how the elements and principles of visual arts can be translated into **music, dance,** or **theater.**

Artists use different types of **forms** to communicate their feelings and ideas and to show how they see the world. They also create forms for use in daily life.

• What is the difference between this sculpture and a drawing?
• Describe the open and solid areas of the sculpture. What basic shape do you see?
• Point out the mother and child in this sculpture. What did Henry Moore do to the figures? Why do you think he did this?
• From how many sides would you view this sculpture? Do you think Moore intended his viewers to observe this sculpture from many angles? Explain why.

Artist Profile

Henry Moore
1898–1986

Sculptor

The English sculptor Henry Moore created many larger-than-life sculptures in stone, wood, and metals such as lead and bronze. He liked to simplify his forms into basic shapes without details. Many of Moore's works have *family* as the theme. He is viewed as one of the greatest and most original sculptors of the twentieth century.

Henry Moore and other sculptors use form to communicate an idea or to create a useful object. In this unit you will learn about using form to express ideas and to understand different ways that artists create forms. Here are the topics you will study.

• Additive Sculpture   • Subtractive Sculpture   • Masks
• Forms   • Assembled Forms

105

Level 4

Balance, Harmony, Variety, and Unity in Dance

Lily Cai Chinese Dance Company: *"The Flying Goddess."*

Lily Cai performs traditional dances from ancient Chinese culture. In the picture above, she performs a Chinese ribbon dance called "The Flying Goddess." The flying and floating of the red ribbons represent the spirit of a goddess. The dance patterns are based on circles. The dancer moves in a variety of visual patterns. She creates balance, harmony, variety, and unity in her dance.

190   Unit 6

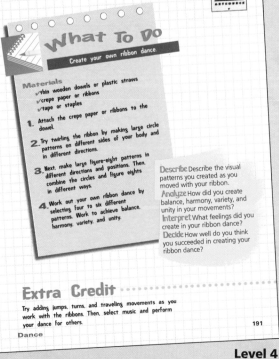

What To Do
Create your own ribbon dance

Materials
✓thin wooden dowels or plastic straws
✓crepe paper or ribbons
✓tape or staples

1. Attach the crepe paper or ribbons to the dowel.
2. Try twirling the ribbon by making large circle patterns on different sides of your body and in different directions.
3. Next, make large figure-eight patterns in different directions and positions. Then, combine the circles and figure eights in different ways.
4. Work out your own ribbon dance by selecting four to six different patterns. Work to achieve balance, harmony, variety, and unity.

Describe Describe the visual patterns you created as you moved with your ribbon.
Analyze How did you create balance, harmony, variety, and unity in your movements?
Interpret What feelings did you create in your ribbon dance?
Decide How well do you think you succeeded in creating your ribbon dance?

Extra Credit
Try adding jumps, turns, and traveling movements as you work with the ribbons. Then, select music and perform your dance for others.

Dance   191

Level 4

• More About . . .

These extra lessons in the back of each book give students an easy-to-access resource for additional information on lesson material in the following areas:

- Art Techniques
- Art Criticism
- Aesthetics
- Art History Around the World
- Art Subject Matter
- Drawing

More About...
Art History

Rembrandt van Rijn.
Self-Portrait.
1660. The Netherlands.

Leonardo da Vinci.
Mona Lisa.
1503–1505. Italy.

Artist unknown.
Bayon Temple Angkor Thom.
1100s–1200s. Cambodia.

Artist unknown.
Shrine Head. (Yorub).
1100–1300. Nigeria.

Torii Kiyotada.
Actor of the Ichikawa Clan.
1710–1740. Japan.

218

More About...Art History

 A.D. 1000–1800

Artist unknown.
Chartes Cathedral.
1145–1220. France.

Thomas Jefferson.
Monticello.
1770–1784. United States.

Artist unknown.
Bayeux Tapestry. (Detail).
1070–1080. England.

Artist unknown.
Anasazi culture petroglyphs.
United States.

Artist unknown.
Taj Mahal.
1632–1648. India.

More About...Art History

219

Level 4

---

2. **Picture plane** is the surface of a drawing. There are three parts of a picture plane—foreground, background, middle ground.
3. **Point of View** is the angle from which the viewer sees an object in artwork.
4. **Tactile Texture** is what artists use to show how things actually feel. (rough, smooth, shiny, matte)

Summing Up

Look at *Old Mesilla Plaza* painted by Leon Trousset. The artist used the techniques covered in this unit to create space and texture.

- Has Trousset used all six perspective techniques? Try to identify at least one example of each technique.
- How many different kinds of textures can you find?
- Does the artist use visual texture to imitate the texture of the wagon, ground, and trees, or does he show the texture of the paint?

Space and texture are important elements in paintings and drawings. By using techniques to create space and textures, artists express to others what they see.

Let's Visit a Museum

The Smithsonian Institution was established in 1846 with funds from the will of the English scientist, James Smithson. Today there are more than 140 million artifacts, exhibits, and works of art at the Smithsonian. It is also a center for research in the arts, sciences, and history. It is made of 16 museums and galleries, several research centers, and the National Zoo. Nine of the museums are located on the National Mall in Washington, DC, between the Capitol and Washington Monument.

The Smithsonian Institution

Level 4

• Museum Profiles help students develop an early appreciation of these fascinating and ever-changing places.

• Career Connections help students discover that art careers are not always defined by a paintbrush and an easel.

- **Alternating rhythm** has a motif that is changed in some way or a second motif is introduced.
- **Flowing rhythm** is created by repeating curved lines or shapes.
3. **Visual movement** is the illusion of motion or change in position. There are two types of visual movement.
- **Frozen** — The movement or action is frozen in time much like a photograph.
- **Progressive** — When a scene or object changes a little each time it is repeated.

Summing Up

Look at the painting by Johnson. He created figures using simplified shapes and repeated areas of color. They create rhythm and movement, which you learned about in this unit.

- Which shapes has Johnson repeated?
- Describe how Johnson created rhythm in his painting.
- Did Johnson use movement? If so, what type?

Shape, rhythm, and movement are important design principles that artists use to communicate to others what they see.

Careers in Art
Landscape Architect

David Barncord is a landscape architect. Landscape architects plan outdoor areas for people. They pay careful attention to protecting the environment. Barncord loved baseball as a boy, but there were no baseball fields near his home. He began laying out his own baseball fields when he was six years old. In his profession he works with architects, engineers, gardeners, building contractors, and various government officials. Barncord got his college degree in landscape architecture. He works long hours and meets many people in his work.

David Barncord, landscape architect

73

With this palette of features, every class will have the signature of a true master.

The Teacher Edition for each grade level K–5, contains all the tools needed to add color and texture to every art class. This easy-to-use resource provides the power to deliver a masterful presentation, page by page, lesson by lesson.

● **Self-contained lessons** enable the presentation of topics in any order to suit individual teaching styles and curriculum.

● **Three-stage "Focus, Teach, Close" lesson cycle** gives complete directions for presenting each lesson in a format that will reach students most effectively.

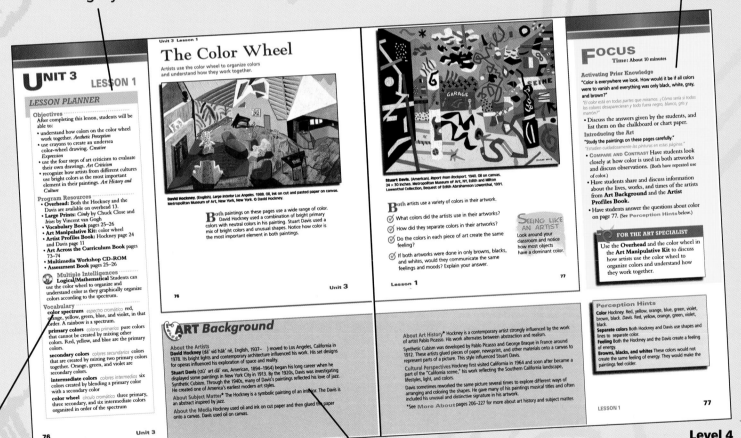

● **Multiple Intelligences** identifies the primary ways of learning in each lesson.

● **Vocabulary** in English and Spanish includes definitions to provide a single-source reference for the new vocabulary words students will master.

● **Art Background** provides the necessary detail to make every art topic more enriching and meaningful.

Level 4

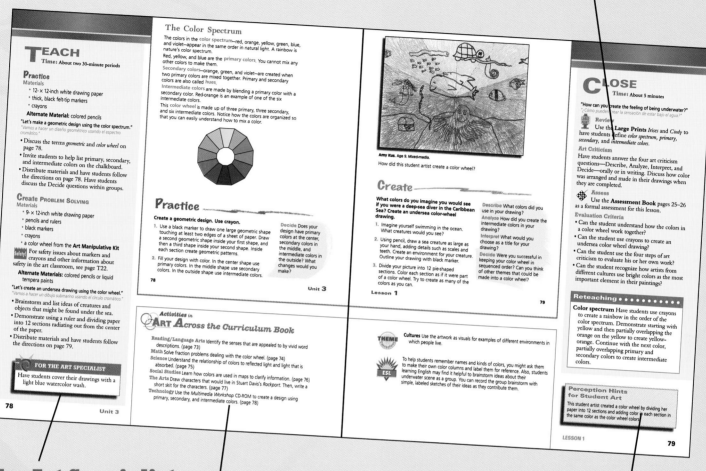

Professional Development

Comprehensive Teacher Edition reference resources at the back of the book include:

- Professional development articles about teaching, assessing, and enriching art education
- Museum Resources
- Program Scope and Sequence
- Program Glossary
- Program Index
- Art Across the Curriculum Index

With Art Connections, support is never an abstract concept.

These materials help send students' imaginations soaring with each new lesson topic they explore.

Fine Art Resources

Overhead Transparency Study Prints K–5

The 36 transparencies of the fine art in each lesson enable teachers to highlight specific elements of the artwork, so students can develop a better understanding of each concept they're studying, and how those concepts apply to actual pieces of art.

Artist Profiles K–5

This teacher/student resource book profiles the artists covered in each **Student Edition**, so students can better understand each artist's inspiration— and the completed work.

Large Prints K–5 (English/Spanish)

There are 12 Large Prints for each grade level featuring art that does not appear in the **Student Edition**. Each one focuses on a specific unit concept to easily integrate additional artwork into every unit. Large Prints are referenced at point of use in the **Teacher Edition** and feature detailed information about the artist, the media, the times, the subject, and the culture on the back of each print in both English and Spanish.

Animals Through History Time Line K–5

Students can use the animal artwork in this time line to trace how animals have been depicted in art throughout history, as they discover that art has always been a fundamental part of life. On the back of the time line, look for profiles of key museums in the United States.

The National Museum of Women in the Arts Collection

Developed in conjunction with the National Museum of Women in the Arts, this program includes 200 works by key women artists. The collection includes Art Prints, Art Cards, a Videodisc, and a CD-ROM to enlist a whole range of media to hold students' attention.

Lesson Enrichment Resources

Art Across The Curriculum Resource Book K–5

The resource book for every grade level includes a one-page blackline master for each of the 36 lessons in the following areas: Reading/Language Arts, Math, Science, Social Studies, The Arts, and Technology.

Vocabulary Book K–5

These blackline master books feature an activity for every lesson that focuses on the core art vocabulary at each grade level. Available in *English and Spanish,* students have the opportunity to practice and integrate new vocabulary words immediately.

Assessment Book K–5

These assessment booklets provide assessment alternatives for each lesson of a grade level. Masters appear in both *English and Spanish.*

Art Manipulative Kit K–5

With this group of art-related objects, teachers can add a new dimension to their presentations of key art concepts, so students can grasp new concepts more quickly. The Kit includes:

- color wheel
- flexible curve
- simple balance
- mirror
- solid shapes and forms
- textured materials
- magnifying glass
- prism
- Flash Cards to help explain the elements and principles of art
- Listening Cassettes of classical music to help inspire students when it's time to create.

Student Portfolios

Students can decorate these oversized folders and use them to hold their artwork and measure what they've learned over the course of the year.

Teacher Support Materials

Multimedia Resources

Literature and Art Video Collection K–5

This set of six videos per grade level provides an opportunity to integrate children's literature into art classes, introducing some well-known picture book illustrators as artists. Including the work of Leo Lionni, Jerry Pinkney, Chris Van Allsburg, Trina Schart Hyman, and others, each video is referenced in the Teacher Edition for easy lesson integration.

Listening Cassettes in the Art Manipulative Kit

These classical music selections featuring Bach, Mozart, Handel, Tchaikovsky, Corelli, and Vivaldi are intended to be played during Create activities to provide opportunities for the integration of music appreciation during art class.

Davidson's MULTIMEDIA WORKSHOP

This multimedia draw-and-paint CD-ROM for elementary students is correlated to activities in the *Art Across the Curriculum* Technology activities. Using computer media, the program provides an engaging alternative for getting young children excited about art projects.

The National Geographic Picture Atlas of the World

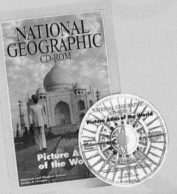

Through this spectacular multimedia CD-ROM, your students have the power to travel to London, Paris, Rome, New York, or any other city where great works of art can be found.

The National Museum of Women in the Arts Collection

This outstanding collection of work by women artists is accessible through CD-ROM and Videodisc technology.

ARTSOURCE Audio/Video Resource

These wonderful Theater, Music, and Drama performances produced by The Music Center of Los Angeles County are related to the ARTSOURCE lessons at the end of each unit in the **Student Edition.** The actual performances are captured on audio- or videotape and provided for each grade level.

Learn how to find the Met on the Net . . . and much more.

Here's a list of Internet addresses for museums profiled throughout *Art Connections* and listed on the reverse side of Animals Though History Time Line. Additional museum education resources are listed on pages T30–T33.

Anchorage Museum of History & Art
121 W. Seventh Ave.
Anchorage, AK 99501
Phone: (907) 343-4326
URL: (WWW address): under development

Albright-Knox Art Gallery
1285 Elmwood Ave.
Buffalo, NY 14222
Phone: (716) 822-8700
http://www.akag.org
Information on exhibitions, educational resources, and art library services.

Art Institute of Chicago
111 South Michigan Ave.
Chicago, IL 60603
Phone: (312) 443-3600
http://www.artic.edu
The numerous resources of the Institute are gathered in this site. An excellent art education site containing many links.

Dallas Museum of Art
1717 N. Harwood
Dallas, TX 75201
Phone: (214) 922-1200
http://www.unt.edu/dfw/dma/www/dma.htm
Includes images from the galleries, views of the sculpture garden, and an education resource center.

The Denver Art Museum
100 West 14th Avenue Parkway
Denver, CO 80204
Phone: (303) 640-7591
http://www.artcom.com/museums/nv/af80204-27.htm

The Detroit Institute of Arts
5200 Woodward Ave.
Detroit, MI 48202
Phone: (313) 833-7900
http://www.dia.org
The DIA is the fifth-largest fine arts museum in the United States, with holdings of more than 60,000 works. More than 300 can be viewed at this site.

Guggenheim Museum
1071 Fifth Ave.
New York, NY 10128
Phone: (212) 423-3500
http://math240.lehman.cuny.edu/gugg
The Guggenheim's vast resources are here to sample. Current exhibits, education helps, images, schedules, and links are included.

The Heard Museum
22 E. Monte Vista Road
Phoenix, AZ 85004-1480
Phone: (602) 252-8840
http://www.heard.org/
The web site of this museum of native cultures and art concentrates on research help.

High Museum of Art
1280 Peachtree St. N.E.
Atlanta, GA 30309
Phone: (404) 733-4400
http://www.high.org
This site features works from the High's folk art and photo gallery. Exhibit, film series, and membership information are available.

Joslyn Art Museum
2200 Dodge St.
Omaha, NE 68102
Phone: (402) 342-3300
http://www.omaha.org/joslyn.htm
Basic museum information and history.

Kimbell Art Museum
3333 Camp Bowie Blvd.
Fort Worth, TX 76107-2792
Phone: (817) 332-8451
URL: (WWW adddress): under development

Los Angeles County Museum of Art
5905 Wilshire Blvd.
Los Angeles, CA 90036
Phone: (213) 857-6000
http://www.lacma.org/
Includes images of masterpieces in LACMA's permanent collection, an exhibition schedule, membership information, and the Museum Shop.

The Metropolitan Museum of Art
5th Ave. at 82nd Street
New York, NY 10028
Phone: (212) 879-5500
http://www.metmuseum.org/
This major museum, often called New York's Louvre, features images from 5,000 years of world culture. Images, schedules, history, and educational resources are included.

Museum of Fine Arts, Houston
1001 Bissonnet
Houston, TX 77005
Phone: (713) 639-7300
http://www.mfah.org/
Images of paintings, sculptures, and decorative art, representing all movements and periods.

National Gallery of Art
4th and Constitution Ave. N.W.
Washington, DC 20565
Phone: (202) 737-4215
http://www.si.edu/newstart.htm
Currently accessed through the Smithsonian web site.

National Museum of Women in the Arts
1250 New York Ave. N.W.
Washington, DC 20005-3920
Phone: (202) 783-5000
http://www.nmwa.org/
A 45-minute video tour or individual image clips can be downloaded.

Nelson-Atkins Museum of Art
4525 Oak St.
Kansas City, MO 64111
Phone: (816) 561-4000
http://www.infozine.com/z9611/anel.html
Includes information about museum resources.

Philadelphia Museum of Art
26th St. & Benjamin Franklin Pkwy.
Philadelphia, PA 19130
Phone: (215) 763-8100
http://www.pma.libertynet.org/
View the galleries, resource lists, images, schedules, and historical data.

San Francisco Museum of Modern Art
151 Third St.
San Francisco, CA 94103
Phone: (415)357-4000
http://www.sfmoma.org/
Schedules, education resources, and a self-guided tour of the museum's online gallery.

Seattle Art Museum
100 University Street
Seattle, WA 98101-2902
Phone: (206) 654-3100
Fax: (206) 654-3191
http://www.ci.seattle.wa.us/sam/default.htm
Includes museum information, education resources, and museum technology.

Smithsonian Museums
8th and G Sts. N.W.
Washington, DC 20560
Phone: (202) 357-2700
http://www.si.edu/newstart.htm
The Smithsonian home page is the door to all the museums under its umbrella.

Wadsworth Atheneum
600 Main St.
Hartford, CT 06103-2990
Phone: (860) 278-2670
http://www.courant.com/hartford/hattract/wadswort.htm
Web site under development.

Walker Art Center
Vineland Place
Minneapolis, MN 55403
Phone: (612) 375-7600
http://www.walkerart.org/
Basic site with schedules and mission statement.

White House (Washington, DC)
Pennsylvania Ave.
Washington, DC
http://www.whitehouse.gov/WH/welcome.html
The White House History and Tours link leads to images of art in the White House.

Authors

Senior Author

Rosalind Ragans, Ph.D., Associate Professor Emerita, Georgia Southern University

Willis Bing Davis, Head of Art Department, Central State University, Ohio

Tina Farrell, Associate Director of Visual and Performing Arts, Clear Creek Independent School District, Texas

Jane Rhoades Hudak, Ph.D., Professor of Art, Georgia Southern University

Gloria McCoy, K–12 Art Supervisor, Spring Branch Independent School District, Texas

Bunyan Morris, Art Teacher, Laboratory School, Georgia Southern University

Nan Yoshida, Former Art Supervisor, Los Angeles Unified School District, California

Contributors

ARTSOURCE Music, Dance, Theater Lessons
The Music Center of Los Angeles County
Education Division, Los Angeles, California

Assessment
Maggie Davis, Lead Teacher, The Performing and Visual Arts Center, Miami Northwestern High School, Miami, Florida

More About Aesthetics
Richard W. Burrows, Executive Director, Institute for Arts Education, San Diego, California

Safe Use of Art Materials
Mary Ann Boykin, Director, The Art School for Children and Young Adults, University of Houston-Clear Lake, Texas

Museum Education
Marilyn JS Goodman, Director of Education, Solomon R. Guggenheim Museum, New York, New York

National Museum of Women in the Arts Collection
National Museum of Women in the Arts, Washington, DC

Contributing Writers

Patricia Carter
Assistant Professor of Art Education, Georgia Southern University, Statesboro, Georgia

Faye Scannell
Art Specialist and Lead Technology Teacher, Bellevue School District, Bellevue, Washington

Marie M. Mennes
Art Supervisor, Dade County Public Schools, Miami, Florida

Jackie Ellett
Elementary Art Teacher, Fort Daniel Elementary School, Dacula, Georgia

Dennis W. Black
High School Art Teacher, Clear Creek Independent School District, Houston, Texas

For more information about SRA products, to place an order, or to follow up on your order, please call SRA Customer Service at 1-888/SRA-4KIDS, from 7A.M. to 5:30 P.M., Central Time.

Teacher Edition

SRA Art Connections

Level 5

Authors

Rosalind Ragans, Ph.D., Senior Author

Willis Bing Davis

Tina Farrell

Jane Rhoades Hudak, Ph.D.

Gloria McCoy

Bunyan Morris

Nan Yoshida

Contributing Writers

Dennis Black

Jackie Ellett

The Music Center of Los Angeles County

Columbus, Ohio

A Division of The McGraw·Hill Companies

SRA Art Connections

Table of Contents

Cover Fine Art Credit
Katsushika Hokusai. (Japanese) *The Great Wave at Kanagawa.*
36 Views of Mount Fuji. 1831-33. Polychrome Woodblock Print.
10 $\frac{1}{8}$ x 14 $\frac{15}{16}$ inches. Metropolitan Museum of Art, NY.

Cover Student Art Credits
Dustin Sandidge. (age 10) *Night City*
Robert Landers. (age 10) *Rainbow Over the Mountain*
Tiffany Hayes. (age 10) *The Encounter*

SRA/McGraw-Hill
A Division of The McGraw-Hill Companies

Copyright ©1998 SRA/McGraw-Hill

Printed in the United States of America

Send all inquiries to:
SRA/McGraw-Hill
250 Old Wilson Bridge Road
Suite 310
Worthington, OH 43085

ISBN 0-02-687817-8

2 3 4 5 6 7 8 9 FED 02 01 00 99 98 97

SRA Art Connections

Level 5

Authors

Rosalind Ragans, Ph.D., Senior Author

Willis Bing Davis
Tina Farrell
Jane Rhoades Hudak, Ph.D.
Gloria McCoy
Bunyan Morris
Nan Yoshida

Contributing Writers

Dennis Black
Jackie Ellett

The Music Center of Los Angeles County

SRA
McGraw-Hill

Columbus, Ohio

A Division of The McGraw-Hill Companies

Credits

Copyright © 1998 SRA/McGraw-Hill

Send all inquiries to:
SRA/McGraw-Hill
250 Old Wilson Bridge Road
Suite 310
Worthington, OH 43085

ISBN 0-02-688319-8

1 2 3 4 5 6 7 8 9 VHP 02 01 00 99 98 97

Authors

Senior Author
Dr. Rosalind Ragans, Ph.D. Associate
Professor Emerita, Georgia
Southern University

Willis Bing Davis, Head of Art
Department, Central State
University, Ohio
Tina Farrell, Associate Director of Visual
and Performing Arts, Clear Creek
Independent School District, Texas
Jane Rhoades Hudak, Ph.D. Professor
of Art Teacher Education, Georgia
Southern University
Gloria McCoy, K–12 Art Supervisor,
Spring Branch Independent School
District, Texas
Bunyan Morris, Art Teacher, Laboratory
School, Georgia Southern University
Nan Yoshida, Former Art Supervisor,
Los Angeles Unified School
District, California

Contributors

**ARTSOURCE Music, Dance,
Theater Lessons**
The Music Center of Los Angeles
County Education Division, Los
Angeles, California
More About Aesthetics
Richard W. Burrows, Executive
Director, Institute for Arts Education,
San Diego, California
Safe Use of Art Materials
Mary Ann Boykin, Visiting Lecturer, Art
Education; Director, The Art School for
Children and Young Adults, University
of Houston-Clear Lake, Houston, Texas
Museum Education
Marilyn JS Goodman, Director of
Education, Solomon R. Guggenheim
Museum, New York, New York
**National Museum of Women in the
Arts Collection**
National Museum of Women in the Arts,
Washington, DC

Reviewers

Mary Ann Boykin
Visiting Lecturer, Art Education;
Director, The Art School for Children
and Young Adults
University of Houston-Clear Lake
Houston, TX

Judy Gong
Multi-age Classroom Teacher
Pacific Elementary School
Lincoln Unified School District
Stockton, CA

Lori Groendyke Knutti
Art Educator
Harrison Street Elementary School
Big Walnut Elementary School
Sunbury, OH

Steven R. Sinclair
Art Teacher
Big Country Elementary School
Southwest Independent School District
San Antonio, TX

Consuelo Tinajero
5th Grade Teacher
Henry B. Gonzales Elementary School
Edgewood Independent School District
San Antonio, TX

Student Activity Testers

Cassie Siler
Sara Gaul
Sabrina Trotter
Charlotte Jobrack
Brenna Wirtz
Jenna Taylor
Jamie Kintz
Abbie Kulju

TABLE OF CONTENTS

Unit 1 Line, Shape, and Value

Unit 2 Color, Rhythm, and Movement

Table of Contents
(continued)

Unit 3 — Space, Form, and Texture

Unit 4 — Proportion and Distortion

Table of Contents
(continued)

More About . . .

OVERVIEW

The purpose of these pages is to open students' minds to the idea that visual arts include many components and take many forms. The arts satisfy the human needs for display, celebration, personal expression, and communication. We use the visual arts to enhance our visual environments, to express our innermost feelings, and to communicate ideas. Art is made by people.

Activating Prior Knowledge

Ask students what they think *art* is. Encourage creative, divergent thinking. In visual art, there are many answers to a question.

Questions to Discuss

Have students look at the images on pages 8–9 and name the things that are visual art.

Then, ask the following questions:

- Which of these things could you hold in your hands?
- Which one could you walk inside of?
- Which ones would you hang on a wall?
- Which one can be worn?
- Do you have any things at home like the images on these pages?
  (See **Perception Hints** below for answers.)

Perception Hints

- All of the images on these pages are visual art.
- They could hold the dish and the jewelry in their hands.
- They could walk inside the architecture, the house.
- They would hang the painting, the drawing, the print, and the photograph on the wall.
- The jewelry can be worn.
- Encourage students to think about things they have at home that fit the categories on these pages. The building they live in is architecture. They have ceramic dishes and other containers. Many of them have things hanging on the walls to enhance their visual environments. Many students wear jewelry, some of it handmade. A few may have sculpture in the home. Many will have seen sculpture in and around public buildings.

What Is Art?

Art is made by people

to communicate personal and social ideas.
to express our deepest hopes and dreams.
to satisfy our need for well-designed objects and buildings.

Art is . . .

Painting is color applied to a surface.

Edward Hopper. (American). *House by the Railroad.* 1925. Oil on canvas. 24 x 29 inches. The Museum of Modern Art, New York, New York.

Drawing is the process of making art with lines.

Wendy Fay Dixon. (British). *Deidre.* 1982. Silverpoint drawing on video paper. $17\frac{3}{4}$ x 17 inches. National Museum of Women in the Arts. Washington, DC.

Sculpture is art that fills space.

Duane Hanson. (American). *Woman with Dog.* 1977. Case polyvinyl polychromed in acrylic with cloth and hair. Collection of Whitney Museum of American Art, New York, New York.

Architecture is the art of designing and constructing buildings.

Frank Lloyd Wright. (American). *Fallingwater.* 1936–1939. Bear Run, Pennsylvania. Glen Allison/Tony Stone Images © 1998 © 1996 Artists Rights Society (ARS), NY/Frank Lloyd Wright Foundation.

8

ART Background

More About Art Terms

Painting is the art of applying color to a surface.

Drawing is the art of creating an image with lines on a surface.

Sculpture is the art of creating three-dimensional images.

Architecture is the art of designing and planning buildings. Architecture includes homes, schools, and other public buildings.

Printmaking is the art of transferring an original image from one prepared surface to another.

Photography is the art of making images by exposing film to light.

Printmaking is a process in which an original image is transferred from one prepared surface to another.

Käthe Kollwitz. (German). *The Downtrodden.* 1900. Etching. $9\frac{3}{4}$ x $12\frac{1}{8}$ inches. The National Museum of Women in the Arts, Washington, DC. Gift of Wallace and Wilhelmina Holladay/© 1998 Artists Rights Society (ARS), New York/Bild-Kunst, Bonn.

Photography is the act of capturing an image on film.

Jerome Leibling. (American). *Boy and Car, New York City.* 1949. Gelatin-silver print. 10 x 10 inches. Modern Museum of Art, New York City, New York.

Ceramics is the art of making objects with clay.

Artist unknown. *Deep Dish*/Spain/from Valencia 1430. Tin-glazed earthenware painted in cobalt blue and lustre. 6.7 x 48.2 cm.

Jewelry is art to be worn.

Iris Sandkühler. (American). *Pyrite Sun Necklace.* 1992. Copper, brass, pyrite, sterling, glass, base metal. Pendant 7×4 inches. Courtesy of © Iris Sandkühler.

... and much more.

9

Using the Credit Line

The credit line is a list of important facts about the work of art. It appears below or next to the work of art and contains much useful information. For example, if you are looking at a photo of a piece of sculpture with your students, you can help them understand the size of the work as it relates to their own size. You can help them understand if the work is a six-inch piece they can hold in their hands, or a six-foot piece that would tower over them. Most credit lines have six or more facts in the following order.

- Name of the artist.
- Title of the work. This always appears in italics. When the word *detail* follows the title, it means that you are seeing a part of the work of art rather than the whole thing.
- Year the work was created. A *c* before the date indicates that the piece was made around the year given.
- Medium used by the artist.
- Size of the work: The first number is the height, the second is the width, and if the work is three-dimensional, the third number indicates the depth.
- Location of the work: This tells the museum, gallery, or collection in which the work is housed and the city, state, and country. The names of the donors may also be included.

Ceramics is the art of making objects with clay. The finished, dry object must be fired in a kiln to make it strong.

Jewelry design is done by jewelry designers. Some pieces are designed to be one of a kind. Many designers work for manufacturers who produce thousands of pieces of jewelry from one design.

All of these works have been made by people. There are many beautiful and exciting things in this world that are natural, such as butterflies, flowers, rolling hills, sunsets, waterfalls, ocean waves, and volcanoes. They are not art. To be art, something must be planned and created by a person.

OVERVIEW

The purpose of these pages is to introduce the students to the names of the art concepts they will be learning in this book. Visual art communicates. It has a language for expressing ideas and feelings.

Activating Prior Knowledge

Ask students what they think of when they hear each of the following words: *line, shape, color.* Encourage them to look around the classroom for examples.

Questions to Discuss

Have students examine the images on pages 10 and 11. Ask them what they can tell about each word by the way it is shown on the page. Encourage them to speculate about the kind of materials that seem to make up the words that are the elements of art. Explore with them possible meanings of the drawing that represent the principles of art, as well. (Share with students information in **Art Background** about the elements and principles of art.)

Art is a language.

The words of the language are the elements of art.

10

ART Background

About the Elements of Art

Each language has its own system of words and rules of grammar. To learn a new language, you need to learn new words and a new set of rules for putting the words together. The language of visual art also has its own system. The words of the language are the **elements** of art. They are the basic visual symbols in the language of art. Just as there are basic kinds of words such as nouns, verbs, adjectives, and adverbs, there are basic kinds of art elements. These are **line, shape, color, value, space, form,** and **texture.**

These elements are the visual building blocks that the artist puts together to create a work of art. No matter what materials are used, the artwork will contain all of the visual elements. Sometimes one element will be more important than the others.

Artists organize these words, or elements, using the principles of art.

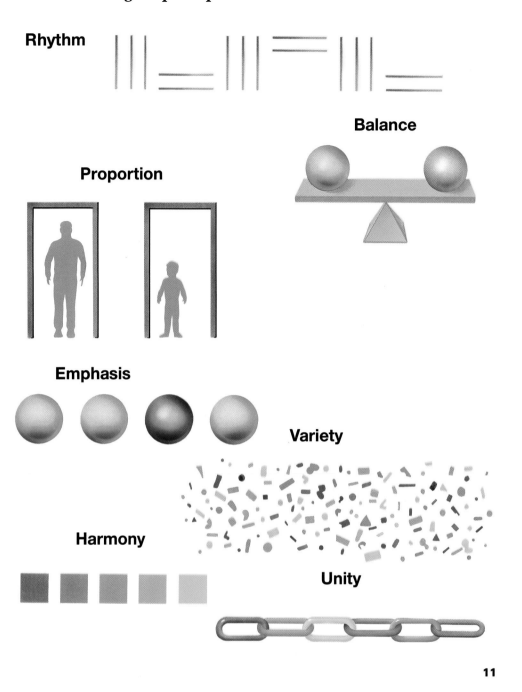

Rhythm

Balance

Proportion

Emphasis

Variety

Harmony

Unity

11

The Principles of Art
Visual images are organized according to rules. In spoken language, these are the rules of grammar. In visual art, the rules for organizing the elements of art are called the **principles** of art. The principles that are covered in this book are **rhythm, balance, proportion, emphasis, variety, harmony, and unity.** These principles are more like guidelines rather than hard-and-fast rules.

OVERVIEW

The purpose of these pages is to introduce the students to the three components that define or make up a work of art: the **subject,** the **composition,** and the **content.**

The **subject** is the image the viewer can easily identify in a work of art. The subject may be one person or many people. It may be things, such as *Pair of Boots.* It can be an event, such as a party, or watching TV. In *At the Milliner's,* the event is the experience of shopping and involves two women, the hats, and the mirror. In recent years, some artists have chosen to create nonobjective art. This is art that has no recognizable subject matter, such as *Eye Dazzler.* In this work, the elements of art become the subject. For more information and additional lessons about subject matter, see pages 222–227.

The **composition** is the way the principles of art are used to organize the elements of art. Notice how Plater-Zyberk has organized line, shape, form, space, color, and texture to create the feeling that the houses fit the environment.

The **content** is the message the work communicates to the viewer. The message may be an idea, such as vanity in *At the Milliner's,* or an emotion or feeling, such as joy, loneliness, independence, or weariness. If the work of art is functional, such as the blanket *Eye Dazzler* or the architectural city planning in *Seaside, Florida, Walkway,* then the function is the meaning. Does the work of art look like it could perform the function it is supposed to?

Every work of art has three parts.

They are

SUBJECT

The objects you can recognize are the subject matter of a work of art. When a work has no recognizable objects, the elements of art such as lines, shapes, colors, and so on become the subject of the work.

COMPOSITION

The composition of the work is the way the artist has used the principles to organize the elements of art.

CONTENT

The content is the message the artwork communicates. Content is the meaning of the work. If the work is functional, such as a chair or clothing, then the content is the function of the object.

Vincent van Gogh. (Dutch). *A Pair of Boots.* 1887. Oil on canvas. 13 x 16$\frac{1}{8}$ inches. Baltimore Museum of Art, Baltimore, Maryland. The Cone Collection.

Artist unknown. Navajo, (United States). *Navajo blanket, Eye Dazzler.* Dallas Museum of Art, Dallas, Texas, Textile Purchase Fund.

Elizabeth Plater-Zyberk. (American). *Seaside, Florida. A Walkway.* Andres Duany & Elizabeth Plater-Zyberk.

Edgar Degas. (French). *At the Milliner's.* 1882. Pastel on paper. 30 x 34 inches. Metropolitan Museum of Art, New York City, New York.

In which work of art do you think the subject matter is very important?
In which artwork do you think composition is most important?
Which work seems to have the strongest message? Explain.
Which artwork's meaning relates to its function?

13

Activating Prior Knowledge

Ask students when they look at a work of art, what is the first thing they look for. (Students may say they look at color, size, or "what it's about." Some may say they look for the feeling or message they get from it. Give students time to explore this question. It will provide a good context for the discussion of these pages.)

Questions to Discuss

- Read with the students the text on page 12 and look at the images on 12 and 13. Share with them some of the information above. Encourage students to think about their responses during the Activating Prior Knowledge discussion as they look at these images and think about the information you have shared with them.

- Read the questions on page 13 and discuss the answers.

(See **Perception Hints** below for answers.)

- Encourage students to think about subject, composition, and content as they view other works of art they encounter in this text and in their environment.

Perception Hints

- The subject matter is important in *Pair of Boots* and *At the Milliner's* .
- Composition is most important in *Eye Dazzler* and *Seaside, Florida, Walkway.*
- Plater-Zyberk's planned town *Seaside, Florida, Walkway* relates most closely to its function.
- Most students will think that *Pair of Boots* and *At the Milliner's* have the strongest message or meaning. However, it is important to point out that the function of a work is an important message.

UNIT 1

UNIT OVERVIEW

This unit covers lines, shapes, and values. It includes types of lines and how lines are used to communicate a movement or gesture, types of shapes, and value techniques.

Lines are how artists control the movement of your eyes. A line is a path created by a moving point or dot. Types of lines are covered in Lesson 1.

Shapes are two-dimensional. They can be measured by length and by height. Lesson 2 is about types of shapes.

Value is the lightness or darkness of a color or an object. Lessons 3 and 4 introduce techniques, and Lesson 5 explains value techniques.

Value contrast is created by using shading techniques such as stippling, cross-hatching, and hatching. It is covered in Lesson 6.

Introducing Unit Concepts

"Artists use the elements of line, shape, and value."
"Los artistas usan los elementos de la línea, la figura y el valor."

Line
- Have students look around the classroom and on their clothing for examples of different types of lines (zigzag, wavy, squiggle).
- Ask students to describe the directions in which some of the lines are moving: vertical, diagonal, or horizontal.

Shape
- Have students look around the room and create categories of similar shapes. For example, a clock and plate are both circles. Next, review shapes in the textbook.

Value
- Ask students to name meanings that come to mind when they hear the word *value*, e.g. "cost of something" or "a standard." Look up the word and discuss definitions.
- Have students find objects or clothing that they are wearing and arrange similarly colored objects of lightest to darkest values.

You may wish to use the **Video** *Jumanji,* which has many examples of lines, shapes, and value, to introduce the unit.

An Introduction to
Line, Shape, and Value

Line, shape, and value are used by artists to create many types of art.

Jaune Quick-to-See Smith. *Rainbow.* 1989. Oil on canvas. 66 × 84 inches. Steinbaum Krauss Gallery, New York, New York.

ART Background

About the Artist
Jaune Quick-to-See Smith (zhōn kwik tū sē smith, American, 1940–) was born into a large family on a Montana reservation in 1940. Her Shoshone grandmother gave her the name "Quick-to-See" because Smith was quick to understand things. After 22 years of supporting herself and her three children, she completed a master's degree in painting. She now lives in New Mexico.

About Subject Matter* In her work, Smith expresses her concern for the destruction of the environment and of Native American cultures.

Artists use **lines** in a work of art to create movement and shapes.

- What area of the picture do your eyes see first? Where do they end up last?
- What types of lines do you see? Do you see any of these lines more than once?

Shapes are used by artists to create objects or people.

- What shapes do you see in this painting?

Artist Profile

Jaune Quick-to-See Smith
1940–

*J*aune Quick-to-See Smith grew up on a Montana reservation. Her Shoshone grandmother gave her the name "Quick-to-See" because she was quick to understand things. As a child, she often went on long trips with her father, who was a horse trainer and trader. She saw the beauty of the rugged northwestern landscape and was inspired to draw. Her paintings reflect her concern about the destruction of the environment and Native American cultrures.

Jaune Quick-to-See Smith and other artists use line and value to help create movement and shapes. In this unit you will learn and practice how artists use line, shape, and value to create art. Here are the techniques.

- Types of Lines
- Shapes
- Value

15

About the Media Smith combines oils with pastels and collage.

About Art History* Smith combines techniques used by the abstract expressionist painters she studied in college with images from her own background.

Cultural Perspectives Years ago, Smith was told she was not college material and that a woman could not have a career in art. She now lectures, teaches, and serves as a guest artist at colleges across the nation. She has been featured in magazines and on television. Her work has been reproduced in books and textbooks, as well as on the inaugural poster for President Clinton's first term.

*See **More About** pages 206–227 for more about art history and subject matter.

Examining the Artwork

"Let's look closely at Quick-to-See Smith's *Rainbow*."
"Vamos a observar detalladamente Rainbow (Arco iris) de Quick-to-See Smith."

- Have students examine *Rainbow.* Have them describe what they see in the print.
- Read the definitions of *line* and *space* to the class and ask students to answer the questions on page 15. (See **Perception Hints** below.)

Artist Profile

Share with the students the information about the artist, including the photograph.

ART JOURNAL You may wish to provide a notebook for each student to use as an **Art Journal** to practice art concepts and record ideas from lesson to lesson.

About Music

Line refers to the way a melody moves higher and lower. Have students sing a song and show the melodic movement by tracing the melody line with their fingers on the notes in their music books.

Shape can pertain to the melodic contour, or the way a musical phrase is "shaped" through gradual changes in volume within phrases.

Value in music relates to the ability of the performer to create subtle differences in tone, sometimes referred to as *warm, cool, dark,* or *light.*

Perception Hints

First and last The eye first sees the light side. This side has vertical and horizontal blue and pale gold lines against a white background. The eye ends up last at the dark side. The curves of the rainbow lead the eye from the light to the left side, which is dark and gray. **Lines** The types of lines seen are curved lines, which are used for the rainbow and Earth. We also see diagonal lines in the boxes. Vertical and horizontal lines are in the boxes and in the background. The wide, curved lines are seen more than once. **Shapes** The shapes seen are the ovals or circles used to shape the cans, and the squares in the bottom of the picture.

UNIT 1 Planning Guide

Lesson	Lesson Title	Suggested Pacing	Create Activities	Materials	
1	**Lines**	45 minutes	Create a mixed-media collage using lines.	12- x 18-inch cardboard glue paper fabric, rope, or sting	
2	**Geometric and Free-Form Shapes**	45 minutes	Create a still life using geometric and free-form shapes.	liquid tempera paints brushes art paper found objects for the still life paint trays	
3	**Value in Shading**	75 minutes	Draw one object using light and dark values from three different points of view.	12- x 18-inch white drawing paper soft lead pencils (4B)	
4	**Value in Lines**	75 minutes	Use lines to create values in a drawing.	pencils 9- x 12-inch drawing paper	
5	**Value**	75 minutes	Illustrate using light and shadow.	12- x 18-inch gray paper white chalk charcoal costumes spotlight	
6	**Value Contrast**	75 minutes	Create a collage using photographs that have strong contrasts of light and dark values.	newspaper and white construction paper scissors, glue, and fine felt-tip black markers cameras black-and-white film white crayons	
Artsource Lesson	**Lines and Shape in a Tableau**	75 minutes	Create a tableau, or "living photograph," to communicate a theme.	pencils paper Artsource audiotape (optional)	

Program Resources (Books)	Art Resources	Literature Resources	*Music Resources
Vocabulary, pp. 1-2 Assessment, pp. 1-2 Art Across the Curriculum Resource Book, pp. 1-6	Overhead Transparency #1, *Maya/Huipil (detail)* and *Incantation* Artist Profile Book, pp. 50, 62 Large Prints, *Current* and *Rembrandt Drawing at a Window*	1. *Shadow* (1982) by Marcia Brown presents stunning examples of collage illustrations in the style of African art. 2. *Draw Me a Star* (1992) by Eric Carle gives a unique look at the story behind Carle's artwork, showcasing his dramatic fingerpaint collage prints.	"El jarabe tapatio," p. T236, CD5:40. "El jarabe tapatio" is an example of Hispanic folk music.
Vocabulary, pp. 3-4 Assessment, pp. 3-4 Art Across the Curriculum Resource Book, pp. 7-12	Overhead Transparency #2, *The Beautiful Bird Revealing the Unknown to a Pair of Lovers* and *Dutch Still Life with Art Books and Field Guide to Western Birds* Artist Profile Book, pp. 36, 58 Large Prints, *Current* and *Rembrandt Drawing at a Window*	1. *Wreck of the Zephyr* (1983) by Chris Van Allsburg provides a look at shapes and solid forms in full-color pastels. 2. *Pish, Posh, Said Hieronymus Bosch* (1991) by Nancy Willard is an imaginative lavishly illustrated poem of medieval beasts and other images from the artist's world.	"Lullaby from the Great Mother Whale to the Baby Sea Pups," by the Paul Winter Consort, p. T339, CD8:18. "Lullaby" is an example of modern music in a free-form shape. It combines jazz style with recordings of animal sounds.
Vocabulary, pp. 5-6 Assessment, pp. 5-6 Art Across the Curriculum Resource Book, pp. 13-18	Overhead Transparency #3, *Drawing Hands* and *Deidre* Artist Profile Book, pp. 16, 17 Large Prints, *Current* and *Rembrandt Drawing at a Window*	1. *Jumanji* (1981) by Chris Van Allsburg is an excellent source for modeling, perspective, and shading with thick and thin lines. 2. *Light and Shadow* (1992) by Myra Cohn Livingston is a collection of poems about viewing light in different settings, accomplished by beautiful photographs.	"Old Abram Brown," by Benjamin Britten and Walter de la Mare, p. T349, CD8:34. "Old Abram Brown" is a round, a style of music in which a single melody overlaps itself several times.
Vocabulary, pp. 7-8 Assessment, pp. 7-8 Art Across the Curriculum Resource Book, pp. 19-24	Overhead Transparency #4, *Sharecropper* and *The Downtrodden* Artist Profile Book, pp. 11, 27 Large Prints, *Current* and *Rembrandt Drawing at a Window*	1. *Once a Mouse* (1961) by Marcia Brown demonstrates use of creating values with lines through woodcut illustrations. 2. *Abuela's Weave* (1993) by Omar Castaneda is a fictional story about a Guatemalan girl and her grandmother using lines to create woven creations they try to sell in a market.	*"Fanfare for the Common Man,"* by Aaron Copland, p. T117, CD3:1. *"Fanfare for the Common Man"* is an example of American Music from the mid twentieth century.
Vocabulary, pp. 9-10 Assessment, pp. 9-10 Art Across the Curriculum Resource Book, pp. 25-30	Overhead Transparency #5, *Mis Hermanos* and *Two Young Girls at the Piano* Artist Profile Book, p. 44 Large Prints, *Current* and *Rembrandt Drawing at a Window*	1. *Knots on a Counting Rope* (1987) by Bill Martin Jr. is an excellent source for showing highlights in portraiture and landscapes. 2. *A Weekend with Renoir* (1990) by Rosabianca Skiri-Venturi joins the reader with the French Impressionist to note important dates in his life and includes lists of locations of his work.	"Sanctus," from *Requiem*, by Gabriel Faure, p. T391, CD10:2. "Sanctus" is an example of late nineteenth-century French music.
Vocabulary, pp. 11-12 Assessment, pp. 11-12 Art Across the Curriculum Resource Book, pp. 31-36	Overhead Transparency #6, *Boy and Car, New York City* and *American Rural Baroque* Artist Profile Book, pp. 29, 52 Large Prints, *Current* and *Rembrandt Drawing at a Window*	1. *Smokey Night* (1994) by Eve Bunting provides a unique look at collage illustration through hand-made paper and photographic images. 2. *The Art of Photography* (1977) by Shirley Glubok represents outstanding photography from the 1830s to the 1970s.	"I Got Rhythm," by George Gershwin, p. T86, CD2:17. "I Got Rhythm" is an American song from the mid twentieth century.

*Music references are from **Share the Music,** Macmillan/McGraw-Hill School Publishers

UNIT 1 LESSON 1

LESSON PLANNER

Objectives

After completing this lesson, students will be able to:

- identify how different kinds of lines are used. *Aesthetic Perception*
- create a mixed-media collage. *Creative Expression*
- use the four steps of art criticism to evaluate their own artwork. *Art Criticism*
- recognize the cultural purpose of both artworks. *Art History and Culture*

Program Resources

- **Overhead:** Both the *Maya/Huipil* and the Sheeler are available on overhead 1.
- **Large Prints:** *Current* by Bridget Riley and *Drawing at a Window* by Rembrandt van Rijn
- **Vocabulary Book** pages 1–2
- **Art Manipulative Kit:** Toobers
- **Artist Profiles Book:** Sheeler page 50 and Artist unknown page 62
- **Art Across the Curriculum Book** pages 1–6
- **Multimedia Workshop CD-ROM**
- **Assessment Book** pages 1–2

Multiple Intelligences

Verbal/Linguistic Students can learn to use lines to create shapes and express ideas through discussion and recall.

Vocabulary

line *línea* a mark drawn by a tool such as a pencil, pen, or paintbrush as it moves across a surface

vertical *vertical* lines that move straight up and down

horizontal *horizontal* lines that move straight across from side to side

diagonal *diagonal* lines that slant and look as if they are full of energy

zigzag *en zigzag* lines that join diagonal direction lines

curved *curva* lines that bend and change gradually or turn inward to form spirals

The following words appear as art in the student edition on page 18: Lines can be **long** or **short, thick** or **thin,** or **rough** or **smooth.**

Lines

Artists use different kinds of lines to create shapes and express attitudes and ideas.

Maya/Huipil (detail) plate 263. c. 1950. Backstrap woven plain weave with supplementary—weft pattern, silk on cotton. 50 × 14½ inches. From the Girard Foundation Collection, in the Museum of International Folk Art, a unit of the Museum of New Mexico, Santa Fe, Photographer: Michel Monteaux.

The *Huipil Weaving* is part of a garment made and worn by the Cakchiquel Maya of Guatemala. Charles Sheeler painted *Incantation* to show the huge machines commonly found in an industrial plant. Notice that both artists use a variety of lines in their work. See how many different kinds of lines you can find in each work. Look for lines that are repeated.

ART Background

About the Artists

Charles Sheeler (chärlz shē′ lər, American, 1883–1965) was born in Philadelphia. He studied classical art and ornamentation. His subjects shifted from American handicraft and architecture to the more modern industrial scene. He painted, drew, and photographed in equal measure. Sheeler, an American Modernist, was the first artist to idealize American technology.

About Subject Matter* The Mayan artwork is a symbolic, or iconographic, weaving. Sheeler's work is a nonobjective oil painting.

About the Media The *Huipil* is a backstrap-woven, plain weave with supplementary weft pattern, made of silk and cotton. *Incantation* is an oil painting on canvas. Oil paint is an opaque, slow-drying medium that comes in a variety of colors and dries to a durable finish.

Charles Sheeler.
(American).
Incantation. 1946.
Oil on canvas.
24 × 20 inches. The
Brooklyn Museum,
Brooklyn, New York.
John B. and
Ella C. Woodward
Memorial Funds.

Study both the weaving and the painting to find a variety of lines.

- ✓ Look for lines that move up and down and side to side.
- ✓ Do you see a line that zigzags?
- ✓ Which lines slant?
- ✓ How do the lines help create a mood?
- ✓ Compare both works of art. Do you see lines that are similar?

Lesson 1

SEEING LIKE
AN ARTIST
Look around for
various lines in the
furniture and in your
classmates' clothing.
Find lines like the ones
you saw in the
weaving and painting.

17

FOCUS

Time: About 10 minutes

Activating Prior Knowledge
"What kinds of lines do you like to use when you create a piece of artwork? Curved lines? Straight lines?"
"¿Qué tipos de línea les gusta usar cuando hacen una obra de arte? ¿Líneas curvas? ¿Líneas rectas?"

- Encourage students to talk about lines they have seen in other pieces of artwork.

Introducing the Art
"Look closely at the Mayan weaving and the oil painting."
"Miren con cuidado el tejido maya y la pintura al óleo."

- Describe: Have students describe the subject matter in each artwork. (Mayan: iconography; Sheeler: nonobjective)
- Share and discuss information with students from **Art Background** and the **Artist Profiles Book.**
- Have the students compare and contrast the use of lines in each work of art. (Vertical lines dominate both works. The weaving uses repeated lines to create a happy mood. The Sheeler uses repeated vertical and slanted lines to indicate strength.)
- Have students answer the questions on page 17. (See **Perception Hints** below.)

FOR THE ART SPECIALIST

Use the **Overhead** and the **Large Print** *Current* or *Drawing at a Window* to discuss how artists use different kinds of lines to create shapes and express attitudes and ideas.

Perception Hints

Vertical lines *Huipil.* Blue, green, and red vertical lines divide each section. *Sheeler.* The piping forms vertical lines of yellow, gray, and white.
Zigzag lines *Huipil.* Uses zigzags within the columns as designs.
Slant *Sheeler.* Contains white slanted lines.
The repeated lines in the *Huipil* create a happy or upbeat mood. The vertical and slanted lines in the Sheeler indicate a mood of strength.
Vertical lines dominate both works.

TEACH

Time: About 30 minutes

Practice

Materials
- 12- × 18-inch white drawing paper
- pencils

Alternate Materials: markers

"How can you illustrate the five different kinds of lines?"

"¿Cómo pueden ilustrar los cinco tipos diferentes de líneas?"

- Discuss the definitions of the five different lines and their variations on page 18.
- Distribute materials and have students follow the directions on page 18 for drawing the different lines. Have them answer the Decide question on the back of their papers.

Create PROBLEM SOLVING

Materials
- 12- × 18-inch cardboard
- glue
- paper
- fabric, rope, or string

Alternate Materials: pipe cleaners, yarn, or straws

"Let's create a mixed-media collage."

"Vamos a crear un collaje usando una mezcla de medios."

- Discuss with students the different lines their materials make. They can cut thick or thin strips of fabric. They can make curved lines out of rope or string. They can make zigzag lines out of paper, fabric, rope, or string.
- Remind them to think about what type of mood they are trying to express in their collages, and have them follow the directions on page 19.
- Review procedures for creating a collage in **More About Technique Tips** on page 202.

Using Lines

A **line** is a mark drawn by a tool such as a pencil, pen, or paintbrush as it moves across a surface. There are five different kinds of lines. Lines have different lengths, widths, and textures. Some curve and move in different directions.

 Vertical lines move up and down, creating a feeling of strength and stability.

 Horizontal lines move side to side, creating a calm feeling.

 Diagonal lines move at a slant and are full of energy.

 Zigzag lines are made by joining diagonal direction lines.

 Curved lines bend and change gradually or turn inward to form spirals.

Lines can be **long** or **short**, **thick** or **thin**, or **rough** or **smooth**.

Practice

Draw each line and its variations. Use markers.

1. Fold a sheet of paper into six equal boxes. Print the name of each of the five types of lines at the top of each box, leaving one box empty.

2. Using a black marker, create the type of line indicated.

3. In the empty box, write your favorite type of line.

Decide Did you use all five types of lines correctly? Did you vary the thickness, length, and texture? What directional lines did you create?

Activities in
ART Across the Curriculum Book

Reading/Language Arts Learn more about the origins of words that describe lines. (page 1)

Math Use division to find the subset of a total number of lines in an artwork. (page 2)

Science Understand the role of industry and recycling resources in the United States as depicted in *Incantation*. (page 3)

Social Studies Study the differences between industrial cultures like the one in *Incantation* and the creators of the *Huipil* weaving. (page 4)

The Arts Learn more about lines made in social dances. (page 5)

Technology Use the *Multimedia Workshop* CD-ROM to draw two pictures using lines. (page 6)

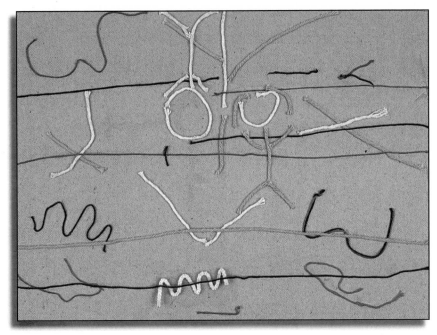

Charlotte Jobrack. Age 10. *There's a Face in Here.* Mixed media on cardboard.

What lines and line variations did the student artist use in this mixed media collage?

Create

In what other way can you make lines besides drawing them? Create a mixed-media collage using lines.

1. Think about the five different types of lines. Collect linear mixed-media materials such as yarn, string, or grass.

2. Use different materials to create lines and line variations. Keep in mind the mood that certain lines suggest.

3. Arrange and glue the collage materials onto a piece of cardboard background.

Describe What lines and materials did you use in your collage?

Analyze Why did you choose certain materials for certain lines? How did you combine your lines?

Interpret What would you title the collage?

Decide Were you successful in creating a variety of lines? If you could do this collage over again, how would you change it?

Lesson 1   **19**

Systems Use the Mayan weaving as a springboard to compare our current calendar system with the elaborate calendar system originated by the Mayans.

Scale and Structure Use Sheeler's oil painting as a visual example to compare the scale and structure of manufacturing in the 1940s with manufacturing today.

ESL You may find if helpful to pantomime **strength** and **stability** when describing vertical lines, **calm** for horizontal lines, and **full of energy** and **at a slant** for diagonal lines. Offer second-language learners the option to practice identifying and describing lines with a partner before they share with the entire class.

CLOSE

Time: About 5 minutes

"Were you able to create a mixed-media collage using lines?"

"¿Pudieron crear un collaje usando una mezcla de medios con líneas?"

 Review Use the Toobers in the **Art Manipulative Kit** to show the five different kinds of lines.

Use the **Large Prints** *Current* and *Drawing at a Window* to have students define the five different kinds of lines. Ask them to compare the use of lines in the **Large Prints** to the lines used in the works in this lesson.

Art Criticism

Have students answer the four art criticism questions—Describe, Analyze, Interpret, and Decide—orally or in writing. Discuss how lines are used in their artwork when they are completed.

 Assess Use the **Assessment Book** pages 1–2 as a formal assessment for this lesson.

Evaluation Criteria

- Can the student identify the use of different kinds of lines to create shapes and express ideas?
- Can the student create a mixed-media collage?
- Can the student use the four steps of art criticism to evaluate his or her own work?
- Can the student demonstrate knowledge of the cultural purpose of both artworks?

Reteaching ● ● ● ● ● ● ● ● ● ●

Lines Using the **Large Prints** *Current* and *Drawing at a Window* as a guide, have students cut small lengths of string to make different kinds of lines. Have them glue the lengths of string onto a piece of cardboard and explain what types of lines they have created.

Perception Hints for Student Art

The student used vertical, horizontal, diagonal, zigzag, curved, long and short, thick and thin, and rough and smooth lines in the mixed-media collage.

UNIT 1
LESSON 2

LESSON PLANNER

Objectives
After completing this lesson, students will be able to:
- identify the function of geometric and free-form shapes in art. *Aesthetic Perception*
- create a still-life painting using geometric and free-form shapes. *Creative Expression*
- use the four steps of art criticism to evaluate their own artwork. *Art Criticism*
- demonstrate knowledge of the lives and works of both artists. *Art History and Culture*

Program Resources
- **Overhead:** Both the Miró and the Wonner are available on overhead 2.
- **Large Prints:** *Current* by Bridget Riley and *Drawing at a Window* by Rembrandt van Rijn
- **Vocabulary Book** pages 3–4
- **Art Manipulative Kit:** flash cards and 2-D simple and geometric shapes
- **Artist Profiles Book:** Miró page 36 and Wonner page 58
- **Art Across the Curriculum Book** pages 7–12
- **Multimedia Workshop CD-ROM**
- **Assessment Book** pages 3–4

Multiple Intelligences
Logical/Mathematical Students can identify relationships and connections as well as abstract pattern recognition. Understanding geometric shapes helps to strengthen math skills along with the ability to see a variety of geometric and free-form shapes in nature and in objects made by people.

Vocabulary
shapes *figuras* two-dimensional forms that can be measured by length and height

geometric shapes *figuras geométricas* shapes described by mathematical formulas

complex geometric shapes *figuras geométricas complejas* a combination of three basic geometric shapes

free-form shapes *figuras abstractas* uneven and irregular shapes

The following words appear as art in the Student Edition page 22: *parallelogram, trapezoid, pentagon, hexagon,* and *octagon*.

Geometric and Free-Form Shapes

Artists use a variety of geometric and free-form shapes to convey an idea and to represent natural objects and artificial objects.

Joan Miró. (Spanish). *The Beautiful Bird Revealing the Unknown to a Pair of Lovers.* 1941. Gouache and oil wash on paper. 18 × 15 inches. The Museum of Modern Art, New York, New York. Acquired through the Lillie P. Bliss Bequest. Photograph © 1998. Artist Rights Society (ARS), New York/ADAGP, Paris.

Miró did not paint realistic-looking objects. He created a lively design of a variety of lines and shapes. Paul Wonner placed natural objects next to artificial ones. Both Miró and Wonner use a variety of shapes and lines in their paintings to express themselves.

ART Background

About the Artists
Joan Miró (hō' än mē rō', Spanish, 1893–1983) was a surrealist artist who lived on the island of Jajarca off the eastern coast of Spain. In 1922 he moved to Paris. In 1925, he took part in the first surrealist exhibition.

Paul Wonner (paul wōn' nər, American, 1920–) was born in Tucson, Arizona. As a high school student he studied art. After the army, he received his master's degree, taught at various universities, and in 1976 moved to San Francisco where he set up his studio.

About Subject Matter* The Miró is nonobjective, and the Wonner is a still life.

About the Media The painting by Miró is done in gouache and oil wash on paper. Gouache is a watercolor mixed with white to obtain an opaque effect. The painting by Wonner is done in acrylic on canvas. Acrylic paint is a synthetic paint that dries quickly.

Paul J. Wonner. (American). *Dutch Still Life with Art Books and Field Guide to Western Birds.* 1982. Acrylic on canvas. 72 × 50 inches. Hunter Museum, Chattanooga, Tennessee. Purchased with funds provided by the Benwood Foundation and the 1983 Collector's Group.

Study both paintings to find a variety of shapes.

- ✓ Where do you see circles, squares, rectangles, or triangles in either work?
- ✓ Do you see a shape with five, six, or eight sides?
- ✓ Find irregular shapes made with curved lines.
- ✓ Point to shapes made with color and created with lines.

SEEING LIKE AN ARTIST

Turn a book around in your hands. How many shapes can you see as you look at it from different angles?

Lesson 2   21

FOCUS

Time: About 10 minutes

Activating Prior Knowledge

"When you look at an object, what do you see first—the shape or the object?"

"Cuando miran un objeto, ¿qué observan primero—la figura u el objeto?"

- Hold up several objects and ask students whether they see the object or the shape first.

Introducing the Art

"Let's look closely at the two paintings."

"Vamos a mirar las dos pinturas detalladamente."

- **Describe:** Ask students to describe the subject matter in each painting. (Miró: nonobjective; Wonner: still-life)

ART MANIPULATIVES Use the **Art Manipulative Kit** to show students 2-D simple and geometric shapes.

- Share and discuss information with students from **Art Background** and the **Artist Profiles Book.**
- Have students answer the questions on page 21. (See **Perception Hints** below.)

FOR THE ART SPECIALIST

Use the **Overhead** and the **Large Print** *Current* or *Drawing at a Window* to demonstrate how the artists use a variety of geometric and free-form shapes to convey an idea and to represent natural and artificial objects.

About Art History* Miró painted during a time when surrealism was an art style. Surrealism proposed that dreams, fantasy, and the subconscious served as inspiration for the artist.

Wonner belongs to the realist revival. Most of the new realists' imagery and compositions were taken directly from photographic sources; however, Wonner's variation is linked to the long historic tradition of representational art.

Cultural Perspectives Miró lived on the island of Jajarca off the eastern coast of Spain. Miró loved his native Catalan landscape. Catalonia is in the eastern region of Spain. Wonner's works are strongly similar to contemporary works by the so-called California figurative painters.

*See **More About** pages 206–227 for more about art history and subject matter.

Perception Hints

Circles, squares, rectangles, and triangles *Miró.* Circles—eyes and throughout work; squares—upper right-hand corner; triangles—the middle of the work. *Wonner.* Circles—oranges; rectangles—books, windows, and shadows.

Shapes with numerous sides are in both works.

Irregular shapes with curved lines *Miró.* The birds and feathers. *Wonner.* The flowers, birds, and shadows.

Shapes made with color and created with lines are included in both works.

TEACH

Time: About 30 minutes

Practice

Materials
- colored construction paper
- scissors
- glue

Alternate Materials: markers or crayons

"How can you create complex geometric shapes?"
"¿Cómo pueden crear figuras geométricas complejas?"

- Discuss the term *geometric* on page 22 and ask students to give examples of geometric shapes.
- Distribute materials and have students follow the directions on page 22 for creating shapes. Discuss the Decide question in groups and share answers.

Create PROBLEM SOLVING

Materials
- liquid tempera paint
- brushes
- paint trays
- art paper
- found objects for the still life

Alternate Materials: markers and drawing paper

"Let's paint a still life using geometric and free-form shapes."
"Vamos a pintar una naturaleza muerta usando figuras geométricas y abstractas."

- Brainstorm ideas to set up a still life.
- Review procedures for working with paint in **More About Technique Tips** on page 199. Have students use a small brush for detail.
- Distribute materials and have students follow the directions on page 23.
- Have students paint with one color at a time and use basic shapes. Repeat colors or lines that express a key mood or idea.

FOR THE ART SPECIALIST

Create a mixed media using watercolors, and enhance the color with oil pastels and colored pencils.

Using Geometric and Free-Form Shapes

Shapes are two-dimensional forms that can be measured in two ways—by length and height. A shape may have an outline or boundary around it, or it can be solid like a shadow. There are two kinds of shapes.

Geometric shapes are shapes that can be described in mathematical formulas. They are shapes with names. The three basic geometric shapes are the square, the circle, and the triangle. When you combine them you create **complex geometric shapes** such as those below.

Parallelogram   Trapezoid   Pentagon   Hexagon   Octagon

Free-form shapes are uneven and irregular. They can be made with curved lines, straight lines, or a combination of the two. They are most often found in nature.

Practice

Create cutout geometric shapes. Use cut paper.

1. Cut out basic shapes such as circles, squares, and triangles.

2. Experiment with the cutout shapes to create complex geometric shapes.

Decide What are the complex geometric shapes you created? How did you make them?

Activities *in*
ART Across the Curriculum Book

Reading/Language Arts Read and write a free-verse poem after studying about Miró. (page 7)

Math Make a picture of an animal using geometric shapes. (page 8)

Science Learn how to use a field guide to study birds like the one featured in Paul Wonner's still-life painting. (page 9)

Social Studies Study how the shape of a graph is used to make information easier to understand. (page 10)

The Arts Write a song about the magical bird in Miró's painting, using questions in the text as a guide. (page 11)

Technology Use the *Multimedia Workshop* CD-ROM to draw a picture using geometric and free-form shapes. (page 12)

Jenna Taylor. Age 10. *Everyday Objects.* Tempera.

What geometric shapes do you see in this student artist's still life?

Create

What objects do you see that are mostly free-form and geometric forms? Create a still life using free-form and geometric shapes.

1. Think about objects you might enjoy drawing. Arrange several objects of different sizes and shapes.

2. Draw one object from the still life in the center of the paper. Draw the other objects around that shape. Paint the shapes.

Describe What objects did you use? What lines, shapes, and colors did you use?

Analyze How did you use lines and color to create shapes?

Interpret What is the main idea or mood of your painting?

Decide Were you able to see a variety of shapes in the still life you set up?

Lesson **2**

23

Stability Use the stability of the shapes in the artworks as a springboard to discuss with students the stability and balance of nature.

Relationships Use the paintings as a springboard for the study of man's relationships with animals, in particular with birds.

ESL students may benefit from structured practice with a fluent English speaker as they respond to the Describe, Analyze, Interpret, and Decide sections. Pair students and explain how they can ask questions, listen, and help each other with missing vocabulary.

CLOSE

Time: About 5 minutes

"Were you able to use geometric and free-form shapes in a still life?"

"¿Pudieron usar figuras geométricas y abstractas en una naturaleza muerta?"

Review
Use the **Large Prints** *Current* and *Drawing at a Window* to have students compare the use of geometric and free-form shapes in both **Large Prints** to those works in this lesson.

Art Criticism
Have students answer the four art criticism questions—Describe, Analyze, Interpret, and Decide—orally or in writing. Discuss how geometric and free-form shapes are arranged in their paintings.

Assess
Use the **Assessment Book** pages 3–4 as a formal assessment for this lesson.

Evaluation Criteria
- Can the student define geometric and free-form shapes in art?
- Can the student create a still-life painting using geometric and free-form shapes?
- Can the student use the four steps of art criticism to evaluate his or her own work?
- Can the student demonstrate knowledge of the lives and works of both artists?

Reteaching • • • • • • • • • • •

Geometric and free-form shapes Have students create a drawing using five geometric and five free-form shapes using both **Large Prints** as a guide.

Perception Hints for Student Art

The geometric shapes seen in the still life include a triangle, a square, and a rectangle. One of the triangles has hexagonal form. The green background is a free-form. The shape on top of the pencil is a free-form shape.

UNIT 1
LESSON 3

LESSON PLANNER

Objectives

After completing this lesson, students will be able to:

- identify the use of shading in art to help an object look more realistic. *Aesthetic Perception*
- create an object from three different points of view using shading techniques. *Creative Expression*
- use the four steps of art criticism to evaluate their own artwork. *Art Criticism*
- demonstrate knowledge of the lives and works of Escher and Dixon. *Art History and Culture*

Program Resources

- **Overhead:** Both the Escher and the Dixon are available on overhead 3.
- **Large Prints:** *Current* by Bridget Riley and *Drawing at a Window* by Rembrandt van Rijn
- **Vocabulary Book** pages 5–6
- **Artist Profiles Book:** Escher page 17 and Dixon page 16
- **Art Across the Curriculum Book** pages 13–18
- **Multimedia Workshop CD-ROM**
- **Assessment Book** pages 5–6

Multiple Intelligences
Visual/Spatial Students can use perception skills to recognize the relationships of objects and to create light and dark values in an object.

Vocabulary

value *valor* the lightness and darkness of a color or object

shading *sombreado* a technique for darkening values by adding black or darkening an area by repeating several lines close together

gradation *degradación* a gradual change from one value to another

point of view *punto de vista* the position from which the viewer looks at an object

---

Value in Shading

Artists use shading to create highlights and shadows so that an object looks more realistic.

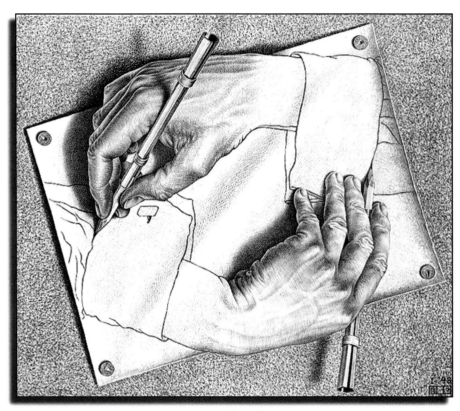

M.C. Escher. (Dutch). *Drawing Hands.* 1948. $11\frac{1}{8} \times 13\frac{1}{8}$ inches. Escher book Lithograph. Cornelius van S. Roosevelt Collection, © 1996 Board of Trustees, National Gallery of Art, Washington, DC.

M. C. Escher creates the illusion of two hands drawing each other. His hands begin as a line drawing, but he gradually darkens and lightens to create the illusion of hands coming to life. Dixon uses a sharpened silver wire to draw the image of a face peering through fish. She draws on special paper, and as the silver ages and tarnishes, the drawing darkens. Both artists used areas of light and dark to create the illusion of reality in these fantasy pictures.

24   Unit **1**

ART Background

About the Artists

M. C. Escher (māu rits kôr nā′ lis esh′ ər, Dutch, 1898–1971) was born in 1898. He made prints depicting a strange inner world filled with unnerving perspectives, impossible situations, and strange creatures that constantly changed identity. He constructed his prints with an almost obsessive mathematical precision.

Wendy Fay Dixon (wen′dē dik′ sən, English, 1931–) became a U.S. citizen in 1991. She was educated in Boston, South Africa, and India. She resides on Hilton Head Island, South Carolina.

About Subject Matter* The Escher is an iconographic lithograph, and the Dixon is a silverpoint drawing.

Wendy Fay Dixon. (British). *Deidre.* 1982. Silverpoint on paper.
$17\frac{3}{4} \times 17$ inches. The National Museum for Women in the Arts,
Gift of Deidre Busenberg and the artist. Washington, DC.

Examine how both artists used value.

- ✓ Where are the darkest and lightest areas in each picture?
- ✓ Where are you in relation to the picture?
- ✓ How did the artists make certain objects look realistic?

SEEING LIKE AN ARTIST

Slowly turn your hand and observe how the light and dark areas change as your hand turns.

Lesson **3**

25

About the Media A lithograph is a printing process where an image to be printed is created on a flat surface. It is treated with ink to create a print. In silverpoint a silver stylus, made of silver wire or a thicker reed of silver in an etching needle or clamp holder, is used for drawing.

About Art History* During the 1960s, Escher's prints were mass-produced as posters. When Dixon uses the traditional approach, her goal is to stretch reality toward a statement in relation to the subject matter.

Cultural Perspectives Escher attempted to create a relationship between what he saw around him and what he remembered from other experiences.

Silverpoint gained in popularity in Italy during the fourteenth century and was used by the old masters for portraits and landscapes.

*See **More About** pages 206–227 for more about art history and subject matter.

FOCUS

Time: About 10 minutes

Activating Prior Knowledge
"Think about values that are shown in your own clothing."
"Piensen en los valores que se muestran en su ropa."

- Have students look at an area of their clothing in sunlight, fluorescent light, and darkness.

Introducing the Art
"Let's look closely at the two pieces of artwork."
"Vamos a observar detalladamente las dos obras de arte."

- **Describe:** Ask students to describe the subject matter in the artwork. (Escher: iconographic; Dixon: silverpoint)
- Share and discuss information with students from **Art Background** and the **Artist Profiles Book.**
- Have students compare and contrast the two works. (Both create the illusion of reality in fantasy pictures through shading. Escher uses gradation in the hands; Dixon uses it in every section of her silverpoint. The viewpoints are different.)
- Have students answer the questions on page 25. (See **Perception Hints** below.)

 FOR THE ART SPECIALIST

Use the **Overhead** and the **Large Print** *Current* or *Drawing at a Window* to demonstrate how artists use shading to create highlights and shadows so that an object looks more realistic.

Perception Hints

Light areas *Escher.* The cuffs of the shirt, the wrist portion, the top part of the fingers, and the center and edges of the paper. *Dixon:* The woman's head and left shoulder.

Dark areas *Escher.* Shadows under the hands and fingers, shadow on side of wrist, and shadow from the pen across the top of the hand. *Dixon.* The dark area is on the viewer's left.

View *Escher.* Viewer is looking down. *Dixon* Viewer is in the front.

Realistic Artists made objects look realistic by using shading for highlights and shadows.

TEACH

Time: About two 30-minute periods

Practice

Materials
- pencils
- 12- × 18-inch white drawing paper

"How can you create a value scale?"

"¿Cómo pueden crear una escala de valores?"

- Discuss value on page 26.
- Help students draw their seven boxes.
- Make sure they leave the first box white and color their last box completely black. Display a picture of a completed value scale.
- On a sheet of paper, show students how to proceed by adding a little more value to each box as they move from box to box.
- Distribute the materials and have students follow the directions on page 26 for using value to create a value scale. Have them discuss the answer to the Decide question.

Create PROBLEM SOLVING

Materials
- 12- × 18-inch white drawing paper
- soft lead pencils (4B)

"Let's use light and dark values to shade an object from three different points of view."

"Vamos a usar valores claros y oscuros para sombrear un objeto desde tres puntos de vista diferentes."

- Have students pick out objects to draw. It should be something that doesn't have too much detail but changes form somewhat when the angle is changed. It should be small.
- Distribute the materials and have students follow the directions on page 27.
- Have students make several quick sketches of each point of view. Have them make a finished drawing by adding as much detail as possible and refine the gradations of light and dark by using their erasers to softly erase or lighten areas.

FOR THE ART SPECIALIST

Use color and oil pastel tints and shades of a single hue to shade each object.

Using Value

Value is the lightness and darkness of a color or object. The values of an object change according to the way the light strikes it. As it is turned, its values change according to the point of view or angle.

 Shading is a technique for darkening values by adding black or darkening an area by repeating several lines close together.

 **Gradation** is a gradual change from one value to another.

Point of view is the position from which the viewer looks at an object.

When you look at an object from different points of view, its shape and values appear to change.

Practice

Draw a value scale. Use a soft lead pencil and white paper.

1. Draw seven boxes. Leave the first box white, and color the last box black.

2. Practice shading in the other boxes to create different values. Make light pencil marks closest to the white box and darker values closest to the black box.

Decide Were you able to create a value scale going gradually from white to black?

Activities in
ART Across the Curriculum Book

Reading/Language Arts Understand how a writer can use a paradox, just as an artist can create an optical illusion. (page 13)

Math Learn more about ratios by studying value in art. (page 14)

Science Learn what living things, like the girl in *Deidre,* need to survive. (page 15)

Social Studies Learn about the purposes of political parties, and how they have a different meaning for the word *value.* (page 16)

The Arts Design props and scenery for the painting *Deidre.* You will need to create the illusion of water on the stage. (page 17)

Technology Use the *Multimedia Workshop* CD-ROM to show value in drawings of a three-dimensional object from different viewpoints. (page 18)

Abbie Kulju. Age 10. *The Clay Pot.* Oil pastel and charcoal.

How does the form of the pitcher change in each view of this student artwork?

Create

Why does the form of an object change when the point of view changes? Draw one object from three different points of view.

1. Think about how to use shading to show form in drawing. Draw a three-dimensional object from three points of view. Move it around under a direct light source.

2. Shade to indicate form. Use lead pencil for detail, and an eraser to lighten.

Describe How does the shape of the shadows change in each point of view?

Analyze How did you create shadows and highlights?

Interpret How does strong light and shadow affect the look of the work?

Decide Do you think strong light and shadow is an interesting way to show form?

Lesson **3**
27

Perspective Use Escher's artwork to facilitate a discussion concerning the difference between perception and reality.

Discovery Use Dixon's silverpoint as a means of introducing the study and understanding of fish as a cold-blooded, strictly water-inhabiting, vertebrate animal.

Second-language learners may need to practice naming different points of view for later discussion. Try sketching a poster with simple pictures that illustrate the following points of view: front, back, side, top, and bottom. Use the poster for ongoing reference.

CLOSE

Time: About 5 minutes

"Were you able to use value to shade an object from three different points of view?"

"¿Pudieron usar valores para sombrear un objeto desde tres puntos de vista diferentes?"

Review
Use the **Large Prints** *Drawing at a Window* and *Current* to have students compare the shading and gradation to the works in this lesson.

Art Criticism
Have students answer the four art criticism questions—Describe, Analyze, Interpret, and Decide—orally or in writing. Discuss the use of value in their drawings.

Assess
Use the **Assessment Book** pages 5–6 as a formal assessment for this lesson.

Evaluation Criteria
- Can the student identify the use of shading in art to help an object look more realistic?
- Can the student create an object from three different points of view using shading techniques?
- Can the student use the four steps of art criticism to evaluate his or her own work?
- Can the student demonstrate knowledge of the lives and works of Escher and Dixon?

Reteaching ● ● ● ● ● ● ● ● ● ● ●

Value Have students watch you demonstrate holding your hand under a light source and turning it so that they can see how light affects the value of your hand.

Use the **Large Print** *Drawing at a Window* to have students recognize value in shading.

Perception Hints for Student Art

The form of the pitcher changes when the point of view changes. One view shows the handle of the pitcher to the left, the other shows it to the right, and the other shows the pitcher on its side.

UNIT 1 LESSON 4

LESSON PLANNER

Objectives

After completing this lesson, students will be able to:

- identify the artists' use of lines to create values in a work of art. *Aesthetic Perception*
- create a portrait using lines to create value. *Creative Expression*
- use the four steps of art criticism to evaluate their own artwork. *Art Criticism*
- demonstrate knowledge of the work and cultures of Catlett and Kollwitz. *Art History and Culture*

Program Resources

- **Overhead:** Both the Catlett and the Kollwitz are available on overhead 4.
- **Large Prints:** *Current* by Bridget Riley and *Drawing at a Window* by Rembrandt van Rijn
- **Vocabulary Book** pages 7–8.
- **Artist Profiles Book:** Catlett page 11, and Kollwitz page 27
- **Art Across the Curriculum Book** pages 19–24
- **Multimedia Workshop CD-ROM**
- **Assessment Book** pages 7–8

Multiple Intelligences

Body/Kinesthetic Students can use lines to create values in art through hatching and cross-hatching by making use of fine motor skills.

Vocabulary

value *valor* the darkness or lightness of an object

hatching *sombreado con rayas* using a series of fine parallel lines

cross-hatching *sombreado con rayas entrecruzadas* using two or more intersecting sets of parallel lines

---

Value in Lines

Artists use lines to create values in a work of art.

Elizabeth Catlett. (American). *Sharecropper*. 1970. Color linocut. 26 × 22 inches. National Museum of American Art, Smithsonian Institution, Washington, DC.

Elizabeth Catlett's print is a linoleum cut. She uses a sharp tool to cut lines in a linoleum plate. The cut lines do not hold ink and appear white in the printed image. Käthe Kollwitz's etching was created by using a tool to draw lines into a metal plate. The lines she made held ink and appear black in the printed image. Both artists use a variety of lines and patterns to create different values in their compositions.

Unit 1

ART Background

About the Artists

Elizabeth Catlett (ē liz′ ə bəth kat′ lət, American 1915–) was born in Washington, D.C. She graduated with honors from Howard University in 1936. She has devoted her entire career to art that represents the struggles of African Americans.

Käthe Kollwitz (kā′ tē kol′ vitz, German, 1867–1945) artist and sculptor, was born in what is now Russia. She was a wife, a mother, and a person who wanted world peace.

About Subject Matter* The Catlett is a linoleum-cut portrait, and the Kollwitz is a narrative etching telling a story about the poor in Germany during the 1940s.

About the Media A linoleum cutting is a design carved into a piece of linoleum. The raised image is then inked with a roller and printed onto a surface. An etching is a design carved into a metal plate rolled with ink. The plate is wiped off, and the "recessed image" is then transferred onto the printing surface.

Käthe Kollwitz. (German). *The Downtrodden.* Etching. $9\frac{3}{4} \times 12\frac{1}{8}$ inches. The National Museum of Women in the Arts, Washington DC. Gift of Wallace and Wilhelmina Holladay. 1998 Artists Rights Society (ARS), New York/VG Bild-Kunst, Bonn.

Study both prints to find out how lines are used to create values.

- What types of lines do you see?
- Where are lines close together or far apart?
- Which areas have dark values and which have light values?
- How did the two artists create these feelings or emotions?

Lesson 4

SEEING LIKE AN ARTIST

Find an example of repeated lines used to make an object darker. How does an artist create a light area on an object?

29

FOCUS

Time: About 10 minutes

Activating Prior Knowledge

"What do you know about using shading techniques?"

"¿Qué saben sobre el uso de las técnicas de sombreado?"

Introducing the Art

"Let's look closely at the two prints."

"Vamos a observar detalladamente los dos grabados."

- **Describe:** Have students describe the subject matter of the artworks. (Catlett: portrait; Kollwitz: narrative)
- Share and discuss information with students from **Art Background** and the **Artist Profiles Book.**
- Have students compare and contrast both artworks. (Both have repeated lines to create shading on the figures, both are black and white prints, and both show the poor of their respective cultures. The Catlett is not as dark, and it is made of repeated curved and straight lines. Kollwitz uses straight lines, and the work is dark except for the child, the face of the woman, and the hands. All those are highlighted with large areas of white.)
- Have students answer the questions on page 29. (See **Perception Hints** below.)

FOR THE ART SPECIALIST

Use the **Overhead** and the **Large Print** *Drawing at a Window* to discuss the different kinds of line patterns found in the print.

About Art History* Kollwitz was one of the best graphic artists of her time. She produced etchings, woodcuts, and lithographs that are sensitive and compassionate portrayals of the working classes. Catlett received the "first honor" in sculpture at the American Negro Exposition in Chicago.

Cultural Perspectives Kollwitz's works were based on tragic subjects that surrounded her. Kollwitz was denounced and expelled by the Nazi regime in Germany in 1933.

Catlett accompanied her artist-husband on his travels in the South, where they directly experienced the racism of the time. She vowed to dedicate her entire career to a socially conscious art that represents the struggles of African Americans.

*See **More About** pages 206–227 for more about art history and subject matter.

Perception Hints

Types of lines *Catlett.* Short, vertical, and parallel lines. *Kollwitz.* Horizontal and parallel lines that intersect.
Close or far apart Lines are close together in the darkest areas. They are far apart in the lightest areas.
Dark values *Catlett.* The neck, left sleeve, folds of the dress, and parts of the dress. *Kollwitz.* Folds of the clothing and hair. **Light values** *Catlett.* The hair. *Kollwitz.* The faces and skin.
Feelings or emotions *Both.* By using lines to create darkness or lightness.

Practice

Materials
- art paper
- pencils

Alternate Materials: pens or markers

"How are parallel lines used to create a value scale going from light to dark values?"

"¿Cómo se usan las líneas paralelas para crear una escala de valores ordenada de valores más claros a valores más oscuros?"

- Discuss value on page 30.
- Demonstrate to the students how to show light value and dark value.
- Explain to students that each box of their rectangle will show a gradual value change from light to dark. In the first box, the lines will be drawn far apart, in the second box slightly closer together, in the third box even closer, and so on until the last box creates the darkest value with the lines so close they are almost, but not quite, touching.
- Distribute the materials and have students follow the directions on page 30 for using lines to create value. Have them answer the Decide question on the back.

Create PROBLEM SOLVING

Materials
- pencils
- 9- × 12-inch white drawing paper

Alternate Materials: pens and markers.

"Let's use lines to create values in a drawing."

"Vamos a usar líneas para crear valores en un dibujo."

- Create a list of different emotions such as sadness or shyness.
- Review value–making techniques.
- Distribute materials and have students follow the directions on page 31.

FOR THE ART SPECIALIST

Have students transfer their drawings onto Styrofoam plates. They can use either a wooden stylus or a dull pencil to draw into the Styrofoam.

Line and Value

The darkness or lightness of an object refers to its **value**. Line patterns create different values. When lines are placed side by side, or parallel, value is created. The closer together parallel lines are, the darker the value. The farther apart the lines are placed, the lighter the object.

Hatching is used to create shading values by using a series of fine parallel lines.

Cross-hatching is used to create shading values by using two or more intersecting sets of parallel lines.

Hatching and cross-hatching are used for shading. The closer together your lines are, the darker your artwork will appear.

Practice

Draw a value scale using parallel lines. Use a pencil.

1. Draw a rectangle and divide it into five sections.

2. Draw parallel lines far apart in one section to show the lightest value. Draw lines as close as you can without having them touch to show the darkest value.

Decide Were you successful in drawing parallel lines to create a value scale going from light to dark?

Activities in
ART Across the Curriculum Book

Reading/Language Arts Write a journal entry or a poem to express feelings like those shown in the artworks. (page 19)

Math Use a grid to find the darkest and lightest points on a painting, then practice finding coordinates of a point on a different grid. (page 20)

Science Use an experimental method to determine how each level of darkness in the value scale is created. (page 21)

Social Studies Learn about sharecropping before the Civil War. (page 22)

The Arts Learn about Spirituals and the feelings expressed in the artworks. (page 23)

Technology Use the *Multimedia Workshop* CD-ROM to create light and dark values in drawings. (page 24)

Dominique Belle. Age 11. *Zephanie.* Pencil.

What technique does the student artist use to create values in the drawing?

Create

How can you use lines in drawing to show different values? Use shading techniques to create values in a drawing.

1. Think about ways to draw emotions on a face. Make sketches of a person's face close-up. Show a different emotion in each sketch.

2. Choose one sketch. Make it simple and use a variety of shading techniques such as cross-hatching and hatching to create value in your drawing.

Describe Describe the shading techniques you used.

Analyze How did you use value to emphasize emotion in your drawing?

Interpret What emotion did you create in your drawing? Give your work a title.

Decide Were you successful in using shading techniques to create different values?

Lesson 4 31

THEME Connections

Identity Use the artwork by Catlett to discover the identity of its subject through the title.

Transitions Use the artwork to study the difficult transition from a comfortable lifestyle to that of an exile under the Nazi regime.

Connection Use both artworks to show the connection of the economically deprived of the United States to the economically deprived of Germany.

ESL

For this lesson, you may want to provide a richer context from which second-language learners can learn about emotions. Consider dramatizing short situations to illustrate a variety of feelings before brainstorming a list of emotions with the class. Second-language learners can help dramatize, while others identify corresponding emotions.

CLOSE

Time: About 5 minutes

"Were you able to draw a portrait using lines to create values?"

"¿Pudieron dibujar un retrato usando líneas para crear valores?"

 Review
Use the **Large Print** *Drawing at a Window* to have students identify lines that create value.

 Use the **Large Print** *Current* to have students compare the lines that create value to the works in this lesson.

Art Criticism

Have students answer the four art criticism questions—Describe, Analyze, Interpret, and Decide—orally or in writing. Discuss the use of lines that create value in their drawings.

 Assess
Use the **Assessment Book** pages 7–8 as a formal assessment for this lesson.

Evaluation Criteria

- Can the student identify the artists' use of lines to create values in a work of art?
- Can the student create a portrait using lines to create value?
- Can the student use the four steps of art criticism to evaluate his or her own work?
- Can the student demonstrate knowledge of the work and cultures of Catlett and Kollwitz?

Reteaching • • • • • • • • • • • •

Value Have students draw four shapes. Using the shading techniques taught in the lesson, shade the four shapes that have been drawn.

Have the students observe the shading techniques used in the **Large Print** *Current* as a guide.

Perception Hints for Student Art

The student artist uses shading to create values. Hatching is used for the hair. Cross-hatching is used on facial areas and on the neck.

U NIT 1 LESSON 5

LESSON PLANNER

Objectives
After completing this lesson, students will be able to:
- identify use the lighting to create highlights and shadows in artwork. *Aesthetic Perception*
- create a drawing of a costumed model using value techniques. *Creative Expression*
- use the four steps of art criticism to evaluate their own drawings. *Art Criticism*
- demonstrate knowledge of the life and work of Renoir. *Art History and Culture*

Program Resources
- **Overhead:** Both the Treviño and the Renoir are available on overhead 5.
- **Large Prints:** *Current* by Bridget Riley and *Drawing at a Window* by Rembrandt Van Rijn
- **Vocabulary Book** pages 9–10
- **Artist Profiles Book:** Renoir page 44
- **Art Across the Curriculum Book** pages 25–30
- **Multimedia Workshop CD-ROM**
- **National Geographic Picture Atlas of the World CD-ROM**
- **Assessment Book** pages 9–10

Multiple Intelligences
Interpersonal Students can express moods and feelings by using lighting to create highlights and shadows in a work of art.

Vocabulary
value *valor* the lightness or darkness of an object

perception *percepción* looking at something carefully and thinking deeply about it

shadows *sombras* shaded areas in a painting or drawing

highlights *claros* small areas of white or light values used to show the brightest spot

---

Value

Artists sometimes use lighting to create highlights and shadows in their artwork.

Jesse Treviño. (American). *Mis Hermanos.* 1976. Acrylic on canvas. 48 × 70 inches. National Museum of American Art, Washington, DC/Art Resource, New York.

J esse Treviño painted what was most important to him—his people, his roots, and the things he grew up with. Renoir was interested in how light reflected off objects, such as the faces of the two girls who are sitting at the piano. Notice how both artists use light and shadow in their paintings.

 **ART Background**

About the Artists
Pierre Auguste Renoir (pyâr ō gūst rən wär, French, 1841–1919) was born into a large and poor family. He was one of the greatest of the Impressionist painters. At 13, he worked in a factory painting china. His paintings were exhibited in the first three Impressionist exhibitions. His works included portraits, still lifes, landscapes, and groups of figures in dance halls, cafés, boats, and riverside landscapes. In his career, Renoir painted about 6,000 paintings.

About Subject Matter* Both the Renoir and the Treviño are narrative paintings.

About the Media The Treviño is acrylic on canvas. Acrylic is a vinyl polymer emulsion. It is a synthetic paint, which dries quickly. The Renoir is in oil, which is an opaque pigment mixed with oil.

Auguste Renoir. (French). *Two Young Girls at the Piano.* 1892. Oil on canvas. 44 × 34 inches. Metropolitan Museum of Art, Robert Lehman Collection, 1975. New York, New York.

Study both paintings for their use of light and shadow.

- ✓ Find the light and dark areas in both paintings.
- ✓ How do the light and shadows affect the clothing?
- ✓ What direction is the light source coming from in these paintings?
- ✓ How does the use of light and shadow create a mood in these paintings?

SEEING LIKE AN ARTIST

Think about how you would draw the natural lighting and shadows you see in your classroom.

Lesson 5 33

About Art History* Renoir was a leader of Impressionism in the late nineteenth century. Impressionists wanted to capture daily life and represent natural sunlight and warm light in their works.

Cultural Perspectives The Hispanic community is an integral part of the family structure and a social organization providing a point of reference for Treviño's work. Renoir painted during a time in history when there was rapid change due to the invention of such things as the telephone, automobile, and electricity. For Renoir, life and art were the same. He painted what he saw around him including his family and friends.

*See **More About** pages 206–227 for more about art history and subject matter.

Activating Prior Knowledge
"What highlights and shadows do you recall seeing in artwork?"
"¿Qué claros y sombras recuerdan haber visto en una obra de arte?"

- Have students look through magazines and identify highlights and shadows. Have them display their examples in front of the class.

Introducing the Art
"Let's look closely at the two paintings."
"Vamos a observar detalladamente estas dos pinturas?"

- **Describe:** Ask students to describe the subject matter in the paintings. (both: narratives.)
- Share and discuss information with students from **Art Background** and the **Artist Profiles Book.**
- **COMPARE AND CONTRAST** (Both tell a story. Both use lighting to create highlights.)
- Have students answer the questions on page 33. (See **Perception Hints** below.)

FOR THE ART SPECIALIST

Use the **Overhead** and the **Large Print** *Portrait of a Lady* to show students how artists use lighting to create highlights and shadows in their artwork.

Perception Hints

Light areas *Treviño.* Highlights the right side of the figures' faces, bodies, and arms. *Renoir.* Highlights the dress and the right side of figures faces and bodies. **Dark areas** *Treviño.* Shades parts of the trees, hair and clothing. *Renoir.* Shades the left side of the faces, arms, and bodies.
Light and shadows Affect the clothing by creating an illusion of form or depth.
Light source In both works it is coming from the right.
Mood By lightness and darkness.

TEACH

Time: About two 30-minute periods

Practice

Materials
- pieces of fabric
- chairs
- pencils
- 12- × 18-inch paper
- spotlight

Alternate Materials: dustless chalk or pens

"How can you illustrate light and shadow?"
"¿Cómo pueden ilustrar la luz y las sombras?"

- Discuss value, highlight, shading, and shadow on page 34.
- Discuss the best way to approach the drawing exercise. Have students start with the outline of the fabric, then start shading.
- Distribute the materials and have students follow the directions on page 34 for using value. Have them discuss the answer to the Decide question.

Create PROBLEM SOLVING

Materials
- 12- × 18-inch gray paper
- white chalk
- costumes
- charcoal
- spotlight

Alternate Materials: pencils or black and white oil pastels

"How can you illustrate light and shadow?"
"¿Cómo pueden ilustrar la luz y las sombras?"

- Have students decide on how to pose their models and where to put the light source.
- Review highlight and shadow techniques.
- Distribute materials and have students follow the directions on page 35.

FOR THE ART SPECIALIST

Have students use school acrylics of black, white, and mixes of gray paints for their pictures.

Using Value

The darkness or lightness of an object is described by its **value**. Value depends on how much light a surface reflects. Artists often draw a scene by creating a perception drawing using highlights and shadows.

Perception is the act of looking at something carefully and thinking deeply about what is seen.

Shadows are the shaded areas in a drawing or painting. They show the surfaces of the subject that reflect the least amount of light. They create the illusion of form or depth and dimension.

Highlights are small areas of white or light values used to show the very brightest spots. They are the opposites of shadows, and they help create illusion of form.

Practice

Illustrate highlight and shadow. Use pencil.

1. Drape a piece of solid-colored fabric over a chair in front of the classroom.

2. Shine a strong light or spotlight on the fabric. Lightly sketch part of the fabric with a pencil. Pay careful attention to highlights and shadows.

Decide How did you create the highlights and shadows?

Activities in ART Across the Curriculum Book

Reading/Language Arts Organize sentences about the men in *Mis Hermanos* and write a paragraph. (page 25)

Math Understand how shading creates the illusion of depth and then find the volume of several three-dimensional objects. (page 26)

Science Study reflections like those in both artworks and its relationship to light. (page 27)

Social Studies Use a political map to find historical information about the changing relationship of Texas and Mexico. (page 28)

The Arts Learn about the music culture of the period in Renoir's painting. (page 29)

Technology Use the *Multimedia Workshop* CD-ROM to show highlights and shadows in a drawing of a classmate. (page 30)

Cassie Siler. Age 10. *Graduate Holly* and *Ref*. Charcoal.

How does the student artist create highlights and shadows in the two drawings?

Create

How can you use value to introduce highlights and dark shadows in a figure drawing? Use value techniques in a drawing.

1. Think about the mood that is created with the use of light. Put a spotlight or strong light on two costumed volunteers from your class.

2. Use shading and perception to draw them. Look at the highlights and dark shadows on the faces and costumes. Make several sketches on gray paper using charcoal and white chalk.

Describe Describe what you included in your drawing.

Analyze What areas have highlights and shadows?

Interpret How did the highlights and shadows affect the mood?

Decide Were you successful in creating highlights and dark shadows? What might you do to improve your drawing?

Lesson 5

35

"Were you able to create a drawing using highlights and shadows?"

"¿Pudieron crear un dibujo usando claros y sombras?"

Review

Use the **Large Print** *Current* to have students recognize value.

Use the **Overhead** to compare the value of the works in the lesson to the value used in the **Large Print** *Drawing at a Window*.

Assess

Have students answer the four art criticism questions—Describe, Analyze, Interpret, and Decide—orally or in writing. Discuss the use of lines, in creating value.

Use the **Assessment Book** pages 9–10 as a formal assessment for this lesson.

Evaluation Criteria

- Can the student identify the use of lighting to create highlights and shadows?
- Can the student create a drawing of a costumed model using value techniques?
- Can the student use the four steps of art criticism to evaluate his or her own work?
- Can the student demonstrate knowledge of the life and work of Renoir?

Reteaching ● ● ● ● ● ● ● ● ● ● ●

Value Use the **Large Print** *Drawing at a Window* to create identical value on paper.

THEME Connections

Relationships Use the artwork by Renoir as an opening to discuss relationships between siblings in the family.

Cultures Use the painting *Mis Hermanos* as an introduction to the study and understanding of the Hispanic culture.

Traditions Use both artworks as a springboard to compare and contrast the differences in the American and German traditions.

 Use the **National Geographic Picture Atlas of the World CD-ROM** to locate Germany.

ESL

Frequent comprehension checks can help you monitor second language learners' ability to follow the lesson. You can ask students for physical responses, or short verbal responses to indicate their understanding. For example: *Point to the brightest highlight in Renoir's picture.*

Perception Hints for Student Art

The student artist created highlights and shadows in the beard, hair, clothing, background, basketball, and net in *Ref. In Graduate Holly*, highlights and shadows appear on the face and facial features and in the hair, graduation cap, and gown.

Value Contrast

Photographers use light to create contrast and to emphasize the subject.

Jerome Liebling. (American). *Boy and Car, New York City.* 1949.
Gelatin-silver print. 10 × 10 inches. © Jerome Liebling Photography.

Both photographs use strong value contrast to tell their stories about the American scene. Liebling uses strong light to show value contrast between the car and the boy in front of the car. Steiner uses the shadow of the chair to create his design. Ralph Steiner's photo was taken eighteen years earlier than Liebling's. How can you tell which photo was taken in the city and which in the country?

36 **Unit 1**

UNIT 1 LESSON 6

LESSON PLANNER

Objectives

After completing this lesson, students will be able to:

- identify the use of light in photography to create contrast and to emphasize a subject. *Aesthetic Perception*
- create a collage of photographs using strong value contrast. *Creative Expression*
- use the four steps of art criticism to evaluate their own artwork. *Art Criticism*
- demonstrate knowledge of the culture and works of both artists. *Art History and Culture*

Program Resources

- **Overhead:** Both the Liebling and the Steiner photographs are available on overhead 6.
- **Large Prints:** *Current* by Bridget Riley or *Drawing at a Window* by Rembrandt Van Rijn
- **Vocabulary Book** pages 11–12
- **Artist Profiles Book:** Liebling page 29 and Steiner page 52
- **Art Across the Curriculum Book** pages 31–36
- **Multimedia Workshop CD-ROM**
- **Assessment Book** pages 11–12

Multiple Intelligences

Intrapersonal Students can gain an awareness of different feelings by looking at subjects in photographs.

Vocabulary

contrast *contraste* the degree of difference between color values, tones, shapes, and other elements in works of art

value *valor* the darkness or lightness of an object

hatching *sombreado can rayas* shading by using a series of repeated parallel lines

cross-hatching *sombreado con rayas entrecruzadas* shading by having two or more sets of parallel lines cross each other

stippling *punteado* shading with dots. The closer the dots, the darker the area.

ART Background

About the Artists

Jerome Liebling (jə rōm' lēb' ling, American, 1924–) was born in New York City. He studied photography at Brooklyn College. While teaching photography at the University of Minnesota, he collaborated on several films. His photographs are often close-ups that focus on a specific area of the figure or the object. Often the figures are dramatically lit.

Ralph Steiner (ralf stī' nər, American, 1899–) was born in Cleveland, Ohio. He used his scientific background as a chemical engineer to help him solve photographic problems. His career alternated between periods of advertising, public relations, film, and editorial photography.

About Subject Matter* By highlighting the figure, Liebling conceals how the figure relates to social concerns. His work is a narrative. The emphasis of Steiner's work is the texture of the rocker. It is a genre.

Ralph Steiner. (American). *American Rural Baroque.* 1930. Gelatin-silver print. $7\frac{9}{16} \times 9\frac{1}{2}$ inches. Museum of Modern Art, New York, New York.

Study the two photographs carefully to see value contrast.

- ✓ What causes the darkest and lightest values in both photographs?
- ✓ Do you see any areas where a highlight is next to a shadow?
- ✓ What do the differing values tell you about the light at the time each photo was taken?
- ✓ How were the different types of moods created in the photographs?

SEEING LIKE AN ARTIST

Look around your classroom. Are there areas of strong light next to dark, shadowed areas like the ones in the photographs?

Lesson **6**   37

About the Media Both were most famous as photographers. Liebling and Steiner were also filmmakers and teachers.

About Art History* Photo journalism—photographs printed in newspapers—influenced the development of documentary and social photography. Both have been important in social movements since the mid-nineteenth century. Photography has been heavily influenced throughout its history by the painters' mediums, and photographs are still judged on how well they imitate paintings and drawings.

Cultural Perspectives Liebling used photography to capture the poverty, social concerns, public events, and the private aspects of public events during his lifetime. Steiner's lyrical and satirical photographs convey, along with sophistication and concern, a sense of wonder about the twentieth century that he entered at the age of one.

*See **More About** pages 206–227 for more about art history and subject matter.

FOCUS

Time: About 10 minutes

Activating Prior Knowledge

"What kind of photographs do you like?"

"¿Qué tipo de fotografías les gusta?"

- Show students a few examples of photographs with value contrast.
- Have students find pictures in magazines that display value and value contrast.

Introducing the Art

"Let's look closely at the two photographs."

"Vamos a observar detalladamente las dos fotografías."

- **Describe:** Have students describe the subject matter in the photographs. (Liebling: narrative; Steiner: genre)
- Share and discuss information with the students from **Art Background** and the **Artist Profiles Book.**
- Have students answer the questions on page 37. (See **Perception Hints** below.)
- Have the students compare and contrast both works. (Both use strong value contrast to tell stories. Liebling uses strong light to show value contrast between the car and the boy. The light helps the viewer focus on the figure. Steiner uses both dark and light values to help the viewer focus on the texture of the chair.)

FOR THE ART SPECIALIST

Use the **Overhead** and the **Large Print** *Drawing at a Window* to show how photographers use light to create contrast and emphasize the subject.

Perception Hints

Darkest and lightest values Caused by using contrast and shading in both.

Highlights *Liebling.* Next to shadows on the boy's face, along the fender of the car, and the shirt. *Steiner.* The shadow of the rocker against the house.

Values *Liebling.* The light came from above and to the left of the photographer. Different values tell the viewer that the light came from the right of the photographer.

Moods Created by using lines to create value contrast and set the mood.

TEACH

Time: About two 30-minute periods

Practice

Materials
- drawing paper
- felt-tip markers

Alternate Materials: pencils

"How can you use shading techniques to create contrast in shapes?"

"¿Cómo pueden usar las técnicas de sombreado para crear contraste en las figuras?"

- Discuss contrast and value on page 38.
- Distribute the materials and have students follow the directions on page 38 for practicing the shading techniques. Have them discuss the answer to the Decide question.

Create PROBLEM SOLVING

Materials
- newspaper and white construction paper
- cameras and black-and-white film
- scissors and glue
- fine felt-tip black markers
- white crayons

Alternate Materials: photographs from a newspaper

"Let's create a collage using photographs that have strong contrasts of light and dark values."

"Vamos a crear un collaje usando fotografías que tengan un contraste fuerte de valoares claros y oscuros."

- Brainstorm ideas for the subjects of photographs with strong contrasts of black and white.
- Discuss which subjects might provide strong contrasts of light and dark values.
- Distribute materials and have students follow the directions on page 39.

FOR THE ART SPECIALIST

Create a pinhole camera image demonstrating the strong contrasts of light and dark values.

38 Unit **1**

Creating Value Contrast

The darkness or lightness of an object is its **value**. Value depends on how much light a surface reflects. Contrast is often created when working with values. **Contrast** is the degree of difference between color values, tones, shapes, and other elements in works of art. Shading techniques such as stippling, cross-hatching, and hatching lines can help create value contrast in a drawing.

   Hatching is made by using a series of repeated parallel lines.

   Cross-hatching is created when two or more sets of parallel lines cross each other.

   Stippling is done by shading with dots. The closer the dots, the darker the area.

Practice

Practice creating contrast in a drawing. Use a black marker.

1. Divide a sheet of paper into three sections. Label each section a shading technique: hatching, cross-hatching, and stippling.

2. Draw a different shape in each box and practice the different shading techniques.

Decide How did you create contrast in your drawing?

38 Unit **1**

Activities in ART Across the Curriculum Book

Reading/Language Arts Use variety to make writing more interesting, just as there is contrast in the artworks in this lesson. (page 31)

Math Use a ruler to measure elements in Steiner's photograph. (page 32)

Science Learn more about mass, force, and movement of objects like those in the photograph. (page 33)

Social Studies Study the changes in automobile technology since 1900. (page 34)

The Arts Learn the relationship of characters and scenery using *American Rural Baroque* as the stage backdrop. (page 35)

Technology Use the *Multimedia Workshop* CD-ROM to draw a shape picture using shading techniques to create value contrast. (page 36)

Sara Gaul. Age 10. *Anything I Want.* Newspaper collage, oil pastel.

How does the student artist create value contrast in her collage?

Create

How would you create value contrast in a black and white photograph? Create a collage using photographs.

1. Take some photographs you like. Select several. Create a collage background from the typeset areas of the newspaper by tearing and gluing the pages together, making sure they overlap.

2. Glue and arrange the photos on the gray background you created. Use a black marker to make shadows darker, and use a white crayon to make highlights lighter.

Describe Describe the objects you used in your design.

Analyze Were you able to create strong or unusual textures with the shading techniques? Do your values change gradually or quickly?

Interpret Give your collage an expressive title.

Decide Were you successful in creating a collage that has strong value contrast?

Lesson 6 39

THEME Connections

Communities Use the artwork as a visual springboard to discuss the way communities lived in the city and in the country.

Perspective Use the main focus in each photograph (the boy and the rocker) to discuss how the viewer perceives life to be at the time the photographs were taken.

Discovery Use the photograph by Liebling as a springboard to discuss the importance of the invention of the automobile.

ESL

You may find it helpful to restate or break down long questions at the beginning of the lesson to make them more comprehensible to ESL students. Pantomime and examples can also provide important clues to help students follow the lesson.

CLOSE

Time: About 5 minutes

"Were you able to create a collage that has strong value contrast using photographic images?"

"¿Pudieron crear un collaje con un contraste de valor fuerte usando imágenes fotográficas?"

 Review

Use the **Large Print** *Current* to have students find value contrast.

 Use the **Overhead** to compare value contrast in their artwork to that in the **Large Print** *Drawing at a Window.*

Art Criticism

Have students answer the four art criticism questions—Describe, Analyze, Interpret, and Decide—orally or in writing. Discuss the use of value contrast in their works.

 Assess

Use the **Assessment Book** pages 23–24 as a formal assessment for this lesson.

Evaluation Criteria

- Can the student identify the use of light in photography to create contrast and to emphasize a subject?
- Can the student create a collage of photographs using strong value contrast?
- Can the student use the four steps of art criticism to evaluate his or her own work?
- Can the student demonstrate knowledge of the culture and work of Liebling and Steiner?

Reteaching • • • • • • • • • • •

Value Use the **Large Print** *Current* to have students find and discuss value contrast.

Use the **Overhead** to compare the value contrast used in the lesson to the value contrast that students see in black-and-white photographs in a magazine.

Perception Hints for Student Art

The student artist created value contrast by using photographs, with emphasis on light against the background made of newsprint.

Objectives

After completing this lesson, students will be able to:

- participate in the process of representing ideas and scenes through a living tableau. *Aesthetic Perception*
- express individual interpretation in creating lines and shapes for a tableau. *Creative Expression*
- use the four steps of art criticism to evaluate their own performances. *Art Criticism*
- demonstrate knowledge of how David Novak uses lines and expressions in storytelling. *Art History and Culture*

FOCUS

Time: About 10 minutes

Activating Prior Knowledge

"Think about how a painting or photograph of a scene captures a specific moment in real life or in our imaginations."

"Piensen acerca de cómo una pintura o una fotografía de un escena captura un momento específico de la vida real o de nuestras imaginaciones."

- Discuss students' answers and talk about how a scene helps us focus on an important moment. Point out that a scene can also stimulate our minds to recall similar situations or lets us imagine an experience.
- Tell students that they will be creating scenes called "tableaux." Explain that a tableau captures a moment and freezes it like a living photograph.

Introducing the Art

"Look at the photograph of storyteller David Novak. Describe what you think he is doing from what you see in the photograph."

"Observen la fotografía de la narración de David Novak. Describan lo que piensan que él está haciendo y lo que ven en la fotografía."

- Discuss students' responses. Share information about David Novak from **Art Background.** If you have the *Artsource* audiocassette, have students listen to the presentation by David Novak.

Lines, Shapes, and Forms in a Tableau

Classic Journeys or Tableau of Contents: *David Novak.*

a tableau is like a still-life photograph, except that the people shown are alive and breathing. Like a photograph, a tableau captures a moment or scene and freezes it. The scene may tell a story or express an emotion or a mood, such as courage or joy. In this living still life, observers can see a variety of lines, shapes, and forms.

ART Background

About the Artist

David Novak is a storyteller, but not in the ordinary sense. His storytelling skills include mime, clowning, juggling, puppetry, and acting. It involves strong physical agility and a clear, flexible voice that creates characters whose fears, joys, frustrations, and dreams are universal. David Novak's creative process begins with daydreaming or envisioning a story and then looking at it from the inside out or the outside in. He works to find universal messages and relationships that he can expand upon in telling the story.

About Subject Matter David Novak has said that "storytelling is a form of animation. The teller brings a tale to life which, after its telling, has new life in the hearts and imaginations of its listeners."

What To Do

Create a tableau, or "living photograph," to communicate a theme.

Materials
✓ pencils
✓ paper

1. Make a list of some themes and values such as family, freedom, love, joy, justice, beauty, and nature.

2. Work in a group. Choose an idea from the list. Try different ways to show that theme using poses, closeness or distance to each other, and facial expressions.

3. Select a pose that communicates the idea. Assume the positions in your tableau and then freeze.

4. Choose a title for your tableau. To perform, use a count of three beats to get into position. Freeze for five beats. Finally, release the "freeze" and stand straight with your hands at your sides.

Describe Describe the tableau you created.

Analyze Explain how you used lines, shapes, and forms to express your theme.

Interpret What mood or feelings did your tableau express?

Decide How well do you think you succeeded in communicating your theme?

Extra Credit

Work with a partner or in a small group. Choose a famous painting or other well-known artwork and re-create it in a tableau. Perform it for the class.

Theater　　　　41

Cultural Perspectives A tableau, or living picture, is a mute, immobile arrangement of performers reproducing a scene from art, literature, or the imagination. Often used in ancient Greek theater in the portrayals of myths, tableaux are now used on floats, at banquets, or at the end of melodramatic plays as devices for allowing spectators to catch all the actor's emotions. More recently, tableaux have been used to portray classic artworks, such as Seurat's *Sunday on the Isle of Grande Jatte*.

About Theater All theater is based on dramatizing stories. Storytelling is one of the oldest arts in history. Storytelling draws upon events in people's lives. Ancient hunters would tell hunt-related stories. Special events, myths, legends, or natural phenomena triggered other story ideas to be presented. Each person brings a specific point of view to a story that may be quite different from others' points of view.

TEACH

Time: **Two 30-minute periods**

Materials
• paper and pencils

"Let's make a list of things we could portray in a living tableau."

"Vamos a hacer una lista de cosas que podríamos representar en un cuadro vivo."

• Have students brainstorm and list universal themes, values, and special events. Examples: family, beauty, conflict, fear, Washington crossing the Delaware, the signing of the Declaration of Independence, and so on.

• Have students show their interpretation of the idea through body posture.

• Have students form small groups and use physical poses, spatial relationships, and facial expressions to express ideas or events in the form of tableaux.

CLOSE

Time: **About 5 minutes**

"What did you learn about capturing a moment or an event in a living tableau?"

"¿Qué aprendieron acerca de capturar un momento o evento en un cuadro vivo?"

◆ Assess
Have students answer the four art criticism questions on page 41—Describe, Analyze, Interpret, and Decide—orally or in writing.

Evaluation Criteria
• Can the student express a scene, emotion, or event through a tableau?

• Can the student demonstrate the ability to express ideas using the lines and positions of the body?

• Can the student use the four steps of art criticism to evaulate his or her own performance?

• Can the student demonstrate knowledge of the work of David Novak and how he uses lines and expressions in storytelling?

UNIT 1

Reviewing Unit Concepts

"A variety of lines, shapes, and values are used by artists to create different kinds of art."

"Los artistas usan una variedad de líneas, figuras y valores para crear diferentes tipos de arte."

• Review line, shape, and value as explained on pages 42 and 43. Have the students list and find examples in their textbooks of the different ways artists use these elements.

Examining the Artwork

"Look closely at the Bishop artwork."

"Observen detalladamente la obra de arte de Bishop."

• Have students look at Bishop's *Men and Girls Walking* and answer the questions on page 43. (See **Perception Hints** below.)

Student Portfolio

Have students review the artwork created during this unit and select the pieces they wish to keep in their portfolios.

School Portfolio

You may wish to confer with students to select one of their artworks, possibly a self-portrait, to be included in a school portfolio to record their developing skills from year to year.

Art Criticism Activity

Have students select an artwork from another unit and study it using the four steps of art criticism. (See pages 206–209 for more information about Art Criticism.)

Perception Hints

Lines The wall and the people walking are vertical lines. The heads and the lines across the person's shirt are horizontal lines. The legs on the man walking, his coat, and the line at the top right wall are all diagonal lines.

Shapes The shapes of the hat and coat and the highlights and shadows are free-form. The head is circular, the legs and bodies are rectangular, and the wall and noses are triangular.

Value is seen in the black of the background and the repeated lines on the people's clothing; the gradual change of light to dark in the man's shirt shows on the front left of the print; small areas of white in this print separate dark areas.

Wrapping Up Unit 1
Line, Shape, and Value
Reviewing Main Ideas

The lessons and activities in Unit 1 are based on how artists use line, shape, and value to create works of art.

• **Line** — When a dot moves and creates a path through space. Although there are five different kinds of lines, all lines move in only three directions.

  1. **Vertical** lines move up and down, creating a feeling of strength and stability.

  2. **Horizontal** lines move side to side, creating a calm feeling.

  3. **Diagonal** lines move at a slant and are full of energy.

• **Shapes** are flat, or two-dimensional. They can be measured by length and by height. All shapes can be categorized into one of two groups.

  1. **Free-form** shapes have uneven or irregular edges. They are most often found in nature.

Isabel Bishop. (American). *Men and Girls Walking.* 1969. Aquatint on paper. $8\frac{3}{8} \times 11\frac{1}{2}$ inches. National Museum of Women in the Arts, Washington, DC. Gift of Mr. and Mrs. Edward P. Levy.

ART Background

About the Artist
Isabel Bishop (iz" ə bəl' bish' əp, American, 1902–   ) was born in Cincinnati, Ohio. She studied art at the New York School of Applied Design for Women. Bishop is best known for her bold colors and her paintings of working women strolling through Union Square in New York City.

About Subject Matter* Isabel Bishop's subject matter was of the scenes she observed from her upper studio window in New York City. The people pass by but do not notice each other.

About the Media *Men and Girls Walking* is an aquatint. This is a print medium in which the image is etched into a copper plate, producing several tones that result in the resemblance to an ink-wash drawing.

2. **Geometric** shapes can be described using mathematical formulas. The three basic geometric shapes are the square, circle, and triangle.

- **Value** is the lightness and darkness of a color or object. There are three ways to create value.
  1. **Shading** is a technique for darkening values by adding black or repeating several lines close together.
  2. **Gradation** is a gradual change of one value to another—from light to dark or dark to light.
  3. **Highlights and shadows** are opposites of each other. Highlights are small areas of white or light values to show bright spots. Shadows are shaded areas that reflect the smallest amount of light.

Summing Up

Isabel Bishop used line, shape, and value to capture the scenes she observed from her studio window in New York City.

- What lines do you see in the artwork?
- What basic shapes did Bishop use to create the figures you see?
- How does the artist create value in the artwork?

Line, shape, and value are all important art elements that artists use to convey a feeling or make a statement. Artists use these art elements to create two-dimensional works of art.

Careers in Art
Medical Illustrator

Marsha Jessup has a profession that combines two of her favorite things—biology and art. Medical illustrators are artists who work in the field of medicine. When Jessup was 14, her mother, who is also an artist, suggested she consider medical illustration as a career. Jessup's training included four years of premedical studies, many courses in art, and a graduate degree in medical illustration. Today she works in Piscataway, New Jersey, combining administrative responsibilities with training people in biomedical computer imaging.

Marsha Jessup

43

Learning About Careers in Art

Marsha Jessup is a medical illustrator. She creates drawings for medical textbooks, research, and for documenting living and nonliving things. She works in an academic setting to create interactive multimedia for medical education.

As a child, Marsha Jessup loved nature, biology, and art. She often went with her mother to the painting studio at Howard University where her mother was a college student. Her mother's activities made art and science appear to be intertwined. This was one reason Jessup knew at age 14 what she wanted to do.

She majored in premedical studies in undergraduate school with a portfolio of nonscientific artwork created from courses in fine arts with special emphasis on drawing (especially life drawing), painting, illustration, color and design, and graphic design.

- Have students collect specimens from outside (shells, rocks, leaves, sticks). Ask them to select items, examine it, and create a detailed pencil drawing showing every crack, scratch, notch, or hole that can be found. Explain that this is how carefully a medical illustrator must observe the objects he or she draws.

About Art History* The art movement known as the Ashcan School was first labeled in 1934 by art critics. The movement began by a group of American painters as a rebellion against the academic paintings that were popular then. This group influenced the work of Isabel Bishop.

Cultural Perspectives Bishop experienced the Depression and both World Wars. She was influenced by the Ashcan School of artists who were greatly interested in naturalism and realistically capturing typical scenes of urban life such as views of alleyways, rooftops, and theater scenes.

*See **More About** pages 206–227 for more about art history and subject matter.

A Final Thought
"Every child is an artist. The problem is how to remain an artist once you grow up."—Pablo Picasso

UNIT 2

UNIT OVERVIEW

Color, rhythm and movement are the focus of this unit. You will review the color spectrum and how to recognize and create the following color schemes: monochromatic, analogous, complementary, and warm and cool colors. Students will also learn how artists use visual rhythm and movement in art. The specific topics in this unit are **color schemes** and **visual rhythm, movement,** and **color.**

Color schemes are a way of organizing colors. Students will learn about five color schemes. They are covered in Lessons 1, 2, 3, and 4.

Visual rhythm is the repetition of shapes, color, or line. Rhythm creates a feeling of movement. Five types of rhythm are studied in Lessons 5 and 6.

Tints and **shades** as values are covered in Lesson 1 with monochromatic colors. A tint is the light value of a color; a shade is the dark value.

Introducing Unit Concepts

"Artists use color in creating all types of art for a variety of reasons."

"Los artistas usan color al crear todo tipo de arte por una variedad de razones."

Color

• Have students create a class list of colors. Write them on the board or on chart paper.

• Create a classroom graph showing favorite colors. Next to each color make a mark indicting if it was voted as a favorite color.

• Ask students to take a color survey of the teachers and staff at the school. Assign each student group a few names. Ask those surveyed the following: What is your favorite color? What color represents sadness to you? Happiness? Anger? Create a graph as a class to show your findings.

• Compare the two graphs and the class and school surveys. Discuss the findings.

44   **Unit 2**

An Introduction to
Color, Rhythm, and Movement

Many artists use color and visual rhythm to create drawings, paintings, prints, and sculptures.

Claude Monet. (French). *Rouen Cathedral, West Facade, Sunlight.* 1894. Oil on canvas. $50\frac{1}{4} \times 36$ inches. Chester Dale Collection, © 1996 Board of Trustees, National Gallery of Art, Washington, DC.

44   **Unit 2**

ART Background

About the Artist

Claude Monet (klōd mō nā', French, 1840–1926) was one of the founders of Impressionism. His work concentrate on the play of light and color, which he produced systematically according to the laws of optics and relationships between complementary colors. Many of his paintings are marine and forest scenes, figures in landscape settings, and flower gardens and townscapes. His wish was to "mingle more closely with nature." By his death, he was blinded by cataracts.

About Subject Matter* Monet's work is one of a series of thirty paintings of the Rouen Cathedrals. He began creating his serial imagery during the mid-1890s as a study of how light and atmosphere affect color. Each painting is named according to weather conditions and the view.

Artists use **color** to express a mood or feeling in their artwork.

- What colors do you see in this painting?
- Monet wanted to express the feeling and quality of light in his paintings. He did this by using dabs of soft colors rather than filling large areas with solid bright colors. How would changing the colors of the painting make it different?

Rhythm is used by artists to create a feeling of movement and add visual excitement to a piece of artwork.

- What shapes do you see repeated in the painting? What color are the shapes?

Artist Profile

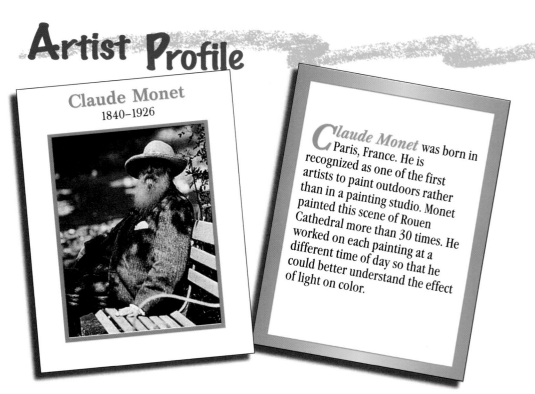

Claude Monet
1840–1926

Claude Monet was born in Paris, France. He is recognized as one of the first artists to paint outdoors rather than in a painting studio. Monet painted this scene of Rouen Cathedral more than 30 times. He worked on each painting at a different time of day so that he could better understand the effect of light on color.

Claude Monet and other artists use color to express a mood or feeling. Many artists also use color to create contrast and visual excitement. In this unit you will learn and practice the techniques that artists use to create color and visual rhythm in their artwork. These are the techniques.

- Color Schemes
- Visual Rhythm
- Value
- Contrast

45

About the Media Monet's work is an oil painting on canvas. Characteristic of his works is the rough, unevenly textured surface created by thickly applying the paints.

About Art History* Impressionism began in the 1860s as a reaction to both romanticism and the academic tradition. The term *impressionism* was coined by an art critic who saw Monet's painting *Impression Sunrise*. The Impressionists recorded the way the color of objects changed and reacted to light and atmospheric conditions.

*See **More About** pages 206–227 for more about art history and subject matter.

Rhythm

- Ask students to explain what they think the term *rhythm* means. Look up the word and and ask students to select the definition that best pertains to art.
- Ask students to find an example of rhythm in the book. Discuss their findings.

 You may wish to use the **Video** *Follow the Drinking Gourd* to introduce the unit. It has examples of color and rhythm.

Examining the Artwork

"Let's look more closely at the artwork."
"Vamos a observar detalladamente la obra de arte."

- Ask students to describe what they see in *Rouen Cathedral, West Facade, Sunlight.*
- Have students answer the questions on page 45. (See **Perception Hints** below.)

Artist Profile

Share with students the information about the artist including the detail from his portrait.

ART JOURNAL Encourage students to practice art concepts and record their ideas from lesson to lesson in their **Art Journals.**

About Music

Color in music refers to the distinctive tone qualities, or *timbre,* of different instruments and voices. With practice in listening to different kinds of instruments and voices, most people develop the ability to differentiate between them and to enjoy their expressive and individual qualities.

- Have the students choose a piece of music to match the color value of their artwork in one of the lessons in this unit.

Perception Hints

Colors The colors you see in Monet's work are tints and shades of blue and gold. The gold portrays the sun reflecting off the facade of the cathedral.
Value Changing the light colors to dark or dark to light might affect the perception of the weather, time of day, or age of the building.
Visual Rhythm The repetition of shapes in the light gold facade, and the vertical lines on the spires create a sense of movement.

UNIT 2 Planning Guide

Lesson	Lesson Title	Suggested Pacing	Create Activities	Materials	
1	Monochromatic Colors	75 minutes	Paint a real or imaginary scene using tints and shades of one hue.	liquid tempera paints brushes white paper newspaper pencils	
2	Analogous Colors	75 minutes	Create a nonobjective painting with an analogous color scheme.	liquid tempera paints brushes white paper pencils	
3	Complementary Colors	45 minutes	Design poster using complementary colors.	posterboard construction paper of complementary colors glue scissors	
4	Warm and Cool Colors	45 minutes	Use warm and cool colors to create a collage.	drawing paper in warm and cool colors tissue paper in warm and cool colors glue scissors white paper	
5	Visual Rhythm and Movement	45 minutes	Create a landscape using visual rhythm.	earth pigments pencils binder, or white glue and water white paper mortar and pestle large and small brushes	
6	Color and Visual Rhythm	45 minutes	Use expressive colors and visual rhythm to illustrate the mood of a piece of music.	white paper oil pastels recorded music	
Artsource Lesson	Rhythm in Dance	75 minutes	Create rhythm patterns using basic steps.	pencils paper Artsource videotape (optional)	

Program Resources (Books)	Art Resources	Literature Resources	*Music Resources
Vocabulary, pp. 13–14 Assessment, pp. 13–14 Art Across the Curriculum Resource Book, pp. 37–42	Overhead Transparency #7, *The King Family* and *Map* Artist Profile Book, pp. 24, 25 Large Prints, *A Sunday on La Grande Jatte, 1884* and *Bookwus Mask*	1. *Introducing Picasso* (1993) by Juliet Heslewood discusses historical and artistic influences on Pablo Picasso's work. 2. *The Great Blueness and Other Predicaments* (1968) by Arnold Lobel is a fictional book that shows the effects of monochromatic colors of the world.	"Everybody Rejoice," from *The Wiz,* by Luther Vandross, p. T102, CD2:31. "Everybody Rejoice" is a song from *The Wiz,* an African American version of *The Wizard of Oz.*
Vocabulary, pp. 15–16 Assessment, pp. 15–16 Art Across the Curriculum Resource Book, pp. 43–48	Overhead Transparency #8, *Red and Pink Rocks and Teeth* and *Eye Dazzler* Artist Profile Book, pp. 40, 63 Large Prints, *A Sunday on La Grande Jatte, 1884* and *Bookwus Mask*	1. *Luka's Quilt* (1994) by Georgia Guback is a fictional story of an argument over the colors that should be put into the making of a traditional Hawaiian quilt. 2. *The Navajo, Native American People* (1989) by Susan Stan discusses Navajo arts, including blankets, rugs, silverworks, and clothing.	"Eka Muda," p. T174, CD4:14. "Eka Muda" is a Native American musical game.
Vocabulary, pp. 17–18 Assessment, pp. 17–18 Art Across the Curriculum Resource Book, pp. 49–54	Overhead Transparency #9, *Featherwork Neckpiece* and *Ancestral Spirit Dance Series* Artist Profile Book, pp. 14, 64 Large Prints, *A Sunday on La Grande Jatte, 1884* and *Bookwus Mask*	1. *Rip Van Winkle* (1992) by Washington Irving illustrates the use of complementary colors in the background of each elegantly drawn scene. 2. *The Art of Ancient Peru* (1976) by Shirley Glubok well illustrates the art of the Incas and other civilizations dating back 2,500 years before the fall of the Inca Empire.	"Los Chiapanecas," p. T237, CD5:41. "Los Chiapanecas" is a Hispanic folk song.
Vocabulary, pp. 19–20 Assessment, pp. 19–20 Art Across the Curriculum Resource Book, pp. 55–60	Overhead Transparency #10, *Baird Trogon* and *Melancholy Metropolis* Artist Profile Book, pp. 32, 33 Large Prints, *A Sunday on La Grande Jatte, 1884* and *Bookwus Mask*	1. *When I Was Young in the Mountains* (1982) by Cynthia Rylant uses soft grays, browns, and blues to create the mood of long-ago memories in remote Appalachia. 2. *The Firebird* (1993) by Selina Hastings provides excellent examples of warm color usage.	"String Quartet in B Minor, 4th Movement," by Theresa Carreno, p. T391K, CD10:3. "String Quartet" was written by Theresa Carreno, a Hispanic composer who lived from 1853–1917.
Vocabulary, pp. 21–22 Assessment, pp. 21–22 Art Across the Curriculum Resource Book, pp. 61–66	Overhead Transparency #11, *Ipuy and his Wife Receiving Offerings from Their Children* and *Deliverance Disco* Artist Profile Book, pp. 35, 65 Large Prints, *A Sunday on La Grande Jatte, 1884* and *Bookwus Mask*	1. *This Quiet Lady* (1992) by Charlotte Zolotowe shows patterns in fabrics and movements in line. 2. *Hieroglyphs from A to Z: A Rhyming Book with Ancient Egyptian Stencils for Kids* (1991) by Peter Der Manuelian shows relationships between the English alphabet and Egyptian hieroglyphs and provides information on Egyptian culture.	"If I Had a Hammer," by Lee Hayes and Pete Seeger, p. T384, CD9:30. "If I Had a Hammer" is an example of American music from the 1960s.
Vocabulary, pp. 23–24 Assessment, pp. 23–24 Art Across the Curriculum Resource Book, pp. 67–72	Overhead Transparency #12, *A Pair of Boots* and *A Frankish Woman and her Servant* Artist Profile Book, pp. 30, 55 Large Prints, *A Sunday on La Grande Jatte, 1884* and *Bookwus Mask*	1. *Van Gogh, Art for Children Series* (1987) presents a brief biography of the artist's life with critical commentary of his work. 2. *Night Sounds, Morning Colors* (1994) by Rosemary Wells explores the senses by reflecting on expressive uses of art elements.	*"Rondeau,"* by Jean-Joseph Mouret, p. T258, CD6:12. *"Rondeau"* is an example of French music from the 1700s.

*Music references are from **Share the Music,** Macmillan/McGraw-Hill School Publishers

UNIT 2
LESSON 1

LESSON PLANNER

Objectives
After completing this lesson, students will be able to:
- identify monochromatic color schemes and how they are used to unite artwork. *Aesthetic Perception*
- create a scene using monochromatic colors. *Creative Expression*
- use the four steps of art criticism to evaluate their own artwork. *Art Criticism*
- demonstrate knowledge of the lives and cultures of both artists. *Art History and Culture*

Program Resources
- **Overhead:** Both the Jones and the Johns are available on overhead 7.
- **Large Prints:** *Sunday Afternoon on the Island of Grande Jatte* by George Seurat and *Bootwus Mask* by Beau Dick
- **Vocabulary Book** pages 13–14
- **Artist Profiles Book:** Jones page 25 and Johns page 24
- **Art Across the Curriculum Book** pages 37–42
- **Multimedia Workshop CD-ROM**
- **Assessment Book** pages 13–14

Multiple Intelligences
Logical/Mathematical Students can discover monochromatic color schemes by recognizing relationships and connections to color.

Vocabulary
monochromatic *monocromático* a color scheme using one color plus all the tints and shades of that color

hue *matiz o color* another name for *color*

tint *tinte* refers to the light value of a hue

shade *sombra* refers to the dark value of a hue

primary hues *color primario* red, blue, and yellow

secondary hues *color secundario* a mix of primary hues

intermediate hues *color intermedio* a mix of primary and secondary hues

---

Monochromatic Colors

Artists use monochromatic colors to bring together or unite their artwork visually.

Ben Jones. (American). *King Family*. Pen drawing. Private Collection.

The *King Family* is a drawing created by Ben Jones. His work shows the faces of familiar people like the Dr. Martin Luther King, Jr., family. Jasper Johns created his collage and wax-based painting *Map* about the map of the United States. His style emphasizes media rather than subject matter. Notice how both artists use color to unify their work.

ART Background

About the Artists
Ben Jones (American, 1942–) began drawing at an early age in his hometown in New Jersey. He attended New York University and Pratt Institute. Jones also traveled and studied in West Africa and Europe. He has exhibited widely in the U.S., Africa, South America, and Paris, France.

Jasper Johns (American, 1930–) served in the army. When he was 24 years of age, he decided to throw away all the art he had ever made. He wanted a fresh start. He was determined to create original art, not copies of other styles or artists. Jasper Johns has been known for his inventive artistic styles ever since.

About Subject Matter* The Jones is a portrait, and the Johns is symbolic.

About the Media The Jones is a pen drawing. The Johns is an oil on canvas.

Jasper Johns. (American). *Map.* 1962. Encaustic and collage on canvas. 60 × 93 inches. The Museum of Contemporary Art, Los Angeles, California. Photo credit: Paula Goldman.

Study the monochromatic color schemes in both pieces of artwork.

- ✅ What one color is used most often in each work of art?

- ✅ Where do you see colors that are lighter or darker than the main color?

- ✅ What type of lines and shapes do you see in each work of art?

- ✅ What feeling is expressed in each artwork? How did these artists create these feelings?

SEEING LIKE AN ARTIST

What objects in nature are made of only one color and variations of that color?

Lesson 1   **47**

About Art History* Jones returned to fine art after 17 years as a successful graphic designer and illustrator. He is known for his use of texture and bright colors.

Johns is a pop artist. Pop artists take everyday objects and transform them into objects of art. They reject abstract painting styles and forms of art making such as splattering paint on canvases. These artists glorify American mass culture, including television, billboard advertising, and cars and bring these images into museums.

*See **More About** pages 206–227 for more about art history and subject matter.

FOCUS

Time: About 10 minutes

Activating Prior Knowledge

"What different shades of the same color do you see in your clothing?"

"¿Qué diferentes tipos de sombras del mismo color ven en su ropa?"

- Have students wearing blue jeans form a line in front of the class. Look at the different values of the blue jeans.

- Tell students that all the jeans are different shades of blue. Mention that this makes them monochromatic. Ask students to name the color of their jeans.

Introducing the Art

"Let's look closely at the two artworks."

"Vamos a observar detalladamente las dos obras de arte."

- Share and discuss information from **Art Background** and the **Artist Profiles Book.**

- Ask students to answer the questions on page 47. (See **Perception Hints** below.)

- **COMPARE AND CONTRAST** Have students list the similarities and differences in the two paintings. (Both use color to create unity. Jones uses blue most often, and Johns uses gray most often. Jones uses curved lines, while Johns uses straight and zigzag lines.)

> **FOR THE ART SPECIALIST**
>
> Use the **Overhead** and the **Large Prints** *Sunday Afternoon on the Island of Grande Jatte* and *Bookwus Mask* to demonstrate how artists use monochromatic colors to bring together or visually unite their artwork.

Perception Hints

Color *Jones.* Uses blue most often. *Johns* uses gray most often.
Colors Both show colors everywhere in the work that are lighter and darker than the main color.
Lines and shapes *Jones* uses curved lines and oval shapes. *Johns* uses straight and zigzag lines and geometric and free-form shapes.
Feelings In both works, students will see various feelings expressed. The artists feelings are created through the use of monochromatic colors.

TEACH

Time: About two 30-minute periods

Practice
Materials

- liquid tempera paints
- white paper
- brushes
- newspaper

Alternate Materials: colored pencils

"How do you mix monochromatic colors?"

"¿Cómo mezclan los colores monocromáticos?"

- Discuss the definition of *monochromatic colors* on page 48.
- Distribute materials and have students follow the directions on page 48 for mixing monochromatic colors. Have students discuss the Decide question in groups and then share their answers with the class.

Create PROBLEM SOLVING
Materials

- pencils
- liquid tempera paints
- newspapers
- brushes
- white paper

Alternate Materials: colored pencils

"Let's paint a real or imaginary scene using tints and shades of one hue."

"Vamos a pintar una escena real o imaginaria usando tintes y sombras de un color."

- Have students discuss ideas for their real or imaginary scenes.
- Review procedures for working with paint.
- Distribute materials and have students follow the directions on page 49.
- When finished, have students place their paintings in a drying area.

FOR THE ART SPECIALIST

Help students avoid a dull decor when they decorate a student lounge in a monochromatic color scheme.

Using Monochromatic Colors

Monochromatic means "one color." A color scheme that is monochromatic uses only one color and the tints and shades of that color.

Hue is another name for color. Red, blue, and yellow are **primary hues**. By mixing primary hues, you get **secondary hues**. Red and blue make violet, red and yellow make orange, and blue and yellow make green. **Intermediate hues** are made by mixing a primary hue with a secondary hue. Red and orange make the intermediate color red-orange. A color wheel is the spectrum bent into a circle. The wheel below is a twelve-color wheel.

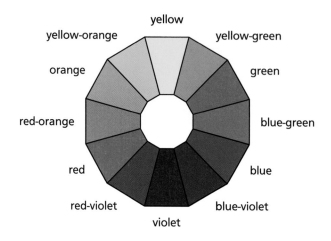

Tint is a light value of a hue made by adding white to a hue.
Shade is a dark value of a hue made by adding black to a hue.

Practice

Practice mixing monochromatic colors. Use tempera paint.

1. Draw three squares. Label the first "hue," the second "tint," and the third "shade." Paint each square.

2. Create a tint in the second square and a shade in the third square.

3. Experiment to create various values of the primary hue.

> **Decide** Did you create monochromatic colors of one primary hue?

Activities in
ART Across the Curriculum Book

Reading/Language Arts Learn about writing biographies by studying Martin Luther King, Jr. (page 37)

Math Measure distances on a map of the United States that is similar to Jasper Johns's *Map*. (page 38)

Science Create a map with materials other than pen and paper, looking at Jasper Johns's *Map* as an example. (page 39)

Social Studies Learn more about the accomplishments of Martin Luther King, Jr. (page 40)

The Arts Learn about the patriotic songs of the United States. (page 41)

Technology Use the *Multimedia Workshop* CD-ROM to create six design motifs filled with monochromatic colors. (page 42)

Dustin Sandidge. Age 11. *Night City.* Tempera.

How does the monochromatic color scheme affect the mood
of the artwork?

Create

**What color dominates your favorite real or
imaginary scene? Paint a real or imaginary
scene using tints and shades of one hue.**

1. Think about imaginary places and real places.
   Select one place and make several simple
   sketches of it.

2. Select your best sketch. Draw it lightly.

3. Mix one hue with white and black paint to
   create a variety of tints and shades. Paint your
   scene using a monochromatic color scheme.

Describe Describe your scene. Is
it imaginary or realistic?

Analyze What hue did you
choose? Describe the tints and
the shades of that hue.

Interpret What kind of mood did
you create?

Decide Were you successful in
creating a monochromatic scene?

Lesson **1**   49

Relationships Use the artwork *The King Family* to facilitate a discussion
about the relationships within the family unit.

Change Use the artwork *Map* to study changes in transportation methods
over the past 100 years.

Discovery Use the collage *Map* to discover the geographical relationship of
states to one another.

ESL

Reinforce ESL students' comprehension and vocabulary with group interviews
during the final discussion portion of the lesson. One or two students can
respond physically or with simple one- or two-word responses to the
questions from the class. You will want to first demonstrate and then allow
time for students to work with small groups later.

CLOSE

Time: About 5 minutes

"Were you able to create a real or imaginary scene using
tints and shades of one hue?"

*"¿Fueron capaces de crear una escena real o imaginaria usando
tintes y sombras de un color?"*

 Review

Use the **Large Prints** *Sunday Afternoon on
the Island of Grande Jatte* and *Bookwus Mask* to
have students explain how the artists used
monochromatic color to give unity to their
work. Ask them to compare the use of color in
the **Large Prints** to the works in this lesson.

Art Criticism

Have students answer the four art criticism
questions—Describe, Analyze, Interpret, and
Decide—orally or in writing. Discuss the use of
monochromatic colors in their paintings.

 Assess

Use the **Assessment Book** pages 13–14
as a formal assessment for this lesson.

Evaluation Criteria

• Can the student identify monochromatic color
schemes and how they are used to unite
artwork?

• Can the student create a scene using
monochromatic colors?

• Can the student use the four steps of art
criticism to evaluate his or her own work?

• Can the student relate information about the
lives and cultures of both artists?

Reteaching ● ● ● ● ● ● ● ● ● ● ●

Monochromatic color Have students look
around them or in their books to find
another example of a monochromatic color
scheme. Ask them to describe the
monochromatic colors they find.

Perception Hints for Student Art

The monochromatic color scheme gives the work a cool or
dark feeling.

U NIT 2
LESSON 2

LESSON PLANNER

Objectives
After completing this lesson, students will be able to:
- identify primary, secondary, and analogous colors. *Aesthetic Perception*
- use an analogous color scheme to create a nonobjective painting. *Creative Expression*
- use the four steps of art criticism to evaluate their own work. *Art Criticism*
- recognize the cultural purpose of each work of art. *Art History and Culture*

Program Resources
- **Overhead:** Both the O'Keeffe and *Eye Dazzler* are available on overhead 8.
- **Large Prints:** *Sunday Afternoon on the Island of Grande Jatte* by George Seurat and *Bootwus Mask* by Beau Dick
- **Vocabulary Book** pages 15–16
- **Art Manipulative Kit:** color wheel
- **Artist Profiles Book** O'Keeffe page 40 and Artist unknown page 63
- **Art Across the Curriculum Book** pages 43–48
- **Multimedia Workshop CD-ROM**
- **National Museum of Women in the Arts Collection CD-ROM**
- **Assessment Book** pages 15–16

Multiple Intelligences
Verbal/Linguistic Students can explain, teach, and define the concept of analogous color schemes.

Vocabulary
analogous colors *colores análogos* colors that sit next to each other and share a common color or hue

color scheme *esquema de color* a plan for organizing colors

nonobjective *abstracto* a piece of art that has no recognizable subject matter. It contains shapes, lines, and colors, not objects or people.

Analogous Colors

Artists use analogous color schemes in their paintings to tie various shapes together.

Georgia O'Keeffe. (American). *Red and Pink Rocks and Teeth.* 1938. 53.5 × 33 cm. The Art Institute of Chicago, Chicago, Illinois. Gift of Georgia O'Keeffe.

Georgia O'Keeffe was interested in painting things that were uniquely American. She used colors found in the New Mexico desert. *Eye Dazzler* is a Navajo blanket. The Navajo of New Mexico are noted for their intricate weavings. Both the painting and the blanket use related colors to bring various shapes and lines together.

ART Background

About the Artists
Georgia O'Keeffe (jôr' jə ō kēf' American, 1887–1986) was raised on a dairy farm in Wisconsin. In the eighth grade, she decided to become an artist. She never veered from that path through a long life of almost 100 years. She was a leader in twentieth-century art because of her strong, personal vision of nature and the western desert. She became best known for her large paintings of desert flowers.

About Subject Matter* The O'Keeffe piece is a landscape. *Eye Dazzler* is nonobjective.

About the Media The O'Keeffe is a painting done in oil, which is an opaque pigment mixed with oil. The blanket is a weaving with brilliant colors. Such weaving takes dexterity of hands, sureness of eyes, and a sense of design balance.

Artist unknown. Navajo Tribe (United States). *Navajo Blanket Eye Dazzler.* 1890. Wool, cotton; tapestry weave; slit tapestry; dovetailed tapestry. 75 × 57 inches. Dallas Museum of Art, Dallas, Texas. Textile Purchase Fund.

Study both works of art to find analogous colors.

- ✓ Find the red colors in the painting and the blanket.
- ✓ What orange areas or lines do you see in each work?
- ✓ Where are the dark red colors in each work?
- ✓ What shapes do you see in both works of art?
- ✓ Find areas in both pieces that are lighter and darker than the main color.

SEEING LIKE AN ARTIST

Find objects or clothing in which similar colors are used. What colors do you see in the painting and the blanket?

Lesson 2 51

About Art History* A pioneer of modernism, O'Keeffe painted the unusual, abstract shapes she saw in her mind rather than painting exact copies of objects. During the early 1900s, other artists experimented with colors and shapes.

When the weavers of the Southwest were introduced to analine dyes in the 1880s, they accepted these brilliant new colors and created interactive diagonal patterns that intensified rather than muted their effect.

Cultural Perspectives The invention of the automobile during the 1920s caused Americans to lead a more rushed life.

The Pueblo revolted against Spanish rule in 1680. The modern Native American populations have preserved their rituals, their art, and their privacy.

*See **More About** pages 206–227 for more about art history and subject matter.

TEACH

Time: About two 30-minute periods

Practice

Materials
- pencils
- brushes
- liquid tempera paints
- white paper

Alternate Materials: colored pencils

"Let's practice mixing hues to create a color wheel using primary, secondary, and intermediate colors."

"Vamos a mezclar colores para crear un círculo cromático usando colores primarios, secundarios e intermedios."

- Discuss the definitions of *primary, secondary, intermediate,* and *analogous colors* on page 52.
- Distribute materials and have students follow the directions on page 52 for making the color wheel. Have them discuss the answer to the Decide questions.

Create PROBLEM SOLVING

Materials
- liquid tempera paints
- brushes
- white paper
- pencils

Alternate Materials: colored pencils

"Let's create a nonobjective painting using an analogous color scheme."

"Vamos a hacer un dibujo abstracto usando un esquema de colores análogos."

- Brainstorm ideas about the different shapes in your environment and use them to create a nonobjective drawing.
- Review analogous color schemes.
- Review procedures for working with paint in **Technique Tips** on page 198.
- Distribute materials and have students follow the directions on page 53.

FOR THE ART SPECIALIST

Work with students to make a weaving on a frame loom using analogous colors.

Using Analogous Colors

On the color wheel, **analogous colors** sit next to each other. They share a common color or hue. For example, violet, blue, blue-green, and green are analogous colors. They share the color blue and are next to each other on the color wheel.

A **color scheme** is a plan for organizing colors. Analogous colors are one type of color scheme. The color scheme on the left shares the color blue. The color scheme on the right shares the color red.

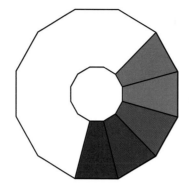 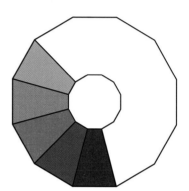

Practice

Create a color wheel using primary, secondary, and intermediate colors. Use paint.

1. Draw a large circle and divide it into 12 equal pie-shaped wedges. Paint primary colors in three wedges and leave three empty wedges.

2. Combine primary colors to make secondary colors. Mix secondary colors with primary colors to create intermediate colors.

Decide Did you mix secondary and intermediate colors? How can you improve them?

Activities in
ART Across the Curriculum Book

Reading/Language Arts Describe a painting using specific, descriptive words. (page 43)

Math Add decimals by identifying numbers in analogous colors. (page 44)

Science Make a loom and create a weaving like *Eye Dazzler*. (page 45)

Social Studies Learn more about the geographic area where the Navajo live. (page 46)

The Arts Create a drum solo that matches the rhythms seen in *Eye Dazzler*. (page 47)

Technology Use the *Multimedia Workshop* CD-ROM to create a design filled with analogous colors. (page 48)

Cedar Brook School. *Analogous Scheme.* Tempera.

What are the analogous colors used in the nonobjective art?

Create

What are the different shapes you see in your environment? Create a nonobjective painting with an analogous color scheme.

1. Think about different shapes. Draw shapes that overlap and vary in size. Draw several sketches.

2. Reproduce one design to create a nonobjective painting. A **nonobjective painting** contains shapes, lines, and colors, not objects or people.

3. Use an analogous color scheme to paint your nonobjective design.

Describe What type of shapes did you use in your nonobjective painting?

Analyze Name the analogous colors you used in your painting.

Interpret What title best reflects the mood of your artwork?

Decide Did you successfully create a nonobjective painting using analogous colors?

Lesson **2**   53

Patterns Use the Navajo piece as a springboard to discuss patterns of tornadoes in the Midwest.

Cultures Use the Navajo piece to compare and contrast our current culture with that of the contemporary Native American.

Second-language students may benefit from extra visual aids in learning concepts presented in this lesson. You might create a large poster with words and simple illustrations describing the color. Students can make individual versions of these graphic organizers for future reference.

CLOSE

Time: About 5 minutes

"Were you able to create a nonobjective painting using analogous colors?"

"¿Fueron capaces de hacer un dibujo abstracto usando colores análogos?"

Review
Use the **Large Print** *Bookwus Mask* to have students define analogous colors. Ask them to compare the use of color in the **Large Print** *Sunday Afternoon on the Island of Grande Jatte* to the works in this lesson.

Art Criticism
Have students answer the four art criticism questions—Describe, Analyze, Interpret, and Decide—orally or in writing. Discuss the use of color in their paintings.

Assess
Use the **Assessment Book** pages 15–16 as a formal assessment for this lesson.

Evaluation Criteria
• Can the student distinguish primary, secondary, and analogous colors?
• Can the student create a nonobjective painting using an analogous color scheme?
• Can the student use the four steps of art criticism to evaluate his or her own work?
• Can the student recognize the cultural purpose of each work of art?

Reteaching • • • • • • • • • • • •

Analogous colors Have the students find examples of analogous colors in their environment.

Use the color wheel in the **Art Manipulative Kit** to have students point out analogous colors.

Perception Hints for Student Art

The first analogous color scheme used by the student artist includes the colors red, orange, yellow, and green. The second scheme ranges from violet to green.

Complementary Colors

Artists use complementary colors to create contrast
and visual excitement in their artwork.

Artist unknown. (Peru).
Featherwork Neckpiece.
1350–1476. 13¼ × 11½ inches.
Cotton, feathers, beads; Late
Intermediate Period; China
Style. Dallas Museum of Art.
The Eugene and Margaret
McDermott Art Fund, Inc.

The *Featherwork Neckpiece* is an example of an
adornment. An **adornment** decorates or adds beauty
to an object or a person. Willis Bing Davis uses historical
African patterns and forms as inspiration for his contemporary
images. In Davis's work, he reflects on the images and
feelings he experienced while attending a ritual dance in
Nigeria. Notice that both artists used contrasting colors. What
emotional qualities were they trying to express?

54   Unit **2**

U NIT 2
LESSON 3

LESSON PLANNER

Objectives
After completing this lesson, students will be
able to:
- recognize complementary color schemes
  used by artists. *Aesthetic Perception*
- design and create a poster using
  complementary colors. *Creative Expression*
- use the four steps of art criticism to evaluate
  their own posters. *Art Criticism*
- recognize the cultural purpose of each work
  of art. *Art History and Culture*

Program Resources
- **Overhead:** Both the *Featherwork Neckpiece*
  and the Davis are available on overhead 9.
- **Large Prints:** *Sunday Afternoon on the Island
  of Grande Jatte* by George Seurat and *Bootwus
  Mask* by Beau Dick
- **Vocabulary Book** pages 17–18
- **Artist Profiles Book:** Davis page 14 and
  Artist unknown page 64
- **Art Across the Curriculum Book** pages
  49–54
- **Multimedia Workshop CD-ROM**
- **Assessment Book** pages 17–18

   Multiple Intelligences
   Visual/Spatial Students can identify
relationships of colors on the color wheel and
use complementary colors to create contrast
in an artwork.

Vocabulary
complementary colors *colores
complementarios* colors opposite each other on
the color wheel

color intensity *intensidad del color* the
brightness or dullness of a color

F OCUS
Time: About 10 minutes

Activating Prior Knowledge
"Try to recall some billboards and posters that you have
seen. What complementary colors do you remember
noticing on them?"

*"Traten de recordar algunas vallas y carteles que hayan visto.
¿Qué colores complementarios recuerdan haber notado?"*

- Discuss students' responses to colors.

54   Unit **2**

ART *Background*

About the Artists
Willis Bing Davis (American, 1937–   ) began his interest in art while in elementary
school. This African American artist attended DePauw University, Miami University (Oxford,
Ohio), Indiana State University, and the Dayton Art Institute. Davis has been an artist and
teacher since 1960.

About Subject Matter* Both works are symbolic. The feather neck piece is a woven
ceremonial object worn around the neck.

About the Media The neck piece is a weaving made of fiber and feathers. Davis's piece
is oil on canvas.

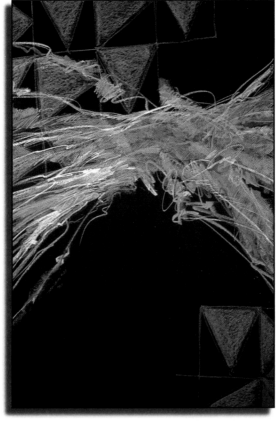

Willis Bing Davis. (American). *Ancestral Spirit Dance Series.*
40 × 60 inches. Courtesy of Bing Davis.

Study both works of art to find their complementary
color schemes.

- ☑ What colors do you see?
- ☑ Do you see different shades or tints of these colors?
- ☑ What colors do you see repeated?
- ☑ Talk about how the artists created contrast in the artwork.

SEEING LIKE AN ARTIST
Do you notice any classmates wearing colors that contrast or look bright next to each other? What colors are they wearing?

Lesson 3 55

Introducing the Art
"Let's look closely at the artwork."
"Vamos a observar detalladamente la obra de arte."

- **Describe:** Ask students to describe the subject matter in both works of art. (both: symbolic)
- Share and discuss information with students from **Art Background** and the **Artist Profiles Book**.
- **Compare** both artworks. (Both use bright colors. Both use different tints from one color, and they are symbolic. They also create contrast with complementary colors.)
- Have students answer the questions on page 55. (See **Perception Hints** below.)

FOR THE ART SPECIALIST

Use the **Overhead** and the **Large Prints** *Sunday Afternoon on the Island of Grande Jatte* and *Bookwus Mask* to demonstrate how artists use complementary colors to create contrast and visual excitement in their artwork.

Perception Hints

Colors *Neckpiece.* Bright orange, violet, and blue. *Davis.* Blue and orange.
Shades and tints Both works have different shades or tints of one color. *Davis.* There are tints of turquoise and blue and violet.
Repeated colors The repeated colors in both works are blue and orange.
Contrast The artists created contrast in the artworks by using complementary colors.

About Art History* The Inca civilization flourished from the twelfth to the sixteenth century.

Davis's works include drawings, paintings, ceramics, and jewelry designing.

Cultural Perspectives Neck pieces were found by archaeologists in Inca burial graves hidden in the Andes mountains.

Davis is influenced by traditional African art and culture. He uses African patterns, motifs, and color to help him express his images of the African American experience.

*See **More About** pages 206–227 for more about art history and subject matter.

TEACH

Time: About 30 minutes

Practice

Materials
- scissors
- colored paper

Alternate Materials: markers

"How do complementary colors affect each other?"

"¿Cómo se afectan entre sí los colores complementarios?"

- Discuss the definition of *complementary colors* on page 56.
- Distribute materials and have students follow the directions on page 56 to see how complementary colors affect each other. Have them discuss the answer to the Decide question.

Create PROBLEM SOLVING

Materials
- posterboard
- construction paper of complementary colors
- scissors
- glue

Alternate Materials: markers, crayons

"Let's design a poster using complementary colors."

"Vamos a diseñar un cartel usando los colores complementarios."

- Have students brainstorm ideas and events to include on a poster.
- Review complementary colors.
- Distribute materials and have students follow the directions on page 57.
- When they are finished, have students present their posters to the class.

 FOR THE ART SPECIALIST

Create a label for your favorite food using complementary colors and combining words and images.

Using Complementary Colors

Colors opposite each other on the color wheel are called **complementary colors**. A complement of a color is the strongest contrast to the color. They are used to create contrast. Red and green, blue and orange, and violet and yellow are all complementary colors.

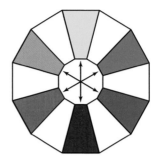

Complementary colors seem to vibrate when they are placed next to each other.

Color Intensities Mixing a color with its complement lowers the brightness or dullness of that color. When two complementary colors are mixed, the color becomes dull. Look at the intensity scale. As you add a small amount of green to red, it becomes dull. More green makes it duller. Equal amounts of red and green make an interesting low-intensity gray. The same thing happens when you add red to green.

Practice

Experiment with pieces of colored paper to see how complementary colors affect each other. Use colored paper.

1. Cut out a hole in a piece of paper. Place the paper with the hole on top of the complementary color to see how they look.

2. Place the hole you cut out on top of the complementary color to see how it looks inside the color.

Decide How did the complementary colors affect each other?

Activities in ART Across the Curriculum Book

Reading/Language Arts Learn how to support opinion with fact to give intensity to words like the opposing relationship of complementary colors. (page 49)

Math Build polygons from simple geometric shapes. (page 50)

Science Learn how data collected from artifacts, like the neckpiece, teach us about the past. (page 51)

Social Studies Learn about textiles, including the one used in the artwork. (page 52)

The Arts Understand how costume and dance are related to special occasions. For example, the neckpiece is worn during a ritual dance in Peru. (page 53)

Technology Use the *Multimedia Workshop* CD-ROM to create a mask filled with complementary colors. (page 54)

Amanda Lee. Age 10. *Earth.* Cut paper.

What are the complementary colors used by the student artist?

Create

What complementary colors would best communicate an idea or event you would like to advertise? Create a poster using complementary colors.

1. Think about an event or idea of interest to you. Create a poster to communicate it. Pick one set of complementary colors for your poster.

2. Using two complementary colors, cut out shapes, letters, and designs. Overlap shapes and have them touch the edges of the background.

3. Glue your shapes and letters onto the background.

Describe What complementary colors, objects, and shapes did you use?

Analyze How did your complementary colors create contrast and visual excitement?

Interpret What is the theme and mood of your poster?

Decide Did your poster successfully communicate your event or idea?

Lesson 3

57

CLOSE

Time: About 5 minutes

"Were you able to create a poster using complementary colors?"

"¿Fueron capaces de hacer un cartel usando los colores complementarios?"

Review
Use the **Large Print** *Sunday Afternoon on the Island of Grande Jatte* to have students compare the use of color in the print with the use of color in the artworks in the lesson.

Art Criticism
Have students answer the four art criticism questions—Describe, Analyze, Interpret, and Decide—orally or in writing. Discuss the use of color in their posters.

Assess
Use the **Assessment Book** pages 17–18 as a formal assessment for this lesson.

Evaluation Criteria
- Can the student identify a complementary color scheme?
- Can the student design and create a poster using complementary colors?
- Can the student use the four steps of art criticism to evaluate his or her own work?
- Can the student recognize the cultural purpose of each work of art?

Reteaching • • • • • • • • • • • •

Complementary colors Have students look through magazines to find five photographs of complementary color schemes used in advertising. Ask them to list the complementary colors.

Perception Hints for Student Art

The complementary colors used by the student artist are blue and green.

Warm and Cool Colors

Artists use warm and cool color schemes to create a mood or feeling in their artwork.

Robert Lostutter. (American). *Baird Trogon*. 1985. Watercolor over graphite. 61.5 × 88 cm. Art Institute of Chicago, Chicago, Illinois. Restricted Gift of the Illinois Arts Council, Logan Fund, 1985.

Lostutter uses the contrast of warm and cool colors to show his expertise with watercolors and his interest in birds. The textures of the feathers contrast with the smooth skin of the man. Mabe uses contrasts between lights and darks and blobs of color to express emotions in his work. Mabe was influenced by his oriental traditions. Both artists have used the contrast of warm and cool colors.

UNIT 2 — LESSON 4

LESSON PLANNER

Objectives

After completing this lesson, students will be able to:

- identify warm and cool colors in art and in the environment. *Aesthetic Perception*
- create a collage using warm and cool colors. *Creative Expression*
- use the four steps of art criticism to evaluate their own artwork. *Art Criticism*
- compare the lives and work of Robert Lostutter and Manabu Mabe. *Art History and Culture*

Program Resources

- **Overhead:** Both the Lostutter and the Mabe are available on overhead 10.
- **Large Prints:** *Sunday Afternoon on the Island of Grande Jatte* by George Seurat and *Bootwus Mask* by Beau Dick
- **Vocabulary Book** pages 19–20
- **Artist Profiles Book:** Lostutter page 32 and Mabe page 33
- **Art Across the Curriculum Book** pages 55–60
- **Multimedia Workshop CD-ROM**
- **National Geographic Picture Atlas of the World CD-ROM**
- **Assessment Book** pages 19–20

Multiple Intelligences

Interpersonal Students can create a mood or a feeling through their use of warm and cool colors in artwork.

Vocabulary

warm color *color cálido* a color that suggests a warm mood and seems to move toward the viewer. Red, orange, and yellow are warm colors.

cool color *color fresco* a color that suggests a cool mood and seems to recede from the viewer. Blue, green, and violet are cool colors.

ART Background

About the Artists

Robert Lostutter (rob′ ərt lō′ stut ər, American, 1939–) is known for his colorful and realistic portrayal of birdmen. *Baird Trogon* shows Lostutter's expertise with watercolors and his personal interest in ornithology, or the study of birds. Notice the intricate textures of the feathers and how they contrast with the soft, smooth skin of the man. A trogon is a brightly colored, fruit-eating, tropical bird.

Manabu Mabe (mä nä bū mä be, Japanese, 1924–) moved from Kumamoto, Japan, where he was born, to Sao Paulo, Brazil, when he was ten years of age. In the 1950s, he was recognized by critics for his lyrical, abstract paintings.

About Subject Matter* The Lostutter is a portrait, and the Mabe is nonobjective art.

About the Media The Lostutter is a watercolor over graphite. The Mabe is oil on canvas.

Manabu Mabe. (Japanese). *Melancholy Metropolis.* Oil on canvas. $72\frac{7}{8} \times 78\frac{7}{8} \times 1\frac{1}{4}$ inches. Collection Walker Art Center, Minneapolis, Minnesota, Gift of the T. B. Walker Foundation 1963.

Study both paintings to find the warm and cool colors.

- What colors do you see that remind you of water, the forest, or a cool winter's day?

- What other colors do you see? Are there any colors that remind you of fire?

- How do these colors affect the mood of these paintings?

SEEING LIKE AN ARTIST

Notice the colors worn most often and least often in class. Do these colors remind you of something warm or something cool?

Lesson 4   **59**

Activating Prior Knowledge
"What colors do you think of when you imagine a day in winter, summer, fall, or spring?"

"¿Qué colores les vienen a la mente cuando se imaginan un día en invierno, verano, otoño o primavera?"

- Discuss students' responses. Help them associate warm colors with warm things, such as the sun and fire, and cool colors with cool things, such as water and ice.

Introducing the Art
"Let's look closely at the paintings."

"Vamos a observar detalladamente las pinturas."

- **Describe:** Ask students to describe the subject matter in both works of art.
- Share and discuss information from **Art Background** and the **Artist Profiles Book.**
  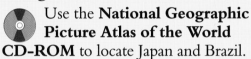 Use the **National Geographic Picture Atlas of the World CD-ROM** to locate Japan and Brazil.
- Have students answer the questions on page 59. (See **Perception Hints** below.)

FOR THE ART SPECIALIST

Use the **Overhead** and the **Large Print** *Sunday Afternoon on the Island of Grande Jatte* to discuss and to demonstrate how artists use warm and cool color schemes to create a mood or feeling in their artwork.

Perception Hints

Colors that remind you of water, the forest, or a cool winter's day are blue in the Lostutter and blue, purple, and green in the Mabe.

Colors that remind you of fire in the Lostutter are red on the cheeks, yellow-orange in the sky, and red on the lips. In the Mabe, you can see red and blue.

Colors Many will associate red with a warm feeling, and blue with cool things.

TEACH

Time: About 30 minutes

Practice

Materials
- scissors
- construction paper in warm and cool colors
- tissue paper in warm and cool colors

Alternate Materials: markers

"Let's experiment with warm and cool colors."
"Vamos a experimentar con colores cálidos y frescos."

- Discuss warm and cool colors on page 60.
- Distribute materials and have students follow the directions on page 60 for experimenting with warm and cool colors. Have them answer the Decide questions by discussing them with partners.

Create PROBLEM SOLVING

Materials
- drawing paper in warm and cool colors
- tissue paper in warm and cool colors
- glue
- scissors
- white paper

Alternate Materials: construction paper in warm and cool colors

"Let's create a collage using warm and cool colors."
"Vamos a hacer un collaje usando colores cálidos y colores frescos."

- Have students brainstorm ideas for creating a collage.
- Review the definitions for *warm* and *cool colors*.
- Distribute materials and have students follow the directions on page 61.
- Have students share their collages with their classmates.

FOR THE ART SPECIALIST

Create a tissue paper collage of warm and cool colors on waxed paper to put onto windows.

Using Warm and Cool Colors

Sometimes colors are divided into warm and cool colors. They make us think about warm or cool things when we see them.

Warm colors are red, orange, and yellow. They suggest warmth and seem to move toward the viewer. They remind us of the sun or fire. Artists use warm color schemes to express a warm mood.

Cool colors are blue, green, and violet. They suggest coolness and seem to move away from the viewer. Cool colors remind us of ice, water, and grass. Artists use cool color schemes to express a cool mood.

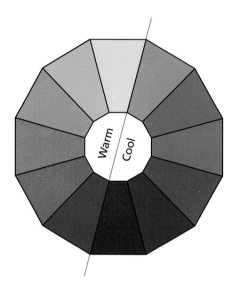

Practice

Experiment with warm and cool colors. Use warm and cool colors of tissue paper.

1. Cut out squares of colored tissue paper. Separate the warm colors and the cool colors.

2. Overlap warm- and cool-colored tissue paper. Hold them up to the light. Then, overlap only warm and only cool colors.

Decide What happened when you overlapped warm and cool colors? Did the colors change when they were placed together?

Activities in ART Across the Curriculum Book

Reading/Language Arts Learn how to use the dictionary to understand word meanings, like *Melancholy Metropolis*. (page 55)

Math Estimate multiplication numbers using rows of feathers. (page 56)

Science Learn about constellations and stargazing, understanding that patterns can be found in nature as well as in the paintings. (page 57)

Social Studies Study how murals convey a message as in the Mabe. (page 58)

The Arts Write a monologue for a person that inspires people to "soar to great heights," noting that birds can soar to great heights. (page 59)

Technology Use the *Multimedia Workshop* CD-ROM to create a design filled with warm and cool colors. (page 60)

Ester Stewart. Age 11. *Panic in the City*. Colored tissue paper and construction paper.

How do the colors and shapes of the artwork contribute to the mood?

Create

How can you create a specific mood in a collage? Use warm and cool colors to create a collage.

1. Think about the warm and cool colors you like.

2. Cut free-form and/or geometric shapes out of colored drawing paper and tissue paper.

3. Arrange your shapes. Combine the warm and cool colors. Allow the tissue paper to overlap some of the drawing paper colors. Glue your shapes onto the white background.

Describe What colors did you overlap? What shapes did you see?

Analyze Did you use warm and cool colors to organize your collage? Did changes occur when you overlapped colored areas with the tissue paper?

Interpret What mood was created by your use of colors?

Decide If you could do this over again, how would you make it different?

Lesson 4   **61**

THEME Connections

Cultures Use the Mabe work as a springboard to explore the Japanese art of origami, the art or process of Japanese paper folding.

Relationships Use the Lostutter as a means to facilitate a discussion regarding the relationship between light and mood disorders.

ESL

Abstract concepts, such as the mood of a painting, should be made concrete for second-language learners in order to ensure their comprehension. You might model some vocabulary that describes mood—and pantomime its meaning—to help build students' knowledge. For example, you might say: *Do you feel hopeful as you look at this picture?*

CLOSE

Time: About 5 minutes

"Were you able to create a collage using warm and cool colors?"

"¿Fueron capaces de hacer un collaje usando colores cálidos y frescos?"

Review

ART MANIPULATIVES Use the **Art Manipulative Kit** color paddles to review warm and cool colors.

LARGE PRINT Use the **Large Print** *Bootwus Mask* to have students compare how color is used in the print with how it is used in the works in this lesson.

Art Criticism

Have students answer the four art criticism questions—Describe, Analyze, Interpret, and Decide—orally or in writing. Discuss the use of color in their collages.

Assess
Use the **Assessment Book** pages 19–20 as a formal assessment for this lesson.

Evaluation Criteria

- Can the student identify warm and cool colors?
- Can the student create a collage using warm and cool colors?
- Can the student use the four steps of art criticism to evaluate his or her own artwork?
- Can the student compare the lives and work of Robert Lostutter and Manabu Mabe?

Reteaching • • • • • • • • • • • •

Warm and cool colors Find two more artworks in the book that use warm and cool colors. What moods do they depict?

Perception Hints for Student Art

The colors and shapes of the student art tend to leave the viewer feeling happy.

UNIT 2
LESSON 5

LESSON PLANNER

Objectives
After completing this lesson, students will be able to:
- identify visual rhythm and movement in art. *Aesthetic Perception*
- create a unique landscape using flowing rhythm. *Creative Expression*
- use the four steps of art criticism to evaluate their own artwork. *Art Criticism*
- recognize the cultural purpose of each artwork. *Art History and Culture*

Program Resources
- **Overhead:** Both the McNeil and *Ipuy and His Wife* are available on overhead 11.
- **Large Prints:** *Sunday Afternoon on the Island of Grande Jatte* by George Seurat and *Bookwus Mask* by Beau Dick
- **Vocabulary Book** pages 21–22
- **Artist Profiles Book:** McNeil page 35 and Artist unknown page 65
- **Art Across the Curriculum Book** pages 61–66
- **Multimedia Workshop CD-ROM**
- **Assessment Book** pages 21–22

Multiple Intelligences
Body/Kinesthetic Students can create rhythm and movement in art by understanding how their own bodies move.

Vocabulary
visual rhythm *ritmo visual* a repeated pattern created by the repetition of shapes, color, or line

visual movement *movimiento visual* a visual rhythm that pulls the viewer's eyes through a work of art

regular rhythm *ritmo regular* repeats motifs with the same amount of space between them

alternate rhythm *ritmo alterno* repeats motifs but changes the positions or adds a second motif to the pattern

random rhythm *ritmo aleatorio* when the motif is repeated in no apparent order

progressive rhythm *ritmo progresivo* when a motif changes each time it is repeated

flowing rhythm *ritmo continuo* rhythm that repeats wavy lines

---

Visual Rhythm and Movement

Artists use visual rhythm and movement to add interest and visual excitement to artworks.

George McNeil. (American). *Deliverance Disco.* Montclair Art Museum, Montclair, New Jersey.

In *Deliverance Disco,* everything seems to be moving quickly. Observe how McNeil uses lines and color to express movement and add interest and excitement. The Egyptian wall fresco was created following strict rules. Certain parts of the body are drawn sideways. Other parts face forward. The artist used repetition to create visual movement. Both artists used different techniques to make our eyes move about the artwork as we observe it.

ART Background

About the Artists
Egyptian Art from 3000 B.C. to the fifth century changed little due to the country's semi-isolation. Art was devoted mostly to the king.

George McNeil (jôrj mək nēl', American, 1908–   ) was a pioneer in the world of abstract painting. Born in New York, he developed his style while studying at the Pratt Institute during the 1920s and 1930s. He was a founding member of the American Abstract Artists group, which encouraged museums to show American abstract art.

About Subject Matter* The Egyptian painting is a narrative. *Deliverance Disco* is symbolic.

About the Media McNeil uses brush strokes that are obvious marks on the texture of the canvas. He applies many layers of paint over one another.

Artist unknown. (Egyptian). *Ipuy and his Wife receiving offerings from their children.* Fresco. 47.5 × 74 cm. Copy of wall painting from the tomb of Ipuy. Egyptian Expedition of the Metropolitan Museum of Art, New York, New York. Rogers Fund 1930.

Study both paintings to find examples of visual rhythm and movement.

- ✓ Where are lines or shapes that appear to move or flow?

- ✓ Where do your eyes look first in each painting and where do they look last? What causes this to happen?

- ✓ Which painting uses free-form shapes and which one uses geometric shapes?

- ✓ What feelings does each painting evoke?

SEEING LIKE AN ARTIST

Do you see repetition of lines, shapes, or colors in any objects around you? Where else have you seen repeated lines, shapes, or colors?

About Art History* *Abstract art* is a term used to describe art that does not realistically portray an object. Modern abstract movements include Fauvism, Cubism, and Abstract Expressionism. There are ancient forms of abstract art, as well. Both Egyptian painting and Byzantine mosaics turn the original object or subject of a painting into a series of shapes, hues, or colors.

Cultural Perspectives McNeil worked as an artist for the WPA (Works Progress Administration) Federal Art Project during the Great Depression of the 1930s. *Egyptology* is a special branch of the science of archaeology that studies ancient Egyptian civilization. It began in 1799 when Napoleon invaded Egypt. He wanted to understand the riches he found in the tombs of the Great Pyramids.

*See **More About** pages 206–227 for more about art history and subject matter.

FOCUS

Time: About 10 minutes

Activating Prior Knowledge

"What do you associate with the word *rhythm*?"

¿Qué asocian con la palabra ritmo?"

- Explain to students that in visual art, rhythm is created by the repetition of shapes, colors, and lines, rather than sound and time as in music.

Introducing the Art

"Let's look closely at the two paintings."

"Vamos a observar detalladamente las dos pinturas."

- **Describe:** Ask students to describe the subject matter in both works of art.

- Share and discuss information from **Art Background** and the **Artist Profiles Book**.

- Ask students to answer the questions on page 63. (See **Perception Hints** below.)

 FOR THE ART SPECIALIST

Use the **Overhead** and the **Large Prints** *Sunday Afternoon on the Island of Grande Jatte* and *Bookwus Mask* to demonstrate how artists use visual rhythm and movement to add interest and visual excitement to artworks.

Perception Hints

Ipuy and His Wife. Objects and patterns are repeated in the way the servants are lined up. There are lines in the clothing of all. *Deliverance Disco.* Pattern is all over. It is on the leopard, the things being held, the neckwear, the headwear, and even in the hair.
Ipuy. The eyes look first at the white of the skirts and last at the top of the picture. *Deliverance.* The eyes look first at the upper-left area of the work because it is the lightest. Eyes look to the right of the work where the dark area is. *Ipuy* uses straight lines and geometric shapes. *Deliverance* uses all free-form shapes.

TEACH

Time: About 30 minutes

Practice

Materials
- colored markers
- white paper

Alternate Materials: crayons

"How can you illustrate five types of visual rhythm?"

"¿Cómo pueden ilustrar cinco tipos de ritmo visual?"

- Have students review the types of rhythms.
- Distribute materials and have students follow the directions on page 64. Have them discuss the answers to the Decide questions.

Create PROBLEM SOLVING

Materials
- earth pigments
- pencils
- binder, or white glue and water
- mortar and pestle
- white paper
- large and small brushes

Alternate Materials: watercolors

"Let's use earth pigments to create a landscape using visual rhythm."

"Vamos a usar pigmentos de tierra para hacer un paisaje usando ritmo visual."

- Have them practice drawing flowing rhythm designs on paper before applying the colors.
- Distribute materials and have students follow the directions on page 65.
- **Natural earth pigments** are anywhere there is dirt, clay, and sand. Collect and grind them finely. (You can use a mortar and pestle.) The finished product will be gritty. For the binder, use one part white glue to one part water. Put a few spoonfuls of pigment into a small container and add some binder. Try different proportions for the color you want. Apply the mixture using a variety of brushes. Stir the mixture to keep the pigment from settling.

FOR THE ART SPECIALIST

Create a landscape scene with flowing rhythms using watercolors.

Using Visual Rhythm and Movement

Visual Rhythm is a repeated pattern created by the repetition of shapes, color, or lines. It pulls the viewer's eyes through a work of art. **Pattern** is another word used to describe visual rhythm.

Movement means creating the illusion of movement through visual rhythm. Artists use movement to control the way a person looks at a work of art.

A **motif** is the object that is repeated or unit of objects that is repeated.

Five Types of Rhythm

 **Regular rhythm** occurs when each motif is repeated with the same amount of space between.

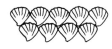 **Alternate rhythm** repeats motifs but changes positions of the motifs or adds a second motif to the pattern.

 **Random rhythm** occurs when the motif is repeated in no apparent order.

 **Progressive rhythm** is a motif that changes each time it is repeated.

 **Flowing rhythm** is rhythm that repeats wavy lines.

Practice

Create designs using five types of visual rhythm. Use colored markers.

1. Fold paper into four sections. Label each section one of the five types of rhythm. Use the back of your paper and label one of your sections the last type of rhythm.

2. Think of a single design or motif. Repeat your design or motif to practice the five types of visual rhythm.

Decide Did you create the five kinds of visual rhythm? Did your designs create a sense of movement?

Activities in ART Across the Curriculum Book

Reading/Language Arts Learn about Egyptian hieroglyphics like those seen in the painting *Ipuy and His Wife*. (page 61)

Math Compare the Egyptian calendar with our calendar. (page 62)

Science Learn about chemical and physical change with both common and art materials, like in the fresco painting. (page 63)

Social Studies Study the geographic features of ancient Egypt. (page 64)

The Arts Describe the kinds of movements the people in the art might make. (page 65)

Technology Use the *Multimedia Workshop* CD-ROM to create several designs showing different kinds of rhythm. (page 66)

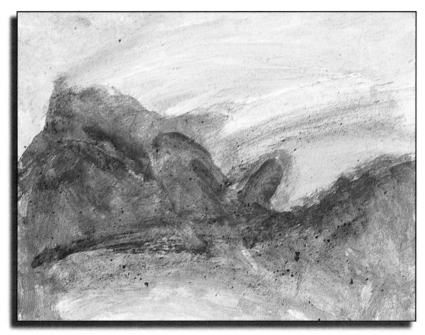

Mandy Tomberlin. Age 9. *A Sunrise on the Mountain.* Dirt and glue.

What lines does the artist use to create a flowing rhythm?

Create ————

What rhythms do you see when you look at the landscape from your window? Create a landscape using flowing rhythm.

1. Think about the colors of the earth. Imagine using them to create a landscape.

2. Collect a variety of earth pigments. Grind your collected pigments. Add them to binder or glue.

3. Lightly draw a landscape using repeated curving lines to create a flowing rhythm.

4. Paint your landscape with the earth pigment paints. Experiment using different amounts of pigment and binder.

Describe How did you create some of your colors?

Analyze Did you use curved lines to create the feeling of flowing rhythm?

Interpret What mood did you create in your landscape?

Decide Were you successful in using flowing rhythm in your landscape?

Lesson 5 65

THEME Connections

Cultures Use both works as examples to discuss cultures that are different from your own.

Systems Use the Egyptian work to compare their system of counting and measuring to our system.

ESL

Guiding ESL students step by step through the text's questions can help you adjust your presentation of the lesson as needed to ensure comprehension. You can ask students to respond physically, with a partner, or chorally to questions to monitor understanding. For example: "*Show your partner a regular rhythm in the picture.*"

CLOSE
Time: About 5 minutes

"Were you able to create a landscape with flowing rhythms?"
"¿Fueron capaces de hacer un paisaje con ritmos continuos?"

LARGE PRINT **Review**
Use the **Large Print** by Seurat to have students compare the use of visual rhythm and movement to the works in this lesson.

Art Criticism
Have students answer the four art criticism questions—Describe, Analyze, Interpret, and Decide—orally or in writing. Discuss the use of visual rhythm and movement in their landscape paintings.

Assesss
Use the **Assessment Book** pages 21–22 as a formal assessment for this lesson.

Evaluation Criteria
• Can the student identify visual rhythm and movement in art?
• Can the student use flowing rhythm to create a unique landscape painting?
• Can the student use the four steps of art criticism to evaluate his or her own artwork?
• Can the student recognize the cultural purpose of each artwork?

Reteaching • • • • • • • • • • • • •

Visual rhythm and movement Have students find other examples of visual rhythm and movement in other works in the book.

Perception Hints for Student Art
The student artist uses curved or wavy lines to create a flowing rhythm.

UNIT 2

LESSON 6

LESSON PLANNER

Objectives

After completing this lesson, students will be able to:

- identify how colors are used to create visual rhythm. *Aesthetic Perception*
- use expressive colors and visual rhythm to illustrate a piece of music. *Creative Expression*
- use the four steps of art criticism to evaluate their own works. *Art Criticism*
- compare the work and lives of both artists. *Art History and Culture*

Program Resources

- **Overhead:** Both the van Gogh and the Liotard are available on overhead 12.
- **Large Prints:** *Sunday Afternoon on the Island of Grande Jatte* by George Seurat and *Bookwus Mask* by Dick Beau
- **Vocabulary Book** pages 23–24
- **Art Manipulative Kit:** music audiotape
- **Artist Profiles Book:** van Gogh page 55 and Liotard page 30
- **Art Across the Curriculum Book** pages 67–72
- **Multimedia Workshop CD-ROM**
- **Assessment Book** pages 23–24

Multiple Intelligences
Intrapersonal Students can express different feelings through use of color or observe the expressive effects of color in artists' works.

Vocabulary

visual rhythm *ritmo visual* created by repeated shapes separated by the area around them

monochromatic color scheme *esquema de colores monocromático* using only one color and its tints and shades

analogous color scheme *esquema de colores análogos* colors that are side by side on the color wheel

complementary color *color complementario* colors that are opposite each other on the color wheel

---

Color and Visual Rhythm

Artists use color to express moods or feelings in their artworks.

Vincent van Gogh. (Dutch). *A Pair of Boots.* 1887. Oil on canvas. $13 \times 16\frac{1}{8}$ inches. Baltimore Museum of Art, Baltimore, Maryland. The Cone Collection, formed by Dr. Claribel Cone and Miss Etta Cone of Baltimore, Maryland.

How are these two paintings similar? Vincent van Gogh painted the shoes of a common man with dull colors to express the poverty that many people suffered. Jean-Étienne Liotard used bold colors to express the luxurious life of a rich woman. Both artists used colors to express certain moods and feelings in their paintings.

ART Background

About the Artists

Vincent van Gogh (vin sent' van gō', Dutch, 1853–1890) was the son of a minister. His religious upbringing influenced his life and, indirectly, his art. His art career spanned just ten years, and during the last five years of his life, he completed more than 800 works.

Jean-Eitienne Liotard (zhän ā tyen lē ō tär, Swiss, 1702–1789) was born in Geneva. He traveled in his youth and in 1736, while in Italy, he became acquainted with a group of wealthy, young Englishmen who invited him to visit Constantinople. He was so taken by the wealth of the culture that he stayed for five years and adopted the dress and manner of a Turk.

About Subject Matter* The van Gogh is a genre, and the Liotard is a narrative painting or a genre.

Jean-Étienne Liotard. (Swedish). *A Frankish Woman and Her Servant.* 1750. Oil on canvas. $28\frac{1}{2} \times 22\frac{1}{2}$ inches. Nelson-Atkins Museum of Art, Kansas City, Missouri. (Purchase Nelson Trust).

Think about how the artists use color to reveal the mood of each painting.

- ✓ What colors are used in both paintings?
- ✓ Which painting uses dull colors for the background?
- ✓ What mood or feeling is created in each painting?
- ✓ How does the artist's use of color affect the mood of each work?

SEEING LIKE AN ARTIST

What colors do your friends use to express themselves? How do you express yourself through color?

Lesson 6   67

About the Media Both works are oil paintings.

About Art History* Van Gogh is considered the greatest nineteenth-century Dutch artist. He was one of the first to express his feelings through painting.

Liotard was best known for his pastels, a medium in which he was an undisputed master.

Cultural Perspectives During the time van Gogh created his work, Queen Victoria celebrated her Diamond Jubilee in England. In France, Louis Pasteur made the first successful inoculation against rabies. The first automobile was produced by Gottlieb in 1886, and in 1895, Marconi sent the first radio transmission.

*See **More About** pages 206–227 for more about art history and subject matter.

FOCUS

Time: About 10 minutes

Activating Prior Knowledge

"What if television were only in black and white?"
¿Qué pasaría si la televisión fuera sólo en negro y blanco?"

- Explain to students that at one time there were no color televisions.
- Ask students what they feel they would be missing without color.
- Discuss how color affects everyday life.

Introducing the Art

"Let's look closely at the two paintings."
"Vamos a observar detalladamente las dos pinturas."

- **Describe:** Ask students to describe the subject matter in both works of art. (van Gogh: genre; Liotard: narrative)
- Share and discuss information from **Art Background** and the **Artist Profiles Book.**
- Have students answer the questions on page 67. (See **Perception Hints** below.)

FOR THE ART SPECIALIST

Use the **Overhead** and the **Large Print** *Bookwus Mask* to demonstrate how artists use color to express moods or feelings in their artworks.

Perception Hints

The artists use color to reveal the mood of each painting. Van Gogh used brown and gray. Liotard used red-orange and green.
Both works used dull colors for the background.
The mood or feeling of each work varies with the viewer. Dark and muted colors are used in the van Gogh to create a solemn or sad mood. Bright, cheerful, and light colors are used in the Liotard to create a happy and cheerful mood.

TEACH

Time: About 30 minutes

Practice

Materials
- crayons

Alternate Materials: markers

"How can you express a different feeling or mood through color?"

"¿Cómo pueden expresar un sentimiento o ánimo diferente a través del color?"

- Discuss how different color schemes create different feelings.
- Distribute materials and have students follow the directions on page 68 for using color to express themselves. Have them discuss the answer to the Decide question.
- **ART MANIPULATIVES** Use the music audiotape in the **Art Manipulative Kit** to play while students create their artwork.

Create PROBLEM SOLVING

Materials
- white paper
- recorded music
- oil pastels

Alternate Materials: markers or crayons

"Let's use expressive colors and visual rhythms to illustrate the mood of a piece of music."

"Vamos a usar colores expresivos y ritmos visuales para ilustrar el ánimo de una pieza musical."

- Bring in cassette tapes or visit your school's library to get recordings for students to use to illustrate the mood of the music. The work can be realistic or nonobjective.
- Distribute materials and have students follow the directions on page 69.

FOR THE ART SPECIALIST

Use tempera or school acrylics to illustrate the mood of a piece of music.

Using Color and Visual Rhythm

A plan for organizing colors is called a **color scheme**. It is used to express a mood.

Visual rhythm is created by repeated shapes separated by the area around them. An artist can use rhythm to control the mood of an artwork.

Monochromatic color schemes use only one color and its tints and shades.

Analogous color schemes use colors that are side by side on the color wheel and have a common hue, such as yellow-green, yellow, yellow-orange, and orange.

Complementary colors cause visual excitement, and they are opposite each other on the color wheel.

Warm colors are red, yellow, and orange. They remind us of warm things and generally give us a feeling of energy.

Cool colors are blue, green, and violet. They are the opposite of warm colors.

Practice

Choose a color scheme to express your feelings. Use crayons.

1. Select a color scheme that best expresses who you are or how you are feeling.

2. With your selected color scheme, use crayons to draw lines or shapes to express your feelings.

Decide Did you use one color scheme to express your feelings?

Activities in

ART Across the Curriculum Book

Reading/Language Arts Do research on shoes as in the van Gogh. (page 67)

Math Using shoes, learn when to estimate, when to measure exactly, and how to judge a reasonable estimate. (page 68)

Science Design a shoe for a specific purpose, like van Gogh's boots. (page 69)

Social Studies Learn about the Kansas homesteader, who may have worn boots like those in van Gogh's painting. (page 70)

The Arts Write stage dialogue for two women as contrasting characters. (page 71)

Technology Use the *Multimedia Workshop* CD-ROM to create a picture using visual rhythm to express your mood. (page 72)

Robert Landers. Age 11. *Rainbow over the Mountains.* Watercolors.

How do the colors and visual rhythms illustrate the mood and rhythm of music?

Create

What colors and visual rhythms can be used to express different moods? Use colors and visual rhythm to illustrate the mood of a piece of music.

1. Think about your favorite music. What emotions are being expressed in the music?

2. Create visual rhythm using different lines and shapes to illustrate the mood and rhythm of the music. Fill the page with color.

3. Select a color scheme that best represents the mood of the music. Fill the page with color.

Describe What was your color scheme? What lines and shapes did you draw?

Analyze How did you arrange your lines, shapes, and colors?

Interpret Does your work express the mood and rhythm of your music?

Decide Explain how the color scheme you chose affected the look of your work.

Lesson 6

69

"What colors and color schemes are used to express the different types of moods or feelings?"

"¿Qué colores y esquemas de colores se usan para expresar las diferentes clases de ánimos o sentimientos"

 Review
Use the **Large Print** *Bookwus Mask* to have students compare the use of color and visual rhythm to the works in this lesson.

Art Criticism

Have students answer the four art criticism questions—Describe, Analyze, Interpret, and Decide—orally or in writing. Discuss the use of color in their illustrations.

Assess
Use the **Assessment Book** pages 19–20 as a formal assessment for this lesson.

Evaluation Criteria

• Can the student identify how colors are used to create visual rhythm in a work of art?

• Can the student illustrate a piece of music using color and visual rhythm?

• Can the student use the four steps of art criticism to evaluate his or her own work?

• Can the student compare the work and lives of both artist?

Reteaching • • • • • • • • • • • •

Color and visual rhythm Ask students to find another artwork in the book that illustrates color and visual rhythm.

Change Use both pieces of art to introduce the study of climate changes across the United States.

Systems Use the Liotard as an introduction to the study of the caste system.

Some students may need focused practice with some of the lesson's vocabulary to discuss the use of color and rhythm. You might begin the lesson with oral questions to check for comprehension. Later, model how to use the vocabulary in describing students' artwork as you point out different characteristics.

Perception Hints for Student Art

Complementary colors cause visual excitement. Warm colors cause a feeling of energy, and cool colors are the opposite. Rhythm is created by the repeated shapes and lines.

UNIT 2

LESSON PLANNER

Objectives

After completing this lesson, students will be able to:

- demonstrate moods through repeated patterns of movement and sound. *Aesthetic Perception*
- express individual and group interpretation of rhythmic patterns. *Creative Expression*
- use the four steps of art criticism to evaluate their own performances. *Art Criticism*
- demonstrate knowledge of how Eddie Brown developed his own style of tap dancing. *Art History and Culture*

FOCUS

Time: About 10 minutes

Activating Prior Knowledge

"What do you know about tap dancing? Have you seen it or tried it yourself?"

"¿Qué saben acerca del baile de tap? ¿Lo han visto o lo han bailado?"

- Discuss students' answers and talk about the importance of rhythm as an element in dance.

Introducing the Art

"Let's look closely at the photograph of the women and man dancing. Describe what you see."

"Vamos a observar detalladamente la fotografía de la mujer y el hombre bailando. Describan lo que ven."

- Share information with students from **Art Background** about Eddie Brown and his experience as a tap dancer. If you have the *Artsource* video, have students view the performance Eddie Brown's *Rhapsody in Taps*.
- If any students in class study tap dancing, ask them if they would be willing to demonstrate a short routine.

Rhapsody in Taps: *Eddie Brown with Linda Sohl-Donnell, Pauline Hagino and bass player:*

artists use color, lines, and shapes to create visual rhythm. Dancers like Eddie Brown use musical beats and their fast-flying feet to tap out rhythms in sound. Artists create moods and a sense of movement with repeated patterns of color, line, and shape. Tap dancers create moods with repeated patterns of movements and sounds.

70   Unit **2**

ART Background

About the Artist

Eddie Brown (1918–1995) created, performed, and taught tap dancing for more than 60 years. His career began in the 1930s with the Bill Robinson Revue at New York's Apollo Theatre. He appeared with Billie Holiday, Joe Turner, and jazz greats Dizzy Gillespie, Count Basie, and Duke Ellington.

About Subject Matter Forms of tap and clogging have their roots in Irish and English dancing. "Buck" dancing was a flat-footed form of tap done by early African Americans. Bill "Bojangles" Robinson took "Buck" dancing to the balls of the feet. John Bubbles, another tap dance pioneer, introduced "rhythm" dancing—dancing done by dropping the heel, thereby cutting the tempo in half so that more taps could be done.

What To Do

Create rhythm patterns using basic steps.

Materials
✓ pencils
✓ paper

1. Make a list of different kinds of steps you do every day.

2. With a partner, take turns clapping out simple rhythmic patterns that your partner can echo. First, echo the rhythmic patterns with your hands, then with your feet.

3. Now try traveling as you make the rhythm patterns with your feet.

4. Sit in a circle with other students. Take turns going into the center and making some moves while everyone else claps the rhythm made by the feet of the solo dancer. Try to get different combinations of movements and rhythmic sounds.

Describe Describe the movements you used in your tap dances.

Analyze Explain how visual rhythms and sound rhythms are alike and different.

Interpret What mood did you create with rhythmic patterns?

Decide Were you more successful in creating rhythm patterns with your hands or with your feet?

Extra Credit

Work out two or three rhythmic patterns that you can do with your feet. Put them in a sequence that includes doing each pattern twice. Perform for others.

Dance   71

Cultural Perspectives Eddie Brown improvised his tap dancing as ideas came to him. Most of his learning took place on neighborhood street corners, dancing with other "hoofers" (tap dancers). Each person would jump in and perform, adding onto each other's ideas. He developed his own style, called "scientific rhythm" because you could hear the rhythm but couldn't see the movement that created it.

About Dance Every dancer develops his or her own style, performing similar steps in different ways. Dancers individualize their movements by using different qualities and intensities of sound and movement. Some movements are bright and bold; others are subtle and soft, or muted. Sometimes dancers perform on sand, changing the quality of both sound and movement—they slide and glide. Other dancers jump up on different-sized boxes, changing the quality of both movement and sound.

TEACH
Time: Two 30-minute periods

Materials
• paper and pencils

"Dancing is based on steps that we all do, like walking, running, and jumping."

"El baile se basa en pasos que hacemos como caminar, correr y saltar."

• Have students name everyday steps: walking, running, shuffling, or jumping. Explain that dancers take these everyday movements and emphasize them with style and rhythm.

• Have students work without bumping others. Ask them to perform without talking. Call out "freeze" when you want students to stop their movements.

• Side-coaching can include suggestions to work at different levels, such as low or high, or to change the size or energy of a movement or the rhythm.

• With partners, have students practice everyday steps. Then, try giving them a rhythm pattern, style, or attitude as they perform.

CLOSE
Time: About 5 minutes

"How are sound rhythms like and unlike visual rhythms?"

"¿En qué se parecen y en qué se diferencian los ritmos sonoros de los ritmos visuales?"

 Assess
Have students answer the four art criticism questions on page 71—Describe, Analyze, Interpret, and Decide—orally or in writing.

Evaluation Criteria
• Can the student demonstrate moods through repeated patterns of movement and sound?

• Can the student demonstrate individual and group interpretation of rhythmic patterns?

• Can the student use the four steps of art criticism to evaluate his or her own performance?

• Can the student demonstrate knowledge of how Eddie Brown and other tap dancers develop their own styles of dance?

UNIT 2

Reviewing Unit Concepts

"Artists often use color to create a feeling, to unify an artwork, or to communicate an idea more clearly."

"Con frecuencia, los artistas usan el color para crear un sentimiento, para unificar una obra de arte o para comunicar una idea con más claridad."

• Review color, rhythm d movement, by asking students to find examples of each in the book.

Examining the Artwork

"How did the artist use color and rhythm in his artwork?"

"¿Cómo usa el artista el color y el ritmo en su obra de arte?"

• Have students look at *Light of the World* and discuss the questions on page 73.
(See **Perception Hints** below.)

Student Portfolio

Have students review all the artwork they have created during this unit and select the pieces they wish to keep in their portfolios.

Art Criticism Activity

Have students select an artwork from the previous unit and study it using the four steps of art criticism. (See pages 206–209 for more information about Art Criticism.)

Perception Hints

Color Schemes

Monochromatic—The sky begins with light blue to dark blue to a medium blue.

Analogous—The red-orange on the hill is next to a yellow-orange color. The light in the open archway is yellow-orange and the shadows are orange.

Complementary—The man behind the post is wearing a bright blue suit and an orange tie.

Warm—The warmth of the hill closest to the viewer is yellow.

Cool—The hills in the distance are a cool green.

Yes, there is more than one color scheme.

Rhythm

Visual—There are repeated squares on the ground and the repetition in the hills.

Regular rhythm—The fence pattern is repeated consistently.

Color, Rhythm, and Movement

Reviewing Main Ideas

The lessons and activities in Unit 2 cover the techniques that artists use to create color and visual rhythm.

• The **color spectrum** is the arrangement of colors seen when light passes through a prism. The **color wheel** is the spectrum bent into a circle. There are three set of colors on the color wheel.

• **Hue** is another name for color. There are three groups of hues.

1. **Primary** hues, or colors, are red, blue, and yellow.

2. **Secondary** hues are violet, orange, and green. They are made by mixing together two primary hues.

3. **Intermediate** hues are made by mixing a primary hue with the secondary hue next to it on the color wheel. Red-violet is an example.

• A **tint** is a light value of a hue made by adding white to it.

• A **shade** is a dark value of a hue that is made by adding black to it.

Peter Blume. (Russian). *Light of the World.* 1932. Oil on composition board. $18 \times 20\frac{1}{4}$ inches. Collection of Whitney Museum of American Art, New York/Purchase/Photography by Robert E. Mates, N.J.

ART Background

About the Artist

Peter Blume (pē' ter blūm, Russian, 1906–1992) came to America in 1911 at the age of five. He first lived on the Lower East Side of New York and then moved to Brooklyn. Blume's artwork reflects the skepticism of politics, which was a part of his childhood. His work is painted in a sharp-focused manner much like the German social realists who painted in the 1920s. His most famous work, *The Eternal City,* focuses on the brutal face of Mussolini.

About Subject Matter* In *Light of the World,* Blume takes a critical look at modern life. Much of his subject matter shows an ironic view of social order.

- A **color scheme** is a plan for organizing colors.
  1. **Monochromatic** means only one color and its tints and shades.
  2. **Analogous** colors are side by side on the color wheel and share a common color.
  3. **Complementary** colors are opposite each other on the color wheel.
  4. **Warm** colors seem to move toward the viewer. They are red, yellow, and orange.
  5. **Cool** colors seem to move away from the viewer. They are blue, green, and violet.
- **Visual rhythm** is a repeated pattern of shapes, color, or line that creates a sense of movement.

Summing Up

In the painting *Light of the World,* Peter Bloom used the techniques for creating color and visual rhythm covered in this unit.

- Look closely at the colors. What color scheme do you recognize? Is there more than one color scheme?
- Where do you see rhythm? Where is there regular rhythm?

Color and rhythm are both art elements used by artists to express a feeling or create visual excitement in a work of art. Color and rhythm are used in all kinds of art.

Careers in Art
Photographer

Richard Tichich is a photographer. There are two different kinds of photographers. Photojournalists are reporters who work for magazines and newspapers and tell stories through photographs. Fine art photographers work with studio, fashion, product and food, and nature photography. Tichich's parents were creative and took him to museums and galleries. He took many photography classes and obtained his graduate degree from the University of Texas at San Antonio. He says the best part about his work is that he can use both his creative and technical skills.

Richard Tichich, photographer

Learning About Careers in Art

Richard Tichich was inspired to become a photographer by the strong presence of creative arts in his family environment. He is a teacher at Georgia Southern College. In his photography, he investigates cultural myths and stereotypes through environmental portraiture. He takes photos of people in their surroundings to maximize the environmental information. An example of this is his series on Mexican sheriffs. Each photo has its own narrative on several levels.

He enjoys the creative challenge of starting with nothing and producing images. This competitive business requires one to pay attention to details.

- Have students collect photographs from magazines and newspapers or original photographs from home. Ask them to categorize the photographs into groupings such as studio photography, fashion photography, product and food photography, moving picture photography, nature photography, and amateur photography (most home photographs).

About the Media Blume's work is painted in oils on composition board. Many of the people in Blume's paintings are caricature-like, but precise, and clearly painted. He uses the oil paints to create a smooth surface.

About Art History* Blume was part of a group of American artists known as the Magic Realists. They were prominent during the 1930s and turned everyday American imagery into fantasy images. Their paintings were detailed and precise and included deep-space perspectives. Peter Blume was one of the most important Magic Realists.

Cultural Perspectives Blume began seriously painting in the 1930s. His work is considered a social commentary on relevant events and issues. He was greatly influenced by such things as the advancement of the modern age, World Wars I and II, and political leaders such as Hitler and Mussolini.

*See **More About** pages 206–227 for more about art history and subject matter.

A Final Thought

"The excellency of every art is its intensity, capable of making all disagreeables evaporate, from their being in close relationship with beauty and truth."—John Keats

UNIT OVERVIEW

Unit 3 covers the elements of space, form, and texture. It explains how artists create space and use form and visual and tactile textures. The specific topics in this unit are **space, texture, form,** and **architectural shape.**

Space refers to the area between, around, above, below, and within objects. Two types of space are reviewed in Lessons 1 and 2.

Texture refers to how things feel, or look as if they might feel if touched. The two ways in which we experience texture are covered in Lessons 3 and 6.

Form refers to any object that can be measured by length, height, and width. Form is covered in Lessons 4 and 6.

Architectural forms are shapes and structures that relate to the rules of architecture. Lesson 5 is about architectural forms.

Introducing Unit Concepts

"Artists use the elements of space, form, and texture in two- and three-dimensional art."

"Los artistas usan los elementos de espacio, forma y textura en arte bidimensional y tridimensional."

Space
- Ask students to develop a concise definition of *space.*
- Place an object like a plant in the center of a table. Have the students describe the open spaces as well as the object itself.

Form
- Have students list examples of form. Create a class list and ask students to defend why an object is considered a form and not a shape.

Texture
- Ask students to name words that come to mind when they hear the word *texture,* e.g. soft, sticky, bumpy, and so on.
- Ask students if all textures can be touched. Discuss how artists create textures. Ask them to look through their books for examples of rough, smooth, or soft textures.

Unit 3

An Introduction to Space, Form, and Texture

Artists use space, form, and texture in both two- and three-dimensional art forms.

Jan Vermeer. (Dutch). *Portrait of a Young Woman.* Oil on canvas. $17\frac{1}{2} \times 15\frac{3}{4}$ inches. Metropolitan Museum of Art, New York, New York.

ART Background

About the Artist
Jan Vermeer (yän vər mir', Dutch, 1632–1675) was born in Holland. Very little is known about his life. His father owned an art-dealing business that he left to Vermeer. The business kept him busy, so he only painted in his spare time. Few people knew about Vermeer's paintings when he was alive; however, today he is one of the best-known artists in the world.

About Subject Matter* The painting is a portrait. Vermeer painted pictures of people doing simple things around the house. His pictures usually contained one or two people in front of a blank wall. He used many details to make the paintings look lifelike. There are only 30 Vermeer paintings in existence today.

Space is used by artists in paintings and drawings to give the illusion of depth on a flat surface.

• Notice the dark negative space around the figure. How did the artist use positive and negative space?

Artists use several techniques to create the illusion of **form** on a two-dimensional, or flat, surface.

• What did Vermeer do to make the figure look so realistic in this painting?

Artists sometimes suggest the **textures** of real objects.

• How did Vermeer suggest the textures of the fabrics and the person?

Artist Profile

Jan Vermeer
1632–1675

Jan Vermeer is an artist who was almost unknown until about a hundred years ago. He made fewer than 40 paintings and very little about his life was written. But those paintings show that he was one of the world's great artists. Vermeer was interested in how scenes of everyday life might look to a person who was standing a short distance away. He created for the viewer the textures, values, and shape and space relationships that natural light on a scene would show. Vermeer was only 43 years old when he died.

Like many artists, Jan Vermeer relied on the use of space, form, and texture to help him create realistic paintings. In this unit you will learn about the following topics:

• Space   • Form   • Types of Textures   • Architectural Form

75

About the Media *Portrait of a Young Woman* is an oil painting. The oil paints allowed Vermeer to paint in a realistic manner.

About Art History* Vermeer is considered one of the great "Dutch Masters". He was one of the first artists to use a technique called *chiaroscuro*. Chiaroscuro is the subtle play of light against dark for dramatic effect. Vermeer's paintings reflect this skillful use of contrast to create quiet yet powerful images.

*See **More About** pages 206–227 for more about art history and subject matter.

Use the **Video** *Yonder* to see how artists use space, form, and texture in landscapes.

Examining the Artwork

"Let's look closely at the painting."
"Vamos a observar detalladamente la pintura."

• Have students look at Vermeer's painting and describe the objects, textures, and spaces they see.

• Read the definitions of *space*, *texture*, and *form*. Have students answer the questions on page 75. (See **Perception Hints** below.)

Artist Profile
Share with students information about the artist, including the details from his portrait.

You may wish to encourage students to practice art concepts and record ideas from lesson to lesson in their **Art Journals.**

About Music
Spaces in music are called rests. Have the students find spaces (musical rests) in a song. *Form* in music relates to the way a composition is organized. For example, ABA form is one in which the first and last sections are the same, and the middle section is contrasting. *Texture* in music refers to combining melody and harmony, or different rhythm patterns, to create layers of sound.

Perception Hints

Space In Vermeer's painting, the face, hair, and shawl are the positive spaces. The bright color draws our attention and brings the image to life. The negative space, or the dark area surrounding the figure, makes the figure the focus of attention.

Detail The figure looks realistic because of the details. Shading makes the figure look three-dimensional. The realism of the shadows creates the illusion of form.

Texture He suggested the textures of the fabrics and the figure through shading techniques. He highlights the eyes, forehead, and nose to make them stand out. The shadows in the fabric are different from those in the skin, creating a visual or tactile texture.

Lesson	Lesson Title	Suggested Pacing	Create Activities	Materials	
1	**Positive and Negative Space**	45 minutes	Draw the negative shapes in a still life.	construction paper markers	
2	**Positive and Negative Space Reversal**	45 minutes	Create a tessellation puzzle design using positive and negative shapes.	white drawing paper felt-tip pens scissors tape	
3	**Texture**	45 minutes	Create a collage of the inside of a fantasy clubhouse using visual textures.	white paper scissors glue samples of visual textures like pictures of a shiny car pencils	
4	**Architectural Form and Texture**	45 minutes	Draw a space station using shading techniques.	12- x 18-inch paper pencils recording of *Star Trek* colored pencils	
5	**Architectural Shape and Visual Texture**	45 minutes	Draw a building using architectural shapes.	white paper felt-tip pens pencils colored pencils	
6	**Form and Tactile Texture**	45 minutes	Build a model out of clay of a unique public building.	clay water carving tools sticks found materials, like small boxes	
Artsource Lesson	**Space, Form, and Texture in Music**	75 minutes	Write a musical score using own musical instruments.	paper and pencils found sources of sound Artsource audiotape (optional)	

Program Resources (Books)	Art Resources	Literature Resources	*Music Resources
Vocabulary, pp. 25–26￼Assessment, pp. 25–26￼Art Across the Curriculum￼Resource Book, pp. 73–78	Overhead Transparency #13, *Cups 4 Picasso* and *Cups 4 Picasso (detail)*￼Artist Profile Book, p. 24￼Large Prints, *Votive Statue of Gudea from Lagash* and *Trade (Gifts for Trading Land with White People)*	**1.** *The Graphic Alphabet* (1996) by David Pelletier has computer-generated illustrations that reinterpret the alphabet in unique perspectives that focus on the shape and space around each letter.￼**2.** *On the Day You Were Born* (1991) by Debra Frasier has brightly colored paper collages that welcome the reader to celebrate the birth of a baby to Earth and utilizes positive and negative space in these integrated designs.	*"Cannon River Wave/Forms,"* by David Means, p. T282, CD6:33. *"Cannon River Wave/Forms"* is an example of modern music that has no tonal center, giving it an ambiguous sound.
Vocabulary, pp. 27–28￼Assessment, pp. 27–28￼Art Across the Curriculum￼Resource Book, pp. 79–84	Overhead Transparency #14, *Sky and Water* and *Reptiles*￼Artist Profile Book, p. 17￼Large Prints, *Votive Statue of Gudea from Lagash* and *Trade (Gifts for Trading Land with White People)*	**1.** *Giving Thanks, A Native American Good Morning Message* (1995) by Chief Jake Swamp reflects progressive reversal illustrations through beauty created by negative space in this educational yet entertaining tribute to Earth.￼**2.** *It's For You* (1995) by John Talbot has positive and negative boundaries that are unleashed in this unique picture puzzle book that explores the shapes and forms of the imagination.	"Fascinating Rhythm," by George and Ira Gershwin, p. T87, CD2:18. "Fascinating Rhythm" is an example of American music from the mid twentieth century.
Vocabulary, pp. 29–30￼Assessment, pp. 29–30￼Art Across the Curriculum￼Resource Book, pp. 85–90	Overhead Transparency #15, *Caravan*￼Artist Profile Book, p. 66￼Large Prints, *Votive Statue of Gudea from Lagash* and *Trade (Gifts for Trading Land with White People)*	**1.** *Baba Yaga and Vasilisa, the Brave* (1994) by Marianna Mayer has dramatic illustrations that feed the eyes with richly textured scenes that show how texture creates moods in art.￼**2.** *The Wave of the Sea Wolf* (1994) by David Wisniewski is a dramatic original story in which Native Americans of the Tlingit culture are engulfed in a flood of cut-paper illustrations that demonstrate the texture of adventure.	"On the Road Again," by Willie Nelson, p. T158, CD3:33. "On the Road Again" is a twentieth-century American travelling song.
Vocabulary, pp. 31–32￼Assessment, pp. 31–32￼Art Across the Curriculum￼Resource Book, pp. 91–96	Overhead Transparency #16, *Space Station #1* and *Homesick Proof Space Station*￼Artist Profile Book, pp. 8, 34￼Large Prints, *Votive Statue of Gudea from Lagash* and *Trade (Gifts for Trading Land with White People)*	**1.** *A City in Winter* (1996) by Mark Helprin will have readers spellbound by this enchanting tale of suspense while observing the textures and forms of the city's architecture.￼**2.** *Architecture and Construction* (1995) from Editions Gallimard Jeuness has clever art and text that journey from the past to the future while exploring architectural creations through interactive elements of design and construction.	"Evergreen, Everblue," by Raffi, p. T336, CD8:15. "Evergreen, Everblue" is a contemporary song about taking care of the Earth.
Vocabulary, pp. 33–34￼Assessment, pp. 33–34￼Art Across the Curriculum￼Resource Book, pp. 97–102	Overhead Transparency #17, *Seaside, Florida, A Sidewalk* and *Fallingwater*￼Artist Profile Book, pp. 42, 59￼Large Prints, *Votive Statue of Gudea from Lagash* and *Trade (Gifts for Trading Land with White People)*	**1.** *The Village of Round and Square Houses* (1986) by Ann Grifalconi has dynamic art that portrays this tale set in the Cameroon hills of Central Africa. The story provides educational information and relative examples of architecture.￼**2.** *Amazing Buildings* (1993) by Philip Wilkinson provides a fascinating introduction to architecture through large-scale constructions with sections cut away to give the viewer a thorough tour of ancient and modern buildings.	Variations on "Simple Gifts," from *Appalachian Spring,* by Aaron Copland, p. T192, CD4:37. *Appalachian Spring* is a mid twentieth-century ballet that celebrates the newly built home of a recently married couple.
Vocabulary, pp. 35–36￼Assessment, pp. 35–36￼Art Across the Curriculum￼Resource Book, pp. 103–108	Overhead Transparency #18, *Chapelle Nôtre Dame-du Haut* and *Opera House*￼Artist Profile Book, pp. 28, 54￼Large Prints, *Votive Statue of Gudea from Lagash* and *Trade (Gifts for Trading Land with White People)*	**1.** *Castle* (1994) by Richard Platt has ten incredible cross-sectioned illustrations that depict an introspective view of a medieval castle combined with facts and stories and details of medieval life.￼**2.** *Cathedral: The Story of Its Construction* (1973) is a Caldecott-winning book that tours the forms and textures of the fictional cathedral Chutreaux whose construction relates to those of Gothic cathedrals.	"Intrada," by Gunild Keetman, p. T211, CD5:10. "Intrada" is an example of twentiethth-century music.

*Music references are from **Share the Music,** Macmillan/McGraw-Hill School Publishers

UNIT 3

LESSON 1

LESSON PLANNER

Objectives

After completing this lesson, students will be able to:

- identify the use of positive and negative spaces by artists to add interest to their work. *Aesthetic Perception*
- create or draw the negative shapes in a still life. *Creative Expression*
- use the four steps of art criticism to evaluate their own drawings. *Art Criticism*
- demonstrate knowledge of the life and work of Jasper Johns. *Art History and Culture*

Program Resources

- **Overhead:** The Johns is available on overhead 13.
- **Large Print:** *Trade* by Jaune Quick-to-See Smith
- **Vocabulary Book** pages 25–26
- **Artist Profiles Book:** Johns page 24
- **Art Across the Curriculum Book** pages 73–78
- **Multimedia Workshop CD-ROM**
- **Assessment Book** pages 25–26

Multiple Intelligences

Visual/Spatial Students can expand their knowledge of shapes and forms when they create negative space in a still life.

Vocabulary

space *espacio* the area between, around, above, below, and within objects

positive space *espacio positivo* the objects, shapes, or forms in works of art

negative space *espacio negativo* the empty space that surrounds objects, shapes, and forms

shape reversal *figura inversa* when a shape or positive space starts out as one image and then in another image turns into negative space

Positive and Negative Space

Artists use positive and negative spaces to add interest to their artwork.

Jasper Johns. (American). *Cups 4 Picasso.* 1972. Lithograph. $14\frac{1}{8} \times 32\frac{1}{4}$ inches. Museum of Modern Art, New York, New York. Licensed by VAGA, New York. Gift of Celeste Bartos.

Jasper Johns's lithographs are examples of optical illusions. He has deliberately organized shapes to create a visual puzzle to confuse the viewer. Johns likes to change a recognizable object to attract more attention to it, as in the way he changed the face of the Spanish artist Pablo Picasso. Notice how Johns arranges shapes and uses color to add interest to *Cups 4 Picasso*.

76　　　　　　　　　　　　　　　　　　Unit **3**

ART Background

About the Artist

Jasper Johns, Jr., (jás pər jänz, American, 1930–) was born in Georgia and spent his childhood in South Carolina. He served in Japan for the United States Army. At 24, he decided to throw away all the art he had made. He wanted a fresh start. He was determined to create original art, not copies of other styles or artists. He has been known for his inventive artistic styles.

About Subject Matter* The subject matter is nonobjective.

About the Media The Johns is a lithograph. A lithograph is a printmaking process in which a flat stone, previously marked with a greasy substance that will retain the ink, is charged with ink and run through a press, producing a print.

Jasper Johns. (American). *Cups 4 Picasso.* 1972.
Lithograph. $14\frac{1}{8} \times 32\frac{1}{4}$ inches. Museum of
Modern Art, New York, New York. Licensed by
VAGA, New York, Gift of Celeste Bartos.

Look closely at both views of *Cups 4 Picasso* by
Jasper Johns.

- What type of shapes do you see in both views?
  Describe the area around each shape.

- How many shapes are in each view?

- What technique did Johns use to show us which shapes
  are most important?

- What changes occur from one image to the next?

SEEING LIKE AN ARTIST

Study a classmate's
face from the side.
What parts look
different from the side
than they do from the
front?

About Art History* Jasper Johns is a pop artist. He takes everyday objects and
transforms them into objects of art. Pop artists glorify American mass culture, including
television, billboard advertising, and cars and bring these images into museums. His work
includes familiar items such as flags, targets, numerals, and maps.

Cultural Perspectives By the end of the 1950s, Johns's paintings showed a freer, looser
arrangement. In some of them, he attached real objects, such as rulers and compasses, to
the canvas. Johns broke ground with a four-painting cycle entitled "The Seasons," shown
in New York City in early 1987. The 75- × 50-inch paintings were considered especially
significant in American art history.

* See **More About** pages 206–227 for more about art history and subject matter.

FOCUS

Time: About 10 minutes

Activating Prior Knowledge

"Have you ever created animal shadow images on the wall
using your hand and strong back light?"
*"¿Alguna vez han hecho sombras de imágenes de animales en la
pared usando sus manos y una luz fuerte de fondo?"*

- Explain and discuss that shadowed images on
  the wall are examples of an optical illusion.
  Ask the students what other optical illusions
  they can think of.

Introducing the Art

"Let's look closely at the two artworks."
"Vamos a observar detalladamente las dos obras de arte."

- **Describe:** Have students describe the subject
  matter in Johns's work. (nonobjective)

- Share and discuss information from **Art
  Background** and the **Artist Profiles Book.**

- Have students answer the questions about
  positive and negative space on page 77.
  (See **Perception Hints** below.)

- **COMPARE AND CONTRAST** Compare and
  contrast the views in Johns's work. (There are
  three shapes in each view. The profiles on the right and
  left are positive shapes. The negative shape is the vase in
  the middle of the painting.)

FOR THE ART SPECIALIST

Use the **Overhead** and the **Large Print**
Trade to demonstrate for students how
artists use positive and negative spaces
to add interest to their work.

Perception Hints

Shapes The profiles on the right and left of the painting
show the most in the first print. They are surrounded by
dark colors. The vase stands out in the second print. It is
surrounded by dark colors. There are three shapes in each
view.
Technique Positive and negative shape reversal.
Shape reversal The profiles become the vase, and the
vase becomes the profiles.

TEACH

Time: About 30 minutes

Practice

Materials
- white drawing paper
- pencils

Alternate Materials: white drawing paper and ink pens

"Can you draw a profile?"

"¿Puede trazar un perfil?"

- Discuss the definition of *positive* and *negative spaces* on page 78.
- Distribute materials and have students follow the directions on page 78 for drawing a profile. Have students discuss the answer to the Decide question.

Create PROBLEM SOLVING

Materials
- construction paper
- markers

Alternate Materials: crayons

"Let's draw the negative shapes in a still life."

"Vamos a trazar las figuras negativas en una naturaleza muerta."

- Review positive and negative spaces.
- Distribute materials and have students follow the directions on page 79.

Safety Tip
- For information about markers and other safety issues in the art classroom, see page T22.

FOR THE ART SPECIALIST

Have the students create the negative spaces in a still life, and have them draw linear patterns in the negative spaces with markers.

Using Positive and Negative Space

The element of art that refers to the area between, around, above, below, and within objects is **space**. Shapes and forms exist in space. It is the air around an object. There are two types of space—positive and negative.

Positive space is the objects, shapes, or forms in works of art.

Negative space is the empty space that surrounds objects, shapes, and forms. When there is a large area of negative space in an artwork, loneliness or freedom is expressed.

 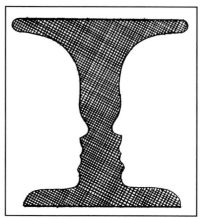

Shape reversal is when a shape or positive space starts out as one image and then in another image turns into the negative space. This is what happens in Johns's lithographs.

Practice

Practice drawing profiles. Use pencil.

1. Draw a profile of your partner's face.

2. Turn your paper upside down and copy the profile backwards just as Jasper Johns did.

Decide What does the negative space between the profiles look like?

Activities in

ART Across the Curriculum Book

Reading/Language Arts Learn about lithography, like the art. (page 73)

Math Look at how artists work with space. Study how to measure it. (page 74)

Science Understand how positive and negative spaces help protect animals in their natural environment. (page 75)

Social Studies Learn more about Picasso's Spain. (page 76)

The Arts Use reversal to show another perspective of the ideas and feelings in a play. (page 77)

Technology Use the *Multimedia Workshop* CD-ROM to create positive and negative spaces, through shape reversal. (page 78)

Where is the negative space in the picture?

Elizabeth Armstrong. Age 10.
The Old Cane Chair. Marker, pencil.

Create

How can you see the shapes of negative space? Draw the negative shapes in a still life.

1. Think about objects for a still life that have large, interesting negative spaces, such as chairs or desks.

2. Look closely at the still life and find an area you like. Concentrate on the negative spaces around the objects.

3. Using markers, fill only the negative spaces with color. Leave the positive spaces white.

Describe Describe the positive shapes in your still-life drawing.

Analyze What shapes did you create when you colored the negative spaces? How do the positive and negative shapes differ?

Interpret How did reversing the positive and negative spaces affect your drawing?

Decide Do you like the way your still life turned out when you reversed the positive and negative spaces?

Lesson 1   79

THEME Connections

Perspective Use the art to discuss how students might have changed their perspective or viewpoint of a subject as a result of getting older and maturing.

Identity Use the artwork to discuss the students' struggle for their own identity.

ESL

Some ESL students may benefit from practice with a more fluent partner before they are ready to discuss their work with the group. Partners can ask each other questions, describing what they see in the artwork, as their partner offers physical and verbal clues to their description: *Are your negative spaces bigger, smaller, or the same size as your positive spaces?*

CLOSE

Time: About 5 minutes

"Were you able to draw the negative shapes in a still life?"
"¿Fueron capaces de trazar las figuras negativas en una naturaleza muerta?"

LARGE PRINT
Review
Use the **Large Print** *Trade* to have students define *positive* and *negative space*. Ask them to compare the positive and negative spaces in the **Large Print** to those used by Johns.

Art Criticism

Have students answer the four art criticism questions—Describe, Analyze, Interpret, and Decide—orally or in writing. Discuss how positive and negative spaces were created in their drawings when they are completed.

Assess
Use the **Assessment Book** pages 25–26 as a formal assessment for this lesson.

Evaluation Criteria

• Can the student identify the use of positive and negative spaces by artists?

• Can the student create or draw the negative shapes in a still life?

• Can the student use the four steps of art criticism to evaluate his or her own work?

• Can the student demonstrate knowledge of the life and work of Jasper Johns?

Reteaching ● ● ● ● ● ● ● ● ● ● ● ●

Positive and negative space Have students look at pictures in magazines to find positive and negative spaces. Ask them to describe what they see.

Perception Hints for Student Art

The negative space in the student art is the area surrounding the chair.

U NIT 3

LESSON PLANNER

Objectives
After completing this lesson, students will be able to:

• identify how artists use reverse positive and negative spaces to add imagination and movement to a piece of artwork. *Aesthetic Perception*

• create a tessellation puzzle design using positive and negative shapes. *Creative Expression*

• use the four steps of art criticism to evaluate their own puzzles. *Art Criticism*

• demonstrate knowledge of the life and work of M. C. Escher. *Art History and Culture*

Program Resources
• **Overhead:** Both Escher's *Sky and Water* and *Reptiles* are available on overhead 14.

• **Large Prints:** *Votive Statue of Gudea from Lagash* c. 2120 B.C. and *Trade* by Jaune Quick-to-See Smith

• **Vocabulary Book** pages 27–28

• **Artist Profiles Book:** Escher page 17

• **Art Across the Curriculum Book** pages 79–84

• **Multimedia Workshop CD-ROM**

• **Assessment Book** pages 27–28

Multiple Intelligences
Visual/Spatial Students can employ their graphic skills when creating their tessellation puzzles.

Vocabulary
progressive reversal *inversión progresiva* when an object starts out as one object or form and slowly changes into another object or form

progressive *progresiva* to change or move forward

tessellation *teselado* a shape reversal that changes quickly and fits together like a puzzle

---

Unit 3 Lesson 2

Positive and Negative Space Reversal

Artists sometimes use reverse positive and negative space to add imagination and movement to a piece of artwork.

M. C. Escher. (Dutch). *Sky and Water.* Woodcut. National Gallery of Art, Washington, DC.

Looking at Escher's artwork is like looking at an optical illusion. *Sky and Water* uses positive and negative space to change the water image to the sky image. Look only at the white shapes and then only at the black shapes. In *Reptiles,* his print draws the viewer's eye toward the reptile that is working its way out of the drawing. The reptiles move around the page, gradually changing from geometric shapes to free-form shapes.

ART Background

About the Artists
M. C. Escher (esh' ər, Dutch, 1898–1971) was born in Holland. He began to study architecture and later quit to study graphics. As an adult, he lived in Italy. He backpacked along the coast of southern Italy with other artists in the summers. In Spain, Escher was delighted by the amazing designs that covered the walls. He spent three days studying tessellations and copying many of the motifs. He began a new way of working he called "periodic space filling."

About Subject Matter* Both works of art are fantasy pieces.

About the Media *Sky and Water* is a woodcut. A woodcutting is a relief print made by cutting a design into the flat surface of a block of wood and applying ink to the raised surface only.

M. C. Escher. (Dutch). *Reptiles*. Lithograph. National Gallery of Art, Washington, DC.

Study both pieces of artwork to notice positive and negative space.

- ✓ Are there negative shapes in the middle of *Sky and Water*?

- ✓ How do the shapes, colors, and details change in *Sky and Water*?

- ✓ Where are the geometric shapes in *Reptiles*? How do they change into free-form shapes?

- ✓ How do the details of the reptiles change in this drawing?

SEEING LIKE AN ARTIST

Can you find positive and negative space in the artwork in your classroom?

Lesson 2

Reptiles is a lithograph. Lithography is a printmaking process in which a flat stone, marked with a greasy substance, is charged with ink and run through a press.

About Art History* Escher's work was important in the fields of art, science, and daily, or popular, culture. He was interested in ideas and how to visually represent ideas. His prints were used to illustrate theories in chemistry, geology, physics, and psychology. During the 1960s, Escher's prints were mass-produced as posters and also used as record jackets for rock music.

Cultural Perspectives Escher's work has become increasingly popular because of its unique combination of humor, logic, and meticulous precision with visual trickery. Escher's amazing images continue to grace thousands of posters, calendars, and record covers. They depict Escher's amazing imagination, talent, patience, and perseverance.

*See **More About** pages 206–227 for more about art history and subject matter.

FOCUS

Time: About 10 minutes

Activating Prior Knowledge

"Can you remember a movie or a story where a character starts out as one character and turns into another character? How does this happen?"

"¿Pueden recordar una película o una historia en donde un personaje comienza un papel y termina haciendo otro? ¿Cómo sucede esto?"

- Discuss the answers given by the students. They might include a movie or a story about a werewolf or a film like *The Nutty Professor*.

Introducing the Art

"Study the artwork on these pages carefully."
"Estudien cuidadosamente la obra de arte de estas páginas."

- **Describe:** Ask students to describe the subject matter of the artwork.

- Share and discuss information from **Art Background** and the **Artist Profiles Book.**

- Ask students to answer the questions about positive and negative space on page 81. (See **Perception Hints** below.)

- **COMPARE AND CONTRAST** changes made by the animals in both. (Both are optical illusions. *Sky and Water* uses positive and negative spaces to change the water image into the sky image. The reptiles move around the page and change from geometric to free-form shapes.)

FOR THE ART SPECIALIST

Use the **Overhead** and the **Large Prints** *Votive Statue of Gudea from Lagash* and *Trade* to illustrate how artists sometimes use reverse positive and negative spaces.

Perception Hints

Negative shapes *Sky and Water*. The white upper part of the drawing; the black part in the bottom of the drawing.

Change in shapes, colors, and details Sky and Water. Water images change to sky when you look at white shapes then black.

Geometric shapes *Reptiles*. The glass, books, cactus, bowl, triangle, and alligator change into free-form through use of positive and negative space, and through color and details.

TEACH

Practice

Materials

- white drawing paper
- black markers

Alternate Materials: pencils

"Let's create a design using progressive change."

"Vamos a crear un diseño usando cambios progresivos."

- Discuss the definition of *progressive reversal* on page 82.
- Distribute materials and have students follow the directions on page 82 for creating a progressive–change design. Have them discuss the answer to the Decide question.

 Safety Tip

- For safety issues about markers, see page T22.

Create PROBLEM SOLVING

Materials

- white drawing paper
- felt-tip pens
- scissors
- tape
- pencils

Alternate Materials: markers

"Let's create a tessellation puzzle using positive and negative shapes."

"Vamos a crear un rompecabezas usando figuras positivas y negativas."

- Review the meanings of positive and negative shapes.

FOR THE ART SPECIALIST

Create a double tessellation by making them on both sides. Paint them with liquid tempera paints.

Using Progressive Reversal

When an object starts out as one object or form and slowly changes into another object or form, it is called **progressive reversal**. This is also known as *progressive rhythm* because it gives the illusion of moving from one image to another.

Progressive means to change or move forward. In progressive reversal, there is a very slow change from one object to another. The object may slowly change size, shape, or color.

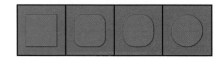

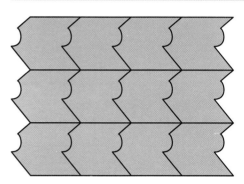

Unlike progressive reversal, which changes gradually, **tessellations** are a type of shape reversal that changes quickly and fits together like a puzzle.

Practice

Create a design using progressive change. Use black marker.

1. Divide your paper into five boxes. Begin by drawing a square in the first box and a circle in the fifth box.

2. Begin to slowly change your square shape into the circle in each of the boxes.

Decide How did you change your image from a square to a circle?

Unit 3

Activities in

ART Across the Curriculum Book

Reading/Language Arts Use writing to create an illusion like an artist would use progressive reversal to do the same. (page 79)

Math Study patterns in *Sky and Water* and then in sets of numbers. (page 80)

Science Understand why some reptiles are endangered species. (page 81)

Social Studies Learn more about the Netherlands, the country where M. C. Escher lived. (page 82)

The Arts Use movement to describe how a reptile, bird, or fish moves, and create a dance using those movements. (page 83)

Technology Use the *Multimedia Workshop* CD-ROM to create a tessellation design. (page 84)

Paula Kramer. Age 11. *Design.* Markers.

Which shapes are positive and which are negative in the tessellation puzzle design?

Create

What kind of puzzle would you like to design? Create a tessellation puzzle design using positive and negative shapes.

1. Think about how the shapes of a puzzle fit together. Draw a perfect square.

2. Cut out a shape from one edge of a square. Tape it onto the opposite edge of the square.

3. Trace around the new shape, locking shapes together like pieces of a puzzle. See the example below.

4. Use color to create a pattern.

Describe Describe the shapes you created. List the steps you followed.

Analyze How does positive and negative space work in your tessellation?

Interpret How do you feel about making a design like this?

Decide Did you successfully create a tessellation design?

Square

Cut shape from paper.

Tape it to opposite side.

Lesson 2

83

CLOSE

Time: About 5 minutes

"Were you able to create a tessellation puzzle using positive and negative shapes?"

"¿Fueron capaces de crear un rompecabezas usando figuras positivas y negativas?"

Review
Use the **Overhead** to have students explain progressive reversal.

Art Criticism

Have students answer the four art criticism questions—Describe, Analyze, Interpret, and Decide—orally or in writing. Discuss the use of progressive reversal in their artwork.

Assess
Use the **Assessment Book** pages 27–28 as a formal assessment for this lesson.

Evaluation Criteria

- Can the student identify positive and negative spaces and progressive reversal?
- Can the student create a tessellation puzzle design using positive and negative shapes?
- Can the student use the four steps of art criticism to evaluate his or her own artwork?
- Can the student demonstrate knowledge of the life and work of M. C. Escher?

Reteaching • • • • • • • • • • • • •

Positive and negative space and progressive reversal Have students look through magazines to find examples of positive and negative spaces.

THEME Connections

Change Use the artowrk to have students trace the change in the civil rights laws from the 1960s to the present time.

Transitions Use the artwork as an introduction to have students research the transitions made by the country of Viet Nam and its people since the end of the war.

ESL

Consider creating a visual wall chart for the class to use as a reference and as a reinforcement during the unit's development. Write concept definitions, create simple sketches or examples as a class, and refer to the chart as you use the terminology throughout the unit.

Perception Hints for Student Art

The negative part that is cut out is filled by the positive space from the next tile or square.

UNIT 3
LESSON 3

LESSON PLANNER

Objectives

After completing this lesson, students will be able to:

- recognize how artists combine a variety of textures to make interior and exterior spaces interesting and appealing. *Aesthetic Perception*
- plan and create a collage of the interior of a fantasy clubhouse using visual textures. *Creative Expression*
- use the four steps of art criticism to evaluate their own drawings. *Art Criticism*
- demonstrate knowledge of the cultural purpose of the *Caravan*. *Art History and Culture*

Program Resources

- **Overhead:** Both views of the *Caravan* are available on overhead 15.
- **Large Prints:** *Votive Statue of Gudea from Lagash* c. 2120 B.C. and *Trade* by Jaune Quick-to-See Smith
- **Vocabulary Book** pages 29–30
- **Artist Profiles Book** Artist unknown page 66
- **Art Manipulative Kit:** fabric swatches on a ring
- **Art Across the Curriculum Book** pages 85–90
- **Multimedia Workshop CD-ROM**
- **Assessment Book** pages 29–30

Multiple Intelligences

Body/Kinesthetic Students can touch various objects, feeling the surfaces.

Vocabulary

texture *textura* the element of art that refers to how things feel or look as if they might feel if touched

tactile texture *textura táctil* texture you see with your eyes

visual texture *textura visual* the way something looks like it might feel if you could touch it

imitated texture *textura imitada* texture that imitates or simulates real texture

---

Texture

Designers combine a variety of textures to make exterior and interior spaces interesting and appealing.

Artist unknown. *Caravan.* Built 1915. Outside view of a gypsy wagon. John Pocketts, owner.

A caravan is a large covered vehicle, like a wagon or a home on wheels. The builders used repeated shapes and lines on the outside of the caravan to create interest. Some areas look rough, while others look smooth. The interior, or inside, of the caravan is a combination of materials. Each surface or material has a different feel. Some look smooth and shiny, while others look bumpy.

ART Background

About the Artists Gypsies first lived in India. They lived in Europe by the fourteenth century. They lived in caravans similar to the one shown here. About 400,000 were killed in Hitler's gas chambers. Today they travel in modern "caravans" of cars and trucks.

About Subject Matter* Paintings on the caravan are symbolic.

About the Media This caravan is wooden inside and out. Inside are painted scenes from the film *Ben Hur*. Outside is more decoration and trim. The only light is a paraffin lamp. Cooking takes place outside.

Artist unknown. *Caravan.* Built 1915. End view of a gypsy wagon. John Pocketts, owner.

Look closely at both photographs. Notice how texture is used.

- ✓ Where do you see a twisted, bumpy surface?
- ✓ Which areas look smooth or shiny?
- ✓ Where do you see repeated shapes or lines? What type of feel do they create?
- ✓ What are some similarities and differences between the materials used on the outside and those used on the inside?

Lesson 3

85

SEEING LIKE AN ARTIST

Think of all the objects and materials that decorate your room. How do these different objects feel?

About Art History* Built in 1915, it has been owned by a nurse who cared for gypsy children. John Pocketts now owns it and is restoring it.

Cultural Perspectives For the past 1,000 years, the gypsies have been roaming Earth. Legend says that gypsies came from India after a war caused them to leave their homeland. They were considered outcasts, and some were even killed by Hitler. Today they often make a living as fortune-tellers, musicians, and entertainers.

* See **More About** pages 206–227 for more about art history and subject matter.

FOCUS
Time: About 10 minutes

Activating Prior Knowledge

"What are the textures of the outside of the buildings in your neighborhood? What are the textures used in the furniture in the main room where you live?"

"¿Qué texturas tienen los edificios en su vecindario? ¿Qué texturas se usaron en los muebles del salón de sus casas?"

- Facilitate a discussion to elicit from students ideas for exterior textures, such as stucco. Interior furniture textures might include leather or wallpaper.

Introducing the Art

"Let's take a close look at the two photographs."

"Vamos a observar detalladamente las dos fotografías."

- **Describe:** Have students describe the subject matter of the photographs. (genre)
- **ART MANIPULATIVES** Use the fabric swatches from the **Art Manipulative Kit** to explain textures.
- Share and discuss information from **Art Background** and the **Artist Profiles Book.**
- Have students answer the questions on page 85 to identify examples of texture. (See **Perception Hints** below.)

FOR THE ART SPECIALIST

Use the **Overhead** to demonstrate to students how designers combine a variety of textures to make exterior and interior spaces interesting and appealing.

Perception Hints

Twisted and bumpy The interior and exterior.
Smooth and shiny The wheel hub, the smokestack on the roof, and the bands on the jug.
Repeated shapes and lines Throughout the interior and exterior.
Feel Both create a bumpy feel.
Materials Both have a lot of texture and design. The inside is lighter and brighter.

LESSON 3 **85**

TEACH

Time: About 30 minutes

Practice

Materials
- thin white paper
- crayons
- found objects with raised textures

Alternate Materials: pencils

"Let's experiment with visual textures."

"Vamos a experimentar con texturas visuales."

- Discuss the definitions of *texture, visual texture,* and *imitated texture* on page 86.
- Distribute materials and have students follow the directions on page 86 for creating visual textures. Have them discuss the answer to the Decide question.

Create PROBLEM SOLVING

Materials
- white paper
- scissors
- pencils
- glue
- samples of visual textures like pictures of a shiny car

Alternate Materials: markers

"Let's create a collage of the inside of a fantasy clubhouse with visual textures."

"Vamos a hacer un collage del interior de un club imaginario con texturas visuales."

- Have students brainstorm ideas for themes to illustrate this special place.
- Distribute materials and have students follow the directions on page 87.

Safety! **Safety Tip•** For safety issues regarding markers, see page T22.

FOR THE ART SPECIALIST

Teach the students how to create invented textures using colored pencils. Use these, with the visual textures from magazines, to decorate the room.

Using Texture in Interior Spaces

Texture is the element of art that refers to how things feel, or look as if they might feel if touched. **Tactile texture** is texture that you see with your eyes. There are two ways in which we experience texture—by sight or by touch.

Visual texture is the way something looks like it might feel if you could touch it. It is the illusion an artist creates to represent texture. A rubbing is one way to show visual texture. Other examples of visual texture are examples you see in magazines.

Imitated textures are also two-dimensional. They imitate real textures. When you look at the textures in a photograph, they are imitated textures.

Practice

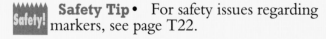

Create some visual textures. Use crayons.

1. To record textures, create rubbings of them.

2. Choose some raised textures, like the soles of a sneaker. Place a thin sheet of paper over each texture to be rubbed. Use the flat side of a crayon while holding the paper in place. Rub the flat side of a crayon over the paper away from your fingers in one direction.

Decide What textures transferred best?

Activities in
ART Across the Curriculum Book

Reading/Language Arts Write dialogue for visitors at the caravan. (page 85)

Math Create a caravan for the year 2000, learning how artists and carpenters use mathematical principles in their designs. (page 86)

Science Learn ways to build a caravan with solar energy to minimize air pollution. (page 87)

Social Studies Study how inventions affect the texture of clothing. (page 88)

The Arts Learn about texture in music as a weaving of words, rhythm, and melody mixed together as a whole. (page 89)

Technology Use the *Multimedia Workshop* CD-ROM to draw a room inside your home with visual texture. (page 90)

Vanesa Garcia. Age 11. *Clubhouse.* Magazines.

What textures do you see in the picture?

Create

What textures would you use to design the interior of a clubhouse? Create a collage of the inside of a fantasy clubhouse using visual textures.

1. Think about creating the inside of a fantasy clubhouse. Choose an idea for a theme.

2. Draw several quick sketches of the inside. Choose one sketch to reproduce. Concentrate on the main shapes.

3. Collect a variety of visual textures, like the texture of frosting or a shiny car. Cut out, then arrange and glue your textures onto your drawing.

Describe Describe the textures and objects in your clubhouse.

Analyze Do the textures you collected copy textures of real objects?

Interpret What kind of mood does your clubhouse have? Is it a quiet space or a space for fun?

Decide What other pictures can be created using this collage technique?

Lesson 3 87

THEME Connections

System Use the artwork as a springboard to study effective mass transit systems.

Culture Use the artwork as a starting point for students to research the culture of the gypsy.

ESL

Before students begin the Create section, you may want to clarify the concept of clubhouses and their cultural context for students unfamiliar with them. Simple sketches on the chalkboard of traditional clubhouses and some sharing time for personal or vicarious experiences with clubhouses can greatly enhance ESL students' interest and ability to fully participate.

CLOSE

Time: About 5 minutes

"Were you able to plan and create a collage of the interior of a fantasy clubhouse using visual textures?"

"¿Fueron capaces de planificar y hacer un collaje del interior de un club imaginario usando texturas simuladas?"

LARGE PRINT **Review**
Use the **Large Print** *Votive Statue of Gudea from Lagash* to have students compare the texture used with that of the texture used in the *Caravan*.

Art Criticism

Have students answer the four art criticism questions—Describe, Analyze, Interpret, and Decide—orally or in writing. Discuss the use of texture in their collages.

Assess
Use the **Assessment Book** pages 29–30 as a formal assessment for this lesson.

Evaluation Criteria

• Can the student recognize the artist's use of textures to make interior and exterior spaces interesting and appealing?

• Can the student create a collage of the interior of a fantasy clubhouse using simulated textures?

• Can the student use the four steps of art criticism to evaluate his or her own work?

• Can the student demonstrate knowledge of the cultural purpose of the *Caravan*?

Reteaching • • • • • • • • • • • •

Texture Have students look around and find examples of how the use of texture for exterior and interior spaces makes them more appealing.

Perception Hints for Student Art

The textures seen in the art include the imitated texture of smoke coming from the chimney, the texture on the house, the sun, the roof, and the bush. Answers may also include the texture of the fence, the flowers, and so on.

UNIT 3
LESSON 4

LESSON PLANNER

Objectives

After completing this lesson, students will be able to:

- identify shading techniques to create the illusion of form and texture on a two-dimensional surface. *Aesthetic Perception*
- plan and create a three-dimensional space station using shading techniques to create the illusion of texture and form. *Creative Expression*
- use the four steps of art criticism to evaluate their own architectural forms. *Art Criticism*
- demonstrate the knowledge of the lives and works of both artists. *Art History and Culture*

Program Resources

- **Overhead:** Both the McCall and the Brown are available on overhead 16.
- **Large Prints:** *Votive Statue of Gudea from Lagash* c. 2120 B.C. and *Trade* by Jaune Quick-to-See Smith
- **Vocabulary Book** pages 31–32
- **Artist Profiles Book:** McCall page 34 and Brown page 8
- **Art Across the Curriculum Book** pages 91–96
- **Multimedia Workshop CD-ROM**
- **Assessment Book** pages 31–32

Multiple Intelligences

Logical/Mathematical Students can identify and name geometric shapes and forms.

Vocabulary

form *forma* objects that have three dimensions. Forms are either geometric or free-form.

Architectural Form and Texture

Artists often use shading techniques to create the illusion of form and texture on a two-dimensional surface.

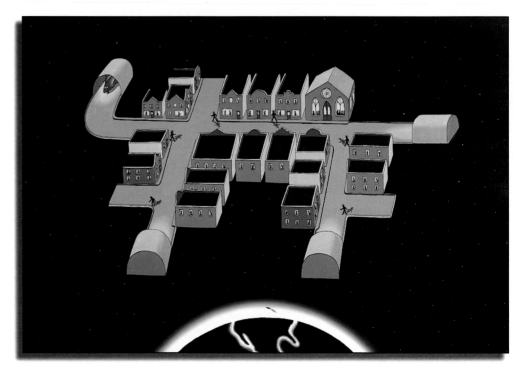

Roger Brown. (American). *Homesick Proof Space Station.* 1987. Oil on canvas. 48 × 72 inches. Courtesy of the Phyllis Kind Gallery.

The painting *Homesick Proof Space Station,* done in 1987, actually makes fun of space travel. The artist is being sarcastic. *Space Station #1* by Robert McCall was created for the MGM movie *2001: A Space Odyssey* in the 1970s. What familiar shapes do you find in the artworks?

88   Unit **3**

ART Background

About the Artists

Robert McCall (American, 1919–) was born in Columbus, Ohio. As the official artist of the U.S. space program, he has been painting pictures of space travel for more than 30 years. He also designed postage stamps for the U.S. government for 16 years.

Roger Brown (American, 1941–), was born in Hamilton, Alabama. He moved to Chicago when he was 21 and studied for several years at the School of the Art Institute of Chicago. He received his Master's degree in Fine Arts. Brown likes to paint scenes of different regions with a focus on the land and people of the United States.

About Subject Matter* The subject matter of both works is narrative.

Robert McCall. (American). *Space Station #1.* Mixed media on canvas. 53 × 40½ inches. Commissioned by MGM for the film *2001: A Space Odyssey.* National Museum of Air and Space, Smithsonian Institution, Washington, DC.

Study both paintings to find textures and forms.

☑ Find a smooth, shiny surface and a rough surface.

☑ Find a cylinder or cube shape. Are there overlapping shapes?

☑ What effect does it have on the subject when an object goes from light to dark?

☑ What was done to create the feeling of floating in space?

SEEING LIKE AN ARTIST

Look around you for shapes similar to the objects in these two paintings.

Lesson **4**   89

About the Media McCall works in oil or acrylic paint on canvases. He has done stained glass, watercolor paint, and ink. Brown also generally works in oil paint on canvas.

About Art History* McCall is an illustrator. He has done paintings for movies such as *Star Trek* and *2001: A Space Odyssey.* His murals are at the Smithsonian Institution and at the Disney World EPCOT Center.

The Chicago Imagists are a group of artists like Brown, who painted pictures of landscapes with few people and simple colors. Their work reflects their feelings.

Cultural Perspectives McCall created his work in the 1970s, a period of turmoil in the United States.

Brown's work was created in 1987, a period of economic growth in the U.S.

*See **More About** pages 206–227 for more about art history and subject matter.

FOCUS

Time: About 10 minutes

Activating Prior Knowledge

"Can you imagine what it would be like to experience a ride into outer space on a spaceship?"

"¿Se imaginan cómo sería experimentar un viaje al espacio en una nave espacial?"

- To give students an idea of the force and speed of a spaceship, have them think about a ride on a roller coaster. Explain to them that roller coasters can reach a "G" force that is a fraction of the force of a spaceship.

Introducing the Art

"Let's take a close look at the two artworks."

"Vamos a observar detalladamente las dos obras de arte."

- **Describe:** Ask students to describe both works. (One shows the layout of a space station; the other shows a spaceship being launched.)
- Share and discuss information from **Art Background** and the **Artist Profiles Book.**
- Have students answer the questions on page 89. (See **Perception Hints** below.)
- **COMPARE AND CONTRAST** Have students compare and contrast the two works. (The McCall shows a launching from a space station. The Brown makes fun of space travel. He uses geometric and free-form forms with smooth texture. McCall uses geometric forms with a mixture of textures.)

FOR THE ART SPECIALIST

Use the **Overhead** and the **Large Prints** *Votive Statue of Gudea from Lagash* and *Trade* to demonstrate how artists use shading techniques to create the illusion of form on a two-dimensional surface.

Perception Hints

Surface *Space Station #1.* The center core is shiny. The surface of Earth appears rough .

Cylinder *Space Station #1.* The center of the space station.

Overlapping cubes *Moore.* The homes appear as overlapping cubes.

Light to dark This sharp contrast creates a feeling of floating.

TEACH

Time: About 30 minutes

Practice

Materials
- white paper
- pencils

Alternate Materials: markers

"How can you change shapes into forms?"
"¿Cómo pueden cambiar las figuras en formas?"

- Discuss the definitions of forms and shapes and the types of shading techniques used to create the illusion of forms on page 90.
- Distribute materials and have students follow the directions on page 90 for using shading techniques. Have students discuss the Decide question.

Create PROBLEM SOLVING

Materials
- 12- × 18-inch paper
- pencils
- recording of *Star Trek*
- colored pencils

Alternate Materials: oil pastels

"Let's draw a space station using shading techniques."
"Vamos a dibujar una estación espacial usando las técnicas de sombreado."

- Play the musical theme from *Star Trek*. (Ask the students to close their eyes and imagine what it would be like to live and travel in space.
- Have students brainstorm ideas for designing a space station and for the kind of forms they would use. Review shading techniques.
- Distribute the materials and have students follow the directions on page 91.

FOR THE ART SPECIALIST

Have students design and build a space station out of cardboard.

Shading to Create Architectural Form and Texture

A **form** is any object that can be measured in three ways: length, width, and depth. In two-dimensional art, artists create the illusion of form using various techniques. They also use shading techniques to create a different quality of texture.

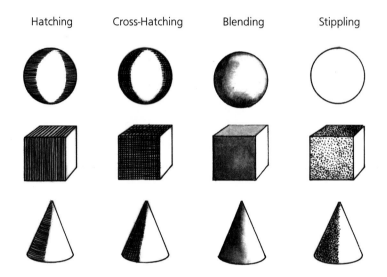

Hatching   Cross-Hatching   Blending   Stippling

To create the illusion of form on a two-dimensional surface, artists use imitated textures. Textures can be used to change a shape into a form.

Practice

Change shapes into forms by using different types of shading techniques. Use pencil.

Decide Which technique did you like best?

1. Lightly draw four different shapes. Beneath each, write *hatching*, *cross-hatching*, *stippling*, or *blending*.

2. Change each shape into a form using the shading technique written below it.

Activities in
ART Across the Curriculum Book

Reading/Language Arts Understand how form is used in writing in contrast to art. (page 91)

Math Compare and contrast the voyages of two space probes after looking at the painting *Space Station #1*. (page 92)

Science Imagine how you would stay healthy in a place like Roger Brown's space station, learning more about ways people stay healthy. (page 93)

Social Studies Learn how mapmakers show forms on a flat surface on topographical maps. (page 94)

The Arts Understand how form is used in music. (page 95)

Technology Use the *Multimedia Workshop* CD-ROM to create a variety of textures to show the forms of an outer space home or space station. (page 96)

Mike Kwon. Age 11. *Silent Steel.* Oil pastel.

How do the shading techniques affect the appearance of the space station?

Create

What types of forms would you use to design your own space station? Draw a three-dimensional space station using shading techniques to create the illusion of texture and form.

1. Think about how both artists used shading techniques to create forms on a flat surface.

2. Sketch your space station using simple shapes. Use the shading techniques to change these shapes into forms.

3. Draw planets using the blending technique to move from light to dark. Try complementary colors for shading. Add white highlights.

4. Add atmosphere by using the side of the oil pastel to make long sweeping marks.

Describe Describe your space station and the shapes you used to build it.

Analyze What shading techniques did you use?

Interpret How did the colors and textures affect the appearance of your station? Would you like to live there?

Decide If you could make another space station, what would you do to improve it?

Lesson 4 91

Exploration Use the artwork as a vehicle to discuss the importance of exploring new space frontiers.

Discovery Use the artwork to help students discover more about the environmental crisis in the United States.

Some ESL students may need guided questioning for successful participation in discussions of their work and techniques. You can simplify, restate, and shorten complex questions to facilitate understanding. Writing the questions down, pantomiming meaning, and showing examples also help increase students' awareness.

CLOSE

Time: About 5 minutes

"Were you able to draw a three-dimensional space station using shading techniques?"

"¿Pudieron dibujar una estación espacial tridimensional usando técnicas de sombreado?"

Review

Use the **Large Print** *Trade* to have students compare the shading techniques used to create the illusion of form and texture with the works in the lesson.

Art Criticism

Have students answer the four art criticism questions—Describe, Analyze, Interpret, and Decide—orally or in writing. Discuss the use of form and texture in their drawings of spaceships.

Assess

Use the **Assessment Book** pages 31–32 as a formal assessment for this lesson.

Evaluation Criteria

• Can the student identify shading techniques to create the illusion of form and texture on a two-dimensional surface?

• Can the student plan and create a three-dimensional space station using shading techniques to create the illusion of texture and form?

• Can the student use the four steps of art criticism to evaluate his or her own artwork?

• Can the student demonstrate knowledge of the lives and works of both artists?

Reteaching ● ● ● ● ● ● ● ● ● ● ●

Architectural forms and textures Have students look in old magazines to find architectural forms similar to the ones in the lesson. Have them cut out the forms and use them to create a space station collage.

Perception Hints for Student Art

The shading techniques give the space station form and texture.

U NIT 3

LESSON PLANNER

Objectives

After completing this lesson, students will be able to:

- identify architectural forms used by artists. *Aesthetic Perception*
- plan and create a painting that will use architectural forms. *Creative Expression*
- use the four steps of art criticism to evaluate their own paintings. *Art Criticism*
- demonstrate knowledge of the lives and work of the architects Elizabeth Plater-Zyberk and Frank Lloyd Wright. *Art History and Culture*

Program Resources

- **Overhead:** Both the Plater-Zyberk and the Wright are available on overhead 17.
- **Large Prints:** *Votive Statue of Gudea from Lagash* c. 2120 B.C. and *Trade* by Jaune Quick-to-See Smith
- **Vocabulary Book** pages 33–34
- **Art Manipulative Kit:** 3-D geometric and free-form shapes with architectural shapes (wood)
- **Artist Profiles Book:** Plater-Zyberk page 42 and Wright page 59
- **Art Across the Curriculum Book** pages 97–102
- **Multimedia Workshop CD-ROM**
- **National Museum of Women in the Arts Collection**
- **Assessment Book** pages 33–34

Multiple Intelligences

Verbal/Linguistic Students can expand their knowledge of architectural shapes through vocabulary and verbal explanations.

Vocabulary

architecture *arquitectura* the art of designing and planning the construction of buildings, cities, and bridges

architect *arquitecto* a person who plans and designs buildings, cities, and bridges

---

Architectural Shape and Visual Texture

Architects are artists who design buildings and structures for living, working, and leisure.

Elizabeth Plater-Zyberk. (American). *Seaside, Florida, Walkway.* Architecture.

Elizabeth Plater-Zyberk designed this group of houses and walkways in the 1980s. Her structures remind us of the pastel sunsets found near the ocean. Architect Frank Lloyd Wright designed homes that were primarily built to blend with their environments. Notice the materials used for the structures by the two architects.

92   Unit **3**

ART Background

About the Artists

Elizabeth Plater-Zyberk (ē liz′ ə bəth plā′ tər zī bûrk, American, 1950–) was educated at Princeton and Yale. She and her husband taught at the University of Miami in Florida. She established Miami's master's program in architecture. In 1980 Plater-Zyberk and Duany, her husband, formed their own company, DPZ architects, so that they could design whole towns.

Frank Lloyd Wright (frangk loid rīt, American, 1867–1959) was destined to become an architect. His mother hung pictures of great cathedrals to inspire him. He designed more than 600 buildings during his long career.

Frank Lloyd Wright. (American).
Fallingwater. Bear Run, Pennsylvania,
1936–1939. Glen Allison/Tony Stone Images
© 1998 © 1996 Artists Rights Society (ARS),
NY/Frank Lloyd Wright Foundation.

Study both photographs to find architectural shapes.

- ✓ Find the geometric and free-form shapes.
- ✓ Where are the windows, doors, and roofs?
- ✓ Do the architectural shapes blend in with the environments that surround them? If so, how?

SEEING LIKE AN ARTIST

What types of details do the homes and buildings in your community have? Do they have unusual windows, roofs, or doors?

Lesson 5

93

About Art History* Plater-Zyberk's work has been featured in the Cuban Museum of Arts and Culture. Her work has been written about in more than 130 publications, including books and magazines from countries around the world.

Wright's most controversial building is the Guggenheim Museum in New York City. Critics say it was his revenge on a city that he hated. Others say it is the most beautiful building in the world.

Cultural Perspectives Wright believed that a house should grow out of the needs and desires of the owner and from the unique character of the setting.

*See **More About** pages 206–227 for more about art history and subject matter.

FOCUS

Time: About 10 minutes

Activating Prior Knowledge

"What do you see when riding in a car and approaching a city that has very tall buildings?"

"¿Qué ven cuando van en un carro y se aproximan a una ciudad que tiene edificios muy altos?"

- Discuss responses, and point out that the buildings are a variety of architectural shapes.

Introducing the Art

"Let's look closely at the architecture."

"Vamos a observar detalladamente la arquitectura."

- **Describe:** Ask students to describe the subject matter. (Both are buildings with no definable subject matter. For examples of landscapes, see the **National Museum for Women in the Arts Collection.**)

- Share and discuss information from **Art Background** and the **Artist Profiles Book.**

- **COMPARE AND CONTRAST** Have students make a list of the similarities and differences in both. (Both suit their environments. The Plater-Zyberk is traditional; the Wright house is contemporary.)

- Ask students to answer the questions on page 93. (See **Perception Hints** below.)

FOR THE ART SPECIALIST

Use the **Overhead** to discuss architectural forms as seen in the photographs.

Perception Hints

Geometric and free-form The houses in both are geometric. *Wright.* The rocks and the landscape are free-form. *Plater-Zyberk.* The bushes, shrubs, and plants are free-form.

Windows, doors, and roofs *Wright.* Set high and almost hidden from view. *Plater-Zyberk.* Windows and roofs are very visable.

Blend into environment Shapes blend into the environment by using materials that match the environment. *Wright.* The river runs through the house. *Plater-Zyber.* The blue of the buildings matches the blue of the water.

TEACH

Time: About 30 minutes

Practice

Materials
- white paper
- pencils

Alternate Materials: pens

"Let's think about architectural forms in our town."

"Vamos a pensar acerca de las formas arquitectónicas en nuestro pueblo."

- Discuss the architectural shapes the students are familar with on page 94.
- Distribute materials and have students follow the directions on page 94 for drawing architectural shapes. Have them discuss the answer to the Decide question.

Create PROBLEM SOLVING

Materials
- white paper
- felt-tip pens
- pencils
- colored pencils

Alternate Materials: watercolors

"Let's draw the building you live in using architectural shapes."

"Vamos a dibujar el edificio en que viven usando figuras arquitectónicas."

- Brainstorm ideas about architectural shapes.
- Distribute materials and have students follow the directions on page 95.
- See page 199 **Technique Tips** for information about watercolors.

FOR THE ART SPECIALIST

Have students do an embossed foil-relief design of the house.

Using Architectural Shapes

Architecture is the art of designing and planning the construction of buildings, cities, and bridges. An **architect** is a person who plans and designs buildings, cities, and bridges.

Types of Architectural Shapes

Practice

Practice drawing some of the architectural shapes you have learned about. Use pencil.

1. Lightly sketch the overall shape of a building or house you have seen. Include an environment.

2. Add architectural shapes to your sketch. Keep the basic structure of your original drawing.

Decide What architectural shapes did you draw?

Activities in

ART Across the Curriculum Book

Reading/Language Arts Write a story using pictures to elaborate on the details just as architects use drawings. (page 97)

Math Understand how mathematics is used in the planning and construction of buildings. (page 98)

Science Use investigative skills to solve a problem, similar to those used by architects to investigate the environment before building. (page 99)

Social Studies Study how architecture reflects the people who live in it. (page 100)

The Arts Create a dance describing a barn raising, using group work. (page 101)

Technology Use the *Multimedia Workshop* CD-ROM to draw a house or an apartment building using architectural shapes. (page 102)

Liliana Jimenez. Age 11. *Town and Country*. Crayons, marker.

What architectural shapes do you see in the picture?

Create

What types of architectural detail does your home have? Draw the building you live in using architectural shapes.

1. Think about the architectural shapes and details in your community. Lightly sketch with pencil the main shapes of the building where you live.

2. Draw architectural shapes such as windows, doors, roofs, and the surrounding environment.

3. Using a black felt-tip pen, outline your drawing. Complete your drawing with colored pencils, adding details.

Describe Describe the shapes and forms used.

Analyze What types of architectural shapes are in your drawing?

Interpret How do the colors, textures, and architectural shapes affect the mood of the drawing?

Decide Could you use these techniques to draw an imaginary building?

Lesson 5   95

THEME Connections

Patterns Use the artwork as a means to open discussion about the pattern of population growth in the sunshine state of Florida.

Scale Use the artwork to help students understand the scale used in maps.

ESL

Second-language learners may need some focused instruction and practice to respond to questions about how they might change their work in the future. *How would your next picture be different? What would you change?* Modeling first and then offering time to practice with a partner can help develop this knowledge.

"Were you able to draw the building you live in?"
"¿Pudieron dibujar el edificio en que viven?"

LARGE PRINT   **Review**
Use the **Overhead** to have students compare the architectural shapes and visual texture used in *Seaside, Florida, Walkway* and *Fallingwater* to the architectural shapes and visual textures of their school building.

ART MANIPULATIVES   Use the 3-D geometric and free-form shapes with architectural shapes from the **Art Manipulative Kit** and compare them to the shapes used in the buildings.

Art Criticism
Have students answer the four art criticism questions—Describe, Analyze, Interpret, and Decide—orally or in writing. Discuss the use of architectural forms in their paintings.

Assess
Use the **Assessment Book** pages 33–34 as a formal assessment for this lesson.

Evaluation Criteria
• Can the student identify architectural forms?
• Can the student incorporate architectural shapes into an original drawing?
• Can the student use the four steps of art criticism to evaluate his or her own work?
• Can the student demonstrate knowledge of the lives and works of both architects?

Reteaching ● ● ● ● ● ● ● ● ● ● ●

Form Have students look through magazines to find photographs of architectural forms and cut them out. Cut the structures in half. Using your imagination, draw the other half of the building, not duplicating what was cut off. Add color using colored pencils.

Perception Hints for Student Art

The architectural shapes seen in the student art include two- and three-dimensional forms, including buildings, roofs, bridges, windows, and roads.

UNIT 3
LESSON 6

Form and Tactile Texture

Artists use form to create three-dimensional works of art.

Objectives

After completing this lesson, students will be able to:

- recognize the use of form and texture in three-dimensional works of art. *Aesthetic Perception*
- create a model of a unique public building using clay. *Creative Expression*
- use the four steps of art criticism to evaluate their own models. *Art Criticism*
- demonstrate knowledge of the lives and cultures of both artists. *Art History and Culture*

Program Resources

- **Overhead:** Both the Le Corbusier and the Utzon are available on overhead 18.
- **Large Prints:** *Votive Statue of Gudea from Lagash* c. 2120 B.C. and *Trade* by Jaune Quick-to-See Smith
- **Vocabulary Book** pages 35–36
- **Artist Profiles Book:** Le Corbusier page 28 and Utzon page 54
- **Art Across the Curriculum** pages 103–108
- **Multimedia Workshop CD-ROM**
- **National Geographic Picture Atlas of the World CD-ROM**
- **Assessment Book** pages 35–36

Multiple Intelligences
Body/Kinesthetic Students can explore form by handling clay, tools, and other materials.

Vocabulary

form *forma* an object that is three dimensional. Forms can also be geometric or free-form.

armatures *armaduras* frameworks for supporting material used in sculpting, such as clay

tactile texture *textura táctil* an actual texture that you can touch and feel

The following words appear as art in the Student Edition page 98 and in the glossary: *rough, smooth, shiny,* and *matte.*

Le Corbusier. (Swiss). *Chapelle Notre Dame-du Haut.* 1950–55. Ronchamp, France.

Le Corbusier was an architect who created *Chapelle Notre Dame-du Haut* in France in 1950. *The Sydney Opera House* in Sydney, Australia, was designed in 1957 by Jorn Utzon of Denmark. Do you think these structures resemble a chapel and an opera house? Both architects used shapes found in nature as a basis for their designs.

ART Background

About the Artists
Le Corbusier (lā kôr bū zyā, Swiss-French, 1887–1965) was the professional name for Charles Edouard Jeanneret. He was an architect, painter, and writer who had a major effect on the development of modern architecture. He studied in Paris, worked in Germany, and finally settled into business in Paris in 1922.

Jørn Oberg Utzon (jôrn ō′ bûrg ut′ zən, Danish, 1918–) learned about building things from his father, a noted yacht designer. He gained international recognition in 1957 when he designed the Opera House in Sydney, Australia. He designs unusual buildings.

About Art History* Among other awards, Le Corbusier's famous buildings include a prize-winning design for the Palace of the League of Nations, Geneva. He was also appointed to plan the permanent building for the United Nations in New York.

Jørn Oberg Utzon. (Danish). *Opera House.* Sydney, Australia.

Study both architectural structures for their use of form and texture.

☑ What two shapes and forms do you see in both structures?

☑ What is unique about these two buildings?

☑ Do you think both structures fit their environments? Why?

SEEING LIKE AN ARTIST

What objects can you think of that are similar to the structures in the photographs?

Lesson 6   97

Activating Prior Knowledge

"As you walk through your town or city, what are the shapes of the buildings you see?"

"A medida que caminan por el pueblo o la ciudad, ¿cuáles son las figuras de los edificios que ven?"

• Discuss the answers with the students. Architecture may be geometric or free-form. Ask students what the dominant texture of the buildings is.

Introducing the Art

"Let's look closely at the two buildings."

"Vamos a observar detalladamente los dos edificios."

• Share and discuss information from **Art Background** and the **Artist Profiles Book** regarding the lives and cultures of both artists.

• Use the **National Geographic Picture Atlas of the World CD-ROM** to find the locations of both structures.

• Have students answer the questions about form and texture on page 97.

(See **Perception Hints** below.)

• **COMPARE AND CONTRAST** both works. (Both used shapes found in nature as a basis for their designs. One is a religious building and the other is an opera house.)

FOR THE ART SPECIALIST

Use the **Overhead** and the **Large Print** *Votive Statue of Gudea from Lagash* to demonstrate how artists use form to create three-dimensional works of art.

Utzon has led the way in designing buildings that are romantic and expressive. His work is influenced by his study of nature and of Islamic and oriental architecture.

Utzon invented the term *additive architecture* when components are joined to form a whole. He was the first to use standard, mass-produced elements to produce complex forms.

Cultural Perspectives Le Corbusier was a functionalist. He sought a twentieth-century style based on engineering. His work did much to bring about acceptance of the now-common style of low-lying, unadorned buildings that depend for aesthetic effect on simplicity of forms and relation to function.

*See **More About** pages 206–227 for more about art history and subject matter.

Perception Hints

Shapes and forms Free-form and rounded triangle shapes in both.
Unique Both are not geometric but free-form shapes.
Environment Both fit because architects used shapes found in nature.

TEACH

Time: About 30 minutes

Practice

Materials:
- found objects

"What objects in your environment have combinations of textures?"

"¿Qué objetos en su ambiente tienen combinaciones de texturas?"

- Discuss the textures rough and shiny, rough and matte, smooth and shiny, and smooth and matte on page 98.
- Have students follow directions on page 98 for finding textures. Have students discuss the Decide question in groups and then share answers with the class.

Create PROBLEM SOLVING

Materials
- clay
- carving tools
- water
- sticks
- found materials, like small boxes

Alternate Materials: posterboard, tape, and paints

"Let's create a unique public building using clay."

"Vamos a crear un edificio público original usando arcilla."

- Brainstorm ideas for a unique public building.
- See **Technique Tips** on page 204 for information about proper clay joining and firing techniques. Distribute materials and have students follow directions on page 99.

FOR THE ART SPECIALIST

Paint all the pieces with school acrylics or artists' acrylic paints.

Using Form and Tactile Texture

A **form** is an object that is three-dimensional. Like a shape, a form has length and width, but it also has depth. Forms can be either geometric or free-form. You must view forms from all angles to truly understand them.

Armatures are frameworks for supporting material used in sculpting, such as clay. An armature helps hold the material up and in place.

Tactile texture is an actual texture that you can touch and feel. The way light reflects off the surface of an object depends on the texture of that object.

 **Rough**-textured surfaces reflect the light unevenly.

 **Smooth**-textured surfaces reflect the light evenly.

 **Shiny**-textured surfaces reflect a bright light.

 **Matte**-textured surfaces reflect a light that is soft with an almost dull look.

Practice

Find objects with combinations of textures.

1. Working in small groups, find textures in your surroundings.

2. Find rough and shiny, then rough and matte-finished. Find smooth and shiny, then smooth and matte.

Decide Do you understand the many combinations of textures?

Activities in
ART Across the Curriculum Book

Reading/Language Arts Learn how to communicate your ideas clearly in support of something, learning how these skills are used in making decisions about public buildings like the Sydney Opera House. (page 103)

Math Use mathematics to compare statistics of Australia. (page 104)

Science Learn more about the Alps where Le Corbusier lived. (page 105)

Social Studies Study how natural forms may be incorporated in the design of public buildings. (page 106)

The Arts Experiment with ways a character might share a tactile experience with an audience. (page 107)

Technology Use the *Multimedia Workshop* CD-ROM to design a public building for your local community. (page 108)

Dung Tran. Rudy Espinbo. Lenny Rodriguez. *Clay Houses.* Clay, paint.

What do you think the purpose of the buildings are?

Create

What is your favorite kind of public building? Build a clay model of a unique public building.

1. Think about a building for your favorite activities. Begin creating it by taping together small boxes or wads of newspaper for an armature. Make clay slabs for the walls and roof.

2. Put your building together. Use proper clay-joining techniques to build your structure.

3. Add details such as windows and doors by adding clay or carving openings. Use found materials to create textures on the clay surface.

Describe What kind of a unique building did you create? Explain how you created the forms and textures.

Analyze Describe the forms and textures you used.

Interpret Does your building look like its function? Give it a name.

Decide Were you able to control the slabs to create the forms you planned?

Lesson 6   99

THEME Connections

Cultures Use the artwork to discuss the cultural differences between Australia and the United States.

Origins Use the artwork to trace the origin of the opera.

ESL

Develop ESL students' understanding, with careful attention to the initial art study section with questions. You can offer synonyms and pantomime meaning as needed for clarification. Students can trace shapes and forms and point out textures to indicate understanding.

CLOSE

Time: About 5 minutes

"Were you able to build a unique public building from clay?"

"¿Fueron capaces de construir un edificio público original de arcilla?"

LARGE PRINT **Review**

Use the **Large Print** *Votive Statue of Gudea from Lagash* to have students compare textures to those in this lesson.

Art Criticism

Have students answer the four art criticism questions—Describe, Analyze, Interpret, and Decide—orally or in writing. Discuss the use of the slab-built technique in their work after the clay is dry.

 Assess

Use the **Assessment Book** pages 35–36 as a formal assessment for this lesson.

Evaluation Criteria

• Can the student identify form and textures used in three-dimensional works of art?

• Can the student create a unique public building using clay?

• Can the student use the four steps of art criticism to evaluate his or her work?

• Can the student demonstrate knowledge of the lives and cultures of both artchitects?

Reteaching ● ● ● ● ● ● ● ● ● ● ● ●

Textures Have students look around them to find examples of the different types of texture.

Perception Hints for Student Art

Possible answers: housing, places of work, restaurants, and so on.

UNIT 3

Objectives

After completing this lesson, students will be able to:

- demonstrate a variety of sounds from materials of different textures and forms. *Aesthetic Perception*
- express individual and group interpretation in creating sounds. *Creative Expression*
- use the four steps of art criticism to evaluate their own performances. *Art Criticism*
- demonstrate knowledge of how the musical group Xochimoki creates music using ancient musical instruments. *Art History and Culture*

FOCUS

Time: About 10 minutes

Activating Prior Knowledge

"Name some musical instruments that you know. Do they produce sound by being shaken, blown, scraped, or struck?"

"Nombren algunos instrumentos musicales que conocen. ¿Producen sonidos al agitarlos, soplarlos, rasparlos o golpearlos?"

- Discuss students' answers and talk about the importance of music as an expression of a culture.

Introducing the Art

"Look at the photograph of Xochimoki and identify the different musical instruments and what they are made of."

"Observen la fotografía de Xochimoki e identifiquen los diferentes instrumentos musicales y de qué están elaborados.

- Point out that instruments of ancient peoples came from materials in the environment, such as plants, wood, seeds, bones, animal skins, and shells.
- Share information from **Art Background** about the musical duo Xochimoki. If you have the *Artsource* audiocassette, have students listen to the music of Xochimoki.

Space, Form, and Texture in Music

Xochimoki: *Jim Berenholtz and Mazatl Galindo.*

 hese musicians use musical instruments like those played by ancient Aztec and Mayan peoples. They make music with things like a log drum, a gourd trumpet, rattles made of seeds, and a turtle shell drum played with deer antlers. Artists use the forms of nature as the basis for their designs. These musicians use the materials of nature as the basis for their music.

ART Background

About the Artists

In 1984, Jim Berenholtz and Mazatl Galindo founded the musical duo known as Xochimoki, which is devoted to the revival of ancient arts. Their focus is to create original music using pre-Columbian instruments of several Mesoamerican civilizations, combined with some contemporary acoustic and electronic instruments.

Cultural Perspectives Xochimoki emphasizes the ancient traditions of the Americas. The name *Xochimoki* derives from the Nahuatl (Aztec) and Hopi languages and means "flower of the ancient one." The two artist-scholars have collected information, music, and instruments from the Hopi, Raramuri, Nahuatl, Maya, and Quechua communities. Ancient murals that depict dancers and musicians have provided images for reconstructing instruments and costumes.

What To Do

Write a musical score.

Materials
- ✔ paper and pencils
- ✔ Found sources of sound

1. Collect common items that create sound. These sound sources will be your classroom collection of instruments.

2. Classify the instruments as to how you make sound with them. Are they shaken, blown, scraped, or struck? On a large chart draw a descriptive symbol for each category. For example, you could draw a simple horn for instruments that are blown and a rattle for those that are shaken.

3. Form a class orchestra, grouping the instruments into their categories. Set a beat by tapping your feet. Then, play your instruments together.

4. Write a musical score using your symbols so that another group could perform your work.

Describe Describe the instruments you created.

Analyze How is your use of nature's materials similar to an artist's use of nature's designs?

Interpret What feelings and moods did you create?

Decide How well do you think you succeeded in creating music? What did you like best about this activity?

Extra Credit

Decorate your musical score in an artistic way, mount it on colorful paper, and display it with a description.

Music 101

About Subject Matter In order to learn about the music of ancient cultures, Jim Berenholtz and Mazatl Galindo have read about the research of musicologists and have done on-site research in museums or at archaeological sites or ruins. They have accumulated more than 500 ancient wind and percussion instruments.

About Music Music is a universal language with many different rhythms, textures, and styles, similar to different dialects. Modern musical instruments fall into four categories, or families. These family names are based on the manner in which the sounds are produced and the materials from which they are made, namely strings, woodwinds, brass winds, and percussion. Modern instruments have become more sophisticated—with extensive ranges and a variety of tone colors—than instruments of the past.

TEACH

Time: Two 30-minute periods

Materials
- paper and pencils
- a variety of found objects, such as shells, blades of grass, gourds, and other items to scrape, blow, shake, or strike

"Let's collect our own musical instruments and create our own music."

"Vamos a reunir nuestros instrumentos musicales y crear nuestra propia música."

- Have each student choose an instrument.
- Have students invent symbols that mean "shake," "blow," "strike," or "scrape" and group themselves according to how their instruments produce sound.
- Choose a conductor to tap or clap a beat, directing students to play their instruments together or separately.
- Assign a small group of students to write down the musical score as other students play.

CLOSE

Time: About 5 minutes

"What do your experiences tell you about the music of ancient cultures?"

"¿Qué les dicen sus experiencias sobre la música de las culturas antiguas?"

Assess

Have students answer the four art criticism questions on page 101—Describe, Analyze, Interpret, and Decide—orally or in writing.

Evaluation Criteria
- Can the student produce sounds from a variety of materials of different forms and textures?
- Can the student express himself or herself in creating musical sounds?
- Can the student use the four steps of art criticism to evaluate his or her own performance?
- Can the student demonstrate knowledge of how Xochimoki creates music by using ancient musical instruments?

UNIT 3

Reviewing Unit Concepts

"Artists use space, form, and texture to add interest in many different types of art."

"Los artistas usan el espacio, la forma y la textura para agregar interés en diferentes tipos de arte."

- Review space, form, and texture and how they are used by artists as explained on page 102.
- Have the students write the different ways artists use these elements and ask them to find examples in the book.

Examining the Artwork

"How did the artist use space, form, and texture in his mobiles?"

"¿Cómo el artista usa el espacio, la forma y la textura en sus móviles?"

- Look at *Untitled Mobile*. Discuss the shapes and colors and how the shapes were arranged so that the mobile would remain balanced within a given space.
- Discuss the questions on page 103.
  (See **Perception Hints** below.)

Student Portfolio
Have students review the artwork they have created during this unit and select the pieces they wish to put into their portfolios.

Art Criticism Activity
Have students select artwork from the previous unit and study it using the four steps of art criticism. (See pages 206–209 for more information about Art Criticism.)

Space, Form, and Texture
Reviewing Main Ideas

The activities and lessons in this unit cover space, form, and texture and how they are used by artists to create works of art.

- **Space**—The element of art that refers to the area between, around, above, below, and within objects. There are two types of space.

1. **Positive space** is the objects, shapes, or forms in all works of art.
2. **Negative space** is the empty space that surrounds objects, shapes, or forms.

- **Texture** is the element of art that refers to how things feel, or look as if they might feel if touched. There are two ways in which we experience texture.

1. **Visual texture** is the way something looks like it might feel if you could touch it. There are two types of visual texture.

a. **Invented textures** are two-dimensional patterns created by repetition of shapes and lines.

b. **Simulated textures** are two-dimensional patterns that imitate real textures.

2. **Tactile texture** is an actual texture. You can touch it and feel it.

Alexander Calder. (American). *Untitled Mobile*. 1976. Aluminum and steel. $35\frac{5}{8} \times 911\frac{1}{2}$ inches. Gift of the Collectors' Committees, © 1996 Board of Trustees, National Gallery of Art, Washington, DC.

ART Background

About the Artist
Alexander Calder (a leg zan' dər kôl' dər, American, 1898–1976) was born in Philadelphia and is considered one of the most innovative sculptors of this century. He first began creating wire sculptures combined with wood. In 1930, after seeing work by abstract artists, Calder began experimenting with free-form and kidney shapes that moved mechanically. By 1932 he was working solely with freestanding sculptures that were wind-propelled. These kinetic sculptures were given the name of "mobiles" by Marcel Duchamp and have been called such ever since.

About Subject Matter* *Untitled Mobile* was purchased by the Collectors Committee for the National Gallery of Art in Washington, DC. Calder usually named his mobiles after they had been installed. Because *Untitled Mobile* was installed after his death, it was left untitled.

- **Form** is any object that can be measured in three ways: length, height, and width.
- **Architectural Forms** are the shapes and structures that relate to the rules of architecture.

Summing Up

Look at *Untitled Mobile* by Alexander Calder. The artist thought carefully about space, form, and texture when he created his mobiles. Several of these techniques were discussed in Unit 3.

- Has Alexander Calder used both types of space in his mobile?
- What basic shapes did Calder use? Why is this mobile considered an example of a three-dimensional form?
- Describe the textures used by Calder. Are they simulated, invented, or tactile?

Space, form, and texture create the illusion of depth on two-dimensional works of art and make three-dimensional works more interesting for the viewer.

Let's Visit a Museum

The National Gallery of Art in Washington, DC, was built for the people of the United States. Upon his death, Andrew W. Mellon, the financier, donated money and his art collection to create the museum. It opened in 1941. The major collection includes more than 100,000 sculptures, paintings, drawings, decorative objects, prints, and photographs. Because the National Gallery of Art was built to give all people access to a museum, there are no admission fees.

The National Gallery of Art

103

Learning About Museums

Museums are used for the preservation and display of artifacts about a particular subject or culture. Every museum has a specialty. The National Gallery of Art in Washington, DC, was created for the people of the United States through a gift of financier and art collector Andrew W. Mellon. The museum has nearly 100,000 pieces of art from the Middle Ages to the present. The collection on view in the West Building concentrates on European works from the thirteenth century through the early twentieth century. The museum represents a partnership of federal and private resources.

- Have students select a work of art from this book and write a description of the type of museum in which the work would be displayed. Have them include other types of art that the museum might hold and what the museum would look like. A drawing of their museum can be included with their written description.

TIMELINE For more information on this and other museums, see pages T13, T30–T33, and the back of the **Animals Through History Time Line.**

About the Media Calder's mobiles are a combination of cut painted sheet aluminum and brass or steel. He uses this type of material for his mobiles so that they will withstand the elements. This type of material also stays constant, which is important to the mobiles because they rely on constant balance.

About Art History* Kinetic Art was begun by the Italian futurists, a group of artists who sought to convey the feeling of motion in their paintings and sculptures. This movement began in the early part of the twentieth century. Kinetic art has come to apply to sculpture that physically moves either by natural forces, like air movement, or by mechanical forces.

See **More About pages 206–227 for more about art history and subject matter.*

A Final Thought

"To us art is an adventure into an unknown world, which can be explored only by those willing to take the risks."—Adolph Gottlieb and Mark Rothko

UNIT 4

UNIT OVERVIEW

The art principles of proportion and distortion are the focus of Unit 4. You will concentrate on proportion as it relates to the size of one part to another in a work of art. Distortion refers to how an artist alters and changes a feature so that it looks unusual or draws the viewer's attention. The topics that are covered in this unit are **proportion, scale, distortion,** and **exaggeration.**

Proportion is concerned with the size relationships of one part to another. Proportion is taught in Lessons 1 and 3 and reviewed in Lesson 6.

Scale refers to size as measured against a standard reference. Lessons 2 and 6 are about scale.

Distortion is a change from expected normal proportions. The focus of Lesson 5 is distortion.

Exaggeration is like distortion, but the feature is changed or altered by enlarging it so that it does not look normal. Lesson 4 is about exaggeration.

Introducing Unit Concepts

"Proportion is an art principle used by artists to show how objects relate to one another in size."

"La proporción es un principio artístico usado por los artistas para mostrar cómo los objetos se relacionan entre sí por el tamaño."

Proportion

• Read the definition of *proportion* to the students. Ask formed groups to find two examples of proportion in the book, but not the two examples used in this unit.

• Have the students within their groups discuss and validate why their chosen works are good examples of proportion. Give each group one minute to share one of their examples.

Distortion

• Have the students remain in their groups and as a group look up the word *distortion.* Have them explain to each other what distortion means and then share the meaning as a class.

An Introduction to
Proportion and Distortion

Proportion and distortion are used by artists in both sculptural forms and pictures.

Frida Kahlo. (Mexican). *Frieda and Diego Rivera.* 1931. Oil on canvas. $39\frac{3}{8} \times 31$ inches. San Francisco Museum of Modern Art, San Francisco, California. Albert M. Bender Collection, gift of Albert M. Bender. Photo by Ben Blackwell.

ART Background

About the Artist

Frida Kahlo (frē′ dä kä′ lō, Mexican, 1907–   ) was born in 1907. Her father was a photographer who had emigrated to Mexico from Germany; her mother was Mexican. Family was very important to Kahlo who painted pictures tracing her ancestry. At 18, she was in an accident that caused her to suffer back ailments and many surgeries. It resulted in her inability to have children. It also motivated her to become a painter. She used her art to help her better understand her pain. Kahlo produced more than 200 paintings, most of which are self-portraits.

About Subject Matter★ Kahlo consistently used the theme of self-exploration. She was trying to better understand the pain and suffering that she endured.

About the Media Kahlo's painting is an oil. She uses bright colors and symbolism in all her works.

Artists use several techniques to create **proportion** in a work of art.

- How does Kahlo use the clothing to increase size? What effect do the full dress and shawl have? How do the hands compare to the size of the palette?
- How tall do you think Frida Kahlo was? To what are you comparing her to get an idea of her height?

Distortion is used by artists in paintings and drawings to express a feeling or idea.

- What message about the relationship of the two figures was Kahlo trying to convey in this painting?

Artist Profile

Frida Kahlo
1907–1954

Self-Portrait with Monkey.

Frida Kahlo was born in Mexico City. During her teens, she was in a bus accident and was severely injured. She had 35 operations and a life of pain as a result. She taught herself to paint and eventually showed her work to famous Mexican artist Diego Rivera, whom she later married. Many of her paintings are based on her marriage, her physical pain, and the history of the Mexican people.

Artists like Frida Kahlo often use proportion in their artwork to show relative sizes and to imitate realism. Other artists choose to use distortion in their artwork to convey a feeling or thought. Unit 4 focuses on the following topics:

- Proportion
- Scale
- Distortion
- Exaggeration

105

Cultural Perspectives In 1910, the Mexican Revolution broke out in retaliation to the conditions of the Mexican people. The majority of the people grew poorer and poorer under the dictatorship of Porfirio Diaz, who became very wealthy. Diaz was overthrown and for several decades the Mexican poor continued to fight for economic reforms.

*See **More About** pages 206–227 for more about art history and subject matter.

- Have students discuss where they have seen distortion used before (comic strips, books, movies, and so on). Create a list on the chalkboard.

You may wish to introduce proportion and distortion in the **Video** *Masks: A World of Diversity.*

Examining the Artwork

"Let's examine the artwork more closely."
"Vamos a examinar detalladamente la obra de arte."

- Have students observe Frida Kahlo's use of both proportion and distortion. Ask them to describe the colors and objects they see.
- Read and discuss the definition of *proportion* and *distortion.* Have students answer the questions on page 105.
(See **Perception Hints** below.)

Artist Profile
Share with students information about the artist, including the portrait she did of herself.

Art Journal
You may wish to encourage students to practice art concepts and record ideas from lesson to lesson in their **Art Journals.**

About Music
Proportion is not a musical term. It is always in the mind of a composer with regard to balancing various aspects of a composition.

- Students can sing a round, such as *Freré Jacques,* and try to balance the sound between parts.

Distortion is sometimes used in music for dramatic effect. Tone colors are sometimes distorted also. In *Tubby the Tuba,* the tuba's sound is distorted when Tubby accidentally "sits" on the tune.

Perception Hints

Proportion Kahlo uses clothing to increase size by adding ruffles and folds to her skirt. The full dress and shawl has the effect of balancing Rivera's solid, heavy form. The hands are very small in proportion to the size of the palette.
Height Kahlo is short in comparison to Rivera. She may feel that Rivera is the dominant person.

UNIT 4 Planning Guide

Lesson	Lesson Title	Suggested Pacing	Create Activities	Materials	
1	**Proportion**	45 minutes	Create a model, using the sighting technique to determine proportion.	white paper oil pastels	
2	**Scale**	75 minutes	Create a collage using unrealistic scale.	white paper magazines glue scissors	
3	**Facial Proportions**	45 minutes	Create a portrait using facial proportions.	white paper pencils ruler or other measuring device spray fix or hair spray	
4	**Exaggeration**	75 minutes	Create an original comic strip character using exaggeration.	pencils white drawing paper	
5	**Distortion**	45 minutes	Create a distorted papier-mâché mask.	papier-mâché paste newspaper paper rolls and tape gallon milk jugs, cut in half liquid tempera paints egg cartons paintbrushes	
6	**Scale and Proportion**	75 minutes	Create a life-size sculpture and place it in a real environment in a school.	life-size clothing, shoes, socks paint or stitchery items newspapers and posterboard knit material or old T-shirts gloves, wigs, panty hose props felt-tip markers	
Artsource Lesson	**Proportion and Distortion in Masks**	75 minutes	Create a two-sided mask that shows contrasting feelings.	paper plates, crayons, felt scraps, paper towel spools, yarn, buttons, Artsource videotape (optional)	

Program Resources (Books)	Art Resources	Literature Resources	*Music Resources
Vocabulary, pp. 37-38 Assessment, pp. 37-38 Art Across the Curriculum Resource Book, pp. 109-114	Overhead Transparency #19, *The Artist Drawing a Young Girl* and *Don Manuel Osorio Manrique de Zuniga* Artist Profile Book, pp. 20, 46 Large Prints, *English Armor of George Clifford, Third Earl of Cumberland (1558-1605)* and *Self-Portrait*	**1.** *The Little House* (1942) by Virginia Lee Burton has balance and proportion that are illustrated in this simplistically drawn picture book. **2.** *What Make a Goya a Goya?* (1994) from the Metropolitan Museum of Art provides insight as to what makes this artist's work and style unique.	"Symphony No. 9 in D Minor, Op. 125, Fourth Movement" (excerpt), by Ludwig van Beethoven, p. T112, CD2:38. This excerpt, containing the famous "Ode to Joy," is an example of music from the early 1800s.
Vocabulary, pp. 39-40 Assessment, pp. 39-40 Art Across the Curriculum Resource Book, pp. 115-120	Overhead Transparency #20, *Francesco Saesetti and His Son Teodoro* and *Emperor Shah Jahan and His Son, Suja* Artist Profile Book, pp. 19, 39 Large Prints, *English Armor of George Clifford, Third Earl of Cumberland (1558-1605)* and *Self-Portrait*	**1.** *Pish Posh, said Hieronymous Bosch* (1991) by Nancy Willard presents scale in this lavishly illustrated poem about the fifteenth-century painter. **2.** *Free Fall* (1988) by David Wiesner brings a young boy's dreams to life in the wildly imaginative pages of this picture book while reflecting superb examples of scale in art.	*"Trumpet Concerto in E-flat Major"* (First movement), by Franz Joseph Haydn, p. T391E, CD9:34. Haydn's *"Trumpet Concerto"* is an example of musical form (AABA, or same-same-different-same) in which one melody predominates.
Vocabulary, pp. 41-42 Assessment, pp. 41-42 Art Across the Curriculum Resource Book, pp. 121-126	Overhead Transparency #21, *Bindo Altoviti* and *Marguerite (Margot) Bérard* Artist Profile Book, pp. 43, 44 Large Prints, *English Armor of George Clifford, Third Earl of Cumberland (1558-1605)* and *Self-Portrait*	**1.** *Heckedy Peg* (1987) by Audrey Wood provides comedic facial expressions in luminous watercolors to complement the vibrant text. **2.** *Amazing Grace* (1991) by Mary Hofman has excellent examples of portraiture brimming from page to page with careful detail to each wrinkle, crinkle, or unique feature of the face.	"Gaudeamus Omnes," p. T391A, CD9:32. "Gaudeamus Omnes" is an example of Gregorian chant, which has been heard in churches and monasteries since about A.D.600.
Vocabulary, pp. 43-44 Assessment, pp. 43-44 Art Across the Curriculum Resource Book, pp. 127-132	Overhead Transparency #22, *Ruben's Wife* and *Portrait of a Polish Woman* Artist Profile Book, pp.7, 37 Large Prints, *English Armor of George Clifford, Third Earl of Cumberland (1558-1605)* and *Self-Portrait*	**1.** *Monster Mama* (1993) by Liz Rosenberg uses vibrant explosions of color and energy that are put into the exaggerated illustrations done in a unique style that all ages will enjoy. **2.** *Chester, The Out of Work Dog* (1992) by Marilyn Singer uses ink and watercolor to create the distorted, misproportioned figures done in caricature style to reflect exaggeration.	"Polonaise in A Major, Op. 40, No. 1," by Frederic Chopin, p. T391G, CD10:1. "Polonaise" is a Polish dance, composed by the famous Polish composer Frederic Chopin, who lived from 1810-1848.
Vocabulary, pp. 45-46 Assessment, pp. 45-46 Art Across the Curriculum Resource Book, pp. 133-138	Overhead Transparency #23, *Dead-Man Mask, False Face Mask, Mask,* and *Bird Snare* Artist Profile Book, p. 57 , 67, 68 Large Prints, *English Armor of George Clifford, Third Earl of Cumberland (1558-1605)* and *Self-Portrait*	**1.** *Masks and Mask Makers* (1961) by Kari Hunt has masks from various cultures that are explored in black-and-white photographic illustrations and researches their purposes and people. **2.** *Masks Tell Stories* (1993) by Carol Gelber studies the uses of masks throughout time for ceremonies, celebrations, theater, and daily life.	"Zuni Sunrise Song," p. T51, CD1:35. "Zuni Sunrise Song" is an example of Native American music.
Vocabulary, pp. 47-48 Assessment, pp. 47-48 Art Across the Curriculum Resource Book, pp. 139-144	Overhead Transparency #24, *Walk Don't Walk* and *Woman with Dog* Artist Profile Book, pp. 21, 49 Large Prints, *English Armor of George Clifford, Third Earl of Cumberland (1558-1605)* and *Self-Portrait*	**1.** *Puss in Boots* (1990) by Charles Perrault has richly illustrated pages that display magnifiscent examples of scale and proportions. **2.** *The Borrowers* (1953) by Mary Norton is a classic story of life on the small side that will enchant readers and provide illustrations of scale and proportion.	"Don't Worry, Be Happy," by Bobby McFerrin, p. T12, CD1:8. "Don't Worry, Be Happy" is an example of late twentieth-century American music.

*Music references are from **Share the Music,** Macmillan/McGraw-Hill School Publishers

UNIT 4 LESSON 1

LESSON PLANNER

Objectives
After completing this lesson, students will be able to:
- identify the use of proportion in art. *Aesthetic Perception*
- create a drawing using the sighting technique. *Creative Expression*
- use the four steps of art criticism to evaluate their own artwork. *Art Criticism*
- demonstrate knowledge of the lives and work of both artists. *Art History and Culture*

Program Resources
- **Overhead:** Both the Robert and the Goya are available on overhead 19.
- **Large Prints:** *Self-Portrait* by Judith Leyster and *English Armor of George Clifford, Third Earl of Cumberland (1558-1605)*
- **Vocabulary Book** pages 37–38
- **Artist Profiles Book:** Robert page 41 and Goya page 20
- **Art Across the Curriculum Book** pages 109–114
- **Multimedia Workshop CD-ROM**
- **Assessment Book** pages 37–38

Multiple Intelligences
Interpersonal Students can explore human proportions by working together in small groups in the Practice activity.

Vocabulary
proportion *proporción* the principle of art concerned with the size relationship of one part to another

---

Proportion

Artists use proportion to show how people or things relate to one another in size.

Hubert Robert. (French). *The Artist Drawing a Young Girl.* 1773. Red chalk on paper. 25.5 cm × 33.8 cm. Metropolitan Museum of Art, New York, New York. Bequest of Walter C. Baker, 1971.

Hubert Robert created *The Artist Sketching a Young Girl.* French artists of the eighteenth century painted portraits of wealthy people enjoying life and having fun. *Don Manuel Osorio Manrique de Zuniga* was painted by Francisco Goya. Goya was well known for his portraits of aristocrats. Each artist uses proportion to show the size of the child.

ART Background

About the Artists
Hubert Robert (ū bûrt rō bâr, French, 1733–1808) studied art in Italy and France and quickly became known for his paintings of landscapes and ruins. Imprisoned for a year during the French Revolution, he continued to paint and draw, recording daily life in jail. He helped create the famous French museum, the Louvre, and served as its curator until 1802.

Francisco Goya (frän sēs' kō gō yä, Spanish, 1746–1828) began learning to paint at the age of 12. His father was a painter and gilder of altarpieces. He had skill in combining light and color. He was the portrait painter for Spanish royalty.

About Subject Matter* Both works are portraits.

About the Media Robert's is a red-chalk study. Goya worked in oils.

About Art History* Robert's work was more airy and light-colored than most of the art of his time.

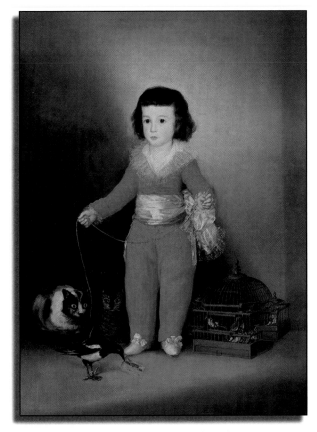

Francisco Goya. (Spanish). *Don Manuel Osorio Manrique de Zuniga.* 1784. Metropolitan Museum of Art, New York, New York.

Study both works of art to notice the proportion.

- What ages do you think the girl and boy are in both works of art?

- How tall do you think they are? What clues in the pictures tell you how tall they are?

- Describe the differences in size between the little girl, the man drawing her, and the woman watching the scene.

SEEING LIKE AN ARTIST

Compare the sizes of your classmates to the objects around them. What are some of your observations?

Lesson 1

107

Goya had three teachers: Rembrandt, Velaquez, and nature. He took on an artistic freedom that was new for those times. He painted his subjects and their personalities.

Cultural Perspectives Robert painted during the French Revolution. When his powerful friends lost their positions, and Robert was arrested for not renewing his citizen's card, he was imprisoned for a year.

Goya was angry about Spain's loss of freedom when the French invaded Spain. He saw firsthand the battles between French soldiers and Spanish citizens during the bloody years of the Napoleonic occupation of Spain. As a painter of the revolution, he sometimes noted in the margins of his drawings of those violent times, "I saw this."

*See **More About** pages 206–227 for more about art history and subject matter.

FOCUS

Time: About 10 minutes

Activating Prior Knowledge
"Think about the height of your teacher."
"Piensen en la estatura de su maestro."

Introducing the Art
"Let's look closely at the artwork."
Vamos a observar detalladamente la obra de arte."

- **Describe:** Have the students describe the subject matter of the artwork. (both: portraits)
- Share and discuss information from **Art Background** and the **Artist Profiles Book**.
- Have students answer the questions on page 107. (See **Perception Hints** below.)
- **COMPARE AND CONTRAST** Have students list the similarities and differences in the two works. (In the Robert, proportion is more obvious. The colorful clothing in the Goya tells us that the young boy is an aristocratic youth.)

FOR THE ART SPECIALIST

Use the **Overhead** and the **Large Prints** *English Armor of George Clifford, Third Earl of Cumberland* and *Self-Portrait* to demonstrate how artists use proportion to show how people or things relate to one another in size.

Perception Hints

Proportion *Robert.* Age 6. *Goya.* About 4.
Body Proportion *Robert.* About 3 feet. Clues include the adults, the level of the artist's sketch pad, and the fact that the artist is sitting down. *Goya.* Slightly shorter than the girl. Clues are the cat, the bird, and the cage.
Size differences *Robert.* The man is the tallest; the woman is taller than the girl; the girl is waist level to the woman and below waist level to the man.

TEACH

Time: About 30 minutes

Practice

Materials
- string
- paper
- pencils

Alternate Materials: yarn

"How can you measure human proportions or height?"

"¿Cómo pueden medir proporciones o alturas humanas?"

- Discuss the definition of *proportion* on page 108.
- Distribute materials and have students follow the directions on page 108 for measuring proportion. Have them discuss the answer to the Decide question.

Create PROBLEM SOLVING

Materials
- white paper
- oil pastels

Alternate Materials: markers

"Let's create a model using the sighting technique to determine proportion."

"Vamos a hacer un modelo usando la técnica de puntería para determinar la proporción."

- Sighting technique: Hold a pencil vertically at arm's length in the direction of the object to be drawn. Close one eye while focusing on the object with your open eye.
- Review procedures for working with oil pastels. See **Technique Tips** on page 197 for using oil pastels.
- Distribute materials and have students follow the directions on page 109.

FOR THE ART SPECIALIST

Have students sketch with chalk and paint with liquid tempera paints or school acrylics.

Using Proportion

Proportion is the principle of art concerned with the size relationships of one part to another such as a hand to a wrist. Artists use several techniques to draw things in proportion.

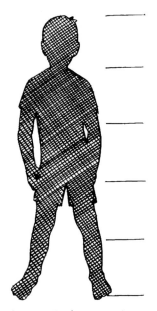

Body Proportions:
Although people vary in size and shape, most people have the same proportions. Artists use the length of the head, from the chin to the top of the skull, to help them in measuring proportion. A child may be five heads long while an infant might be only three heads long.

Average Body Proportions of 10 year old.

Practice

Measure body proportions. Use string.

1. With a string, measure a partner's head from the top of the skull to the bottom of the chin. Using the length of the head as a unit of measurement, measure the rest of the body. For example, the length of an arm might be two head lengths.

2. Record and compare your findings.

Decide What did you learn about proportion by doing this activity?

Activities in
ART Across the Curriculum Book

Reading/Language Arts Learn about proportion in writing. (page 109)

Math Learn how proportions can be expressed in mathematical terms. (page 110)

Science Investigate color as used by Goya. (page 111)

Social Studies Study the changes in America and France in the eighteenth century. Learn how poor people fought for power from noble people, like those portrayed in Goyas's painting. (page 112)

The Arts Write a monologue. Imagine you are a person in Hubert's drawing. (page 113)

Technology Use the *Multimedia Workshop* CD-ROM to create a proportional drawing of a human. (page 114)

Ginger Hall. Age 11. *Saturday Mornings.* Oil pastels.

How many heads tall is the girl in the artwork? How old do you think she is?

Create

How can you use the sighting technique to draw a person in proportion? Sketch a model, using the sighting technique to determine proportion.

1. Think about proportion as it relates to people. Looking at a class model, use the sighting technique to determine the proportions of the model.

2. Lightly sketch the basic body parts of the model using a light color. Oil pastels cover the color beneath them.

3. Fill your paper with colors.

Describe Describe the colors, lines, and shapes you used.

Analyze How did you place your lines using the sighting technique?

Interpret What is the mood of your finished work?

Decide Were you able to successfully use the sighting technique to draw the model in proportion?

Lesson 1 109

THEME Connections

Relationships Use the artworks to explain the relationship of children to their parents in the 1700s.

Origins Use Goya's work as a springboard to discuss the origins of different animals as pets.

ESL

When you are presenting new techniques, it can be helpful to have students watch and follow along as you model procedure and read the instructions aloud. This creates an oral-to-print connection with the text for students to rely on later in independent practice.

"Were you able to draw a model using the sighting technique to determine the proportions of the model?"

"¿Pudieron dibujar un modelo usando la técnica de percepción para determinar las proporciones del modelo?"

LARGE PRINT **Review**

Use the **Large Prints** *English Armor of George Clifford, Third Earl of Cumberland* and *Self-Portrait* to have students compare to the works in this lesson.

Art Criticism

Have students answer the four art criticism questions—Describe, Analyze, Interpret, and Decide—orally and in writing. Discuss the use of proportion techniques in their works after the drawings are dry.

Assess

Use the **Assessment Book** pages 37–38 as a formal assessment for this lesson.

Evaluation Criteria

• Can the student identify the use of proportion in a drawing?

• Can the student create a drawing using the sighting technique?

• Can the student use the four steps of art criticism to evaluate his or her own artwork?

• Can the student demonstrate knowledge of the lives and work of both artists?

Reteaching • • • • • • • • • • • • •

Body proportions Have students look through magazines to find photographs of well-proportioned people, cut them out, and create a collage.

Perception Hints for Student Art

The girl in the student art is about six to seven heads tall. She is probably a teenager.

UNIT 4
LESSON 2

Scale

Artists use scale to relate one object to another in a work of art.

LESSON PLANNER

Objectives
After completing this lesson, students will be able to:
- identify the use of scale by artists. *Aesthetic Perception*
- plan and create a collage using unrealistic scale. *Creative Expression*
- use the four steps of art criticism to evaluate their own work. *Art Criticism*
- compare the lives and cultures of both artists. *Art History and Culture*

Program Resources
- **Overhead:** Both the Ghirlandaio and the Nanha the Mughal are available on overhead 20.
- **Large Prints:** *Self-Portrait* by Judith Leyster and *English Armor of George Clifford, Third Earl of Cumberland* (1558–1605)
- **Vocabulary Book:** pages 39–40
- **Art Manipulative Kit:** music audiotape
- **Artist Profiles Book:** Ghirlandaio page 19 and Nanha the Mughal page 39
- **Art Across the Curriculum Book** pages 115–120
- **Multimedia Workshop CD-ROM**
- **National Geographic Picture Atlas of the World CD-ROM**
- **Assessment Book** pages 39–40

Multiple Intelligences
Logical/Mathematical Students can discover the use of scale by recognizing size relationships in works of art.

Vocabulary
scale *escala* similar to proportion in that it deals with size relationships

realistic scale *escala real* a work of art where everything seems to fit together and make sense in size relationship

unrealistic scale *escala irreal* size relationships that do not make sense

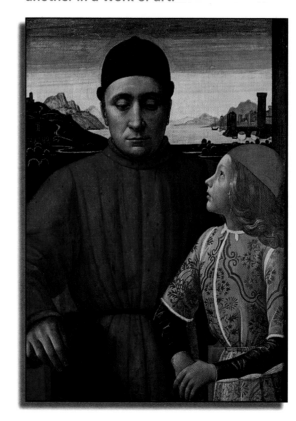

Domenico Ghirlandaio. (Italian). *Francesco Saesetti and His Son Teodoro.* 1949. Tempera on wood. $29\frac{1}{2} \times 20\frac{1}{2}$ inches. Metropolitan Museum of Art, New York, New York.

Ghirlandaio was best known for his portraits during a period in history called the Renaissance. He often included architecture in his paintings to create the illusion of space. Nanha painted during the Mughal Period of art in India. His subject, the Emperor Shah Jahan, built the Taj Mahal. Notice how differently each father is interacting with his son. What does this tell you about each relationship? Notice how both artists use scale to relate one subject to another.

110

Unit **4**

ART Background

About the Artists
Domenico Ghirlandaio (dō mä' nē kō gēr län' dā ō, Italian, 1449–1494) was born in Florence, Italy, son of a garland maker. He inherited his nickname from his father, and he was trained in the same trade. He left that trade to become one of Florence's most famous painters. He is known for his sacred paintings.

Nanha the Mughal's (nän hä the mū' gəl, India, c. 1582–c. 1635) works epitomize the stylistic and typological changes that occurred during the reigns of the three emperors who were his patrons. He was a designer, painter, and portraitist.

About Subject Matter* The Ghirlandaio and the Nanha the Mughal are both portraits and narratives.

Nanha the Mughal. (Indian). *Emperor Shah Jahan and His Son, Suja.* 1625–30. Colors on gilt on paper. $15\frac{5}{16} \times 10\frac{5}{16}$ inches. Metropolitan Museum of Art, New York, New York. Purchase, Rogers Fund and The Kevorkian Foundation Gift, 1955.

Study both paintings to learn about scale.

- How big are the people in both works of art? What clues suggest their sizes?

- If the bed were not in Nanha the Mughal's painting, how would you be able to tell the sizes of the people?

- Do you see anything unusual about the child in one of the paintings in relation to his father?

- As a viewer, where are you in relation to each picture? How does this affect the way you see the people in these paintings?

Lesson 2

SEEING LIKE AN ARTIST

How can you show an object in a drawing so that someone looking at it will know how big that object is?

111

About the Media The Ghirlandaio is a fresco. Fresco wall painting is a medium that resembles watercolor on plaster. Nanha the Mughal's work bears two distinct types of figures: one whose thickest neck and shoulders impart a notable stockiness and another whose slender physique is accentuated by strong contours and a small but heavily mottled face.

About Art History* During the Renaissance, math was used in art. Mathematical principles were used in creating the illusion of deep space. Nanha the Mughal's artistic identity has been somewhat obscured by his association with other artists with similar names.

Cultural Perspectives Ghirlandaio is known for his sacred paintings. His works show his deep love for his city, Florence. His paintings show luxury, drama, beauty, and courtly manners.

*See **More About** pages 206–227 for more about art history and subject matter.

FOCUS

Time: About 10 minutes

Activating Prior Knowledge

"Find examples of scale in your environment."
"Busquen ejemplos de escala en su ambiente."

- Discuss the examples.

Introducing the Art

"Let's look closely at the two paintings."
"Vamos a observar detalladamente las dos pinturas."

- **Describe:** Have students describe the subject matter in each painting. (both: portraits)

- Use the **National Geographic Picture Atlas of the World CD-ROM** to help students locate cities and countries where the artists lived and worked.

- Share and discuss information from **Art Background** and the **Artist Profiles Book**.

- Have students answer the questions on page 111. (See **Perception Hints** below.)

- **COMPARE AND CONTRAST** Have students make a list of the similarities and differences in the two paintings. (Both works deal with the same subject and media. In the Ghirlandaio, the subjects are closer, and the artist uses less scale.)

FOR THE ART SPECIALIST

Use the **Overhead** and the **Large Print** *Self-Portrait* to demonstrate how artists use scale to relate one object to another in a work of art.

Perception Hints

Size *Ghirlandaio* and *Nanha.* Both boys are smaller than the fathers. *Nanha.* The bed suggests the sizes of the two; also, items in their hands, and their size relationship to each other.

Unusual *Nanha.* The child is not looking at the father.

Point of view Answers may vary, but point of view may affect the size of the people in each work.

TEACH

Time: About two 30-minute periods

Practice

Materials
- white drawing paper
- pencils

Alternate Materials: black markers

"Let's draw an object to scale using one of our hands as a standard size."

"Vamos a dibujar un objeto a escala usando una de nuestras manos como una medida patrón."

- Discuss the definitions of *realistic* and *unrealistic scale* on page 112.
- Distribute materials and have students follow the directions on page 112 to draw a realistic-scale object. Have them discuss the answer to the Decide question.

Create PROBLEM SOLVING

Materials
- white paper
- glue
- magazines
- scissors

Alternate Materials: photographs, newspaper photographs

"Let's create a collage using unrealistic scale."

"Vamos a hacer un collaje usando la escala irreal."

- Review procedures for creating a collage in More About Technique Tips on page 202.
- Brainstorm ideas to create the collage.
- Play one of the music audiotapes from the **Art Manipulative Kit** to stimulate student activity as they work.
- Distribute materials and have students follow the directions on page 113.

Safety! For information about glue and other safety issues in the classroom, see page T22.

FOR THE ART SPECIALIST

Paint a realistic landscape or indoor scene. Cut out objects from magazines and draw and glue them onto the scene. Have two or more objects that are out of scale.

Using Scale

Scale is similar to proportion in that it deals with size relationships. The difference is that scale refers to size as measured against a standard reference, like the human body. Scale can be created realistically or unrealistically.

Realistic Scale: When an artist creates a work of art where everything seems to fit together and make sense in size relation, it is called realistic scale.

Unrealistic Scale: When an artist makes size relationships that do not make sense, the scale becomes unrealistic. Making a small object, such as a coin, larger than the hand holding it creates unrealistic scale.

Practice

Practice drawing an object using realistic scale. Use pencil.

1. Draw your hand to create an object of standard size.

2. Select an object that is either larger or smaller than your hand. Draw the object in scale to your hand. The entire object may not fit on your paper.

Decide What are some other ways to create realistic scale?

Activities in
ART Across the Curriculum Book

Reading/Language Arts Write a short story about the relationships between the fathers and sons portrayed in the paintings. (page 115)

Math Identify the geometric forms in the architecture. (page 116)

Science Study the Himalayan mountains, where the emperor lived. (page 117)

Social Studies Create bar graphs comparing the mountain ranges of the world, noting the Himalayas. (page 118)

The Arts Use unrealistic scale to show that a scary character is not very powerful, considering the use of scale by artists. (page 119)

Technology Use the *Multimedia Workshop* CD-ROM to draw a scene that includes one item of unrealistic scale. (page 120)

Jason Peoples. Age 11. *Collage.* Magazines.

What kind of scale did the artist use in his collage to create drama?

Create

How can you make a point through your artwork using unrealistic scale? Create a collage using unrealistic scale.

1. Think about objects and an indoor or outdoor background to use in your collage. Cut out pictures of objects, some that are in proper scale and one or two images that are too large or too small for the other objects.

2. Arrange your collected images so that they overlap and touch the edges of your paper. Keep the arrangement organized so that it is almost realistic.

3. Glue down the background. Next, glue the remaining objects. Make sure that at least one object shows unrealistic scale.

Describe Describe the objects you selected for your collage.

Analyze How are the objects arranged to create unrealistic scale?

Interpret Does your collage convey humor?

Decide Do you feel you were able to clearly portray unrealistic scale in an organized manner?

Lesson 2 113

THEME Connections

Stabililty Discuss the stability of the family unit of today versus the family unit we see in the works of art.

Culture Use the Ghirlandaio as a source to begin the study of the Italian culture in the 1400s.

ESL

For most ESL students, the art vocabulary presented in the text may need clarification and frequent exposure before students are ready to use it in their descriptions. You can provide this extra exposure by discussing the art, using both familiar and new language and asking students to respond with the new vocabulary. *Is this scale realistic or unrealistic?*

CLOSE

Time: About 5 minutes

"Were you able to create a collage using unrealistic scale?"
"¿Fueron capaces de hacer un collaje usando la escala irreal?"

 Review
Use the **Large Print** *Self-Portrait* to have students compare their work to the work in this lesson.

Art Criticism
Have students answer the four art criticism questions—Describe, Analyze, Interpret, and Decide—orally or in writing. Discuss the use of scale and proportion in their work.

Assess
Use the **Assessment Book** pages 39–40 as a formal assessment for this lesson.

Evaluation Criteria
- Can the student identify the use of scale?
- Can the student create a collage using unrealistic scale?
- Can the student use the four steps of art criticism to evaluate his or her own work?
- Can the student compare the lives and work of Ghirlandaio and Nanha the Mughal?

Reteaching ● ● ● ● ● ● ● ● ● ● ●

Unrealistic scale Have students look through magazines to find examples of scale that look realistic but are actually unrealistic. Have them redraw the objects so that they are realistically scaled.

Perception Hints for Student Art

The student artist used an unrealistic scale by making the bear so large.

UNIT 4
LESSON 3

LESSON PLANNER

Objectives
After completing this lesson, students will be able to:
- identify the use of facial proportions in portraits. *Aesthetic Perception*
- create a portrait drawing using facial proportions. *Creative Expression*
- use the four steps of art criticism to evaluate their own work. *Art Criticism*
- demonstrate knowledge of the lives and work of both artists. *Art History and Culture*

Program Resources
- **Overhead:** Both the Raphael and the Renoir are available on overhead 21.
- **Large Prints:** *Self-Portrait* by Judith Leyster and *English Armor of George Clifford, Third Earl of Cumberland* (1558-1605)
- **Vocabulary Book** pages 41–42
- **Art Manipulative Kit:** mirror
- **Artist Profiles Book:** Raphael page 43 and Renoir page 44
- **Art Across the Curriculum Book** pages 121–126
- **Multimedia Workshop CD-ROM**
- **Assessment Book** pages 41–42

Multiple Intelligences
Intrapersonal Students can become sensitive to the feelings of others as they use facial proportions to create portraits.

Vocabulary
facial proportion *proporción facial* used to help artists place features correctly on the human face

central axis *eje central* the vertical center line used to divide a view

profile proportion *proporción de contorno* the relationship of one feature of a face to another feature when looking from the side view

Facial Proportions

Artists use proportion to help them correctly organize the features of a face.

Raphael. (Raffaello Sanzio, Italian) *Bindo Altoviti.* National Gallery, Washington, DC.

Raphael's paintings have the sculptural quality of Michelangelo, the grace and feeling of Leonardo Da Vinci, and the detail of his first teacher, Perugino. Renoir was interested in the bright and cheerful effect of light and air, which was typical of his style of painting. His interest was in painting people in pleasant surroundings. Both artists painted portraits with character and expression.

ART Background

About the Artists
Raphael (ra' fē el, Italian, 1483–1520) was born in a small town in central Italy. His first teacher was probably his father, who was a painter for a noble family. After learning to create gentle landscapes, he went to Florence to study the works of the leading artists of the day. His teachers included da Vinci and Michelangelo. Raphael is one of the great artists of the Renaissance.

Pierre-Auguste Renoir (pyâr ō gŭst rən wär, French, 1841–1919) was born into a large and poor family in Limoges. His father was a tailor. Renoir was a modest man who, despite his poverty, was optimistic. By 13, he was already making a living as an artist painting scenes on china. He was interested in painting the human figure. For Renoir, life and art were the same.

Pierre Auguste Renoir.
(French). *Marguerite (Margot)*
Bérard. 1879. Oil on canvas.
$16\frac{1}{8} \times 12\frac{3}{4}$ inches.
Metropolitan Museum of Art,
New York, New York. Bequest
of Stephen C. Clark, 1960.

Study both paintings to understand facial proportions.

- What is the difference in the position of each face?

- How does the eye look different in a side view compared to a front view? How does the mouth look different?

- Where are the ears in relation to the eyes and nose?

- What differences do you notice in the features of the child compared with those of the young man?

SEEING LIKE AN ARTIST

Observe the differences in side views and front views of your classmates. Notice how their features change.

Lesson 3 115

About Subject Matter* The Raphael and the Renoir are both portraits.

About the Media The Raphael and the Renoir are both oil paintings.

About Art History* Renoir was a leader of Impressionism in the late nineteenth century. Impressionists wanted to capture daily life in their paintings. Impressionists studied how to represent natural sunlight and warm light in their paintings. Living in Paris, Renoir often met other artists and writers at cafés to talk about art.

Cultural Perspectives Raphael was born a year after Columbus went on his voyage of discovery to the New World. Renoir's work reflected the happiness in his life. He painted with bright colors.

*See **More About** pages 206–227 for more about art history and subject matter.

Activating Prior Knowledge

"Are faces symmetrical?"

"¿Las caras son simétricas?"

- Discuss students' answers to the question. Have students look closely at their own faces in the mirror in the **Art Manipulative Kit** and observe that one eyebrow is slightly larger, or one ear is higher than the other, and so on.

Introducing the Art

"Let's look closely at the art."

"Vamos a observar detalladamente el arte."

- **Describe:** Have students describe the subject matter in the painting. (both: portraits)

- Share and discuss information from **Art Background** and the **Artist Profiles Book.**

- Ask students to answer the questions on page 115. (See **Perception Hints** below.)

FOR THE ART SPECIALIST

Use the **Overhead** and the **Large Prints** *English Armor of George Clifford, Third Earl of Cumberland* and *Self-Portrait* to discuss facial proportions.

Perception Hints

Position *Raphael.* Farther away and a right front view. *Renoir.* Closer and left front view.

View *Raphael.* Part of mouth not seen. *Renoir.* Eyes look bigger in front view. Mouth is seen in its entirety in front view.

Facial proportions *Raphael.* Top of the ear begins at the top of the eye and ends at the bottom of the nose.

Features *Raphael.* The man's are farther away. *Renoir.* The child's are closer.

TEACH

Time: About 30 minutes

Practice

Materials:

- paper
- pencils

Alternate Materials: pens or crayons

"Let's draw a profile."

"Vamos a trazar un perfil."

- Discuss the definitions of facial proportions on page 116.
- Distribute materials and have the students follow the directions on page 116 for drawing a profile. Have them discuss the answer to the Decide question.

Create PROBLEM SOLVING

Materials:

- white paper
- pencil
- ruler or other measuring device
- spray fix or hair spray

Alternate Materials: crayons

"Let's create a portrait using facial proportions."

"Vamos a hacer un retrato usando proporciones faciales."

- Brainstorm ideas to draw the face.
- Distribute materials and have students follow the directions on page 117.

FOR THE ART SPECIALIST

Have the students add watercolor washes and details with colored pencils over the dry watercolor paints.

Using Facial Proportions

Artists use **facial proportions** to help place features correctly on the human face. Lines, lightly drawn on a shape, are guidelines used by the artist to draw both full-face and profile portraits more accurately.

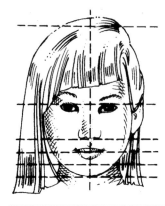

Facial Proportions: A front view of the head can be divided by drawing three horizontal lines across a vertical center line called the **central axis**. In the example, notice how the eyes are drawn on the center line, the lips just below the bottom line, and the ears between the center and lower horizontal lines. The nose is above the bottom line on the central axis. The hairline is near the top line.

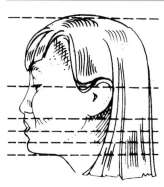

Profile Proportions: When you view a head in profile, or side view, all the horizontal proportion lines remain the same as in the front view. The shape of the head and the shapes of the features change. Notice the space between the eye and the ear and the chin. Notice that the shape of the head in the profile is different from the front view.

Practice

Practice drawing a profile. Use pencil.

1. Draw the shape of the head in profile. Add guidelines, using the second drawing shown above as a reference.

2. Add eyes, nose, mouth, chin, ear, hair, and neck.

Decide Were you able to create a profile using guidelines?

Activities in
ART Across the Curriculum Book

Reading/Language Arts Write a business letter to Renoir or Raphael and invite one to America to create a new painting. (page 121)

Math Learn how symmetry is used in mathematics as well as art. (page 122)

Science Learn more about the sense organs found in the head. (page 123)

Social Studies Learn about women in history who may have changed the lives of girls like Marga Berard. (page 124)

The Arts Study the faces in the portraits of Altoviti and Berard and respond in music to the mood shown in their expressions. (page 125)

Technology Use the *Multimedia Workshop* CD-ROM to draw your face using the correct proportion. (page 126)

Where is the central axis of this portrait?

Esmirna Elizabeth Hernandez. Age 10. *Self-Portrait*. Felt-tip marker.

Create

What is the best way to draw features on a portrait? Working with a partner, draw a portrait using facial proportions.

1. Think about the shape and size of your partner's head.

2. Measure the size of your partner's head. Mark off the dimensions on paper. Next, lightly draw guidelines for the eyes.

3. Use shading to draw hair, eyebrows, and clothing. Also use it to draw around the neck and shoulders and to add shadows to the skin.

Describe Describe the shapes and lines used to draw the features in your portrait.

Analyze How can this technique of drawing portraits be used to draw anyone?

Interpret What does the person in your portrait seem to be thinking?

Decide Were you successful in getting the features of your portrait in proportion? What would you do to make it better?

Lesson **3**   117

Models Use both artworks to learn more about modeling as a career.
Tradition Use the Renoir to study the traditional expectations of a female child in the late 1800s versus the expectations of today's female child.

Many ESL students can become confused with long lists of detailed instructions. You can read the instructions aloud, modeling procedures on the board as students follow instructions at their seats.

CLOSE

Time: About 5 minutes

"Were you able to draw a portrait using facial proportions?"

"¿Fueron capaces de hacer un retrato usando proporciones faciales?"

 Review
Use the **Large Prints** *English Armor of George Clifford, Third Earl of Cumberland* and *Self-Portrait* to have students compare their works to the works in this lesson.

Art Criticism
Have students answer the four art criticism questions—Describe, Analyze, Interpret, and Decide—orally or in writing. Discuss the use of facial proportions after the drawings are dry.

Assess
Use the **Assessment Book** pages 41–42 as a formal assessment for this lesson.

Evaluation Criteria
• Can the student identify the use of facial proportions in artwork?
• Can the student create a portrait using facial proportion?
• Can the student use the four steps of art criticism to evaluate his or her own work?
• Can the student demonstrate knowledge of the lives and cultures of Raphael and Renoir?

Reteaching • • • • • • • • • • • •

Vertical and horizontal lines Have students look through magazines to find large portraits. Compare the photograph to the artwork in the lesson in terms of proportion.

Perception Hints for Student Art
The central axis of the girl's face is a slightly left-of-center vertical line.

LESSON PLANNER

Objectives

After completing this lesson, students will be able to:

- identify how artists use exaggeration in works of art. *Aesthetic Perception*
- plan and create an original comic strip character using exaggeration. *Creative Expression*
- use the four steps of art criticism to evaluate their own drawings. *Art Criticism*
- demonstrate knowledge of the lives and work of both artists. *Art History and Culture*

Program Resources

- **Overhead:** Both the Botero and the Modigliani are available on overhead 22.
- **Large Prints:** *Self-Portrait* by Judith Leyster and *English Armor of George Clifford, Third Earl of Cumberland* (1558–1605)
- **Vocabulary Book** pages 43–44
- **Artist Profiles Book:** Botero page 7 and Modigliani page 37
- **Art Across the Curriculum Book:** pages 127–132
- **Multimedia Workshop CD-ROM**
- **National Museum of Women in the Arts Collection CD-ROM**
- **Assessment Book** pages 43–44

Multiple Intelligences
Visual/Spatial Students can show exaggeration by drawing imaginative images.

Vocabulary

exaggeration *exageración* a change from expected, normal proportion by increasing part or all of a person or object

---

Exaggeration

Artists sometimes use exaggeration rather than real proportion to express their ideas or feelings.

Fernando Botero. (Colombian). *Ruben's Wife.* 1963. Oil on canvas. $72\frac{1}{8} \times 70\frac{1}{8}$ inches. Guggenheim Museum, New York, New York. Photograph by David Heald © The Solomon R. Guggenheim Foundation, New York.

Fernando Botero is best known for giving all his models plump proportions that he calls "plasticity." This creates a whimsical mood. Modigliani painted extended figures with few details, which creates a feeling of elegance. Both artists used exaggeration.

118   Unit **4**

FOCUS

Time: About 10 minutes

Activating Prior Knowledge

"Have you ever used exaggeration to tell a story?"

"¿Han usado alguna vez la exageración para decir un cuento?"

- Remind students of stories that include exaggeration, such as *Pinnochio*, *Paul Bunyan*, and *James and the Giant Peach*.

ART *Background*

About the Artists

Fernando Botero (fer nän' dō bō tā' rō, Colombian, 1932–   ) spent two years learning to be a matador. He changed his career plans and studied art in Colombia, Spain, France, and Italy. After he began painting in a rounded style in 1956, his pictures sold well. After one son died in a car accident, he often included images of the boy in his art.

Amedeo Modigliani (ä mā dā ō mō'' dē yä' nē, Italian, 1884–1920) often was ill during his youth. He studied in France and Italy. Beginning as a painter, Modigliani found that he enjoyed sculpture more. He returned to painting and often reproduced his sculptures as paintings.

About Subject Matter* Both works are portraits.

About the Media The Botero and the Modigliani are both oil paintings. Oil is an opaque, slow-drying medium that comes in a variety of colors.

Amadeo Modigliani. (Italian). *Portrait of a Polish Woman.* 1918. Oil on canvas. $39\frac{1}{2} \times 25\frac{1}{2}$ inches. Philadelphia Museum of Art, Philadelphia, Pennsylvania. The Louis E. Stem Collection.

Study the paintings on these pages to find exaggeration.

- Where do you see a lengthened or stretched figure? A figure that is puffed up?

- What are some descriptive words to explain what these artists have done to the people in their paintings?

- Why do you think the artists changed the figures in this way?

- What emotional qualities do these figures suggest to you?

SEEING LIKE AN ARTIST

Look in books and newspapers to find examples of exaggeration.

Lesson 4 119

About Art History* In his early years, Botero was influenced by modern French and Spanish painters, along with the Renaissance masters.

Modigliani was influenced by Cézanne, Toulouse-Lautrec, and Picasso. Much of his early work seemed to copy the style of one of his favorite artists. His own style edged toward abstraction in his later life.

Cultural Perspectives Much of Botero's work shows the influence of his South American background, such as its food, music, Catholicism, and architecture.

Modigliani's subjects of his portraits included famous artists of the time such as Diego Rivera, Picasso, Henri Laurens, Paul Guillaume, and others.

*See **More About** pages 206–227 for more about art history and subject matter.

- Ask students to provide examples of exaggeration they are familiar with. Write some of these examples on the chalkboard, and include illustrations, if possible.

Introducing the Art

"Let's look closely at the two paintings."
"Vamos a observar detalladamente las dos pinturas."

- **Describe:** Have students describe the subject matter in each painting. (Botero: portrait; Modigliani: portrait)

- Share and discuss information from **Art Background** and the **Artist Profiles Book.**

- For more works dealing with portraits, see the **National Museum of Women in the Arts Collection CD-ROM.**

- Have the students answer the questions on page 119. (See **Perception Hints** below.)

- **COMPARE AND CONTRAST** Compare and contrast the two portraits in the lesson. (The Botero shows exaggeration in the face and body. The Modigliani shows exaggeration in the neck of its subject. Both works are portraits and use exaggeration.)

FOR THE ART SPECIALIST

Use the **Overhead** and the **Large Prints** *English Armor of George Clifford, Third Earl of Cumberland* and *Self-Portrait* to demonstrate how artists use exaggeration rather than real proportion to express their ideas or feelings.

Perception Hints

Exaggeration *Botero.* The figure is puffed. *Modigliani.* The figure's neck is stretched.
Descriptive words *Botero.* Puffed and distorted. *Modigliani.* Stretched, lengthened, distorted, misshapen, twisted, out of proportion.
Purpose *Botero* and *Modigliani.* To prove a point.
Emotional qualities *Botero* and *Modigliani.* Stress, sadness, wealth, and so on.

TEACH

Time: About two 30-minute periods

Practice

Materials
- newspapers

Alternate Materials: magazines

"Can you find examples of exaggeration featuring a politician?"

"¿Pueden encontrar ejemplos de exageración caracterizando a un político?"

- Discuss the definition of *exaggeration* on page 120.
- Distribute materials and have students follow the directions on page 120 for finding cartoons using exaggerated features.

Create PROBLEM SOLVING

Materials
- pencils
- white drawing paper

Alternate Materials: markers

"Let's use exaggeration to create an original comic strip character."

"Vamos a usar la exageración para crear un personaje de una tira cómica original."

- Brainstorm ideas for a comic strip character.
- Distribute materials and have the students follow the directions on page 121.

FOR THE ART SPECIALIST

Have the students create an entire comic strip with the character in one box, then using the other three boxes to tell a story with a beginning, a middle, and an end. They may also make a flip book showing movements of the character.

Using Exaggeration

Exaggeration is a change from expected normal proportion by increasing part or all of a person or object. Some artists use exaggeration rather than accurate proportion to express strong feelings and ideas.

Exaggeration occurs in drawings, paintings, and even in sculptures. Artists can lengthen, enlarge, or bend parts of the body. By making these changes, they can show moods and feelings that are easy to understand.

Practice

From a newspaper, collect editorial cartoons featuring a politician.

1. Look through your newspaper for an editorial cartoon of a politician. Next, find a photo of that same politician.

2. Compare the exaggerated features of the person in the cartoon with his or her features in the photo.

Decide Why was the feature exaggerated by the cartoonist? What effect did that exaggeration have?

Activities in
ART Across the Curriculum Book

Reading/Language Arts Learn some synonyms that will help you understand art and artists. (page 127)

Math Understand the use of exact, accurate information to compare two things, unlike artists who exaggerate to create mood. (page 128)

Science Study rock materials used for paint pigments or sculptures. (page 129)

Social Studies Learn more about Botero's Colombia. (page 130)

The Arts Interpret a mood by using exaggerated body movements in a dance. (page 131)

Technology Use the *Multimedia Workshop* CD-ROM to draw a cartoon character using exaggeration. (page 132)

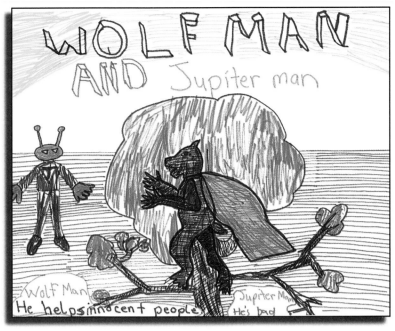

Chad Ethridge. Age 10. *Wolfman and Jupiter Man.* Markers.

What parts did the artist exaggerate?

Create

What kind of a character would you create if you were a cartoonist? Create an original comic strip character using exaggeration.

1. Think about comic strip characters you see every day. Then, draw several sketches of your own original comic strip character.

2. Choose one sketch. Exaggerate one or more features to show whether the character is funny, an action character, a superhero, or a fantasy creature. Give your character a name.

Describe Describe the features you exaggerated on your character.

Analyze Explain how you decided which feature to exaggerate and how you exaggerated that feature.

Interpret What emotional qualities does your character show?

Decide Do you like the way the exaggerated feature changed the mood of your drawing? Explain.

Lesson 4

121

THEME Connections

Change Use the artwork as a visual example of how fashion trends change.
Perspectives Use the artwork to begin a discussion of how we view ourselves versus how others view us.

ESL

Pantomime and sketch examples to help ESL students learn the basic vocabulary needed to be successful in this lesson. You might begin with a rough sketch on a poster and have students demonstrate the meaning of words such as *lengthen*, *enlarge*, *twist*, and so on. Students can compare work with a partner for extra vocabulary practice.

CLOSE

Time: About 5 minutes

"Were you able to create an original comic strip character using exaggeration?"

"¿Fueron capaces de crear un personaje de una tira cómica original usando la exageración?"

LARGE PRINT **Review**
Use the **Large Print** *Self-Portrait* to have students define exaggeration. Ask them to compare the use of exaggeration in the **Large Print** to the works in this lesson.

Art Criticism
Have students answer the four art criticism questions—Describe, Analyze, Interpret, and Decide—orally or in writing. When they are completed, discuss how exaggeration was created in their drawings.

Assess
Use the **Assessment Book** pages 43–44 as a formal assessment for this lesson.

Evaluation Criteria
• Can the student identify exaggeration in a work of art?
• Can the student create an original comic strip character using exaggerated features?
• Can the student use the four steps of art criticism to evaluate his or her own work?
• Can the student demonstrate knowledge of the lives and work of Botero and Modigliani?

Reteaching ● ● ● ● ● ● ● ● ● ● ●

Exaggeration Have the students look through magazines to find examples of exaggeration.

Perception Hints for Student Art

The student artist exaggerated *Jupiter Man's* hands and *Wolfman's* hands.

Distortion

Distortion is used by artists to create an expressive effect in a work of art.

Artist unknown. Tlingit (Alaska). *Dead-man Mask.* Nineteenth century. Wood, paint, hide metal. $13\frac{5}{8}$ inches high. Metropolitan Museum of Art, New York, New York.

Elon Webster. Iroquois. *False Face Mask.* 1937. *Wood.* Cranbrook Institute of Science, Bloomfield Hills, Michigan.

Masks are used in many cultures as a part of religious ceremonies and rituals. In many cases, the features of the masks are distorted for expressive purposes. *False Face Mask* was carved directly into a living tree by an Iroquois and separated after the carving was completed. *Ritual Object* is made of carved wood with shell inlay. What materials were used to make the other masks?

UNIT 4 LESSON 5

LESSON PLANNER

Objectives

After completing this lesson, students will be able to:

- identify how artists use distortion in a work of art. *Aesthetic Perception*
- plan and create a mask using distortion. *Creative Expression*
- use the four steps of art criticism to evaluate their own masks. *Art Criticism*
- demonstrate knowledge of the cultural purpose of the four masks. *Art History and Culture*

Program Resources

- **Overhead:** All the masks are available on overhead 23.
- **Large Prints:** *Self-Portrait* by Judith Leyster and *English Armor of George Clifford, Third Earl of Cumberland* (1558–1605)
- **Vocabulary Book** pages 45–46
- **Art Manipulative Kit:** distortion mirror
- **Artist Profiles Book:** Artists unknown pages 67 and 68
- **Art Across the Curriculum Book** pages 133–138
- **Multimedia Workshop CD-ROM**
- **National Geographic Picture Atlas of the World CD-ROM**
- **Assessment Book** pages 45–46

Multiple Intelligences

Body/Kinesthetic Students can expand their understanding of distortion by making faces in the mirror or manipulating faces they have created out of a variety of materials.

Vocabulary

distortion *distorsión* a change from expected, normal proportions

FOCUS

Time: About 10 minutes

Activating Prior Knowledge

"Does it take more muscles to smile than it does to frown?"

"¿Se usan más músculos para sonreír que para arrugar la frente?"

- Discuss the students' answers to the questions. It does take more muscles to frown than to smile. Discuss with students that smiling and frowning are ways to distort the face.

ART Background

About the Artists The Tlingit lived in houses filled with carvings and paintings expressing the power and prestige of the inhabitants.

The Mayan civilization was an advanced culture whose astronomers had a precise mathematics that allowed them to predict solar eclipses.

The *Ritual Object's* use is a mystery. It has been suggested that the grooved sides held the cords of a bird snare.

About Subject Matter* All the masks are symbolic.

About the Media *Dead-man Mask* is made from wood, paint, hide metal. The Mexican mask is ceramic. The mask from New Zealand is made of wood and shell inlay.

Artist unknown. Tlaticlo Valley of Mexico. *Mask.* 800–400 B.C. Ceramic pigment. $5\frac{1}{4}$ inches high. Metropolitan Museum of Art, New York, New York.

Artist unknown. Maori (New Zealand). *Ritual Object.* Wood, shell inlay. $9\frac{3}{4}$ inches long. Metropolitan Museum of Art, New York, New York.

Study the four masks to learn more about distortion.

- What features have been changed in each of these masks?

- What do you think was the purpose in changing these masks? How does this affect the viewer's reaction?

- What do you think each mask was used for?

- What do all four masks have in common? What are their differences?

Lesson 5

SEEING LIKE AN ARTIST
Think of different ways masks are used today. What are some ways that artists have changed masks to suit special occasions?

123

Introducing the Art
"Let's look closely at the masks."
"Vamos a observar detalladamente las máscaras."

- **Describe:** Have students describe the subject matter of each mask. (The subject matter of each mask is symbolic.)
- Share and discuss information from **Art Background** and the **Artist Profiles Book.**
- Use the distortion mirror in the **Art Manipulative Kit** to explain distortion.
- Use the **National Geographic Picture Atlas of the World CD-ROM** to find the areas where the masks originated.
- Have students answer the questions on page 123. (See **Perception Hints** below.)
- **COMPARE AND CONTRAST** Have students make a list of the similarities and differences in the four masks. (All were made for ceremonial purposes. All were made of different materials.)

FOR THE ART SPECIALIST

Use the **Overhead** and the **Large Prints** *English Armor of George Clifford, Third Earl of Cumberland* and *Self-Portrait* to demonstrate how artists use distortion to create an expressive effect in a work of art.

About Art History* Since at least Paleolithic times, people have used masks made of wood, basketry, bark, corn husks, cloth, leather, skulls, papier-mâché, and other materials. Masks may cover the face, the entire head, or the head and shoulders, and they are sometimes part of an accompanying costume. Masks vary widely in their realism or abstraction, their use of symbols, and their ornamentation.

Cultural Perspectives The making of masks is a primary artistic outlet in many cultures, and masks from Africa, Oceania, and the Native American cultures of North America are highly prized by art collectors.

*See **More About** pages 206–227 for more about art history and subject matter.

Perception Hints

Change The eyes have been changed in each mask.
Purpose To create an expressive effect. Viewer is more impressed.
Use Each mask was used for ceremonial purposes and initiations.
Likenesses All are based on faces and covers for faces. None are realistic; all are distorted.
Differences They are made of different materials and come from different cultures.

Practice

Materials
- white drawing paper
- pencils

Alternate Materials: felt-tip markers

"How can you illustrate distortion in a mask design?"

"¿Cómo pueden ilustrar la distorsión en un diseño de una máscara?"

- Discuss the definition of *distortion* on page 124.
- Distribute materials and have students follow the directions on page 124 for designing a mask. Have them discuss the answer to the Decide question.

Create PROBLEM SOLVING

Materials
- papier-mâché paste
- gallon milk jugs (cut in half)
- newspaper
- liquid tempera paints
- paint brushes
- paper rolls
- egg cartons
- tape

Alternate Materials: cardboard and found materials

"Let's create a papier-mâché mask using distortion."

"Vamos a hacer una máscara de cartón piedra usando distorsión."

- Brainstorm ideas to create your design.
- Review procedures for working with papier-mâché in the **Technique Tips** on page 203.
- Distribute materials and have students follow the directions on page 125.

FOR THE ART SPECIALIST

Add yarns, fabrics, and found materials to enhance the mask. Put holes for the eyes. Students might role-play a drama with it.

Using Distortion

Distortion is a change from expected normal proportions. Artists can distort a figure by bending, warping, stretching, squashing, or twisting it. Artists use distortion in paintings, drawings, and sculptures.

Practice

Design a mask. Use pencil.

1. Design a mask that will address a problem you are interested in such as poverty or crime. Make sketches of your mask.

2. Distort the features of the mask to emphasize the problem you are addressing.

Decide Did you create some good sketches? What features did you distort?

Activities in
ART Across the Curriculum Book

Reading/Language Arts Identify distortion in a speech, learning three different ways that facts can be distorted in writing and speech. (page 133)

Math Learn about topology, the study of how bending, stretching, shrinking, and twisting affect the properties of geometric figures. (page 134)

Science Study the concerns for the natural environment. Understand that masks help celebrate people's relationship with nature. (page 135)

Social Studies Study the two ways of life of the Tlingit. (page 136)

The Arts Understand that distortion is used in music as well as art. (page 137)

Technology Use the *Multimedia Workshop* CD-ROM to create an expressive mask with a distorted feature. (page 138)

What did the artist distort in her mask?

Deidre. Age 11. *Mask.* Papier-mâché and tempera.

Create

How does a mask express a certain feeling or idea? Create a distorted papier-mâché mask.

1. Think what you want your mask to look like. Tear strips of newspaper 1 inch wide. Dip strips into the paste and wipe off excess liquid. Lay the strips over the outside of a plastic milk container. Overlap two layers of newspaper.

2. Dry the base, then add the features. Tape the shapes onto the base. Distort the features. Apply two more layers of papier-mâché, and let the mask base dry overnight.

3. When it is dry, pop your mask off the container and trim the edges. Paint the mask and apply other objects.

Lesson 5

Describe Describe the shapes, colors, and textures of your mask.

Analyze How did you distort the features on your mask?

Interpret What feelings does your mask suggest? Which parts affect the feeling most?

Decide Were you successful in creating a distorted mask that expressed a certain feeling or idea?

125

"Were you able to create a mask using distortion?"

"¿Fueron capaces de hacer una máscara usando distorsión?"

LARGE PRINT **Review**
Use the **Large Print** *Self-Portrait* to have students define *distortion*. Ask them to compare the use of distortion in the **Large Print** to the works in this lesson.

Art Criticism
Have students answer the four art criticism questions—Describe, Analyze, Interpret, and Decide—orally or in writing. Discuss how distortion was created in their masks when they are completed.

Assess
Use the **Assessment Book** pages 45–46 as a formal assessment for this lesson.

Evaluation Criteria
- Can the student identify distortion in works of art?
- Can the student create a mask using distortion?
- Can the student use the four steps of art criticism to evaluate his or her own work?
- Can the student demonstrate knowledge of the cultural purpose of the four masks?

Reteaching • • • • • • • • • • •

Distortion Find two more artworks in the book that use distortion to create an expressive effect.

THEME Connections

Origins Use the artwork to learn about the origins of the mask.
Celebration Use the artwork to learn more about celebrations using masks.

ESL

ESL students can benefit from structured and paired practice with discussion questions before sharing in front of the group. You can hold a mock interview, modeling possible responses and recording phrases to use on the chalkboard. As students share with partners, you might write down the emotions evoked by their artwork for later group reference.

Perception Hints for Student Art

The student artist distorted the nose into a horizontal tube. The mouth is an elongated tube.

UNIT 4
LESSON 6

LESSON PLANNER

Objectives

After completing this lesson, students will be able to:

- identify how artists use scale and proportion. *Aesthetic Perception*
- plan and create a life-size sculpture, using scale and proportion. *Creative Expression*
- use the four steps of art criticism to evaluate their own sculptures. *Art Criticism*
- demonstrate knowledge of the lives and work of both artists. *Art History and Culture*

Program Resources

- **Overhead:** Both the Segal and the Hanson are available on overhead 24.
- **Large Prints:** *Self-Portrait* by Judith Leyster and *English Armor of George Clifford, Third Earl of Cumberland* (1558–1605)
- **Vocabulary Book** pages 47–48
- **Artist Profiles Book:** Segal page 49 and Hanson page 21
- **Art Across the Curriculum Book** pages 139–144
- **Multimedia Workshop CD-ROM**
- **Assessment Book** pages 47–48

Multiple Intelligences

Verbal/Linguistic Students can expand their knowledge of scale and proportion through group discussion.

Vocabulary

body proportions *proporciones del cuerpo* ratios of one part of the body to another

ratio *radio* a comparison of size between two things

scale *escala* deals with size relationship; refers to size as measured against a standard reference, like the human body

Scale and Proportion

Artists use proportion and scale to create life-size sculptures and place them in realistic settings.

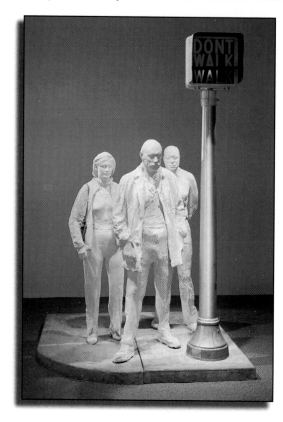

George Segal/Licensed by VAGA, New York, NY. (American). *Walk Don't Walk*. 1976. Plaster, cement, metal, painted wood and electric light. 104 × 72 × 72 inches. Whitney Museum of American Art, New York, New York.

Segal began his career as a painter but then turned to creating life-size sculptures by covering people with gauze-embedded plaster. Hanson produced lifelike sculptures and dressed them in real clothes. They were so realistic they were mistaken for live people. Both artists placed their life-size figures in settings with realistic objects from everyday life.

ART Background

About the Artists

George Segal (jôrj sē′ gəl, American, 1924–) after graduating started a chicken farm and taught art in a high school to support his family. In 1958, he sold his chickens and used the buildings as his studio. He created plaster figures on wood and chicken wire frames. Then, he started making a plaster cast, removing the cast, and placing the hollow figure in a real-life setting. Soon he was at the center of the pop art movement.

Duane Hanson (dwān han sən, American, 1925–) grew up in Minnesota where, as a boy, he carved wooden figures out of logs. His sculptures are a three-dimensional answer to works of the "New Realism" movement of the 1960s and 1970s.

Duane Hanson. (American). *Woman with Dog.* 1977. Cast polyvinyl, polychromed in acrylic with cloth and hair. Whitney Museum of American Art, New York, New York. Purchased with funds from Frances and Sydney Lewis.

Study both sculptures to find things that are realistic and lifelike.

- ✓ Which artist's work looks more realistic? Explain.
- ✓ What are the people doing in each sculpture?
- ✓ Why did the artists include a realistic environment with their sculptures? What objects did they use?

SEEING LIKE AN ARTIST

If they were creating sculptures to place within your school, what activities do you think these artists would represent?

Lesson **6**

127

About Subject Matter* Both sculptures are considered to be portraits.

About the Media The three figures called *Walk, Don't Walk* are made of plaster. Plaster is a mixture of lime, sand, and water, which hardens when dry. Hanson's figure is a mixture of resin and fiberglass. His entire process takes six weeks or more.

About Art History* The New Realists, who were inspired by pop artists of the 1960s, worked from photos, which transformed reality into a new reality. Both Segal and Hanson are considered New Realists.

Cultural Perspectives Hanson's most famous sculptures are of everyday stereotypical Americans, such as tourists or football players. Segal's work focuses on the "presence of man in his daily life."

FOCUS

Time: About 10 minutes

Activating Prior Knowledge

"Have you ever noticed the mannequins in the stores?"
"¿Alguna vez han notado los maniquíes en las tiendas?"

- Discuss how real they often look, and relate them to life-size sculptures.

Introducing the Art

"Look closely at the two sculptures."
"Observen detalladamente las dos esculturas."

- **Describe:** Have students describe the subject matter in each sculpture. (both: portraits)
- Share and discuss information from **Art Background** and the **Artist Profiles Book.**
- Have students answer the questions on page 127. (See **Perception Hints** below.)
- **COMPARE AND CONTRAST** Compare and contrast both sculptures. (The Segal is made of gauze-embedded plaster, while the Hanson is made of polyester resin and fiberglass. Both are realistic.)

FOR THE ART SPECIALIST

Use the **Overhead** and the **Large Prints** *English Armor of George Clifford, Third Earl of Cumberland* and *Self-Portrait* to demonstrate how artists use scale and proportion to create life-size sculptures.

Perception Hints

Realistic *Hanson.* It looks more realistic because of the color of the figure.

Activity *Segal.* The people are waiting at a walk sign. *Hanson.* The woman is reading a letter.

Environment *Segal.* The walk sign. *Hanson.* The dog, the letter, and the chair.

TEACH

Time: About two 30-minute periods

Practice

Materials
- white drawing paper
- pencils
- props

Alternate Materials: felt-tip pens

"Can you find examples of scale and proportion for a living sculpture?"

"¿Pueden hallar ejemplos de escala y proporción para una escultura viviente?"

- Discuss the definitions of *body proportion* and *scale* on page 128.
- Distribute materials and have students follow the directions on page 128 for finding scale and proportion examples. Have them discuss the answer to the Decide question.

Create PROBLEM SOLVING

Materials
- life-size clothing, shoes, socks
- knit material or old T-shirts
- paint or stitchery items
- gloves, wigs, panty hose
- newspapers   • props
- posterboard   • felt-tip markers

Alternate Materials: papier-mâché

"Let's create a life-size sculpture of a person and place it somewhere in your school."

"Vamos a hacer una escultura de tamaño natural de una persona y colocarla en algún lugar de la escuela."

- Brainstorm ideas to create a sculpture.
- Distribute materials and have students follow the directions on page 129.
- Make heads from knitted material or T-shirts. Use panty hose or a leotard and stuff it with newspapers for the body. Dress it with regular clothing, a wig, a hat, gloves, and shoes. Facial features may be painted or sewn on. Place the work in the school.

> ### FOR THE ART SPECIALIST
> Work in groups and make life–size papier-mâché figures. Paint and dress them.

Using Scale and Proportion

Body proportions are defined in ratios of one part of the body to another.

A **ratio** is a comparison of size between two things. Often artists will use the head as a ratio of one to the length of an adult body, which is about seven and a half head lengths. Therefore, the ratio would be 1 (the head) to 7 (heads per body length) and be written as 1:7.

Scale is similar to proportion in that it deals with size relationships. The difference is that scale refers to size as measured against a standard reference, like the human body.

Practice

Find examples of scale and proportion.

1. Divide into small groups. Think of a scene that Hanson or Segal might create. Collect props that are either in scale or out of scale to your body proportions.

2. Set up your living sculpture for the class to see.

Decide Do your classmates recognize whether you are working in scale or out of scale with your objects?

Activities in
ART Across the Curriculum Book

Reading/Language Arts Create a story about the sculptures. (page 139)

Math Plan a realistic sculpture, using ratio to develop a small model of the work into a larger sculpture. (page 140)

Science Learn about car safety, looking first at the people in the Segal. (page 141)

Social Studies Study and compare the judgments made about a historical person. (page 142)

The Arts Use pantomime to dramatize the reactions of a visitor coming upon one of the sculptures. (page 143)

Technology Use the *Multimedia Workshop* CD-ROM to create a drawing of a friend using realistic proportions and a realistic scale. (page 144)

Fort Daniels Elementary fifth-grade class. *Life-size Sculpture.*
Ektachrome film.

How can you tell scale and proportion were used?

Create

What effect would a life-size sculpture have if you placed it somewhere in the school? Create a life-size figure using scale and proportion. Place it in a real environment in your school.

1. Think about available items you have to make a life-size soft sculpture. Work in small groups. Plan and make sketches of your figure and environment.

2. Divide responsibilities. Some can create the soft sculpture head. Others can stuff clothes with newspapers. Others can construct the environment. Make sure your figure is in scale with the environment.

3. Make a sign showing the title of the work.

Describe Describe the materials used to create your sculpture and environment.

Analyze Who does your character represent? What is the setting of your sculpture?

Interpret What is the mood of your sculpture? What are observers likely to think your sculpture represents?

Decide Were you successful in creating a life-size sculpture that is in realistic scale and proportion?

Lesson 6   **129**

Culture Use the Hanson as a springboard to discuss the problems of the elderly in our culture.

Communities Use the artwork to learn more about how to keep our communities safe from crime.

All students, ESL students in particular, will find it easier to follow instructions when working in small groups if each group has a specific list of instructions to follow. You can have students role-play their instructions as a group or tell a partner what comes next.

CLOSE
Time: About 5 minutes

"Were you able to create a sculpture using scale and proportion?"

"¿Fueron capaces de hacer una escultura usando escala y proporción?"

 Review

Use the **Large Print** *English Armor of George Clifford, Third Earl of Cumberland* to have students compare the use of scale and proportion to the works in this lesson.

Art Criticism

Have students answer the four art criticism questions—Describe, Analyze, Interpret, and Decide—orally or in writing. Discuss the use of form and proportion in their work after it is dry.

 Assess

Use the **Assessment Book** pages 47–48 as a formal assessment for this lesson.

Evaluation Criteria

• Can the student identify scale and proportion in artwork?

• Can the student create a sculpture of a person, using scale and proportion?

• Can the student use the four steps of art criticism to evaluate his or her own artwork?

• Can the student demonstrate a knowledge of the lives and works of George Segal and Duane Hanson?

Reteaching ● ● ● ● ● ● ● ● ● ●

Proportion Ask students to think about where another sculpture like those in the lessons might be in the community.

Perception Hints for Student Art

You can tell scale and proportion were used by observing the size of the sculpture in relationship to its surroundings (books, erasers, and so on).

UNIT 4

Faustwork Mask Theater:
Robert Faust.

 y wearing different masks, Robert Faust can make himself into many different characters. He surprises everyone with the funny faces and strange features of his masks. In many cultures throughout the world, masks are worn at festivals, celebrations, and rituals. Wherever they are used, masks make it possible for a person to pretend to be someone or something else.

130   Unit 4

LESSON PLANNER

Objectives

After completing this lesson, students will be able to:

- demonstrate a variety of expressions and movements that convey emotions. *Aesthetic Perception*
- express individual interpretation in the use of exaggerations to create masks and convey feelings. *Creative Expression*
- use the four steps of art criticism to evaluate the experience of communicating with masks and movements. *Art Criticism*
- demonstrate knowledge of how Robert Faust uses exaggeration in masks and movements to show emotions. *Art History and Culture*

FOCUS

Time: About 10 minutes

Activating Prior Knowledge

"Think about different emotions you experience and how you communicate these through facial expression, movement, and body posture."

"Piensen sobre las diferentes emociones que han experimentado y cómo las comunican a través de la expresión facial y del movimiento y la postura corporal."

- Discuss students' responses and talk about expressing emotions. Stress that emotions are universal to the human experience.

Introducing the Art

"Look at the photograph of Robert Faust and his masks and describe the many different emotions or characters you can identify."

"Observen la fotografía de Robert Faust y sus máscaras y describan las diferentes emociones o personajes que pueden identificar."

- Share information about Robert Faust and masks in **Art Background.** If you have the *Artsource* video, have students view the presentation by Robert Faust.
- Have students identify and list as many pairs of emotions as possible. Examples: happy/sad, angry/calm, laughing/crying, and so on.

ART Background

About the Artist

Robert Faust founded Faustwork Mask Theater in 1983, creating shows that tour theaters, festivals, and schools. Faust is an actor, athlete, dancer, choreographer, and mask maker. In his one-man show "The Masked Man," he transforms himself into more than 20 different characters. Through the portrayal of these characters, he demonstrates the power of masks. Some characters speak, wearing half-masks. Other characters wear full masks on top or on the back of the head, transforming the performer into a four-legged creature or creating distortions that baffle or surprise.

Cultural Perspectives Since ancient times, masks have been used in ceremonies and rituals to transform people. Masks still hold enchantment and fascination. In some parts of the world today, masks still retain a deep and complex meaning.

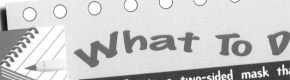

What To Do

Create a two-sided mask that shows contrasting feelings.

Materials

- ✔ paper plates, glue, and scissors
- ✔ paper towel tubes, yarn, buttons, fabric
- ✔ crayons and markers
- ✔ beans, rice, seeds, or other natural materials

1. Discuss pairs of emotions: happy/sad, mean/kind. Then, show an exaggeration of each of these feelings in your face.

2. Create two contrasting masks. Use a paper plate to sketch each face. Use distortion in the features. Decorate your masks. Then, fasten them back to back.

3. Make a slit in the end of the paper towel tube. Put the masks in the slit. Use the tube as a handle.

4. Develop movements that express the feelings on each mask. Perform your idea of two contrasting characters.

Describe Describe your two-sided mask.

Analyze Explain how you used distortion and exaggeration in creating your masks.

Interpret What opposite feelings did you create with your masks and your body?

Decide How well did you succeed in communicating two different emotions?

Extra Credit

Make a self-portrait mask. Present a pantomime of a particular event in your life.

Theater 131

About Subject Matter The mask has been an important aspect of the religious and social life in many cultures. As a device in the theater, the use of masks evolved from religious practices of ancient Greece. The first masks were used to imitate a god and were made primarily of animal skins. As these ceremonies became more theatrical, the masks became more elaborate. The traditional masks depicting tragedy and comedy are derived from Greek theatrical traditions.

About Theater One advantage of using masks in performance is that they can be seen from a distance because they are often larger than the human head. To use a mask, an actor must be well trained because the actions must be large, clear, and complement the character of the mask. Vocal projection within a mask also requires skill and the ability to express a range and depth of emotions.

TEACH
Time: Two 30-minute periods

Materials
- paper plates, glue, scissors
- paper towel rolls, yarn, buttons, fabric scraps
- crayons, markers
- beans, rice, seeds, or other natural materials

"Let's make two-sided masks portraying two opposing emotions."

"Vamos a hacer máscaras de dos lados representando dos emociones opuestas."

- Have students vary facial expression to show appropriate, opposing feelings. Examples: happiness and sadness.

- Have students explore movements that express these opposing feelings. Examples: drooping posture and dragging feet could express sadness.

- Point out to students that distortion and exaggeration in their masks and movements can help make emotions obvious.

CLOSE
Time: About 5 minutes

"How is expressing emotions using a mask different from working without a mask?"

"¿En qué se diferencia la expresión de las emociones usando una máscara que sin una máscara?"

◆ Assess
Have students answer the four art criticism questions on page 131—Describe, Analyze, Interpret, and Decide—orally or in writing.

Evaluation Criteria
- Can the student demonstrate a variety of expressions and movements that convey emotions?
- Can the student use exaggeration in the construction of masks and of body posture and movement?
- Can the student use the four steps of art criticism to evaluate his or her masks and movements?
- Can the student demonstrate knowledge of how Robert Faust uses exaggeration in masks and movements to show emotions?

UNIT 4

Reviewing Unit Concepts

"Artists use proportion and distortion to communicate an emotion or idea in a work of art."

"Los artistas usan la proporción y la distorsión para comunicar una emoción o idea en una obra de arte."

- Review the use of proportion and distortion as discussed throughout Unit 4.
- Ask students to list examples of how artists use proportion and distortion.

Examining the Artwork

"How did the artist use proportion, scale, exaggeration, or distortion in his artwork?"

"¿Cómo usó el artista la proporción, la escala, la exageración o la distorsión en su obra de arte?"

- As a class study Degas's painting. Discuss how Degas used proportion to relate size in his painting.
- Have the students answer the questions on page 133. (See **Perception Hints** below.)

Student Portfolio

Have students review all the artwork they have created during this unit and select the pieces they wish to put into their portfolios.

Art Criticism Activity

Have students select an artwork from the previous unit and study it using the four steps of art criticism. (See pages 206–209 for more information about Art Criticism.)

Perception Hints

Proportion Degas uses proportion to help him make the likenesses of the people seem more realistic.

Scale Degas uses realistic scale to relate the size of the two women. We can tell how tall the women are by comparing them to the sizes of the hats and the stand-up mirror.

Exaggeration Degas does not appear to have exaggerated any features. The nose is centered on the face, the mouth a finger width below the nose, and the eyes are spaced evenly apart and on an imaginary line that can be traced with a finger.

Wrapping Up Unit 4
Proportion and Distortion
Reviewing Main Ideas

The lessons and activities in this unit show how proportion and distortion are used by artists to create both two- and three-dimensional works of art.

- **Proportion** is the principle of art concerned with the size relationships of one part to another.
- **Scale** is the principle of art referring to size as measured against a standard reference, like the human body. Scale can be created in two ways.
  1. **Realistic scale** is when an artist creates a work of art in which various elements seem to fit together well and they resemble size relations in real life.
  2. **Unrealistic scale** is when an artist intentionally makes size relationships that do not resemble real life.
- **Facial proportions** guidelines are used by an artist to correctly place features on the human face.

Edgar Hilaire Germain Degas. (French). *At the Milliner's.* 1882. Pastel on paper. 30 × 34 inches. Metropolitan Museum of Art, New York, New York. Bequest of Mrs. H. O. Havermeyer, 1929. The H. O. Havermeyer Collection.

ART Background

About the Artist
Edgar Degas (ed' gär dā gä', French, 1834–1917) was concerned with portraying movement in his art and the continuity of contours. Degas was the son of a wealthy banker. He studied art in Paris, and the Renaissance works in Italy. He painted contemporary scenes of the theater with an emphasis on props and setting. The female ballet dancer eventually became his favorite theme. He would draw from a model in his studio and combine several of his sketches to portray the dancers in various settings. As his eyesight failed, he turned to making sculptures.

About Subject Matter* *At the Milliner's* is an example of the work Degas typically created after 1880. His subject matter dealt with milliners, laundresses, and dancers against sketchy backgrounds.

- **Exaggeration** is when an artist changes an object or person by enlarging a feature.
- **Distortion** is when an artist changes an object or person by changing a feature in any way except by enlarging it.

Summing Up

Look at the *At the Milliner's* by Edgar Degas. The artist used several of the proportion techniques taught in this unit.

- How does Degas use proportion in his painting?
- What type of scale does he use to relate the size of the two women in this painting?
- Has Degas exaggerated or distorted any of the features of the two women? Explain.

Proportion and distortion are used to create the illusion of realism or fantasy in a work of art. Artists use these principles to evoke the strong feelings they want to communicate.

Let's Visit a Museum

The Metropolitan Museum of Art in New York City is one of the world's largest museums. It has more than 2 million works of art spanning 5,000 years of culture. The museum was founded in 1870 and is located in the city's Central Park. Its Egyptian collection is second only to the one in Cairo, Egypt. Major collections in the museum in addition to the paintings include arms and armor, Chinese art, costumes, musical instruments, primitive art, French and American furniture, and photography. More than 4.5 million people from around the world visit the Metropolitan Museum each year.

The Metropolitan Museum of Art. 1991.

133

Learning About Museums

The Metropolitan Museum of Art was one of the first museums to be established in the United States. It is one of the world's largest and finest museums. It is visited by 4.5 million people annually. The American Wing houses the world's most comprehensive collection of American artwork. Prior to the museum's founding in 1870, the only public museums were in Europe.

- Divide the class into groups. Have each group design a "museum" in Greek architectural style.

TIMELINE For more information on this and other museums, see pages T13, T30–T33, and the back of the **Animals Through History Time Line.**

A Final Thought

"...art is something which, although produced by human hands, is not created by these hands alone, but something which wells up from a deeper source in our souls."
—Vincent van Gogh

About the Media Degas drew *At the Milliner's* with pastels. This became his favorite medium because he was able to get sharper colors and surface textures.

About Art History* Impressionism was the leading French development in art during the late 1900s. It was a reaction against the academic traditions where art was created primarily in the studio. The Impressionists concentrated on the reaction of light and atmosphere on various objects. The group included the artwork of several artists who had exhibited in Paris between 1874 and 1886 in a series of group exhibitions. Edgar Degas had participated in all but one of these exhibitions.

*See **More About** pages 206–227 for more about art history and subject matter.

UNIT 5

UNIT OVERVIEW

Unit 5 focuses on the principles of balance and perspective. Balance is used to arrange visual elements in a work of art. Perspective is used to create the illusion of depth on a flat surface. The specific topics in this unit are types of **balance, depth and perspective,** and **point of view.**

Balance refers to how the art elements are arranged. Balance is taught in Lessons 1, 2 and 3.

Perspective is the technique used to create depth. Lessons 4 and 5 are about perspective.

Point of view is the angle from which you see an object. Lesson 6 covers point of view.

Introducing Unit Concepts

"The art principle of balance is used by artists in all types of art; perspective is used only in two-dimensional art."

"El principio artístico de equilibrio lo usan los artistas en todas los tipos de arte; la perspectiva sólo se usa en el arte bidimensional."

Balance

- Ask students to work in groups to find an example of balance according to the definition you read to them.
- Ask the groups to take things from their desks to create a balanced arrangement.

Perspective

- Have the students look up the word *perspective* and discuss the meaning.
- Take the students into a long hallway. Select three students of equal height. Have one stand toward the end of the hallway, another a few feet in front of the class, and the third halfway between the other two students. Ask the class to observe what happens to the sizes of their classmates the farther away they are. Ask them to compare details that they can see. Have them close one eye and observe where each student would be placed in a drawing. Who would be drawn higher and lower on the picture plan?

An Introduction to Balance and Perspective

Some artists use balance and perspective to create a work of art.

Andrew Wyeth. (American). *Ground Hog Day.* 1959. Egg tempera on board. 31 × 31¾ inches. Philadelphia Museum of Art, Philadelphia, Pennsylvania. Given by Henry DuPont and Mrs. John Wintersteen.

ART Background

About the Artist

Andrew Wyeth (an′ drū wī′ əth, American, 1917–   ) was born in Chadds Ford, Pennsylvania. Wyeth received his artistic training from his father, the illustrator N.C. Wyeth. Wyeth draws his subject matter primarily from two locales: his hometown of Chadds Ford and the fishing village of Cushing, Maine, his summer home. His paintings are accurately drawn with fine details. Wyeth's son, Jamie, is one of America's most popular portrait artists.

About Subject Matter* Andrew Wyeth often painted scenes about the people who lived near him. The painting *Ground Hog Day* is a realistic picture of the kitchen inside his neighbor's house.

Balance is used by artists to arrange visual elements in a work of art.

- When you look at this painting, what objects do you notice first?
- If you were to divide this painting in half, would both sides be identical?

Artists use **perspective** in paintings to create the illusion of depth.

- How does Wyeth create a feeling of depth in this painting?

Artist Profile

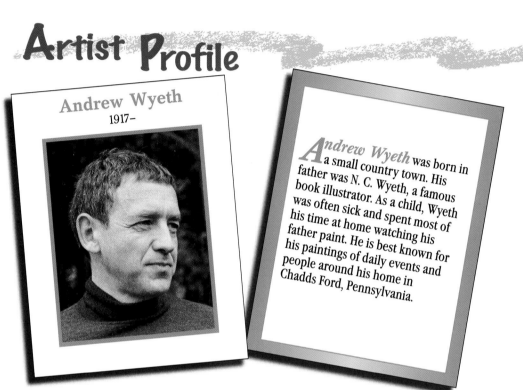

Andrew Wyeth
1917–

Andrew Wyeth was born in a small country town. His father was N. C. Wyeth, a famous book illustrator. As a child, Wyeth was often sick and spent most of his time at home watching his father paint. He is best known for his paintings of daily events and people around his home in Chadds Ford, Pennsylvania.

Andrew Wyeth and other artists use balance and perspective to arrange visual elements and create the illusion of depth. In this unit you will learn and practice the techniques that artists use to create balance and perspective in artworks. Here are the techniques.

- Types of Balance
- Depth
- Perspective
- Points of View

135

About the Media Wyeth uses both watercolor and tempera. He has adopted the technique of dry brush in watercolors to give him more control. His best-known works are painted in egg tempera, which gives him great precision.

About Art History* Andrew Wyeth is considered part of a group of painters who became well known in the 1950s as the New Realists. This is a group of American artists who portray their subject matter realistically.

Cultural Perspectives Wyeth experienced the Great Depression and World War II, which influenced his work. During the 1950s when he became well known, Rock and Roll was born, the Korean War took place, and the Russians initiated the space race.

*See **More About** pages 206–227 for more about art history and subject matter.

Use the **Video** *Rumpelstiltskin* to show perspective in interior and exterior scenes in buildings. It also illustrates weaving.

Examining the Artwork

"Let's look more closely at the artwork."
"Vamos a observar detalladamente la obra de arte."

- Have students look at Andrew Wyeth's painting and describe the objects they see.
- Discuss the definitions of *balance* and *perspective.* Have students answer the questions on page 135.
 (See **Perception Hints** below.)

Artist Profile
Share with students information about the artist, including the photograph.

You may wish to encourage students to practice art concepts and record their ideas from lesson to lesson in their **Art Journals.**

About Music
Balance in music is associated with symmetrical forms such as ABA—music having three sections with the middle one different from the two outer sections. Have students sing an example of this by singing *Au Clair de la Lune.*

Perspective is not a term in music. However, there are examples of compositions that simulate aurally the effect of something disappearing into the distance or of something coming closer and closer.

Perception Hints

Perspective The objects you see first are the dishes on the table. Your eyes are then drawn to the object (wood) through the window.
Balance If you divided this painting in half, it would not be evenly balanced. It is informally balanced. The plate, cup, and window are all arranged to the right of the central point of the picture.
Depth A feeling of depth is created in the logs and pathway as they become smaller and have less detail the farther back they appear to be. Perspective is used by placing the cup and plate toward the bottom of the painting and larger than the logs, which are seen outside of the window and higher on the picture plan.

Lesson	Lesson Title	Suggested Pacing	Create Activities	Materials	
1	Formal Balance	45 minutes	Design a robot using symmetrical balance.	two pieces of cardboard brayers and ink scissors, glue, and pencils black felt-tip markers watercolor paints	
2	Informal Balance	45 minutes	Create a still-life painting using asymmetrical balance.	white drawing paper liquid tempera paints pencils found objects	
3	Radial Balance	45 minutes	Create a collage design that uses radial balance.	posterboard old magazines yarn and found objects or pasta shapes glue and scissors paper and pencils	
4	Perspective Techniques	45 minutes	Create a fantasy setting for a music video using perspective technique.	white paper colored markers pencils	
5	Linear Perspective	45 minutes	Create a real or imaginary scene using linear perspective.	white drawing paper pencils watercolor paints	
6	Point of View and Direct Observation	45 minutes	Create a drawing of an object from three different points of view.	white drawing paper colored markers	
Artsource Lesson	Balance and Perspective in Dance	75 minutes	Create dance designs that are symbols of the sun.	a variety of sun symbols and sun designs based on the image of the sun Artsource videotape (optional)	

Program Resources (Books)	Art Resources	Literature Resources	*Music Resources
Vocabulary, pp. 49–50 Assessment, pp. 49–50 Art Across the Curriculum Resource Book, pp. 145–150	Overhead Transparency #25, *Cow's Skull: Red White and Blue* and *Self-Portrait* Artist Profile Book, pp.13, 40 Large Prints, *Path through the Tall Grass* and *Belt Mask, Court of Benin, Bini Tribe, Nigeria*	**1.** *Grandfather's Journey* (1993) by Allen Say has exquisite paintings that illustrate the formal balance of both photographs and life experiences captured in grandfather's life and provides excellent lesson examples of art and cross-cultural experiences. **2.** *On the Day You Were Born* (1991) by Debra Frasier has brightly colored paper collages that celebrate the birth of a baby to Earth and utilizes positive and negative space in these integrated designs.	"On the Trai,l, from *Grand Canyon Suite,* by Ferde Grofe, p. T178, CD4:18. "On the Trail" is an example of American music from the twentieth century.
Vocabulary, pp. 51–52 Assessment, pp. 51–52 Art Across the Curriculum Resource Book, pp. 151–156	Overhead Transparency #26, *Women of Paris: The Circus Lover* and *The Sisters of the Artist and Their Governess* Artist Profile Book, pp. 1, 53 Large Prints, *Path through the Tall Grass* and *Belt Mask, Court of Benin, Bini Tribe, Nigeria*	**1.** *A Child's Book of Art: Great Pictures, First Words* (1993) by Lucy Michelthwait introduces well-known pieces of art from all around the world to illustrate familiar words. One section is entitled "Pets" and is perfect for this lesson. **2.** *Ashanti to Zulu: African Traditions* (1976) by Margaret Musgrove explains the traditions and customs of 26 African tribes and uses numerous patterns and example of informal balance.	*"Finlandia,"* Op. 26, No.7, by Jean Sibelius, p. T132, CD3:10. *"Finlandia"* is an example of European music from the late 1800s.
Vocabulary, pp. 53–54 Assessment, pp. 53–54 Art Across the Curriculum Resource Book, pp. 157–162	Overhead Transparency #27, *Ardabil Carpet* and *Deep Dish/Spain/from Valencia* Artist Profile Book, pp. 69, 70 Large Prints, *Path through the Tall Grass* and *Belt Mask, Court of Benin, Bini Tribe, Nigeria*	**1.** *Arrow to the Sun* (1974) by Gerald McDermott has Native American patterns of line and color to create shapes and illustrate uses of radial balance. **2.** *Flowers* (1993) by Gallimard Jeuness, Claude Delafosse, and Rene Mattler will help students observe the radial balance found in nature by exploring the interactive pages of this educational book.	"Mi Gallo" (My Rooster), p. 347, CD8:29. "Mi Gallo" is an example of a canon, a "round" form in music in which several repetitions of the same melody overlap.
Vocabulary, pp. 55–56 Assessment, pp. 55–56 Art Across the Curriculum Resource Book, pp. 163–168	Overhead Transparency #28, *The Arrival of the Normandy Train at the Gare Saint-Lazare* and *The Guide's Home Algonquin* Artist Profile Book, pp. 31, 38 Large Prints, *Path through the Tall Grass* and *Belt Mask, Court of Benin, Bini Tribe, Nigeria*	**1.** *Jumanji* (1981) by Chris Van Allsburg manipulates space and points of view to bring to life the black-and-white illustrations of this adventure book. **2.** *The Polar Express* (1985) by Chris Van Allsburg is another excellent example of distorted perspectives and unique points of view that will captivate students by both the illustrations and the story.	"Tsiothwatase:tha" (Round Dance), p. T229, CD5:23. "Tsiothwatase:tha" is an example of Native American music.
Vocabulary, pp. 57–58 Assessment, pp. 57–58 Art Across the Curriculum Resource Book, pp. 169–174	Overhead Transparency #29, *Interior of St. Peters, Rome* and *Cornell Farm* Artist Profile Book, pp. 22, 41 Large Prints, *Path through the Tall Grass* and *Belt Mask, Court of Benin, Bini Tribe, Nigeria*	**1.** *Up North at the Cabin* (1992) by Mary Wilson Chall has exquisite paintings that describe a young girl's memories that demonstrate scenes of linear perspective. **2.** *The Nutcracker Ballet* (1992) retold by Melissa Hayden reinterprets in masterful illustrations that reflect lesson concepts.	"Santa Lucia," p. T313, CD7:24. "Santa Lucia" is an Italian folk song about an early Christian saint.
Vocabulary, pp. 59–60 Assessment, pp. 59–60 Art Across the Curriculum Resource Book, pp. 175–180	Overhead Transparency #30, *House by the Railroad* and *American Interior* Artist Profile Book, pp. 23, 50 Large Prints, *Path through the Tall Grass* and *Belt Mask, Court of Benin, Bini Tribe, Nigeria*	**1.** *Christmas at Long Pond* (1992) by William T. Goerge uses unique perspectives to give visually refreshing quality to this holiday tale.\ **2.** *Jim Hedgehog and the Lonesome Tower* (1990) by Russel Hoban will have students loving to read about the exciting adventure of a heavy metal fan set to solid images reflecting points of view and observation.	"California, Here I Come," by B.G. De Sylva, Al Jolsen, and Joseph Meyer, p. T364, CD9:15. "California, Here I Come" is an example of American music from the first half of the twentieth century.

*Music references are from **Share the Music,** Macmillan/McGraw-Hill School Publishers

UNIT 5 LESSON 1

LESSON PLANNER

Objectives

After completing this lesson, students will be able to:

- identify the use of formal balance and symmetry in art. *Aesthetic Perception*
- create a relief print of a robot using symmetrical balance. *Creative Expression*
- use the four steps of art criticism to evaluate their own artwork. *Art Criticism*
- demonstrate knowledge of the lives and work of both artists. *Art History and Culture*

Program Resources

- **Overhead:** Both the O'Keeffe and the Close are available on overhead 25.
- **Large Prints:** *Path through the Tall Grass* by Auguste Renoir and *Belt Mask, Court of Benin, Bini Tribe, Nigeria*
- **Vocabulary Book** pages 49–50
- **Artist Profiles Book:** O'Keeffe page 40 and Close page 13
- **Art Across the Curriculum Book** pages 145–150
- **Multimedia Workshop CD-ROM**
- **Assessment Book** pages 49–50

Multiple Intelligences
Visual/Spatial Students can explore formal balance as they visually identify and illustrate examples of this concept.

Vocabulary

central axis *eje central* the central dividing line, sometimes imaginary

balance *equilibrio* the principle of design that deals with visual weight in a work of art

formal balance *equilibrio formal* when equal, or very similar, elements are placed on opposite sides of a central line called an axis

symmetry *simetría* a special type of formal balance in which two halves of a balanced composition are identical

relief point *grabado en relieve* a technique in which the design to be printed is raised from the background

Formal Balance

Artists use formal balance to organize an artwork so that its opposite sides are equal or very similar.

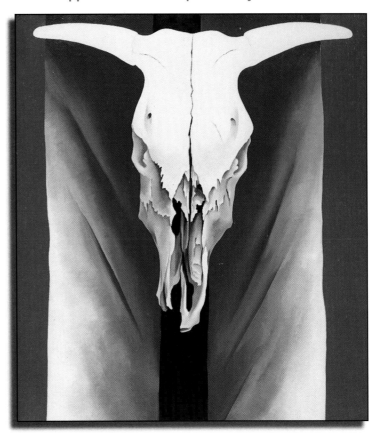

Georgia O'Keeffe. (American). *Cow's Skull: Red White and Blue.* $39\frac{7}{8} \times 36\frac{7}{8}$ inches. 1931. Oil on canvas. The Metropolitan Museum of Art, New York, New York. Alfred Stieglitz Collection, 1952.

Georgia O'Keeffe often painted images incorporating the New Mexico landscape and the remains of animals. Notice how the painting appears as if there were a line running down the middle of the cow's skull. In both paintings, the two sides are almost mirror images of each other. Chuck Close's *Self-Portrait* is an example of formal balance.

136   Unit **5**

ART Background

About the Artists

Georgia O'Keeffe (jôr' jə ō kēf', American, 1887–1986) was born in Sun Prairie, Wisconsin. By age 13, she had decided to become an artist. She became famous for her spectacular, larger-than-life paintings of natural objects such as bones, shells, and flowers. She loved nature, especially the desert of New Mexico, where she spent the last half of her life.

Chuck Close (chək klōs, American, 1940–   ) was born in Seattle. He had learning disabilities but he always felt special because he could create art, and his friends could not. He left Seattle to attend Yale Graduate School. He was paralyzed from the shoulders down in 1988; however, he found a way to paint his physically demanding portraits.

About Subject Matter* The O'Keeffe is a still-life composite. The Close is a portrait.

Chuck Close. (American). *Self Portrait.* 1987. Oil on canvas. 72 × 60 inches. Pace Wildenstein Gallery, New York, New York. Photo by Bill Jacobson.

Compare both paintings to find formal balance.

✓ Describe how the objects, colors, and lines are arranged in both works of art. How are they similar? How are they different?

✓ Find the center of each painting. What happens on either side of the center line?

✓ Are both sides of each painting identical? Where do you see differences?

Lesson 1

137

SEEING LIKE AN ARTIST

Can you think of any objects in nature that if divided in half would be identical on both sides?

About the Media The Close and O'Keeffe are both oil paintings.

About Art History* A pioneer of modernism in the United States, O'Keeffe painted the unusual, abstract shapes she saw in her mind rather than painting exact copies of objects. O'Keeffe is known for her dazzling, jewel-toned colors, large scale, and unusual perspectives, such as very close up or far away. She never painted people.

Close is not a portrait painter in the traditional sense. He created paintings based on photographs. For 20 years, he was known as a photo-realist. His new work is no longer photo-realistic, but he still works with a grid from photographs. He is widely praised for his abundance of color and light in these new paintings.

*See **More About** pages 206–227 for more about art history and subject matter.

FOCUS

Time: About 10 minutes

Activating Prior Knowledge

"Think about a stereo that has two speakers. What happens when you turn the balance knob to the right? What if you turned it to the center?"

"Piensen en un equipo de sonido con dos cornetas. ¿Qué sucede cuando le dan vuelta hacia la derecha al botón del volumen? ¿Qué sucede si lo voltean al centro?"

• Discuss students' answers to the questions and why balance is appealing to the ear and eye.

Introducing the Art

"Let's look closely at the paintings."

"Vamos a observar detalladamente las pinturas."

• **Describe:** Have students describe the subject matter in the paintings. (O'Keeffe: symbolic; Close: portrait)

• Share and discuss information with students from **Art Background** and the **Artist Profiles Book.**

• Have students discuss the questions on page 137. (See **Perception Hints** below.)

• **COMPARE AND CONTRAST** Have students make a list of the similarities and differences in the two paintings. (Both use approximate symmetry. The O'Keeffe's is a still life, and the Close is a realistic portrait.)

FOR THE ART SPECIALIST

Use the **Overhead** and the **Large Print** *Belt Mask, Court of Benin, Bini Tribe, Nigeria,* to demonstrate how artists use formal balance to organize an artwork so that its opposite sides are equal or very similar.

Perception Hints

Description Objects, colors, and lines are arranged using approximate symmetry in both works. Both have the head in the center, and the features are arranged symmetrically.
Center *Both.* The head. The center line on each is like an imaginary axis with features organized outward from there.
Sides *Both.* are not identical. They are balanced but are not mirror images. *O'Keeffe.* Slight changes in the bone structure. *Close.* More hair on the left side than on the right side. The shirt is a little off center, and the left shoulder is higher.

TEACH

Time: About 30 minutes

Practice

"How do you recognize formal balance in an artwork?"

"¿Cómo reconocen el equilibrio forma en una obra de arte?"

• Discuss the definitions of *formal balance* and *symmetry* on page 138.

• Have students follow the directions on page 138 to find examples of symmetrical balance. Have them discuss the answer to the Decide question.

Create PROBLEM SOLVING

Materials

- two pieces of cardboard
- brayers
- scissors
- ink
- glue
- pencils
- black felt-tip markers

Alternate Materials: drawing paper and liquid tempera paints

"Let's design a robot using symmetrical balance."

"Vamos a diseñar un robot usando equilibrio simétrico."

• Brainstorm ideas to use symmetry in a robot design. Review the concepts of formal balance and symmetry.

• Review procedures for printmaking in **More About Technique Tips** on page 200.

• Distribute materials and have students follow the directions on page 139.

• Have the students use the felt-tip markers to add details to their robots.

FOR THE ART SPECIALIST

Have students make a linoleum relief and print on a tissue collage.

Using Formal Balance

Balance is the principle of design that deals with visual weight in a work of art. One type of balance is **formal balance.**

Formal balance occurs when equal, or very similar, elements are placed on opposite sides of a central line called a **central axis.** The axis may be part of the design, or it may be an imaginary line. The axis, or central line, divides the design in half.

Symmetry is a special type of formal balance. The two halves of a symmetrically balanced object are the same. They are mirror images of each other.

Practice

Find examples of symmetrical balance in this book.

1. See if you can find individual objects in an artwork that you think are symmetrical.

2. Discuss why the work or objects are an example of symmetrical balance. Share with your class one example of symmetrical balance.

Decide Explain why you think your selection is a good example of symmetrical balance.

Activities in ART Across the Curriculum Book

Reading/Language Arts Learn to achieve balance in sentences by using contrasting words like artists create balance in their work. (page 145)

Math Study shapes that are congruent and identify whether a shape uses slide, flip, or rotation to change its appearance. (page 146)

Science Study the use of symmetry in nature by studying plants. (page 147)

Social Studies Study robots. Note that most do not have bilateral symmetry. (page 148)

The Arts Imagine the movements that a robot with bilateral symmetry would make and invent a robot dance step. (page 149)

Technology Use the *Multimedia Workshop* CD-ROM to create an imaginary creature with formal balance. (page 150)

How do you know where the imaginary axis of the robot is?

Anthony Strayer. Age 11. *Robot*. Tempera, marker.

Create

If you could design a personal robot, what would you have it do for you? Create a relief print of a robot using symmetrical balance.

1. Think about what tasks you want your robot to do. Draw your robot using symmetrical balance. Create a cardboard relief print. In a **relief print**, the image to be printed is raised from the background.

2. Draw on cardboard so that it has a central axis. Cut the shapes from the cardboard and glue them onto a printing plate (another piece of cardboard), keeping the symmetrical balance.

3. Use brayer and ink to make three prints of the robot.

Describe Describe the types of shapes you used to design your robot.

Analyze How did you use symmetry to arrange these shapes?

Interpret Does your robot look like what it is supposed to do? Give it a name.

Decide Do you think using symmetrical balance in this project was helpful?

Lesson **1**   **139**

Identify Using the Close as a springboard, discuss the importance of students maintaining their own identity in a group of their peers.

Exploration Using the location of many of O'Keeffe's works—New Mexico—explore the natural resources found there.

You may want to check frequently for ESL students' comprehension of a concept before moving to independent work. As you explain or demonstrate a concept's meaning, you might ask quick questions designed for one- or two-word responses. Students can respond as a group or to partners before sharing individual responses with the group.

CLOSE

Time: About 5 minutes

"Were you able to create a relief print of a robot using symmetrical balance?"

"¿Fueron capaces de crear un grabado en relieve de un robot usando equilibrio simétrico?"

LARGE PRINT **Review**

Use the **Large Prints** *Path Through the Tall Grass* and *Belt Mask, Court of Benin, Bini Tribe, Nigeria,* to compare the use of formal balance to the artists' use of formal balance in the lesson.

Art Criticism

Have students answer the four art criticism questions—Describe, Analyze, Interpret, and Decide—orally or in writing. Discuss the use of formal balance in their paintings.

Assess

Use the **Assessment Book** pages 49–50 as a formal assessment for this lesson.

Evaluation Criteria

- Can the student identify formal balance and symmetry in art?
- Can the student create a relief print of a robot using symmetrical balance?
- Can the student use the four steps of art criticism to evaluate his or her own artwork?
- Can the student demonstrate knowledge of

Reteaching • • • • • • • • • • • • •

Formal balance Have students look through magazines to find formal balance compositions and cut out the photographs for discussion.

Perception Hints for Student Art

You know that the imaginary axis is in the center because the two sides of the robot are almost symmetrical. The arms are alike, the feet are alike, and so on.

UNIT 5
LESSON 2

Informal Balance

Informal balance occurs when two unlike objects in an artwork have equal visual weight.

LESSON PLANNER

Objectives

After completing this lesson, students will be able to:

- identify the use of informal balance in works of art. *Aesthetic Perception*
- plan and create a still-life painting using asymmetrical balance. *Creative Expression*
- use the four steps of art criticism to evaluate their own drawings. *Art Criticism*
- demonstrate knowledge of the lives and work of both artists. *Art History and Culture*

Program Resources

- **Overhead:** Both the Tissot and the Anguissola are available on overhead 26.
- **Large Prints:** *Path Through the Tall Grass* by Auguste Renoir and *Belt Mask, Court of Benin, Bini Tribe, Nigeria*
- **Vocabulary Book** pages 51–52
- **Artist Profiles Book:** Tissot page 53 and Anguissola page 1
- **Art Across the Curriculum Book** pages 151–156
- **Multimedia Workshop CD-ROM**
- **National Museum of Women in the Arts Collection CD-ROM**
- **Assessment Book** pages 51–52

Multiple Intelligences

Body/Kinesthetic Students can expand their understanding of informal balance as they create examples of it with their bodies in the Practice section.

Vocabulary

informal balance *equilibrio informal* a way of organizing parts of a design so that unlike objects have equal eye attraction

asymmetry *asimetría* another name for "informal balance." Something asymmetrical looks balanced even if it is not the same on both sides.

negative space *espacio negativo* the areas around an object or group of objects

The following words appear in the Student Edition page 142 as art: *size, texture, color,* and *position*.

J. J. Tissot. (French).
Women of Paris, The Circus Lover.
Oil on canvas. 58 × 40 inches.
Juliana Cheney Edwards Collection.

James Tissot was interested in portraying urban life at the turn of the century. Notice how he arranged the people in this painting. He has larger figures and darker colors in the lower half, and smaller figures and brighter colors in the upper half. In Sofonisba Anguissola's Italian Renaissance painting, the placement of the figures is different. The figures on the right are farther away from the center of the painting. Notice how both artists use informal balance.

140   Unit **5**

ART Background

About the Artists

James Tissot (jāmz tē sō, French, 1836–1902), like the Impressionists, recorded the diversions of modern urban life but in a style that retained much of the polish of the academic painting that the Impressionists avoided. Tissot's works are tightly executed and anecdotal in the best sense of this nineteenth-century concept.

Sofonisba Anguissola (sō fa nēz′ bä äng gwēs′ sō lä, Italian, 1532–1625) was internationally famous in her own lifetime when only men achieved such celebrity. She was born into an aristocratic family in Italy. In her early years, she studied with local artists.

About Subject Matter★ The Tissot is a narrative. The Anguissola is a group portrait.

About the Media Both works are oil on canvas.

Sofonisba Anguissola. (Italian). *The Sisters of the Artist and their Governess/A game of chess, involving the painter's three sisters and a servant.* 1555. Oil on canvas. 72 × 97 cm. National Museum Poznan, Poland. Erich Lessing/Art Resource, New York.

Analyze both works of art to better understand informal balance.

- ✓ What are the important figures in each painting?

- ✓ How are the figures in these paintings arranged?

- ✓ Do objects take up one area or several areas in these two works?

- ✓ Where are the darkest and lightest areas in both paintings? How does this placement affect the mood of each?

SEEING LIKE AN ARTIST

Look for an area in your school where the items are arranged using informal balance.

Lesson 2

141

About Art History* *Women of Paris, The Circus Lover* belongs to a series of 18 large paintings entitled *La Femme a Paris* that Tissot created between 1883 and 1885.

Anguissola was a student of Michelangelo and was a court painter to King Philip II of Spain, the sixteenth century's most important patron of the arts. She assumes her rightful place as a key figure in Renaissance art. She created genre paintings long before they were popularized.

Cultural Perspectives Tissot's series records Parisian women of different social classes at various occupations and amusements. The curious gender segregation of the audience in this picture has yet to be explained.

Anguissola remained for almost 20 years as a court painter and close friend of the Spanish royal family. Her work provides a critical link between Italian and Spanish court portraiture.

*See **More About** pages 206–227 for more about art history and subject matter.

FOCUS

Time: About 10 minutes

Activating Prior Knowledge

"What is the best way to arrange three items from your desk?"

"¿Cuál es la mejor manera de ordenar tres objetos de sus pupitres?"

- Discuss the question and have students arrange items using informal balance.

Introducing the Art

"Let's look closely at the painting."

"Vamos a observar detalladamente la pintura."

- For more examples of Anguissola's work or those with similar subjects, see the **National Museum of Women in the Arts Collection CD-ROM.**

- Share and discuss information from **Art Background** and the **Artist Profiles Book.**

- Have students answer the questions on page 141. (See **Perception Hints** below.)

- **COMPARE AND CONTRAST** Have students list the similarities and differences in the two paintings. (The Tissot is a public scene, while the Anguissola is an intimate family scene. Both use informal balance.)

> ### FOR THE ART SPECIALIST
>
> Use the **Overhead** and the **Large Prints** *Path Through the Tall Grass* and *Belt Mask, Court of Benin, Bini Tribe, Nigeria,* to demonstrate that informal balance occurs when two unlike objects in an artwork have equal visual weight.

Perception Hints

Figures *Tissot.* The woman in the audience and the performers. *Anguissola.* The oldest sister.

Arranged Both use informal balance, or asymmetry.

Objects *Tissot.* In the circus, the railing, the chairs, and the fans divide the viewer from the performer. *Anguissola.* The board is in the center. The trees and landscape behind them are dividing the figures.

Dark and light areas *Tissot.* The performing area is the lightest. The foreground and the background where the audience is sitting are the darkest. *Anguissola.* The lightest area is the distance, or the landscape. The faces and hands are also light. The dark area includes the trees in the middle ground. The sister on the right is wearing dark colors. Light areas appear to be placed for special emphasis in both works.

TEACH

Time: About 30 minutes

Practice

"How could you demonstrate informal balance?"

"¿Cómo pueden demostrar equilibrio informal?"

- Discuss informal balance, asymmetry, and negative space on page 142.
- Have the students follow the directions on page 142 for demonstrating informal, or asymmetrical, balance. Have them discuss the answer to the Decide questions.

Create PROBLEM SOLVING

Materials
- white drawing paper
- pencils
- liquid tempera paints
- found objects

Alternate Materials: colored pencils

"Let's create a still-life painting using asymmetrical balance."

"Vamos a crear una pintura de naturaleza muerta usando equilíbrio asimétrico."

- Brainstorm ideas to illustrate informal balance.
- Review procedures for working with liquid tempera paints in **More About Technique Tips** on page 198.
- Distribute materials and have students follow the directions on page 143.
- For safety issues about liquid tempera and other issues about safety in the classroom, see page T22.

Using Informal Balance

Informal balance is a way of organizing parts of a design so that unlike objects have equal visual weight. **Asymmetry** is another name for "informal balance." The **negative space**, or the areas around an object or group of objects, is often larger on one side of an asymmetrical piece than on the other side. There are several ways that artists create asymmetrical balance.

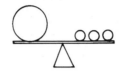 **SIZE:** A large shape or form will appear to be heavier than a small shape. Several small shapes can balance one large shape. To create informal balance, place large shapes closer to the center and small shapes farther away.

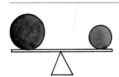 **COLOR:** A brighter color has more visual weight than a dull color.

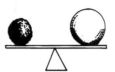 **TEXTURE:** A rough texture has an uneven pattern of highlights and shadows. For this reason, a rough surface attracts the viewer's eyes more easily than a smooth, even surface.

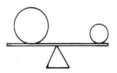 **POSITION:** A large, positive shape and a small, negative space can be balanced by a small, positive shape and a large, negative space.

Practice

Demonstrate informal or asymmetrical balance.

1. Form groups of four or five students. Choose one of the ways that artists use informal or asymmetrical balance.

2. Create a pose with your body to illustrate that particular type of balance. Have your classmates guess which type of balance technique your group is demonstrating.

Decide How did you communicate your technique? What pose did you use to help you communicate your technique?

Activities in
ART Across the Curriculum Book

Reading/Language Arts Learn the differences in the English language between the time of Anguissola's painting and today. (page 151)

Math Solve for missing numbers to make both sides of an equation equal. (page 152)

Science Understand the concepts of force and motion. (page 153)

Social Studies Understand the influence of inventions on people's lives. (page 154)

The Arts Choose a circus performer. Answer questions about their character. (page 155)

Technology Use the *Multimedia Workshop* CD-ROM to create a still life with informal balance. (page 156)

Rachel Young. Age 11. *Potted Plant.* Watercolor.

How did the student artist create balance in the painting?

Create

What are the different types of objects around you that could be used for a still life? Create a still-life painting using asymmetrical balance.

1. Think about arranging an asymmetrically balanced still life. Collect the objects you have selected, then arrange them.

2. Use your thumb and index finger to form a frame around the still life to help you look at only one section of it. Lightly draw your selected section of the still life.

3. Add color and details to your drawing.

Describe What objects or section of the still life did you select to draw? What colors did you use?

Analyze Why did you select that particular area of the still life? How did you arrange the objects on your paper?

Interpret What feeling do you get when you look at your asymmetrical still life? Give it a title.

Decide Does your painting show asymmetrical balance? How?

Lesson 2

143

Tradition Use the Tissot to discuss the tradition of the circus as entertainment.

Origin Use *The Chess Game* to begin a study on the origin of chess.

ESL students in particular can benefit from multiple opportunities to define abstract and difficult concepts. As you describe examples of informal balance around the room, you might refer to key words and phrases written on the chalkboard. Students can also point to the corresponding illustrations in the book.

"Were you able to create a still-life painting using asymmetrical balance?"

"¿Fueron capaces de crear una pintura de naturaleza muerta usando equilibrio asimétrico?"

LARGE PRINT **Review**

Use the **Large Prints** *Path Through the Tall Grass* and *Belt Mask, Court of Benin, Bini Tribe, Nigeria,* to have students compare the use of informal balance to the works in this lesson.

Art Criticism

Have students answer the four art criticism questions—Describe, Analyze, Interpret, and Decide—orally or in writing. Discuss the use of asymmetrical balance in their artworks.

Assess

Use the **Assessment Book** pages 51–52 as a formal assessment for this lesson.

Evaluation Criteria

- Can the student identify informal balance in artworks?
- Can the student create a still-life painting using asymmetrical balance?
- Can the student use the four steps of art criticism to evaluate his or her own artwork?
- Can the student demonstrate knowledge of the lives and work of both artists?

Reteaching • • • • • • • • • • • • •

Asymmetry Have the students find two examples of asymmetry in their environment.

Perception Hints for Student Art

The student artist placed the poinsetta and stand on the right side. She created balance by leaving a large, white space and a strong, horizontal line on the left side.

UNIT 5
LESSON 3

LESSON PLANNER

Objectives
After completing this lesson, students will be able to:
- identify radial balance in works of art. *Aesthetic Perception*
- create a collage design using radial balance. *Creative Expression*
- use the four steps of art criticism to evaluate their own artwork. *Art Criticism*
- recognize the cultural purpose of each work of art. *Art History and Culture*

Program Resources
- **Overhead:** Both the *Ardabil Carpet* and the *Deep Dish from Valencia* are available on overhead 27.
- **Large Prints:** *Path Through the Tall Grass* by Auguste Renoir and *Belt Mask, Court of Benin, Bini Tribe, Nigeria*
- **Vocabulary Book** pages 53–54
- **Artist Profiles Book:** Artists unknown pages 69 and 70
- **Art Across the Curriculum Book** pages 157–162
- **Multimedia Workshop CD-ROM**
- **Assessment Book** pages 53–54

Multiple Intelligences
Interpersonal Students can work together in small groups to create radial designs.

Vocabulary
radial balance *equilibrio radial* when elements of a design are based on a circle with features radiating from the central point

mandala *mandala* a radial design divided into sections or wedges, each of which contains a different image.

Radial Balance

Artists use radial balance to enhance shapes and forms. Radial balance is found in natural objects and objects made by people.

Artist unknown. (Iran). *Ardabil Carpet.* 1540. Wool and silk. $23\frac{1}{2} \times 13$ feet. Los Angeles County Museum of Art, Los Angeles, California. Gift of J. Paul Getty.

Both works of art on these two pages once served as functional pieces. This means they were used and not just admired as works of art. The *Ardabil Carpet* was one of a pair of carpets that was donated as a gift to a royal shrine. It was used within the shrine, possibly as a prayer rug. The *Deep Dish* was once used as a serving bowl. The center section is a replica of a family coat of arms. The designs on both pieces are arranged very similarly. Notice how lines, shapes, and color are used and arranged.

ART Background

About the Artists
Ardabil Carpet and its mate are located in the Victoria and Albert Museum in London. They are among the world's most famous textiles. Both versions are signed and dated by Maqsud of Kashan. It took eight to ten weavers more than three years to tie the 35 million knots that make up this carpet.

About Subject Matter* Both works are symbolic.

About the Media *Ardabil Carpet* is a woven wool-and-silk carpet. *Deep Dish from Valencia* is a ceramic bowl.

Artist unknown. (Spain). *Deep Dish/Spain/from Valencia*. 1430. Tin-glazed earthenware painted in cobalt blue and lustre. 6.7 × 48.2 cm. Hispanic Society of America, New York, New York.

Study both works of art to see examples of radial design.

✓ Where is the center of each design?

✓ Find the shapes that start in the center and repeat as they move away from the center.

✓ Describe the designs you see. How are they arranged?

✓ Can you find where these designs begin and end?

Seeing Like an Artist

What objects have you seen at school or at home that have designs that start in the center and repeat in a circular pattern?

Lesson 3   145

About Art History* The carpet was created during the reign of Shah Tahmasp I, a renowned patron of the arts. The carpet's subtle design, dominated by a large central medallion, is typical of Tabriz work. The artwork is symbolic of a Persian garden because a Muslim believes this symbolizes the pleasures of paradise—physical and spiritual peace in the Muslim world.

Cultural Perspectives The carpet is believed to have been created in Tabriz, which is located in the northwestern part of Iran near the Turkish border. The site of Ardabil was sacred.

The coat of arms represented on the dish is believed to be from the Despujol family of Catalonia. The Catalonians are an ethnic group from Spain. In Spain, the official language is Spanish, but Catalonians also speak their own language of Catalan and have their own flag.

* See **More About** pages 206–227 for more about art history and subject matter.

FOCUS

Time: About 10 minutes

Activating Prior Knowledge

"Imagine that you are riding a Ferris wheel. What do you notice about the wheel's movement, the arrangement of its spokes and cars, and its colors and lights?"

"Imagínense que van en una rueda mágica. ¿Qué observan acerca del movimiento de la rueda, la disposición de los rayos y los carros, y los colores y las luces?"

• Discuss students' responses.

Introducing the Art

"Let's look closely at the art."

"Vamos a observar detalladamente el arte."

• Share and discuss information from **Art Background** and the **Artist Profiles Book**.

• Have students answer the questions on page 145. (See **Perception Hints** below.)

• **COMPARE AND CONTRAST** Have students note the similarities and differences in both works. (Both are functional and use radial design to organize the design. The carpet is woven fiber and used in a religious shrine; the dish is made with fired clay and is used by a family.)

FOR THE ART SPECIALIST

Use the **Overhead** and the **Large Prints** *Belt Mask, Court of Benin, Bini Tribe, Nigeria,* to demonstrate how artists use radial balance to enhance shapes and forms.

Perception Hints

Center *Both*. The radial design or the circle.
Shapes *Carpet*. Free-form, curvy lines. move away. *Deep Dish*. Teardrops, with the points toward the center.
Designs *Deep Dish*. The rim of the plate is dark blue with the imitation of calligraphy.
Ardabil Carpet. The teardrops are radiating.
Arrangement *Both*. They begin in the center and end at the edge.

TEACH

Time: About 30 minutes

Practice

Materials

- found objects in the classroom

"How could you create a radial design?"

"¿Cómo podrían crear un diseño radial?"

- Discuss the definition of *radial balance* and the examples of radial balance found in nature on page 146.
- Assign students to small groups. Have them collect materials and follow the directions on page 146 for creating a radial design. Students should answer the Decide questions in their small groups.

Create PROBLEM SOLVING

Materials

- posterboard
- scissors
- yarn and found objects or pasta shapes
- old magazines
- paper
- glue
- pencils

Alternate Materials: clay

"Let's create a collage that uses radial design."

"Vamos a hacer un collaje que use un diseño radial."

- Have students brainstorm ideas for creating a radial design.
- Distribute materials and have students follow the directions on page 147.

FOR THE ART SPECIALIST

Have students do the project with clay. Have them press or draw objects into the clay, then fire and paint it.

Using Radial Balance

Radial balance occurs when the elements of design (line, shape, color, and form) seem to radiate or come out from a center point. In almost every case, the elements are spaced evenly around the center of the design and create circular patterns.

Radial balance happens frequently in nature. Many plants follow radial patterns of growth. Cut an orange in half and you will see the radial pattern of the segments.

People have imitated nature in many objects by creating radial designs. You often see radial balance in architecture such as stained glass windows. The design always radiates out from a central point. Another example of radial balance is the bicycle wheel.

Practice

Create examples of radial designs using objects found in your classroom.

1. In small groups, collect objects from your desk or room.

2. Using your collected objects, arrange them into a design that has radial balance. Experiment with several arrangements.

Decide Look at all the designs in the class. Which design do you like best? Why?

Activities in
ART Across the Curriculum Book

Reading/Language Arts Edit a paragraph about functional art. (page 157)

Math Study missing parts of a pattern to determine what would fill in the blanks and then draw the missing portion. (page 158)

Science Study flowers that show radial and bilateral symmetry. (page 159)

Social Studies Understand how folk art was created by craftspeople and family members for functional purposes. (page 160)

The Arts Use the "Riddle Song" to learn more about folk music and how its repetitions are similar to a symmetrical work of art. (page 161)

Technology Use the *Multimedia Workshop* CD-ROM to create a design with radial balance. (page 162)

How did the student artist arrange the collage?

Sandy Clemens. Age 11. *My Future.* Marker.

Create

How would you create a balanced design to show your dreams for future? Create a collage design that has radial balance.

1. Think about your dreams of the future. Create a mandala of your dreams. A **mandala** is a radial design divided into sections or wedges, each of which contains a different image.

2. Cut out a round piece of posterboard for the background. Use yarn and found materials to divide the circle into wedges, creating the radial pattern. All wedges should be identical in size and have identical designs for a successful radial design.

3. Draw or cut out from magazines images that represent ideas you have for your future. Glue a different picture into each wedge.

Describe What objects did you use to press shapes into your design? What types of shapes did you use?

Analyze How did you organize your design?

Interpret What does your radial design remind you of? Why?

Decide Do you like the way you used your shapes and lines to create radial balance in your design? Can you think of other ways to create radial balance?

Lesson 3 147

CLOSE

Time: About 5 minutes

"What have you learned about radial design?"
"¿Qué han aprendido acerca de un diseño radial?"

Review
Use the **Large Prints** *Path Through the Tall Grass* and *Belt Mask, Court of Benin, Bini Tribe, Nigeria,* to have students identify radial design. Have them compare the use of radial design in the prints to the artworks in this lesson.

Art Criticism
Have students answer the four art criticism questions—Describe, Analyze, Interpret, and Decide—orally or in writing. Discuss the use of radial design in their artworks.

Assess
Use the **Assessment Book** pages 53–54 as a formal assessment for this lesson.

Evaluation Criteria
• Can the student identify radial balance in works of art?
• Can the student create a collage design using radial balance?
• Can the student use the four steps of art criticism to evaluate his or her own work?
• Can the student recognize the cultural purpose of each work?

Reteaching ● ● ● ● ● ● ● ● ● ● ●

Radial balance Look through a magazine to find examples of radial balance.

Discovery Using the carpet as a springboard, study the discovery and uses of wool.

Celebrations Using *Deep Dish* as a springboard, have students research the most popular celebrations in Spain today.

To help hesitant ESL students gather the knowledge and confidence needed to discuss their artwork with the group, offer rehearsal time with a partner or small group. Rewrite questions as needed in more familiar language and have members of the small group extend ESL students' language as they point out balance techniques in their work.

Perception Hints for Student Art

The student artist arranged the collage using a radial design to break the circle into quarters. Each quarter shows something about her and her desire to teach. The lower right shows what she is good at doing; the lower left that she plans to go to college; the upper right that she wants to teach; the upper left reflects some rewards of teaching.

Perspective Techniques

Perspective techniques help artists make objects appear closer or farther away from the viewer.

Claude Monet. (French). *The Arrival of the Normandy Train at the Gare Saint-Lazare.* 1877. Oil on canvas. $23\frac{1}{2} \times 31\frac{1}{2}$ inches. Art Institute of Chicago, Mr. and Mrs. Martin Ryerson Collection, 1933. Chicago, Illinois.

Claude Monet is one of the greatest French Impressionist painters. Notice how he has portrayed the light and steam in this painting. Lismer grew as an artist when he painted the wild northern landscapes of Canada. He adopted the Impressionistic style for *The Guide's Home Algonquin,* using reflected light and broken brush strokes. Observe how both artists used lines, shapes, and colors.

148   Unit **5**

UNIT 5   LESSON 4

LESSON PLANNER

Objectives

After completing this lesson, students will be able to:

- identify perspective techniques used by artists. *Aesthetic Perception*
- plan and create a fantasy setting for a music video using perspective techniques. *Creative Expression*
- use the four steps of art criticism to evaluate their own artwork. *Art Criticism*
- demonstrate knowledge of the lives and cultures of both artists. *Art History and Culture*

Program Resources

- **Overhead:** Both the Monet and the Lismer are available on overhead 28.
- **Large Prints:** *Path Through the Tall Grass* by Auguste Renoir and *Belt Mask, Court of Benin, Bini Tribe, Nigeria*
- **Vocabulary Book** pages 55–56
- **Artist Profiles Book:** Monet page 38 and Lismer page 31
- **Art Across the Curriculum Book** pages 163–168
- **Multimedia Workshop CD-ROM**
- **Assessment Book** pages 55–56

Multiple Intelligences

Verbal/Linguistic Students can increase their vocabulary and learn about perspective through explanations and discussions.

Vocabulary

perspective *perspectiva* the method used to create the illusion of depth on a flat surface like a drawing or painting

depth *profundidad* the appearance of distance on a flat surface

The following words appear as art in the Student Edition page 150: *overlapping, size, location, detail, lines,* and *color.*

ART Background

About the Artists

Claude Monet (klōd mō nā′, French, 1840–1926) was born in France. Painter Eugene Boudin encouraged Monet to paint. Artists were "supposed" to paint in studios, but Boudin urged Monet to paint outside, in the open air. There, Monet learned to capture his first impressions on canvas. He recorded these impressions during a long and productive life, outliving two wives. His greatest wish was to "mingle more closely with nature." By the time of his death at 86, Monet was blinded by cataracts.

Arthur Lismer (är′ thûr lis′ mər, English, 1885–1969) was born and raised in Sheffield, England. He taught for 50 years in Halifax, Toronto, and Montreal. He is remembered for his work with the many children who attended his classes in Toronto and Montreal.

About Subject Matter* Both works are narratives.

Arthur Lismer. (Canadian). *The Guide's Home Algonquin.* 1914. Oil on canvas. 102.6 × 114.4 cm. National Gallery of Canada. Ottawa, Ontario, Canada.

Study both paintings to see how perspective techniques are used.

- Where is the middle ground of each painting? What objects are painted there?

- What objects are partially covering other objects?

- How do the colors, lines, and shapes change from the foreground to the background of each painting?

- Do you see a set of lines in Monet's work where the lines look like they are getting closer together?

Lesson 4 **149**

SEEING LIKE AN ARTIST

Look across your classroom. How do the objects look that are far away from you? How do those objects look when you get closer to them?

About the Media Both artists used oil on canvas.

About Art History* Monet painted landscapes and people, but he especially loved scenes that included water. Toward the end of his life, Monet painted huge landscapes of the garden and lily ponds he had created near his home in Giverny, France. He was known as the father of Impressionism.

Lismer found it a slow and difficult process to break free from his own background in the European landscape-painting traditions and respond to the rich, wild character of the northern landscape.

Cultural Perspectives Monet's 73-year career was a bridge from true Impressionism to a later, more abstract style, typical of the late water lily paintings.

Lismer attended evening classes at art school while apprenticing as a photoengraver.

* See More About pages 206–227 for more about art history and subject matter.

FOCUS

Time: About 10 minutes

Activating Prior Knowledge

"Imagine that you are standing on the beach looking far out over the water. What do you notice about the sky in relation to the water?"

"Imagínense que están parados en una playa mirando el agua. ¿Qué observan sobre el cielo en relación con el agua?"

- Discuss students' answers to the question. (They may say that the sky and the water appear to meet.)

Introducing the Art

"Let's look closely at the two paintings."

"Vamos a observar detalladamente las dos pinturas."

- Share information from **Art Background** and the **Artist Profiles Book.**

- Have students answer the questions about perspective techniques on page 149. (See **Perception Hints** below.)

- **COMPARE AND CONTRAST** Have students note the similarities and differences in the two works. (Both use deep space. The Monet is an urban scene, and the Lismer is a rural, woodland scene.)

FOR THE ART SPECIALIST

Use the **Overhead** and the **Large Print** *Path Through the Tall Grass* to demonstrate how perspective techniques help artists make objects appear closer or farther away from the viewer.

Perception Hints

Middle ground *Monet.* The middle ground is the train, the crowds, and the lamppost. *Lismer.* The house, the tree stump, and some trees are the middle ground.

Objects *Monet.* The train and the people cover the building in the distance, and the steam covers the roof. *Lismer.* The trees cover the house. The house covers trees in the distance. The stump covers part of the house.

Colors, lines, and shapes *Lismer.* The colors are orange and yellow-orange in the foreground, and in the distance they turn into tints of the same colors. The lines of the edge of the tree trunk are clear in the foreground. In the distance, they are blended together as a mass of foliage. *Monet.* The color, lines, and shapes are darker and more distinct in the foreground than in the background.

Lines In the roof.

TEACH

Time: About 30 minutes

Practice

Materials
- white paper
- pencils

Alternate Materials: colored pencils

"Let's find examples of each perspective technique."

"Vamos a buscar ejemplos de cada una de las técnicas de perspectiva."

- Discuss the definitions of *perspective* and *depth*—and the techniques of overlapping, size, location, detail, lines, and color—on page 150.
- Have students follow the directions on page 150 to discover perspective techniques in the classroom. Have them discuss the answer to the Decide questions.

Create PROBLEM SOLVING

Materials
- white paper
- pencils
- colored markers

Alternate Materials: colored pencils

"Let's use perspective techniques to create a fantasy scene for a music video."

"Vamos a usar técnicas de perspectiva para crear una escena fantástica para un video musical."

- Brainstorm ideas for a fantasy scene.
- Distribute materials and have students follow the directions on page 151.

FOR THE ART SPECIALIST

Have students build a 3-dimensional stage setting for the music video, using action figures.

Using Perspective Techniques

Perspective is the method used to create the illusion of depth on a flat surface, like a drawing or painting. **Depth** is the appearance of distance on a flat surface. There are six different perspective techniques that artists can use to create the feeling of depth.

 OVERLAPPING: When one object partially covers another object, the object in front appears to be closer.

 SIZE: Large objects seem to be closer to the viewer than small objects. The smaller the object, the farther away it appears to be, unless it is placed on top of something large in the front of the picture.

 LOCATION: Objects placed near the bottom of a picture seem to be closer to the viewer. Objects placed near the top of a picture seem to be farther away.

 DETAIL: Objects with clear, sharp edges and details appear to be closer to the viewer. Objects with fuzzy edges and without details seem to be farther away.

 **LINES:** Parallel lines seem to move toward the same point as they move farther away from the viewer.

 **COLOR:** Brightly colored objects seem closer to the viewer. Objects with pale, dull colors seem to be farther away.

Practice

Discover perspective techniques.

1. Look around the classroom. List examples of each perspective technique that you observe.

2. Describe the techniques that you see.

Decide Why do some objects look closer? Why do some objects look larger than others?

Activities in ART Across the Curriculum Book

Reading/Language Arts Identify the viewpoint of a writer when describing an object. Write a similar description using two perspectives. (page 163)

Math Read a train schedule and decide which trains to take in order to make certain appointments. (page 164)

Science Learn about steam power used by trains. (page 165)

Social Studies Use details from Monet's work and your own knowledge to answer questions regarding travel in a steam locomotive. (page 166)

The Arts Create a character like the Algonquin guide. (page 167)

Technology Use the *Multimedia Workshop* CD-ROM to create a landscape scene using perspective techniques. (page 168)

Chris Soto. Age 11. *Because You Love Me.* Marker.

What techniques did the student artist use to create an illusion of depth in the picture?

Create

What are some scenes that come to mind when you hear your favorite song? Design a fantasy setting for a music video using perspective techniques.

1. Think about your favorite song. Make a sketch of a fantasy scene that could be used as the background for a music video.

2. Think about the perspective techniques that create depth. Use at least four of the six perspective techniques in your scene.

3. Add color to your fantasy scene, and title your work. Write the name of the song you were thinking of on the back of your paper.

Describe Describe the lines, shapes, colors, and objects in your fantasy scene.

Analyze Which perspective technique did you use to create depth?

Interpret What mood did you create in your fantasy scene? Does the scene suggest the mood of your song?

Decide Were you successful in creating illusion of depth? What techniques were most effective? Explain.

Lesson **4**   **151**

Models Use the Monet to open a discussion regarding the hobby and popularity of model trains.

Communities Use the Lismer as a springboard to study how communities were organized in northern Canada in the early 1900s.

Complex, written instructions can be confusing for beginning and intermediate ESL students. Try writing a simple sentence and drawing a sketch of the step on the chalkboard. After modeling procedures, students can refer to the board for questions.

CLOSE

Time: About 5 minutes

"Were you able to design a fantasy setting for a music video using perspective techniques?"

"¿Fueron capaces de diseñar un escenario fantástico para un video musical usando las técnicas de perspectiva?"

 Review

Use the **Large Print** *Belt Mask, Court of Benin, Bini Tribe, Nigeria,* to have students identify the perspective techniques used and compare the print to the works in this lesson.

Art Criticism

• Have students answer the four art criticism questions—Describe, Analyze, Interpret, and Decide—orally or in writing. Discuss the use of perspective techniques in their fantasy scenes.

Assess

Use the **Assessment Book** pages 55–56 as a formal assessment for this lesson.

Evaluation Criteria

• Can the student identify perspective techniques used in artworks?

• Can the student use perspective techniques to design a fantasy setting for a music video?

• Can the student use the four steps of art criticism to evaluate his or her own artwork?

• Can the student relate information about the lives and cultures of Monet and Lismer?

Reteaching • • • • • • • • • • • •

Perspective techniques Have students look through magazines to find photographs of landscape paintings. Have students draw lines on the photograph and label the perspective techniques used.

Perception Hints for Student Art

The student artist used color, location, detail, and overlapping to create an illusion of depth. The trees are darker and more detailed than the mountain. Trees are closer to the bottom of the page, and the mountain is the center of the page. People overlap the mountain and buildings on the mountain.

LESSON 4   **151**

Linear Perspective

Artists use linear perspective to create the illusion of depth in a piece of artwork.

Giovanni Paolo Pannini. (Italian). *Interior of St. Peters, Rome.* 1754. Oil on canvas. 60¾ × 77½ inches. National Gallery, Washington, DC. Ailsa Mellon Bruce Fund.
© 1996 Board of Trustees, National Gallery of Art, Washington, DC.

Interior of St. Peters, Rome, was painted by Pannini. He was the first artist to specialize in painting architectural ruins. Edward Hicks used flat forms with clearly defined edges. He was considered a primitive artist. This means he had no formal training. He painted scenes from the Bible, the farm, and historical America. Both artists use similar techniques to make the viewer look into the distance.

152   Unit 5

UNIT 5 LESSON 5

LESSON PLANNER

Objectives

After completing this lesson, students will be able to:

- identify linear perspective techniques used by artists. *Aesthetic Perception*
- create a real or imaginary scene that has the illusion of depth and uses linear perspective. *Creative Expression*
- use the four steps of art criticism to evaluate their own artwork. *Art Criticism*
- compare the lives and cultures of both artists. *Art History and Culture*

Program Resources

- **Overhead:** Both the Pannini and the Hicks are available on overhead 29.
- **Large Prints:** *Path Through the Tall Grass* by Auguste Renoir and *Belt Mask, Court of Benin, Bini Tribe, Nigeria*
- **Vocabulary Book** pages 57–58
- **Artist Profiles Book:** Pannini page 41 and Hicks page 22
- **Art Across the Curriculum Book** pages 169–174
- **Multimedia Workshop CD-ROM**
- **Assessment Book** pages 57–58

Multiple Intelligences

Logical/Mathematical Students can learn linear perspective using measurements, rulers, and other math tools and skills.

Vocabulary

perspective *perspectiva* the method used to create the illusion of depth on a flat surface

linear perspective *perspectiva lineal* the use of lines to show distance and depth

horizon line *línea de horizonte* the point at which Earth and the sky meet

vanishing point *punto de la vista* a point on the horizon where all the lines moving back into space meet

---

ART Background

About the Artists

Edward Hicks (ed' wərd hiks, American, 1780–1849) was the leading folk, or naive, artist of the first half of the 1800s. An untutored artisan, he was apprenticed to a coach maker at the age of 13 and later set up his own successful workshop for the painting of signs, clocks, furniture, and other utilitarian items.

Giovanni Pannini (jō vän' nē pän nē' nē', Italian, 1692–1765) probably received his first painting lesson in his hometown of Piacenza, Italy, while still very young. He moved to Rome in 1711 for more art training. Pannini painted several pictures in Rome and its inns, which quickly became popular among tourists and art collectors.

About Subject Matter* Pannini often exaggerated proportions and lighting to enhance the awe of real-life scenes. Hicks's work is a landscape.

About the Media Both works are oil on canvas.

Edward Hicks. (American). *Cornell Farm*. 1848. Oil on canvas. $36\frac{3}{4} \times 49$ inches. National Gallery of Art, Washington, DC. Gift of Edgar William and Bernice Chrysler Garbisch, © 1996 Board of Trustees, National Gallery of Art, Washington DC.

Analyze both paintings to discover linear perspective.

- ✓ Follow the lines of the walls and fields that lead to the area that looks farthest away from the viewer.

- ✓ What types of shapes are repeated in each painting? What happens to these shapes the farther away they become?

- ✓ Find objects in both paintings that overlap.

- ✓ Where are the largest and smallest objects?

- ✓ Describe the use of details in both works of art.

SEEING LIKE AN ARTIST

What does a road look like as you move away from it in a car? Does the road really get smaller?

Lesson 5

153

Activating Prior Knowledge

"Imagine looking down a long tunnel. What do you see? How big is the opening of the tunnel?"

"Imagínense que ven hacia un túnel. ¿Qué observan? ¿De qué tamaño es la boca del túnel?"

- Discuss with students how the imaginary lines of the tunnel meet at a single point in a one-point perspective.

Introducing the Art

"Let's look closely at the two paintings."

"Vamos a observar detalladamente las dos pinturas."

- Share and discuss information from **Art Background** and the **Artist Profiles Book.**

- Have students answer the questions on page 153. (See **Perception Hints** below.)

- **COMPARE AND CONTRAST** Have students note the similarities and differences in the two paintings. (Both use receding lines or one-point perspective. Pannini's is an interior scene by a skilled professional, and Hicks's is an outdoor scene by a primitive, or untrained, artist.)

FOR THE ART SPECIALIST

Use the **Overhead** and the **Large Print** *Path Through the Tall Grass* to demonstrate how artists use linear perspective to create the illusion of depth in a piece of artwork.

About Art History* Pannini combined the classical Baroque art of his times with the beginnings of Romanticism. He often painted things as he wished they were. He taught perspective, and one of his students, Hubert Robert, also became well known.

After Hicks became a Quaker preacher, he painted canvases illustrating scenes from the Scriptures. His principal subject was the *Peaceable Kingdom.* There are 40 versions of this work. In them, the background always includes a scene of the Quaker colonist William Penn making a peace treaty with the Native Americans.

Cultural Perspectives As Pannini's art became popular, he hired assistants to help him keep up with the demand. Many young artists did this to learn from established painters.

Edward Hicks was involved in a separatist faction within the Society of Friends. His paintings were "sermons" about living peacefully together.

*See **More About** pages 206–227 for more about art history and subject matter.

Perception Hints

Lines *Pannini.* The lines seem to meet in the center of the farthest arc. *Hicks.* The horizon line seems most distant.

Shapes *Pannini.* Geometric shapes are repeated in the picture frames. The people are free-form shapes and get smaller. *Hicks.* The animals in the foreground are repeated. The people are repeated free-form shapes. All the shapes get smaller the farther away they become.

Overlapping *Pannini.* The people and the columns overlap. *Hicks.* The animals, trees, and houses overlap.

Largest and smallest In each painting, the largest object is in the foreground, and the smallest object is in the background.

Details Details in the foreground are very sharp in both works. The edges are clear. *Pannini.* You can almost recognize the paintings in the foreground. *Hicks.* You can see the hair on the horse and the eyes on the animals.

Time: About 30 minutes

Practice

"Were you able to see linear perspective?"

"¿Fueron capaces de ver la perspectiva lineal?"

• Discuss the definition of *linear perspective* on page 154.

• Have students follow the directions on page 154 for seeing linear perspective. Have students discuss the answer to the Decide questions.

Create PROBLEM SOLVING

Materials
  • white drawing paper
  • pencils
  • watercolor paints
  Alternate Materials: felt-tip pens

"Let's create a real or imaginary scene using linear perspective."

"Vamos a crear una escena real o imaginaria usando la perspectiva lineal."

• Brainstorm ideas for a real or imaginary scene that has the illusion of depth. Such places might include a train station, a carnival, an island, and a faraway planet.

• Review **More About Technique Tips** on page 199 for working with watercolors.

• Distribute materials and have students follow the directions on page 155.

FOR THE ART SPECIALIST

Have students sketch with chalk and paint with school acrylics.

Using Linear Perspective

Perspective is the method used to create the illusion of depth on a flat surface. Often when artists want to make viewers think they are looking at an object moving back into space, they use one-point linear perspective.

Linear perspective is one way of using lines to show distance and depth. All lines that move back into space meet at a single point in one-point perspective.

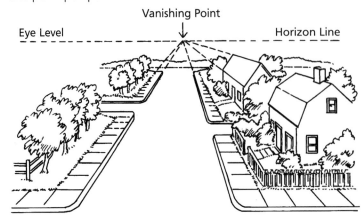

Eye Level　　　Vanishing Point　　　Horizon Line

The **horizon line** is the point at which the earth and sky meet. In the example above, the horizon line is at eye level.

The **vanishing point** is the point on the horizon line where all the lines moving back into space meet. Can you find the vanishing point in Panini's painting?

Practice

Practice seeing linear perspective.

1. Look down the end of a hallway to the farthest possible point. Close one eye and raise your index fingers to the lines where the wall and ceiling meet. Move your fingers along those lines until they reach the end of the hall. Notice how your arms move down to eye level.

2. Do this again, pointing to the lines where the walls meet the floor. How did your arms move?

Describe What did you observe when doing this sighting technique? Where did your hands meet? Do you see how linear perspective is created?

Activities in
ART Across the Curriculum Book

Reading/Language Arts Write a journal entry about spending a day on Cornell's farm, putting the day's events in chronological order. (page 169)

Math Learn about planning fractions of a garden. (page 170)

Science Imagine how the farm in the painting has changed in 150 years. Include changes in buildings, land, machinery, and technology. (page 171)

Social Studies Learn how cultural values are reflected in architecture. (page 172)

The Arts Learn how songs and paintings can describe a time and place. (page 173)

Technology Use the *Multimedia Workshop* CD-ROM to draw a scene using linear perspective techniques. (page 174)

Hoshi Min. Age 11. *Beautiful Florida*. Marker.

What objects are clues to finding the vanishing point in the student artwork?

Create

How can you use linear perspective in a real or imaginary scene? Draw a real or imaginary scene that has the illusion of depth. Include at least one building that uses linear perspective.

1. Think of a real or imaginary place. Make several sketches of objects you want to include in your scene. Include at least one building.

2. Lightly draw a horizon line and mark a point on it where the lines will meet. Draw at least four lines coming out from the point on the horizon line. This is the vanishing point. Using these guidelines, draw the building first, then the other objects. Make the objects touch the top and bottom of the guidelines.

3. Paint your drawing.

Describe Did you draw a real or imaginary scene? What objects did you include in your scene?

Analyze How did you use linear perspective in your work?

Interpret What objects communicate the kind of scene you created? Give your work a title.

Decide How could you apply the technique of linear perspective to another drawing?

Lesson 5   155

THEME Connections

Change Use *Cornell Farm* to begin a class study of the changes in the family farm in the last 75 years.

Discovery Use Pannini's work to discover and identify the many architectural ruins of Rome.

ESL

You can help second-language learners bridge the gap between more the formal, academic language presented in the text and the informal, conversational language to which they may be more accustomed. As you read instructions and explanations aloud, embellish them with descriptions and examples in colloquial and informal language.

CLOSE

Time: About 5 minutes

"Were you able to create a real or imaginary scene using linear perspective?"

"¿Fueron capaces de crear una escena real o imaginaria usando la perspectiva lineal?"

LARGE PRINT **Review**

Use the **Large Print** *Belt Mask, Court of Benin, Bini Tribe, Nigeria,* to have students compare the uses of linear perspective to the works in this lesson.

Art Criticism

Have students answer the four art criticism questions—Describe, Analyze, Interpret, and Decide—orally or in writing. Discuss the use of linear perspective in their artwork.

♦ **Assess**

Use the **Assessment Book** pages 57–58 as a formal assessment for this lesson.

Evaluation Criteria

• Can the student identify linear perspective used in artwork?

• Can the student create a real or imaginary scene that has the illusion of depth and uses linear perspective?

• Can the student use the four steps of art criticism to evaluate his or her own artwork?

• Can the student compare the lives and cultures of Pannini and Hicks?

Reteaching ● ● ● ● ● ● ● ● ● ●

Linear perspective Ask the students to find examples of linear perspective in other artwork in their books.

Perception Hints for Student Art

The objects that are clues to finding the vanishing point in the student artwork include the fence, the palm trees, and the boats. All lead to a vanishing point.

UNIT 5
LESSON 6

Point of View and Direct Observation

Artists will often study an object from different points of view before creating an artwork.

LESSON PLANNER

Objectives

After completing this lesson, students will be able to:

- identify point of view and direct observation in works of art. *Aesthetic Perception*
- create a drawing of an object from three different points of view. *Creative Perception*
- use the four steps of art criticism to evaluate their own artwork. *Art Criticism*
- demonstrate a knowledge of the lives and work of both artists. *Art History and Culture*

Program Resources

- **Overhead:** Both the Hopper and the Sheeler are available on overhead 30.
- **Large Prints:** *Path Through the Tall Grass* by Auguste Renoir and *Belt Mask, Court of Benin, Bini Tribe, Nigeria*
- **Vocabulary Book** pages 59–60
- **Artist Profiles Book:** Hopper page 23 and Sheeler page 50
- **Art Across the Curriculum Book** pages 175–180
- **Multimedia Workshop CD-ROM**
- **Assessment Book** pages 59–60

Multiple Intelligences

Intrapersonal Students can enrich their knowledge of point of view in art by comparing it to personal points of view. You might ask them to think about how their point of view on a certain subject has changed from the fourth grade to the fifth grade.

Vocabulary

point of view *punto de vista* the angle from which you see an object or scene

direct observation *observación directa* when an artist studies an object from various viewpoints and looks closely at the important details and records them in his or her drawings

Edward Hopper. (American). *House by the Railroad.* 1925. Oil on canvas. 24 × 29 inches. The Museum of Modern Art, New York, New York. Given anonymously. © 1998.

Notice how both artists created images from different angles. *House by the Railroad* was painted during a time of migration from farms to the cities. Charles Sheeler is best known for his simplified paintings of industrial landscapes. He uses simple shapes and flat colors. Can you tell where each artist is standing in relation to his work?

Unit **5**

ART Background

About the Artists

Edward Hopper (ed′ wərd häp′ ər, American, 1882–1967) was a giant of American art. He is considered a major twentieth-century realist. His work seems to embody the very character of our time. He was born in upstate New York and worked as a commercial artist for many years. He loved the simple architecture of New England.

Charles Sheeler (chärlz shē′ lər, American, 1883–1965) was a painter and photographer in the precisionist style. He was born in Philadelphia and educated at the School of Industrial Art and at the Pennsylvania Academy of the Fine Arts.

About Subject Matter* The Hopper is a landscape, and The Sheeler is an interiorscape.

About the Media Hopper's work is oil on canvas. Light was important in Sheeler's work. He used light to create harmony.

Charles Sheeler. (American). *American Interior.* 1934. Oil on canvas. $32\frac{1}{2}$ x 30 inches. Yale Art Gallery. Gift of Mrs. Paul Moore.

Study both paintings for their use of viewpoint.

- Where are you in relation to the paintings? Are you looking up at the paintings, down onto the paintings, or directly at the paintings?

- Do the shapes and lines look like they are drawn from a particular angle? How does this affect the use of shadows?

- Why do you think each artist chose to create his painting from these angles?

SEEING LIKE AN ARTIST

Hold up this book and look at it from different angles. What happens to the shape, shadows, and lines?

Lesson 6 157

About Art History* Many American artists painted large canvases showing the grandeur of America's unspoiled wilderness. Hopper wanted to show another side of America, the sense of loneliness, emptiness, and alienation.

Sheeler was influenced by the highly structured work of Paul Cézanne and the Cubists. He developed his own precisionist style combining the naturalistic and the abstract.

Cultural Perspectives Hopper's paintings are not dominated by people. Rather, the solitary figures in his painting are dominated by the space in which they sit or stand.

American Interior reflects Sheeler's house in South Salem, New York. The painting pays homage to the unpretentious American-made objects. It suggests that this sort of simple interior represents the best of American values.

* See **More About** pages 206–227 for more about art history and subject matter.

F OCUS

Time: About 20 minutes

Activating Prior Knowledge

"What do you see when standing in front of your school? What do you see when you move ten feet back?"

"¿Qué ven cuando se paran frente a la escuela? ¿Qué ven cuando retroceden 10 pies?"

- Discuss students' responses.

Introducing the Art

"Let's look closely at the two paintings."

"Vamos a observar detalladamente las dos pinturas."

- **Describe:** Have students describe the subject matter in each painting. (Hopper: landscape; Sheeler: interiorscape)

- Share and discuss information from **Art Background** and the **Artist Profiles Book.**

- Have students answer the questions on page 157. (See **Perception Hints** below.)

- **COMPARE AND CONTRAST** Have students note the similarities and differences in the two paintings. (Both use unusual viewpoints. Both are paintings. Hopper's is an outdoor scene, while Sheeler's is an interior scene.)

FOR THE ART SPECIALIST

Use the **Overhead** and the **Large Prints** *Path through the Tall Grass* and *Belt Mask, Court of Benin, Bini Tribe, Nigeria,* to demonstrate how artists will often study an object from different points of view before creating an artwork.

Perception Hints

Point of view *Hopper.* Looking up at the railroad tracks and the house. *Sheeler.* Looking down from the ceiling.
Shapes and lines Yes, the Hopper is drawn as if he viewer is standing below, and the Sheeler is dawn as if the viewer is above. The shadows appear with the point of view.
Create *Hopper.* Chose to create his painting from a certain angle to create a mood of loneliness. *Sheeler.* Wanted us to think about interiors in a different way.

TEACH

Time: About 30 minutes

Practice

"Describe an object from one point of view."

"Describan un objeto desde un punto de vista."

- Discuss point of view and direct observation on page 158.
- Have students follow the directions on page 158 for describing an object from one viewpoint. Have them discuss the answer to the Decide questions.

Create PROBLEM SOLVING

Materials

- white drawing paper
- colored markers

Alternate Materials: pencils or felt-tip markers

"Let's create a drawing of an object from three different points of view."

"Vamos a hacer un dibujo de un objeto desde tres diferentes puntos de vista."

- Have students discuss points of view and direct observation.
- Have students look for an object in the classroom to draw.
- Distribute materials and have students follow directions on page 159.

Using Point of View and Direct Observation

Point of view is the angle from which you see an object or scene. Depending on the point of view, the way you perceive, or see, an object can change. There are four common points of view. Notice how your perception changes as you look at the same object from various points of view.

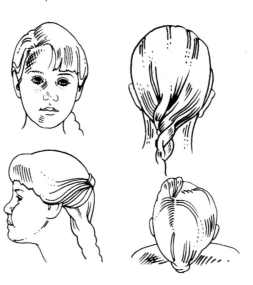

Often artists study an object from various viewpoints. They look closely at the important details and record them in their drawings. This approach is called **direct observation**.

Practice

Select one object and describe it from one viewpoint.

1. Working in small groups, take turns selecting one object from the classroom and describing what it looks like from your viewpoint.

2. Use the elements of art, shape, line, and texture to help you describe your object. Let the group guess what your object is.

Decide Could your friends tell what you were describing? Were they able to guess which angle you were viewing the object from?

Activities in
ART Across the Curriculum Book

Reading/Language Arts Write descriptions of a painting from the perspective of different objects in *House by the Railroad* and *American Interior*. (page 175)

Math Identify geometric forms of objects from different perspectives. (page 176)

Science Learn about levels of sound, thinking of a train passing the house. (page 177)

Social Studies Use a bar graph and time line to answer questions regarding the railroads and expansion of the United States. (page 178)

The Arts Study the words and rhythms of American songs describing the railroad. (page 179)

Technology Use the *Multimedia Workshop* CD-ROM to draw a scene from different points of view. (page 180)

Larry Vaughn. Age 11. *Softball.* Colored pencil.

What are the changes in the point of view in the student artwork?

Create

How does shape change as you change your point of view? Create one drawing of an object from three different points of view.

1. Think about how an object looks from different points of view. Notice how the shadows and shapes of an object change when you are looking at it from different points of view.

2. Draw an object from three points of view.

Describe Describe the object that you observed and the details you noticed.

Analyze What three points of view did you select? Why?

Interpret Give your work a title.

Decide How does drawing an object from more than one point of view change your understanding of the object?

Lesson **6**

159

"Were you able to draw an object from three different points of view?"

"¿Fueron capaces de dibujar un objeto desde tres diferentes puntos de vista?"

 Review
Use the **Overhead** and the **Large Prints** *Path through the Tall Grass* and *Belt Mask, Court of Benin, Bini Tribe, Nigeria,* to have students compare the points of view in the artwork.

Art Criticism
Have students answer the four art criticism questions—Describe, Analyze, Interpret, and Decide—orally or in writing. Discuss the use of point of view in their drawings after they are completed.

 Assess
Use the **Assessment Book** pages 59–60 as a formal assessment for this lesson.

Evaluation Criteria
• Can the student identify points of view and direct observation in works of art?
• Can the student create a drawing of an object from three different points of view?
• Can the student use the four steps of art criticism to evaluate his or her own artwork?
• Can the student demonstrate knowledge of the lives and works of both artists?

Reteaching • • • • • • • • • • •

Point of view Find two more artworks in the book with similar points of view as Hopper's and Sheeler's.

Energy Use Hopper's work to discuss energy-saving methods to heat the house in the artwork.
Traditions Use *American Interior* as a means of beginning a discussion of the traditions of the American family of 50 years ago versus the traditions of the current American family.

Some ESL students may need oral practice before they are ready to write detailed descriptions as in the Practice section. Consider pairing beginning- or intermediate-level learners with more confident writers and have students work in pairs to create their written descriptions.

Perception Hints for Student Art
The changes in the point of view in the student artwork involve the softball seams and shadowing.

UNIT 5

LESSON PLANNER

Objectives

After completing this lesson, students will be able to:

- translate visual symbols into movement designs. *Aesthetic Perception*
- express individual and group interpretation in creating symbols for a sun dance. *Creative Expression*
- use the four steps of art criticism to evaluate the balance and perspective of sun designs. *Art Criticism*
- describe how the Ballet Folklorico de Mexico uses movement and costumes in the sun dances. *Art History and Culture*

FOCUS

Time: About 10 minutes

Activating Prior Knowledge

"Think about folk dances you have seen performed by groups from Mexico or other nations. What kinds of feelings or ideas did the dancers express?"

"Piensen acerca de los bailes folclóricos ejecutados por grupos de México u otras naciones. ¿Qué tipos de sentimientos o ideas expresan los bailarines?"

- Discuss students' answers and talk about how the movements of a dance can express feelings and ideas about the natural world.

Introducing the Art

"Look at the photograph of the Ballet Folklorico de Mexico. How do the dancers' costumes and postures remind you of the sun?"

"Observen la fotografía del Ballet Folclórico de México. ¿Cómo los trajes y las posturas de los bailarines les hacen recordar al sol?"

- Discuss students' responses. Point out the importance of the sun in Aztec and Mayan cultures and explain that the sun is featured in much of Mexican folk art.
- Share with students some of the information in **Art Background** about Amalia Hernández, the choreographer, and the ancient cultural dances of Mexico. If you have the *Artsource* video, have students view the dance by the Ballet Folklorico de Mexico.

160   **Unit 5**

Balance and Perspective in Dance

"Los Concheros": *Ballet Folklorico de Mexico.*

In ancient cultures, people performed folk dances that connected them to life and the universe. They used dance movements as symbols of things in nature such as the moon and the sun. In their folk dances, they achieved balance through repetition of lines and forms. They showed depth through their movements.

ART Background

About the Artist

At the age of eight, Amalia Hernández decided to make dance her life's work. Her parents supported her interest, designing a private course of study for Amalia and her two sisters. The study of classical dance forms gave Amalia a strong technical foundation, but she was more interested in the folk music and dance of her country. She has presented authentic folk dances from different Mexican ethnic groups for more than 25 years. She has also created exciting new dances based on ancient traditions.

About Subject Matter
Amalia Hernández has said, "Folklore all over the world is alive and influenced by its changing surroundings." In researching a piece, she goes to the geographic source of the folklore, then shapes the work to communicate her perception. The music for her ancient dances is inspired by ancient texts.

What To Do

Create dance designs that are symbols of the sun.

Materials

✓ a variety of symbols and designs based on the image of the sun

1. Look at the different symbols or designs of the sun. In each work, notice the use of balance and perspective.

2. Brainstorm elements of these works that could be shown in a dance design.

3. With a group, explore ways that you can use the shapes and lines of your bodies to create symbols of the sun.

4. Select three of your best designs, and put them in an interesting sequence.

5. Perform your designs for other groups.

Describe Describe the main design elements that you used in creating your sun dance.

Analyze Explain how you used balance and depth in your dance.

Interpret How did your dance portray the sun expressively?

Decide How well did you succeed in capturing the image of the sun? What would you change if you did this again?

Extra Credit

Add sounds to your dance with percussion instruments, such as a gong, drum, woodblock, finger cymbals, and shakers.

Dance 161

Cultural Perspectives Between the time of the Olmec Indians and the birth of modern Mexico, more than 30 distinct cultures have flourished, each influencing Mexican culture before being supplanted by another. Amalia Hernández created one dance called "Los Mitos," which means "the myths." It features the pageantry and ritual of indigenous cultures before the arrival of the Spaniards.

About Dance Dance is a form of expression that has been shaped and formed by each culture. It builds upon the dances of previous generations and will, in turn, be used by future generations as the basis for their dances. Dance reflects the beliefs, values, and myths of each culture, as well as the artistic choices.

TEACH

Time: Two 30-minute periods

Materials

• a variety of symbols and designs based on the image of the sun

"Let's look at the way in which different artists have created symbols or designs inspired by the sun and create our own sun dance."

"Vamos a observar la manera en que diferentes artistas han creado símbolos o diseños inspirados en el sol y crear nuestro propio baile solar."

• Have students brainstorm elements of the sun that could be shown in dance designs. Ideas might include rays, symmetry, or round shapes.

• Form students into groups of four or five. Tell them to try several movements that have variation in levels. Encourage them to convey the feeling of exploding energy.

• For transitions in the sequences, students can add stretching, turning, falling-in-slow-motion, and rising-upward movements.

CLOSE

Time: About 5 minutes

"What would you add to or change about your group work?"

"¿Qué le agregarían o cambiarían a sus grupos de trabajo?"

Assess

Have students answer the four art criticism questions on page 161—Describe, Analyze, Interpret, and Decide—orally or in writing.

Evaluation Criteria

• Can the student translate visual symbols into movement designs?

• Can the student express individual and group interpretations in creating symbols for a sun dance?

• Can the student use the four steps of art criticism to evaluate his or her own performance?

• Can the student demonstrate knowledge of how the Ballet Folklorico de Mexico uses costumes and movements in their sun dances?

U NIT 5

Reviewing Unit Concepts

"Artists use balance to arrange the elements of art and perspective to create depth in a work of art."

"Los artistas usan el equilibrio para ordenar los elementos artísticos y la perspectiva para crear profundidad en una obra de arte."

- Review how artists use balance and perspective as discussed on page 162.
- Have students create a list of examples from the text of how artists use balance and perspective.

Examining the Artwork

"How did the artist use balance and perspective in his painting?"

"¿Cómo usó el artista el equilibrio y la perspectiva en su pintura?"

- Have students look at Caillebotte's work and answer the questions on page 163.
  (See **Perception Hints** below.)

Student Portfolio

Have students review the artwork created during this unit and select the pieces they wish to keep in their portfolios.

Art Criticism

Have students select an artwork from another unit and study it using the four steps of art criticism. (See pages 206–209 for more information about Art Criticism.)

Perception Hints

Balance The type of balance used in the painting is asymmetrical or informal balance. The street lamp in the middle ground divides the picture into halves. The figures of the people on the right are large and take up half of the painting. The large buildings in the background on the left take up almost the same amount of room so the two balance each other. Although these are unlike objects, they both have equal visual weight.

Perspective Caillebotte used all six perspective techniques to create the illusion of depth. The people in the foreground overlap the buildings in the background and are larger with more detail than the people painted smaller and farther back in the painting. All of the lines move toward two vanishing points. They are on either side of the large building on the left in the background. The darker, more vivid colors are in the front, right side of the painting.

Balance and Perspective

Reviewing Main Ideas

The lessons and activities in this unit cover the techniques that artists use to create balance and perspective.

- **Balance** — A principal of design that deals with arranging visual elements equally in a work of art. There are two types of balance.
  1. **Formal or symmetrical balance** occurs when equal, or very similar, elements are placed on opposite sides of a central line called an axis.
  2. **Radial balance** occurs when the elements of design seem to radiate or come out of a center point.
  3. **Informal or asymmetrical balance** is a balance of unlike objects. It is a way of organizing part of a design so that unlike objects have equal visual weight. It is not exactly the same on both sides.
- **Depth** is the appearance of distance on a flat surface.
- **Perspective** is the method used to create the illusion of depth on a flat surface.

Gustave Caillebotte. (French). *Paris Street Rainy Day.* 1876–1877. Oil on canvas. 212.2 × 276.2 cm. Art Institute of Chicago, Chicago, Illinois. Charles H. and Mary F. S. Worcester Collection.

ART Background

About the Artist

Gustave Caillebotte (gūs′ täv kā″ yə bôt′, French, 1848–1894) was born into a wealthy family. He earned a degree in law and was then drafted into the French army. He was attracted to the artistic rebels of his time, the Impressionists. He had inherited a fortune from his family and helped support other Impressionists by buying their work. Caillebotte later moved from Paris to a French village.

About Subject Matter* The work may be considered a cityscape.

About the Media The work is done in oils.

There are six perspective techniques: overlapping, size, location, detail, lines, and color.

- **One-point perspective** is when lines move back into space and meet at a single point to show distance and depth on a two-dimensional surface.
- **Horizon line** is the point at which the earth and sky meet.
- **Vanishing point** is the point on the horizon line where all the lines moving back into space meet.
- **Point of view** is the angle from which you see an object or scene. There are four common points of view: front, side, back, and overhead.

Summing Up

Look at *Paris Street, Rainy Day* by Gustave Caillebotte. In this painting, he used the techniques of creating balance and perspective covered in this unit.

- Explain the type of balance the artist used in the painting.
- Did Caillebotte use all six perspective techniques? Give examples of each perspective technique he used.

Balance and perspective are important elements in paintings and drawings. With balance and perspective, Caillebotte and other artists are able to arrange visual elements so that they are pleasing to the eye and create the illusion of depth.

Let's Visit a Museum

The Art Institute of Chicago was originally called the Chicago Academy of Fine Arts when it was established in 1879. Today, its membership is 150,000, the highest of any art museum in the country. Its collection has more than 225,000 works of art. There are ten different departments and galleries. The museum is known for its architectural displays and collection of French Impressionist works. A large part of the museum is a school. People from all over the world attend classes in photography, painting, fashion design, and other visual arts.

The Art Institute of Chicago

163

Learning About Museums

The Art Institute of Chicago was established in 1879 as the Chicago Academy of Fine Arts, and it changed its name in 1882. It is known for its architectural displays and collection of French Impressionist works. Its collections include 225,000 objects, and its membership—150,000—is the highest of any museum in the United States. The library of The Art Institute of Chicago, a research collection of national and international significance, is the second largest museum library in the U.S. The school of the Institute is accredited to confer the Bachelor and Masters of Fine Arts Degrees.

- Have students describe a museum where they would want their work to be exhibited. They should give the location and the types of works the museum would specialize in.

TIMELINE For more information on this and other museums, see pages T13, T30–T33, and the back of the **Animals Through History Time Line.**

A Final Thought

"I believe that if it were left to artists to choose their own labels, most would choose none."—Ben Shahn

About Art History* First painting in a French Realist style, Caillebotte soon began to use light and shade in an Impressionistic way. He was deeply influenced by his friends Degas, Renoir, and Monet.

Cultural Perspectives Impressionism was a reaction against academic traditions where art was created mostly in the studio. This group concentrated on the reaction of light and atmosphere on different objects.

*See **More About** pages 206–227 for more about art history and subject matter.

UNIT 6

UNIT OVERVIEW

This unit covers emphasis, variety, harmony, and unity. Emphasis is used to draw attention to an area in a work of art, variety adds interest to the artwork, harmony is concerned with similarities of separate but related parts, and unity brings all of the elements together in an artwork. The specific topics in this unit are **emphasis, focal point, variety, harmony,** and **unity.**

Emphasis stresses one area of an artwork. It is covered in Lessons 1 and 2.

Focal point refers to the area that is emphasized. Lesson 2 is about focal point.

Variety is the principle of design concerned with difference or contrast. Lesson 3 covers variety.

Harmony is concerned with similarities of separate but related parts. The focus of Lesson 4 is harmony.

Unity is the quality of wholeness or oneness that is achieved through the effective use of the elements and principles of art. Both Lessons 5 and 6 are based on unity.

Introducing Unit Concepts

"Artists use the art principles of emphasis, variety, harmony, and unity in all kinds of art."

"Los artistas usan los principios artísticos de el énfasis, la variedad, la armonía y la unidad en todos los tipos de arte."

Emphasis and Focal Point
- Read the definitions of *emphasis, variety, harmony,* and *unity.*

- Have several students wearing the same colors of clothing stand in the front of the class. Select one student who has on clothing that is a different color, preferably brighter, to stand up with the group. Have the class close their eyes and open them, noting which student stands out. Discuss the answers.

- Have the students point out examples of harmony in the room (repeated shapes and colors, like the desks, color of the walls, and so on).

- Have students create a still life of a variety of objects in the same color scheme. Explain that it is interesting because it has a variety of objects, but it works together or harmonizes because of like colors.

164   **Unit 6**

An Introduction to
Emphasis, Variety, Harmony, and Unity

Artists sometimes use emphasis, variety, harmony, and unity in paintings and sculptural forms.

John Biggers. (American). *Shotguns Fourth Ward.* 1987. Acrylic and oil on board. $41\frac{3}{4} \times 32$ inches. Hampton University Museum, Hampton, Virginia.

164   **Unit 6**

ART Background

About the Artist

John Biggers (jon big' ərs, American, 1924–) was born in Gastonia, North Carolina. Much of his work explores the role of elders and the young, of men and of women, and the meaning of family and community to the African American. He borrows on the African traditions of storytelling, rituals, dress, and quilting and incorporates these images into his intricate paintings. He teaches at Texas Southern University.

About Subject Matter* Biggers created a series of shotgun houses in 1987. Shotgun houses have a long hall down the middle with a door at each end and rooms on each side of the hall. His paintings illustrate the African-influenced architecture that was so common during the first half of the twentieth century.**About the Media** *Shotgun, Fourth Ward* is an acrylic and oil painting on board. Biggers mixes the two paint mediums to gain better precision and to have a wide range of color.

Emphasis is used by artists to attract attention to a certain area in a piece of artwork.

- What area of this painting do you see first?

Variety is used to make a drawing or painting more interesting.

- What shapes, lines, and colors are used more than once in this painting?

Artists sometimes use variety and **harmony** to create unity in a work of art.

- What element of this painting gives you a feeling of oneness and wholeness?

Artist Profile

John Biggers
1924–

John Biggers was born in Gastonia, North Carolina. He gives his parents the credit for encouraging his interest in human nature and for his ability to see beauty in almost anything. He first entered college to study heating and engineering, but a teacher inspired him to change his major to art. In addition to his work as an artist, he has also made important contributions as an art educator. His artworks include painting, sculpture, and murals.

John Biggers and other artists use emphasis, variety, harmony, and unity to attract attention to certain art elements, make a work of art more interesting, and create oneness or wholeness within a work of art. In this unit you will learn and practice the techniques that artists use. Here are the topics you will study.

- Emphasis   • Focal Point   • Variety   • Unity   • Harmony

165

- Have students write a short description of unity in nature.

📼 Use the **Video** *Meet the Caldecot Illustrator: Jerry Pinkney* to discuss the life of Jerry Pinkney and his inspiration.

Examining the Artwork

"Let's look more closely at the artwork."
"Vamos a observar más detalladamente la obra de arte."

- Read and discuss the definitions of *emphasis, variety, harmony,* and *unity.* Have the students answer the questions on page 165.
(See **Perception Hints** below.)

Artist Profile

Share with students information about the artist, including the photograph.

🎨 You may wish to encourage students to practice art concepts and record ideas from lesson to lesson in their **Art Journals.**

About Music

Harmony in music refers to different pitches played or sung at the same time, producing chords. Have students play combinations of three pitches with one pitch in between them (C–D–E) and observe the inharmonious effect. *Unity* and *variety* are much of what gives each composition identity and character. Have students sing a song or listen to a recording and hear what seems to create unity and variety (repeated and contrasting melodies, rhythm patterns, speeds, and so on).

About Art History* John Biggers was greatly influenced by many of the murals that were created during the Works Progress Administration (WPA) between 1935 and 1943. Many artists created murals for public buildings and depicted the American scene or social protest during this time.

Cultural Perspectives The 1930s was the decade of the Depression, the beginning of World War II, and President Franklin D. Roosevelt's New Deal. The New Deal (1933–1939) was created to give relief, recovery, and reform to help solve the economic problems created due to the Depression. Its aims were to prevent future economic crises through reforms and guarantee a minimum standard.

*See **More About** pages 206–227 for more about art history and subject matter.

UNIT 6 Planning Guide

Lesson	Lesson Title	Suggested Pacing	Create Activities	Materials	
1	Emphasis Through Contrast	45 minutes	Create an appliqué design that uses contrast for emphasis.	fabric scissors needles and yard or thread paper pencils	
2	Emphasis as a Focal Point	45 minutes	Create a focal point in a mixed-media work of art.	cardboard loom masking tape string or yarn paper pencils	
3	Variety	45 minutes	Use variety to change an area of a school to make it more interesting.	12- x 18-inch white paper colored markers pencils	
4	Harmony	45 minutes	Create an assemblage using found objects.	found objects glue thick paper or cardboard liquid tempera paints	
5	Environmental Unity	45 minutes	Create a paper sculpture of a piece of equipment found at a playground.	cardboard liquid tempera paints construction paper glue paper pencils	
6	Unity	45 minutes	Create a piece of jewelry using found objects.	found objects, such as electrical material, buttons, wires, beads, or old bits of jewelry glue string or chain	
Artsource Lesson	Emphasis, Variety, Harmony, and Unity in Music	75 minutes	Write a song.	paper and pencils Artsource audiotape (optional) selection of songs (on audiocassette or CD)	

Program Resources (Books)	Art Resources	Literature Resources	*Music Resources
Vocabulary, pp. 61–62 Assessment, pp. 61–62 Art Across the Curriculum Resource Book, pp. 181–186	Overhead Transparency #31, *Rodeo Jacket* and *Blouse* Artist Profile Book, pp. 2, 71 Large Prints, *The Letter* and *The Dancing Couple*	**1.** *Abuela's Weave* (1993) by Omar Castaneda tells the story of a young Guatemalan girl who weaves special creations reflecting differences in patterns, designs, and cultures. **2.** *Talking to the Sun* (1985) by Kenneth Koch and Kate Farrell is good for providing various examples of differences found in forms correlated with poems.	"Go, My Son," by Carnes Burson and Arliene Williams, p. T254, CD6:9. "Go, My Son" is an example of a modern Native American song.
Vocabulary, pp. 63–64 Assessment, pp. 63–64 Art Across the Curriculum Resource Book, pp. 187–192	Overhead Transparency #32, *Navajo Loom with Wool Blanket and Tools* and *Crow, Crow* Artist Profile Book, pp. 48, 72 Large Prints, *The Letter* and *The Dancing Couple*	**1.** *Jumanji* (1981) by Chris Van Allsburg manipulates space and points of view to bring to life the black-and-white illustrations of this adventure book. **2.** *The Polar Express* (1985) by Chris Van Allsburg is another excellent example of distorted perspectives and unique points of view that will captivate students by both the illustrations and captivating story.	*"Musette,"* by J.S. Bach, performed by Bobby McFerrin, singer and Yo-Yo Ma, cellist, p. T255, CD6:10. *"Musette"* is an example of centuries-old music that is performed in a modern way, just as modern Native Americans still practice ancient arts.
Vocabulary, pp. 65–66 Assessment, pp. 65–66 Art Across the Curriculum Resource Book, pp. 193–198	Overhead Transparency #33, *After Leslie Left* and *She Ba* Artist Profile Book, pp. 3, 18 Large Prints, *The Letter* and *The Dancing Couple*	**1.** *Caddie Woodlawn* (1973) by Carol Brink has variety as the only description of this spunky girl whose misadventures are skillfully captured to add to the spontaneity of the story. **2.** *The Ballad of Biddy Early* (1989) by Nancy Willard uses mysterious watercolor illustrations to intrigue the reader into this collection of poems, limericks, and ballads that are useful for expanding on variety.	"Brandenburg Concerto No. 2, Third Movement," by J.S. Bach, p. T391C, CD9:33. Bach's *Brandenburg Concertos* show contrast in music by alternating between a small group of soloists and a large orchestra.
Vocabulary, pp. 67–68 Assessment, pp. 67–68 Art Across the Curriculum Resource Book, pp. 199–204	Overhead Transparency #34, *Tree House* and *Detroit Industry, South Wall* Artist Profile Book, pp. 4, 45 Large Prints, *The Letter* and *The Dancing Couple*	**1.** *Ox-Cart Man* (1979 by Donald Hall uses low-intensity colors that are united harmoniously to depict the daily life of an early nineteenth century New England family in folk art style paintings. **2.** *Christmas at Long Pond* (1992) by William T. George uses soft, subtle colors to harmoniously create the moods and setting of this visually refreshing picture book.	"The Dream of Martin Luther King," by Merle Gartell, p. T328, CD8:8. "The Dream of Martin Luther King" is an American song from the late twentieth century.
Vocabulary, pp. 69–70 Assessment, pp. 69–70 Art Across the Curriculum Resource Book, pp. 205–210	Overhead Transparency #35, *The Park* and *Playground* Artist Profile Book, p. 12 Large Prints, *The Letter* and *The Dancing Couple*	**1.** *Free Fall* (1988) by David Wiesner is a fantastical dream sequence in which students can note the perfected balance and unity that drifts from page to page. **2.** *Ashanti to Zulu: African Traditions* (1976) by Margaret Musgrove is a Caldecott-winning book that explains the traditions and customs of 26 African tribes and uses numerous patterns as examples of balance and harmony.	*"Suite for Wind Quintet,"* by Ruth Crawford Seeger, p. T251, CD6:7. *"Suite for Wind Quintet"* is an example of American music.
Vocabulary, pp. 71–72 Assessment, pp. 71–72 Art Across the Curriculum Resource Book, pp. 211–216	Overhead Transparency #36, *Composition in Brown and Gold* and *Pyrite Sun Pendant* Artist Profile Book, p. 47 Large Prints, *The Letter* and *The Dancing Couple*	**1.** *The Hidden Jungle* (1992) by Simon Henwood has fresh and vibrant examples of subject and unity that are portrayed in this colorful entanglement of lines, shapes, and forms. **2.** *It's for You* (1995) by John Talbot is a unique picture-puzzle book that allows viewers to discover the hidden relms of the imagination in twisted illustrations of subject and unity.	"Kalinka" (Little Snowball Bush), p. T358, CD9:8. "Kalinka" is an example of a Northern European folk song.

*Music references are from **Share the Music,** Macmillan/McGraw-Hill School Publishers

UNIT 6
LESSON 1

LESSON PLANNER

Objectives

After completing this lesson, students will be able to:

- identify the use of color, shape, and size to emphasize or draw attention to an area in a work of art. *Aesthetic Perception*
- create an appliqué design to show emphasis through contrast on an article of clothing or a piece of material. *Creative Expression*
- use the four steps of art criticism to evaluate their own artwork. *Art Criticism*
- demonstrate knowledge of the cultural purpose of both artworks. *Art History and Culture*

Program Resources

- **Overhead:** Both the Beard and the *Blouse* are available on overhead 31.
- **Large Prints:** *The Letter* by Mary Cassatt and *The Dancing Couple* by Jan Steen
- **Vocabulary Book** pages 61–62
- **Artist Profiles Book:** Beard page 2 and Artist unknown page 71
- **Art Across the Curriculum Book** pages 181–186
- **Multimedia Workshop CD-ROM**
- **Animals Through History Time Line**
- **Assessment Book** pages 61–62

Multiple Intelligences

Intrapersonal Students can discover contrast in their own lives as they choose symbols to represent themselves in the Create section.

Vocabulary

appliqué *aplicación* fabric shapes glued or sewn onto fabric

emphasis *énfasis* the principle of design that stresses one area in a work of art

contrast *contraste* when one element stands out from the rest of the work

isolation *aislamiento* when an object is placed alone and away from all the other objects in an artwork

location *ubicación* when the eyes are naturally drawn toward the center of an artwork

---

Emphasis Through Contrast

Artists use color, shape, and size to emphasize or draw attention to an area in an artwork.

Anne Beard. (American). *Rodeo Jacket.* Courtesy of Ms. Anne Beard. U.S. Seminole.

Anne Beard created *Rodeo Jacket* using a technique called appliqué. **Appliqué** is made by attaching fabric shapes onto a fabric background by gluing or sewing. *Ponca Blouse* was created out of cloth and ribbon work. Traditionally, Ponca artists added an odd bead to their costumes or broke the pattern in some other way so that the costumes weren't perfect. They felt this was a way to be humble. Both works of art are examples of emphasis through contrast.

ART Background

About the Artists

Anne Beard (an bērd, American, 1951–) a fiber artist, grew up in Washington State on a mountain ranch. She married into a family who managed a rodeo stock contracting company. She has lived in England, all over the U.S., and has moved 20 times in 20 years. The most important artistic influence was Beard's mother. She was "an incredible seamstress."

All clothing of the Ponca was naturally made by the women of the tribe. The Ponca tribe traded with western pioneers, which influenced the choice of material and design.

About Subject Matter* The Beard is a narrative; *Blouse* is nonobjective.

About the Media Beard uses Indian, Thai, or Italian silks and gabardine wool.

The Ponca blouse is made of pieces of dyed cloth, ribbon, and small, rounded buttons from animal bone.

Artist unknown. *Blouse.* Ponca Tribe. Woman's cloth waist shirt decorated with ribbon work. Smithsonian National Museum of the American Indian, New York, New York.

Compare both works of art to better understand emphasis through contrast.

- Describe how the objects, colors, and lines are arranged in both works of art.

- Close your eyes, then open them, looking at one of the images. What was the first thing that you saw? Why do you think this happened?

- Which one of the two pieces tells a story?

- Which of these two works of art would you like to wear?

Lesson 1

167

Seeing Like an Artist

Think about an advertisement you may have seen that you really liked. What objects or colors drew your attention? Why?

About Art History* The Ponca were a small, peaceful Native American tribe. At one time, the tribe was nearly wiped out by smallpox. They now live in Oklahoma.

Beard uses many of these American themes, but she also gains inspiration from traditional Seminole cloth work.

Cultural Perspectives This type of blouse was worn only for ceremonial purposes. Ponca members wrapped themselves in blankets. They communicated to each other by using various ways to wrap themselves.

During the past five years there has been a resurgence of western culture in the U.S.

* See **More About** pages 206–227 for more about art history and subject matter.

FOCUS

Time: About 10 minutes

Activating Prior Knowledge

"Have you ever highlighted an important word in your study notes or in a book?"

"¿Han resaltado alguna vez una palabra importante en sus notas de estudio o en un libro?"

- Discuss with students the fact that highlighting is an example of emphasis. Ask the students for other examples.

Introducing the Art

"Let's look closely at the two works of art."

"Vamos a observar detalladamente las dos obras de arte."

- For more information regarding horses in art, see the **Animals Through History Time Line.**

- Have students answer the questions on page 167.

- Share and discuss information from **Art Background** and the **Artist Profiles Book.** (See **Perception Hints** below.)

- **COMPARE AND CONTRAST** Have students make a list of similarities and differences in the art. (*Blouse* has all geometric designs, while the Beard has free-form shapes. The Beard is narrative, while the *Blouse* is nonobjective.)

> ### FOR THE ART SPECIALIST
>
> Use the **Overhead** and the **Large Prints** *The Letter* and *The Dancing Couple* to demonstrate the use of color, shape, and size to emphasize or draw attention to an area in an artwork.

Perception Hints

Objects, colors, and lines *Beard.* Arranged in a linear pattern along the bottom. *Blouse.* Horizontal and vertical stripes with diagonal ones are around the cuffs and the back. There is a row of leaves and free-form shapes at the bottom of the collar.

First thing Answers will vary, but the majority will probably say that the white stripes or the red diagonal in the center of the back came first in the *Blouse*. In the jacket, the light horse is the focal point. The white ribbon in the collar also catches the eye.

Story The Beard tells a story.

Like to wear Answers will vary.

TEACH

Time: About 30 minutes

Practice

Materials
- newspapers and magazines
- light-colored markers

Alternate Materials: textbook

"Let's look for examples of emphasis through contrast."

"Vamos a buscar ejemplos de énfasis a través del contraste."

- Discuss the definitions of *emphasis* and *contrast* on page 168.
- Distribute materials and have students follow the directions on page 168 to find examples of emphasis through contrast. Have students discuss the answer to the Decide question.

Create PROBLEM SOLVING

Materials
- fabric
- scissors
- needles and yarn or thread
- paper
- pencils

Alternate Materials: Stitch Witchery

"Let's create an appliqué design that uses contrast for emphasis."

"Vamos a hacer un diseño de una aplicación que use contraste por énfasis."

- Brainstorm ideas for symbols that represent students' interests.
- Distribute materials and have students follow the directions on page 169.

FOR THE ART SPECIALIST

Have students use either fabric paint or fabric crayons to put in the bottom layer of the design. Add appliqué and stitchery to it. Use paint for details.

Using Emphasis

Emphasis is the principle of design that stresses one area in a work of art. Have you ever underlined or highlighted an important word in your study notes? Have you ever seen an advertisement or video in which one object seemed to jump out and catch your attention? These are examples of emphasis.

There are several techniques that artists use to create emphasis.

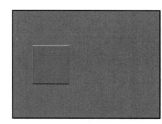

Contrast occurs when one element stands out from the rest of the work. A bright color will stand out from a dull color. A large shape will stand out from small shapes. An angular shape among round shapes will catch your attention.

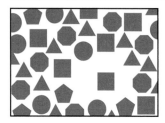

Isolation happens when an object is placed alone and away from all the other objects in an artwork. The viewer's eye then looks at the isolated object.

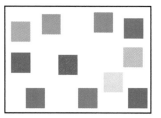

Location occurs when the eyes are naturally drawn toward the center of an artwork. Anything placed near the center of the picture will be noticed first.

Practice

Find examples of emphasis through contrast. Use newspapers and magazines.

1. What word or object in each attracts your eye first? Is it because of size, color, or an unusual shape? Locate three examples of emphasis through contrast.

2. Highlight the word or object emphasized in each example.

Decide What about the word or object in each example caught your attention first?

Activities in ART Across the Curriculum Book

Reading/Language Arts Write sentences using contrast to bring attention to an object or event. (page 181)

Math Use a grid to describe the location of objects in a wall hanging, after studying the placement of objects in *Rodeo Jacket*. (page 182)

Science Study types of clouds in order to predict the weather. (page 183)

Social Studies Study rodeos and western culture, as seen in *Rodeo Jacket*. (page 184)

The Arts Imagine you are a Ponca, and create a coming-of-age dance showing contrasting steps and movements. (page 185)

Technology Use the *Multimedia Workshop* CD-ROM to design a personal logo, using emphasis. (page 186)

What kind of emphasis did the student artist use?

Camille Blue. Age 10. *My Symbols.* Yarn, burlap.

Create

What symbol best represents your interests or tells something about you? Use appliqué to create a design showing emphasis through contrast on an article of clothing or a piece of material.

1. Think about a symbol to draw and cut out from fabric that represents something about you. Your symbol will become your appliqué and the point of emphasis.

2. Use emphasis techniques to draw several sketches of your symbol. Select one sketch for your symbol.

3. Trace the symbol onto the fabric and cut it out. Stitch the symbol onto your selected fabric. Decorate your appliqué with different types of stitches.

Describe Describe the symbol that you selected and the types of stitches that you used to complete your appliqué.

Analyze How does the symbol create a point of emphasis on the background?

Interpret Does your appliqué clearly communicate something about you and your interests?

Decide Did strong contrast make the clothing or fabric look better? Why?

Lesson 1 169

THEME Connections

Communities Use the *Ponca Blouse* as an introduction for a discussion about the community structure of the Ponca tribe.

Exploration Use the Beard work as a springboard to study early explorers in the United States.

ESL

To prepare ESL students to discuss their techniques and artwork, involve the class in a review of the entire lesson's activities. Some students might pantomime while others describe aloud. You can record key phrases on the board for later reference, if necessary.

CLOSE

Time: About 5 minutes

"Were you able to create a design showing emphasis through contrast on an article of clothing or piece of material?"

"¿Fueron capaces de crear un diseño mostrando énfasis a través del contraste en una prenda de vestir o en un pedazo de tela?"

LARGE PRINT **Review**

Use the **Large Prints** *The Letter* and *The Dancing Couple* to have students compare the use of emphasis to the works in this lesson.

Art Criticism

Have students answer the four art criticism questions—Describe, Analyze, Interpret, and Decide—orally or in writing. Discuss the use of emphasis in their works.

Assess

Use the **Assessment Book** pages 61–62 as a formal assessment for this lesson.

Evaluation Criteria

• Can the student identify the use of color, shape, and size to emphasize or draw attention to an area in a work of art?

• Can the student create an appliqué design to show emphasis through contrast on an article of clothing or a piece of material?

• Can the student use the four steps of art criticism to evaluate his or her own artwork?

• Can the student demonstrate knowledge of the cultural purpose of both artworks?

Reteaching • • • • • • • • • • • •

Emphasis Have students look through their books to find two examples of emphasis through contrast.

Perception Hints for Student Art

The student artist used contrast as a method of emphasis by using yellow as a background, monochromatic lines, and one green piece. She used isolation by having one green triangle piece. The location of two triangle pieces, outlined with white stitching, draw the eye in from the edges.

LESSON PLANNER

Objectives

After completing this lesson, students will be able to:

- identify the use of emphasis to draw attention to a specific area in a work of art. *Aesthetic Perception*
- plan and create a focal point in a mixed-media work of art. *Creative Expression*
- use the four steps of art criticism to evaluate their own artwork. *Art Criticism*
- demonstrate knowledge of the cultural purpose of both works of art. *Art History and Culture*

Program Resources

- **Overhead:** Both the the blanket and the Scanlin are available on overhead 32.
- **Large Prints:** *The Letter* by Mary Cassatt and *The Dancing Couple* by Jan Steen
- **Vocabulary Book** pages 63–64
- **Artist Profiles Book:** Scanlin page 48 and Artist unknown page 63
- **Art Across the Curriculum Book** pages 187–192
- **Multimedia Workshop CD-ROM**
- **Animals Through History Time Line**
- **Assessment Book** pages 63–64

Multiple Intelligences

Interpersonal Students can use emphasis as a focal point as they work in small groups in the Practice activity.

Vocabulary

emphasis *énfasis* the most important area of an artwork

focal point *punto focal* the area that is emphasized

warp *urdimbre* the vertical threads attached to the loom

weft *trama* the threads that are woven over and under the warp threads

Emphasis as a Focal Point

Emphasis is used by artists to draw attention to a specific area in a work of art.

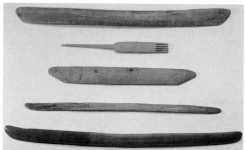

Artist unknown. Top: Navajo loom with wool blanket. Bottom: Battens, comb, and spreading stick. 113.1 × 104.2 cm. Loom with partly woven blanket. New York, New York. Smithsonian Institution National Museum of the American Indian, William M. Fitzhugh Collection.

Although *Navajo Loom* is a half-completed, woven blanket, you can see that the emphasized area, or the focal point, is the two small figures. Both weavings have a distinct design that represents the individual woman who wove it, her people, and a story. In *Crow, Crow,* the focal point is the crow. Both artists used symbols and designs to create their weaving patterns. The first thing that attracts the viewer's attention in each work is the focal point.

ART Background

About the Artists

Tommye Scanlin (tom' ē scan' lin, American, 1947–) was born in Georgia and worked for 20 years as an art teacher before deciding to concentrate her work in weaving and, eventually, tapestry weaving.

About Subject Matter* *Crow, Crow* is a narrative. The loom is symbolic.

About the Media The Navajo piece is the beginning of a handwoven blanket from hand-spun wool. The Scanlin piece is also woven. She works with wool and natural fibers.

About Art History* The earliest surviving Navajo blankets date from the late 1700s and early 1800s. Most of the blankets remain only as fragments and were found in caves. The most important blanket fragments were found in the Canon del Muerto, remembered in Navajo history as "Massacre Cave."

Tommye Scanlin. (American). *Crow, Crow.* 6 × 6 inches. Wool, cotton. Courtesy of Tommye Scanlin.

Analyze both works of art to better understand emphasis as a focal point.

- What do you think are the most important objects or areas in both these works of art? Why?

- How are the lines, shapes, and colors in these works of art arranged?

- What area of each piece attracts your eye? Why?

SEEING LIKE AN ARTIST

Close your eyes, then open them. What is the first thing you see? What about it drew your attention?

Lesson 2   **171**

Thousands of years ago, people discovered how to weave baskets from grasses. Historians do not know when the process of weaving cloth developed, but civilizations in central Europe, the Middle East, and Pakistan had probably learned to weave textiles by 2500 B.C. Ancient wall paintings illustrate weaving techniques mastered by the Egyptians as early as 5000 B.C.

Cultural Perspectives Today most Navajo weavers sell their work. Traditionally, weavings were sold to tourists or used for trading. Navajo families rarely have these pieces hanging in their dwellings. Weavings were once used as clothing—wearing blankets and wool dresses—but now are worn only for special occasions.

The Industrial Revolution brought the greatest improvements in machinery for weaving. This was a period of rapid industrial growth in Europe during the 1700s and early 1800s.

*See **More About** pages 206–227 for more about art history and subject matter.

FOCUS
Time: About 10 minutes

Activating Prior Knowledge
"Think about billboards you see along a highway when you're in a car. Where is your eye attracted first?"
"Piensen acerca de las vallas que ven en las autopistas cuando van en un carro. ¿Qué es lo que atrae primero tu atención?"

- Discuss students' answers to the question. Explain that the focal point on a billboard is the area that is emphasized by contrasting color, shape, or size or the location near the center. Also discuss the fact that the human form is a focal point.

Introducing the Art
"Let's look closely at the two weavings."
"Vamos a observar detalladamente los dos tejidos."

- For further information regarding animals through history, see the **Animals Through History Time Line.**

- Share information from **Art Background** and the **Artist Profiles Book.**

- Have students answer the questions on page 171. (See **Perception Hints** below.)

- **COMPARE AND CONTRAST** Have students make a list of the similarities and differences in the two weavings. (The Scanlin is a finished piece and the loom is only half finished. The Scanlin is predominately free-form, while the weaving is geometric. Both are woven and both have common colors.)

FOR THE ART SPECIALIST

Use the **Overhead** and the **Large Prints** *The Letter* and *The Dancing Couple* to demonstrate the use of emphasis to draw attention to a specific area in a work of art.

Perception Hints

Important objects or areas *Loom.* The white zigzag at the bottom stands out because it is white and is outlined in black. *Scanlin.* The crow. The black stands out on the yellow background.
Lines, shapes, and colors *Loom.* Under the white. *Scanlin.* Around the area of emphasis.
Area *Loom.* The people stand out because they are below the white line. *Scanlin.* The crow attracts your eye because it is the largest shape. It has strong contrast of value and size.

LESSON 2   **171**

TEACH

Time: About 30 minutes

Practice

"What is the focal point of the school?"

"¿Cuál es el punto focal de la escuela?"

• Discuss the definitions of *emphasis* and *focal point* on page 172.

• Have students brainstorm and then follow the directions on page 172 for discussing the focal point of the school. Have them discuss the answer to the Decide questions.

Create PROBLEM SOLVING

Materials

• cardboard loom	• string or yarn
• masking tape	• paper
	• pencils

"Let's create a focal point in a mixed-media work of art."

"Vamos a crear un punto focal en una obra de arte de medios mixtos."

• Brainstorm ideas to create a mixed-media landscape with a focal point.

• Distribute materials and have students follow the directions on page 173.

• Shape the outline with your fingers and tape with masking tape to hold it in place. Using yarn, weave this shape.

• To make a cardboard loom, string warp thread from top to bottom through notches cut $\frac{1}{4}$ inch apart and $\frac{1}{2}$ inch deep, taping the end of the thread to the back. Start to weave horizontally at the bottom of the loom in an over-one-under-one motion. Do not pull too tightly.

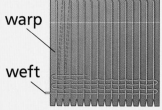

warp

weft

FOR THE ART SPECIALIST

Have students use layers of white paint to block out the brown cardboard, and paint the landscape with school acrylics.

Using Emphasis as a Focal Point

Emphasis is usually the most important area of an artwork. It helps unify a work of art. Emphasis controls the order in which the viewer notices the parts and the amount of attention the viewer gives each part. The area emphasized is called the **focal point**. Artists use different techniques to create a focal point:

Using a contrasting color on one object or shape creates a focal point. The orange square is the focal point

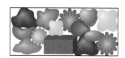

Using a contrasting shape or form will create a focal point. The solid rectangle is the focal point.

Using a contrasting size will create a focal point. The focal point is the large shape.

Location near the center of a work creates a focal point. Placing one object near the center of a composition will make that object the focal point of the work.

Difference will create a focal point. The human form is the focal point.

Practice

Talk about the focal point of your school.

1. Form groups. Discuss within the groups the emphasis or focal point of your school.

2. What physical characteristics make up its focal point? Compare opinions and share with the class.

Decide How did you decide what made up the focal point of the school? Did everyone in your group agree?

Activities in ART Across the Curriculum Book

Reading/Language Arts Understand the importance of a topic sentence in a paragraph in order to create a focus. (page 187)

Math Study the loom in the lesson to calculate the amount of thread you will need to string the loom accurately. (page 188)

Science Learn more about wool used to make blankets. (page 189)

Social Studies Study changes in the Navajo culture. (page 190)

The Arts Understand how musical signs placed under notes direct a musician to give different kinds of emphasis. (page 191)

Technology Use the *Multimedia Workshop* CD-ROM to design a rug with a focal point. (page 192)

What objects does the student artist use as a focal point?

Nikolas Eches. Age 11. *Sunset Mountain.* Yarn, marker.

Create

What part of a landscape scene do you find most interesting? Create a focal point in a mixed-media work of art.

1. Think about part of a landscape you like. Draw several sketches.

2. Make a cardboard loom and draw one sketch onto it. Fill your drawing with color. String the warp threads over the drawing. **Warp** threads are the vertical threads attached to the loom.

3. Outline with yarn onto the warp threads the shape that will be the focal point of your work. Hold the outline in place with pieces of tape. Fill the shape with weft threads. **Weft** threads are threads that are woven over and under the warp threads.

Describe What type of landscape did you create? What object did you select to weave onto your loom?

Analyze Why did you select that particular area of the landscape to weave your object?

Interpret Give your work a title.

Decide Do you think that other people will recognize where the focal point of your work is? What will cause them to look there first?

Lesson **2**   **173**

THEME Connections

Communication Use the work *Crow, Crow* to study ways that animals communicate with each other and with people.

Traditions Use the Navajo loom to teach some of the traditions of early America.

ESL

In small group discussions, support ESL students with some discussion guidelines. A speaker's turn can be indicated by holding an object and passing it to the next person. Students may also ask for assistance when it is their turn.

CLOSE

Time: About 5 minutes

"Were you able to create a focal point in a mixed-media work of art?"

"¿Pudieron crear un punto focal en una obra de arte de medios mixtos?"

LARGE PRINT **Review**

Use the **Large Prints** *The Letter* and *The Dancing Couple* to have students compare the use of focal point in their work to the works in this lesson.

Art Criticism

Have students answer the four art criticism questions—Describe, Analyze, Interpret, and Decide—orally or in writing. Discuss the use of focal point in the students' landscapes.

Assess

Use the **Assessment Book** pages 63–64 as a formal assessment for this lesson.

Evaluation

- Can the student identify focal points in works of art?
- Can the student plan and create a focal point in a mixed-media work of art?
- Can the student use the four steps of art criticism to evaluate his or her own artwork?
- Can the student demonstrate knowledge of the cultural purpose of both works of art?

Reteaching ● ● ● ● ● ● ● ● ● ● ●

Emphasis Have the students look through magazines to find two more works of art illustrating the use of emphasis by the artist to draw attention to a specific area in a work of art.

Perception Hints for Student Art

The object used as a focal point includes the red sun. It suggests a whole, circular feeling in the center of the piece. This is emphasized by the points of the mountain ranges, as well as the vertical blue yarn pieces, which pull your eyes to the sun.

U NIT 6

LESSON PLANNER

Objectives
After completing this lesson, students will be able to:

- identify the use of variety to add interest in artwork. *Aesthetic Perception*
- create a new design using variety to make an area of the school more interesting. *Creative Expression*
- use the four steps of art criticism to evaluate their own artwork. *Art Criticism*
- demonstrate knowledge of the lives and work of both artists. *Art History and Culture*

Program Resources
- **Overhead:** Both the Fish and the Bearden are available on overhead 33.
- **Large Prints:** *The Letter* by Mary Cassatt and *The Dancing Couple* by Jan Steen
- **Vocabulary Book** pages 65–66
- **Artist Profiles Book:** Fish page 18 and Beardon page 3
- **Art Across the Curriculum Book** pages 193–198
- **Multimedia Workshop CD-ROM**
- **Assessment Book** pages 65–66

Multiple Intelligences
Visual/Spatial Students can enhance their understanding of variety through observation and drawing.

Vocabulary
variety *variedad* the principle of design concerned with difference or contrast

contrast *contraste* when different elements like lines, shapes, or colors are placed next to each other in a work of art

assemblage *montaje* a work of art in which a variety of objects are assembled to create one complete piece

---

Variety

Artists use variety to add interest to their artwork.

Janet Fish. (American). *After Leslie Left.* 1983–84. Oil on canvas. 48 × 62 inches. Albright Knox Art Gallery, Buffalo, New York. Norman E. Boasberg, George Cary, and Charles W. Goodyear Funds, 1984.

Janet Fish is best known for her realistic paintings of objects. She is interested in showing how light plays on surfaces such as mirrors, glass, and metals. Romare Beardon is best known for his collages made from pieces of old photographs, scraps of paper, and painted papers. Both artworks express variety.

174   Unit **6**

ART Background

About the Artists
Janet Fish (jan' ət fish, American, 1938–) was born in Boston and raised in Bermuda. She earned degrees at Smith College and Yale University. For a period of time, she painted bars of soap for a department store. She is best known for her still lifes of glassware in which specific color areas appear to dissolve and the objects themselves are integrated with each other and their setting. The quality of light is the main focus of her work.

Romare Bearden (rō mar' bēr' dən, American, 1912–) was born in Charlotte, North Carolina. He moved to Harlem at a young age. His parents were at the center of the Harlem Renaissance. Their home became a meeting place for artists, intellectuals, writers, and musicians. Over the years, Bearden studied art in New York City and in Paris, worked as a social worker, served in the army, and wrote several songs and books.

About Subject Matter* Fish's work is a still life, while Bearden's is narrative.

Romare Beardon. (American). *She Ba*. 1970. Paper cloth, paint, board. Wadsworth Atheneum, Hartford, Connecticut. The Ella Gallup Sumner and Mary Catlin Sumner Collection Fund.

Compare both works of art to learn about variety.

- ✓ Compare the types of lines, colors, and shapes used by both artists.

- ✓ What did both artists do to add interest to their works of art?

- ✓ Describe the different objects you see in each picture. How are they arranged?

Lesson 3

175

SEEING LIKE AN ARTIST

What is your favorite display in a shop window or at the mall? Are the colors, patterns, and objects the same or different?

About the Media Both works are oil on canvas.

About Art History* In the 1960s, Fish was part of a group of painters who were not bound to tradition. She is a realist, but her work often has abstract qualities.

Bearden experimented with abstract expressionism, but his style is called "social realism."

Cultural Perspectives Janet Fish credits her years of growing up in Bermuda for stimulating her taste for paintings with very active surfaces.

Bearden grew up during the Harlem Renaissance. He knew people like Charles Alston, Langston Hughes, and Duke Ellington. After serving and studying in Europe, he returned to the United States to face the Civil Rights Movement. This movement was of great influence on Bearden's work.

*See **More About** pages 206–227 for more about art history and subject matter.

FOCUS

Time: About 10 minutes

Activating Prior Knowledge

"Do all your friends wear the same clothes and have the same personality?"

"¿Usan sus amigos la misma ropa y tienen la misma personalidad?"

- Discuss the answers with the students. Explain that it is the differences in the personalities and tastes of their friends that makes life interesting.

Introducing the Art

"Let's look closely at the two works of art."

"Vamos a observar detalladamente las dos obras de arte."

- Have students answer the questions on page 175. (See **Perception Hints** below.)
- **COMPARE AND CONTRAST** Have students discuss the similarities and differences in the two works of art. (Both have variety. The Fish is a watercolor, and the colors are light. She paints a realistic scene with lots of highlights. Bearden uses bright, flat abstract colors made with cloth and paint on cardboard.)

FOR THE ART SPECIALIST

Use the **Overhead** and the **Large Prints** *The Letter* and *The Dancing Couple* to demonstrate the use of variety to add interest to artwork.

Perception Hints

Lines, shapes, and colors *Fish.* Delicate colors that create the illusion of realism; intricate, complex shapes; curved and straight lines. *Bearden.* Curved and straight lines as well as flat, intense colors; geometric and free-form shapes.

Interest *Fish.* Strong highlights and reflections. *Bearden.* Bright lights.

Objects *Fish.* Bananas in a transparent bowl, a stack of magazines and coupons, a sponge, a half-full cup of coffee, a feather duster, a Windex bottle, keys, a plant with green leaves, and wrinkled plastic. Behind all these items are transparent curtains with a print on them. The objects are arranged asymmetrically with the sponge as the focal point. *Bearden.* A man holding an umbrella and a woman holding a stick. The arrangement is asymmetrical.

TEACH

Time: About 30 minutes

Practice
Materials
- 12- × 18-inch white paper
- colored markers

Alternate Materials: crayons

"How could you make a household item look better?"

"¿Cómo podrían hacer lucir mejor un artículo doméstico?"

- Discuss the definition of *variety*.
- Distribute materials and then follow the directions on page 176 for using variety to redesign a common household item. Have students discuss the answer to the Decide questions.

Create PROBLEM SOLVING
Materials
- 12- × 18-inch white paper
- colored markers
- pencils

Alternate Materials: crayons

"Let's make an area of the school more interesting by using variety."

"Vamos a hacer más interesante un área de la escuela usando variedad."

- Brainstorm ideas to select and improve an area of the school.
- Discuss the three elements of art used to create variety.
- Distribute materials and have students follow the directions on page 177.

FOR THE ART SPECIALIST

Have the students re-create environmental designs to add variety to an area in the school.

Using Variety

Variety is the principle of design concerned with difference or contrast. If a work has no variety—for instance, it is a painting of one shape in one color—it probably will not hold the viewer's attention. When different elements, like lines, shapes, or colors, are placed next to each other in a work of art, they are in **contrast**. This adds interest to the artwork and gives it a lively quality.

Lines, shapes, and colors are three of the elements of art that are used to create variety in a work of art.

Variety in Lines

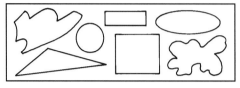

Variety in Shapes

Variety in Colors

Practice

Use variety to redesign a common household item. Use markers.

1. Think of a common household object, such as a tube of toothpaste, a box of laundry detergent, a bar of soap, or a spoon.

2. Use colored markers to draw the object. Add variety or contrast to your selected object by using contrasting lines, shapes, or colors.

Decide Do you think your new design is more interesting than the original design? Did you create variety or contrast?

Activities in
ART Across the Curriculum Book

Reading/Language Arts Write a story using details from the Fish painting. (page 193)

Math Learn how to use diagrams to solve problems. (page 194)

Science Make a collage expressing your point of view about recycling. (page 195)

Social Studies Gather information from the painting *After Leslie Left* to describe the person. (page 196)

The Arts Create an opening scene for a play using the setting of *After Leslie Left*. (page 197)

Technology Use the *Multimedia Workshop* CD-ROM to create variety in a design of common objects. (page 198)

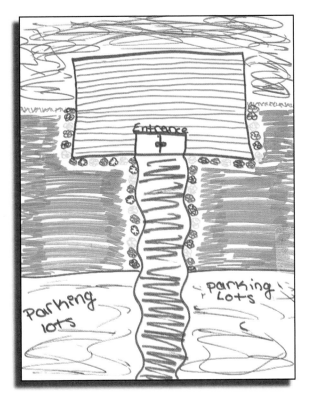

How did the student artist use variety to make the work more interesting?

Brent Lennox. Age 11. *Colorful Building*. Marker.

Create

What area of your school could be improved? Use variety to change an area of your school to make it more interesting.

1. Think about an area in or around your school that you think is dull or uninteresting. What are some changes you can make without losing the area's purpose?

2. Create two sketches of the area. Experiment with some ways to add variety or contrast using either color, lines, or shapes.

3. Reproduce one onto your paper. Add color. The area needs to remain functional but should be more interesting than before.

Describe What changes did you make to your selected area?

Analyze How did you organize your design?

Interpret What one word best describes your design?

Decide Do you like the changes you made? Can you think of other ways to create variety or contrast in this area of your school?

Lesson 3 177

Cultures Use the painting *She Ba* as a springboard to open a discussion regarding African culture.

Change Use the painting by Janet Fish to discuss the changing roles of women in today's world.

ESL students may benefit from hearing the lesson vocabulary in a large group brainstorm session before moving on to their individual project ideas. Consider visually recording the group brainstorm session with a simple, labeled sketch for ongoing student reference.

CLOSE

Time: About 5 minutes

"Were you able to use variety to change an area of your school to make it more interesting?"

"¿Fueron capaces de usar variedad para cambiar un área de su escuela y hacerla más interesante?"

Review

Use the **Large Prints** *The Letter* and *The Dancing Couple* to have students compare the artists' use of harmony to the use of harmony in the works in this lesson.

Art Criticism

Have students answer the four art criticism questions—Describe, Analyze, Interpret, and Decide—orally or in writing and discuss the use of variety in their drawings.

Assess

Use the **Assessment Book** pages 65–66 as a formal assessment for this lesson.

Evaluation Criteria

• Can the student identify the use of variety to add interest in artwork?

• Can the student create a new design using variety to make an area of the school more interesting?

• Can the student use the four steps of art criticism to evaluate his or her own artwork?

• Can the student demonstrate knowledge of the lives and work of both artists?

Reteaching • • • • • • • • • • •

Variety Have students look through the book to find three works of art that demonstrate techniques used to add variety. Ask them to make a list of the artworks and describe the technique used.

Perception Hints for Student Art

The student artist used different lines to shade the sky, lawn, school, walk, and parking lot to give the work variety and make it more interesting. Some lines squiggle and some are thin, straight lines. He also used a variety of color and circular lines to make rows of flowers.

LESSON PLANNER

Objectives

After completing this lesson, students will be able to:

- identify how artists use harmony in a work of art to create a feeling of unity. *Aesthetic Perception*
- design an assemblage using color to create harmony. *Creative Expression*
- use the four steps of art criticism to evaluate their own artwork. *Art Criticism*
- demonstrate knowledge of the lives and works of both artists. *Art History and Culture*

Program Resources

- **Overhead:** Both the Biggers and the Rivera are available on overhead 34.
- **Large Prints:** *The Letter* by Mary Cassatt and *The Dancing Couple* by Jan Steen
- **Vocabulary Book** pages 67–68
- **Artist Profiles Book:** Biggers page 4 and Rivera page 45
- **Art Across the Curriculum Book** pages 199–204
- **Multimedia Workshop CD-ROM**
- **National Geographic Picture Atlas of the World CD-ROM**
- **Assessment Book** pages 67–68

Multiple Intelligences

Verbal/Linguistic Students can develop a greater comprehension of harmony by writing a descriptive paragraph about a work of art.

Vocabulary

harmony *armonía* concerned with similarities of separate but related parts

---

Harmony

Artists use harmony in their artwork to create a feeling of unity.

John Biggers. (American). *Tree House.* 1989. 240 × 120 inches. Acrylic on canvas. Hampton University Museum, Hampton, VA. William R. and Norma B. Harvey Library.

John Biggers has painted about twenty murals using the topic of the black experience in America and Africa. The people in Biggers's work are unique and dignified. Diego Rivera was a muralist who was invited to paint many murals in the United States in the 1930s. He emphasized the dignity of working people.

FOCUS

Time: About 10 minutes

Activating Prior Knowledge

"How many different voices are there in your school choir?"

"¿Cuántas voces diferentes hay en la coral escolar?"

- Discuss the students' answers. Explain that even though there are several types of voices, alto, soprano, and so on, they are all combined in harmony to create a unified voice for the choir.

ART *Background*

About the Artists

John Biggers (jon big' ərs, American, 1924–) was born in South Carolina, the youngest of seven children. His father was the principal of a three-room school. At Hampton University, an art instructor encouraged Biggers to sculpt and paint. He graduated from Penn State. He taught art, and in 1957, he was one of the first African American artists to travel to Africa to study.

Diego Rivera (dē ā' gō rē bā' rä, Mexican, 1886–1957) is one of the most controversial and most productive Mexican artists. He began studying art in Mexico. He was a large man with strong opinions. His love for his country showed in his art.

About Subject Matter* Both works are narratives.

About the Media Both works are murals. Biggers used pencils, oils, and tempera. Rivera's is a fresco—a mural that is painted on fresh, moist lime plaster.

Diego Rivera. (Mexican). Detail of *Detroit Industry*, South Wall. 1932–33. Fresco. Photograph © 1996. Detroit Institute of Arts, Gift of Edsel B. Ford.

Observe how harmony is used in both paintings.

- ✓ Do you see any lines, shapes, or colors repeated in either mural?

- ✓ Is there any one area in either mural that seems to stand out? If so, what area is it?

- ✓ How would you describe the use of color in both works?

- ✓ Do you think these artists took a long time to plan these murals? Why or why not?

SEEING LIKE AN ARTIST

Think about a costume or a uniform. What made the costume or uniform look like the pieces were meant to be worn together? Was it a particular color, texture, or pattern?

Lesson 4

179

Introducing the Art

"Let's look closely at the artwork."

"Vamos a observar detalladamente la obra de arte."

- Share and discuss information with students from **Art Background** and the **Artist Profiles Book.**
- Use the **National Geographic Picture Atlas of the World CD-ROM** to help locate the countries where the artists were born.
- Have students answer the questions on page 179. (See **Perception Hints** below.)
- **COMPARE AND CONTRAST** the two works of art. (The Biggers is a drawing of a mural, while the other is an actual painted mural. Both use symbols. The Rivera machinery on the right looks like a Mexican idol or god; everything in the Biggers represents something.)

FOR THE ART SPECIALIST

Use the **Overhead** and the **Large Prints** *The Letter* and *The Dancing Couple* to demonstrate the use of harmony in artwork to create a feeling of unity.

Perception Hints

Lines, shapes, or colors *Biggers.* The geometric shapes, lines, and colors are repeated. *Rivera.* The working man figures and colors are repeated.

Area *Both.* The center area. *Biggers.* The women wearing white. *Rivera.* The men in the center wearing yellow.

Color *Biggers.* Low-intensity colors, or dull colors, contrasting with the white of the people's clothing. *Rivera.* Low-intensity, cool colors to contrast with the warm colors used in the center.

Plan Both artists took a long time to plan these murals because they are both very elaborate and full of complex shapes and forms. Rivera went to the factory to do his sketches.

About Art History* Biggers was influenced by his Hampton teacher, Viktor Lowenfeld, who encouraged students to express the feelings in their lives.

Rivera's painting style was influenced by the work of Klee, Cezanne, Picasso, and other modern painters. He wanted to paint art that could be understood and enjoyed by ordinary people.

Cultural Perspectives After Biggers's trip to Africa, he focused his art on African traditions and symbols. One of the first well-known African American artists, he has worked to see that other talented African Americans are also recognized.

For an enormous stairway at the National Palace in Mexico City, Rivera painted 124 panels that trace the entire history of his nation.

*See **More About** pages 206–227 for more about art history and subject matter.

TEACH

Time: About 30 minutes

Practice

Materials
- found objects of the same color

"How can you use items of the same color to arrange a still life?"

"¿Cómo pueden usar artículos del mismo color para ordenar una naturaleza muerta?"

- Discuss the definitions of *harmony* on page 180.
- Distribute materials and have students follow the directions on page 180 to arrange a still life with harmony. Have them discuss the answer to the Decide questions.

Create PROBLEM SOLVING

Materials
- found objects
- thick paper or cardboard
- glue
- liquid tempera paints

"Let's create an assemblage using found objects."

"Vamos a hacer un montaje usando objetos."

- Brainstorm ideas to create an assemblage using found objects. Discuss the definition of *assemblage*. The assemblage may be freestanding or flat.
- Discuss how color can create harmony and unity. Students may also paint their assemblage one color.
- Distribute materials and have students follow the directions on page 181.
- **Safety!** For safety issues about liquid tempera, glue, and other information about safety in the art classroom, see page T22.

> ### FOR THE ART SPECIALIST
> Have students create a larger assemblage, and cover it with papier-mâché made with paper towels.

Using Harmony

Harmony is the principle of design that is concerned with similarities of separate but related parts. Artists use these art elements to create harmony.

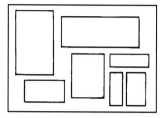

Shapes create harmony when related shapes of various sizes are repeated. A design using one type of shape is more harmonious than a design using two types of shapes.

Color creates harmony when a work is limited to only cool or warm colors.

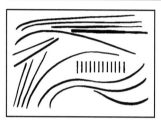

Line creates harmony by limiting lines to either straight or curved lines.

Practice

Arrange a still life to observe harmony. Use items of the same color.

1. As a class, choose one color. Have each person in the class bring in an item of the selected color.

2. Form small groups and create a still life using the objects brought to class. Discuss in small groups how color creates harmony in the still life.

Decide What types of objects were displayed in your group's still life? How did the use of color create harmony?

Activities in
ART Across the Curriculum Book

Reading/Language Arts Write a poem about *Tree House* or *Detroit Industry* using rhyming words and rhythm to create harmony and unity. (page 199)

Math Identify shapes as congruent or similar after looking at the shapes in the artwork. (page 200)

Science Imagine you are in charge of a factory that manufactures bikes. Describe the steps in this process, and explain the duties of each worker. (page 201)

Social Studies Understand the relationship between people and the natural environment using *Tree House* as an example. (page 202)

The Arts Learn how chords create harmony in music. (page 203)

Technology Use the *Multimedia Workshop* CD-ROM to create a scene that shows harmony. (page 204)

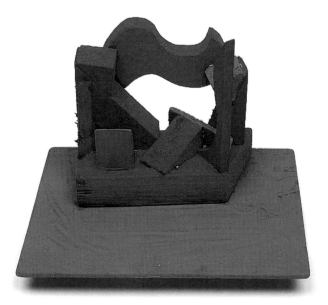

Tiffany Hayes. Age 9. *The Encounter*. Wood scraps, tempera.

How does the student artist create harmony in the assemblage?

Create

How can you arrange unrelated objects in an artwork to create harmony? Design an assemblage using color to create harmony.

1. Think about harmony and how one element, such as color, can pull a variety of objects together.

2. Collect all found materials. These items will be used to create an assemblage. An **assemblage** is a sculpture in which a variety of objects are assembled to create one complete piece.

3. Arrange a few items at a time. Glue them into place. Let your assemblage dry, then paint it using related colors.

Describe Describe the objects you used in your assemblage. Are textures similar or different? Are the objects of various sizes?

Analyze Was there any particular order to the arrangement of your objects?

Interpret Were you able to create the feeling of harmony within your assemblage? What differences do you notice when you look at your piece by itself and when you add it to a group?

Decide What color did you choose as a class? Did this color bring together the completed work?

Lesson 4

181

"Were you able to design an assemblage using color to create harmony?"

"¿Fueron capaces de diseñar un montaje usando colores para crear armonía?"

LARGE PRINT **Review**
Use the **Large Prints** *The Letter* and *The Dancing Couple* to have students compare the use of harmony to the works in this lesson.

Art Criticism
Have students answer the four art criticism questions—Describe, Analyze, Interpret, and Decide—orally or in writing. Discuss the use of harmony in their works after they have finished.

Assess
Use the **Assessment Book** pages 67–68 as a formal assessment for this lesson.

Evaluation Criteria
• Can the student identify harmony in works of art?
• Can the student create an assemblage using color to create harmony?
• Can the student use the four steps of art criticism to evaluate his or her own artwork?
• Can the student demonstrate knowledge of the lives and work of both artists?

Reteaching ● ● ● ● ● ● ● ● ● ● ●

Harmony Have the students look through magazines to find two pictures that use harmony to create a feeling of unity.

Discovery Use the Biggers work as a springboard to identify African Americans who have made major discoveries in the fields of science and medicine.

Celebrations Use the Rivera work to identify and discuss celebrations that are popular in Mexico.

Some ESL students may find it helpful to move away from oral language into print as they write descriptions of their artwork for this lesson. You might have students form small groups. Then, have each student in the group offer an oral comment or two about the group's piece. Each group can then combine and number sentences as needed to form the basis of their paragraph.

Perception Hints for Student Art

The student artist creates harmony through her use of color and arrangement of shapes. The inner sculpture is outlined in blue and surrounded by green. The addition of smaller purple and green pieces keeps the space broken up and interesting. The big blue swirl creates a line that is continued through the sloped piece and back down to the blue base.

UNIT 6
LESSON 5

LESSON PLANNER

Objectives

After completing this lesson, students will be able to:

- identify how harmony and variety create unity in works of art. *Aesthetic Perception*
- design and create a paper sculpture of one piece of playground equipment. *Creative Expression*
- use the four steps of art criticism to evaluate their own artwork. *Art Criticism*
- demonstrate knowledge of the cultural purpose of each work of art. *Art History and Culture*

Program Resources

- **Overhead:** Both the Chase and the *Playground* are available on overhead 35.
- **Large Prints:** *The Letter* by Mary Cassatt and *The Dancing Couple* by Jan Steen
- **Vocabulary Book** pages 69–70
- **Art Manipulative Kit:** Toobers and flexible curve
- **Artist Profiles Book:** Chase page 12
- **Art Across the Curriculum Book** pages 205–210
- **Multimedia Workshop CD-ROM**
- **Assessment Book** pages 69–70

Multiple Intelligences

Logical/Science Students can develop a greater knowledge of unity by studying a plant and its related parts.

Vocabulary

unity *unidad* the feeling of wholeness or oneness achieved by properly using the elements and principles of art

harmony *armonía* a technique for creating unity by using related or similar elements

variety *variedad* the opposite of harmony

Environmental Unity

Artists often use harmony and variety to create unity in a work of art.

William M. Chase. (American). *The Park.* 1888. Oil on canvas. $13\frac{5}{8} \times 19\frac{5}{8}$ inches. Art Institute of Chicago, Chicago, Illinois. Bequest of Dr. John J. Ireland.

William Merritt Chase was a very successful artist best known for his portraits, landscapes, and still lifes. Chase became interested in the effects of light. Playground equipment sometimes looks like sculpture when the playground is designed by an artist. This piece of equipment is a slide. The forms around the slide have been designed to look like a futuristic creature. Both artists use harmony and variety to create unity in their artwork.

ART Background

About the Artists

William Merritt Chase (wil' yem mer' ət chās, American, 1849–1916) was born in Indiana. He studied art in New York City and in Germany. Upon his return from Germany in 1877, he was well known in the art world. He taught art and established his own art school, the Chase School of Art.

About Subject Matter* Chase's work may be considered a landscape, a genre, or a narrative. The *Playground* is a genre.

About the Media Chase's work is oil on canvas. The *Playground* is a photograph of a playground in Israel.

Artist unknown. (Jerusalem). *Playground*. National Geographic Image Collection.

Study both works of art to find harmony and variety in each.

- What colors stand out most in both works of art?

- What types of shapes and lines do you see repeated in each artwork?

- Is there any one element that you notice more than others?

- What are some differences you notice between the two? Do these differences create a particular mood?

SEEING LIKE AN ARTIST

Think about how all the separate parts of your home, though they are different, work together to create a whole.

Lesson 5   183

About Art History* Chase influenced thousands of young artists. His classes in New York, Philadelphia, and Europe attracted many students. He took classes to Europe to study art and meet his artist friends. His vigor as a painter was equaled by his long and successful career as a teacher.

Cultural Perspectives Chase was one of the most influential painters in America at the turn of this century. He demonstrated his extraordinary versatility painting portraits, landscapes, still lifes, and everyday scenes. Chase believed that nature was a combination of color and form that could be translated into a painting.

The *Playground* in Israel provides a much needed break for children in their country.

*See **More About** pages 206–227 for more about art history and subject matter.

FOCUS

Time: About 10 minutes

Activating Prior Knowledge

"What is the one thing that all parks have in common?"

"¿Qué cosa tienen los parques en común?"

- Discuss the fact that all parks have a uniqueness, but most have a sense of unity.

Introducing the Art

"Let's look closely at the two artworks."

"Vamos a observar detalladamente las dos obras de arte."

- Share and discuss information from **Art Background** and the **Artist Profiles Book.**

- **ART MANIPULATIVES** Use Toobers and the flexible curve in the **Art Manipulative Kit** to duplicate the shapes used for the equipment.

- **COMPARE AND CONTRAST** Have students compare the artworks. (Both deal with parks. The playground is for children; all ages use *The Park*. The playground appears to be noisy; *The Park* appears quiet.)

- Have students answer the questions on page 183. (See **Perception Hints** below.)

FOR THE ART SPECIALIST

Use the **Overhead** and the **Large Prints** *The Letter* and *The Dancing Couple* to demonstrate how artists use harmony and variety to create unity in a work of art.

Perception Hints

Colors *Chase.* Pink and black. *Playground.* White, blue, and magenta

Shapes and lines Both make use of free-form shapes and vertical lines. The *Chase* also has geometric shapes.

Element *Chase.* Harmony and variety. *Playground.* Variety is used in the colors. Shapes help unify it.

Differences The colors are brighter in the playground scene. Chase's work appears more serene, while the *Playground* appears whimsical.

TEACH

Time: About 30 minutes

Practice

"What types of harmony and variety can you find in your neighborhood?"

"¿Qué tipos de armonía y variedad pueden encontrar en sus vecindarios?"

- Discuss the definitions of *harmony* and *variety*. Divide the class into small groups.
- Have students follow the directions on page 184 for discussing harmony and variety. Have them discuss the answers to the Decide questions.

Create PROBLEM SOLVING

Materials

- paper
- liquid tempera paints
- construction paper
- cardboard
- pencils
- glue

Alternate Materials: clay

"Let's create a paper sculpture of a piece of equipment found at a playground."

"Vamos a hacer una escultura de papel de un equipo que encontramos en el patio de recreo."

- Brainstorm ideas to create a piece of playground equipment.
- Review procedures for working with paint in **More About Technique Tips** on page 198.
- Distribute materials and have students follow the directions on page 185.
- Use either construction paper or painted cardboard for the ground.

FOR THE ART SPECIALIST

Have small groups design an entire playground. Have them create a large model using clay and found materials.

Using Unity

Unity is the feeling of wholeness or oneness that is achieved by properly using the elements and principles of art.

Unity is oneness. A plant is an example of unity in nature. It is made of a root system, a stem and leaves, and flowers. Each part has a purpose or job that gives life to the growing plant. Unity is created when harmony and variety work together.

Harmony and variety are two principles of art that work together to create unity. **Harmony** is the principle of art concerned with similarity or how separate parts relate. **Variety** is the opposite of harmony. It is about difference or contrast. A good balance between harmony and variety creates unity.

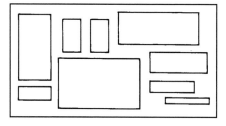

Harmony of Shapes

Variety of Shapes

Practice

Discover harmony and variety in your neighborhood.

1. Discuss in small groups what elements or objects create variety in your neighborhood. Discuss how the elements relate to create harmony.

2. Describe how variety and harmony work together.

Decide What elements did you describe? How is unity created through variety and harmony?

Activities in ART Across the Curriculum Book

Reading/Language Arts Learn about unity created by subject/verb agreement compared to the way unity is created in art. (page 205)

Math Learn to estimate distances to solve problems. (page 206)

Science Study levers and learn about a pivot, fulcrum, effort force, and resistance force, using a seesaw on a playground as an example. (page 207)

Social Studies List the rights and responsibilities of children using a playground. (page 208)

The Arts Describe the body movements, gestures, and facial expressions of a group in harmony and a group in conflict. (page 209)

Technology Use the *Multimedia Workshop* CD-ROM to create a group theme drawing that shows unity. (page 210)

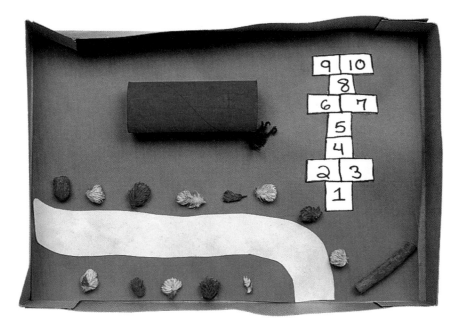

Ophelia Darst. Age 10. *Playground.* Found objects.

How does the student artist create unity for the piece of equipment she designed?

Create

What was your favorite playground when you were younger? Design one piece of equipment for a playground.

1. Think about a playground you remember. Choose one piece of equipment to create and make a sketch of it.

2. What does each separate part look like and how are the parts attached? Use paper and sculpture techniques to create your playground equipment.

3. Create the ground. Paint or glue down pathways, a hopscotch outline, or some flowers. Arrange your completed form on your prepared playground area.

Describe What piece of equipment did you select and how did you form it? What color is your playground equipment?

Analyze How did you arrange the various pieces? Describe how you used variety to create your equipment.

Interpret What title would you give the finished piece?

Decide What part of the scene do you like most? Do you feel that you were able to create unity by balancing harmony and variety?

Lesson 5   **185**

"Were you able to create a paper sculpture using harmony and variety to create unity?"

"¿Fueron capaces de crear una escultura de papel usando armonía y variedad para crear unidad?"

LARGE PRINT **Review**
Use the **Large Prints** *The Letter* and *The Dancing Couple* to have students compare the uses of unity to the works in this lesson.

Art Criticism

Have students answer the four art criticism questions—Describe, Analyze, Interpret, and Decide—orally or in writing. Discuss the use of unity in their works after they are completed.

Assess
Use the **Assessment Book** pages 69–70 as a formal assessment for this lesson.

Evaluation Criteria

- Can the student identify how harmony and variety create unity in works of art?
- Can the student design and create a paper sculpture of one piece of playground equipment?
- Can the student use the four steps of art criticism to evaluate his or her own artwork?
- Can the student demonstrate knowledge of the cultural purpose of the artworks in this lesson?

Reteaching • • • • • • • • • • • •

Unity Have students look through magazines to find two additional artworks that use harmony and variety to create unity.

THEME Connections

Systems Use the photograph of the playground in Israel as a means of introducing the study of the democratic system of governing in Israel and the United States.

Energy Use Chase's painting to discuss ways that scientists can use waste to build parks and produce energy.

ESL

It can be difficult for students in the early and intermediate stages of learning English to talk about a subject, such as their neighborhood. Use rough sketches and photographs to help with the lessons. Students may point out characteristics and describe them.

Perception Hints for Student Art

The student artist created unity through a variety of shapes such as the round tube, hopscotch squares, and a walkway. Harmony is created by the grass, which is the backdrop for the whole design. Unity is further achieved with the enclosure of all the elements.

Unity

Artists create unity by bringing different objects or elements together in a work of art so that everything fits together.

Iris Sandkühler. *Composition in Brown and Gold.* 1995. Costume jewelry, copper, brass, glass, and amber. 24-inch length × 3-inch fringe. Private Collection

The artist, Iris Sandkühler, uses many unusual materials to create jewelry. In *Composition in Brown and Gold,* she uses recycled jewelry. In the pendant, *Pyrite Sun Pendant,* she uses a unique process called *copper electroforming.* This process actually allows a designer to "grow" copper by combining chemical and electrical techniques. Notice how both pieces contain a variety of art elements yet create the feeling of wholeness.

LESSON PLANNER

Objectives

After completing this lesson, students will be able to:

• identify the use of unity by bringing together objects or elements in a work of art so that everything fits together. *Aesthetic Perception*

• create an original piece of jewelry using found objects, while maintaining unity. *Creative Expression*

• use the four steps of art criticism to evaluate their own artwork. *Art Criticism*

• demonstrate knowledge of the life and work of the artist. *Art History and Culture*

Program Resources

• **Overhead:** Both works of Sandkühler are available on overhead 36.

• **Large Prints:** *The Letter* by Mary Cassatt and *The Dancing Couple* by Jan Steen

• **Vocabulary Book** pages 71–72

• **Art Manipulative Kit:** Baroque music audiotape

• **Artist Profiles Book:** Sandkühler page 47

• **Art Across the Curriculum Book** pages 211–216

• **Multimedia Workshop CD-ROM**

• **Assessment Book** pages 71–72

Multiple Intelligences
Body/Kinesthetic Students can apply their knowledge of unity by manipulating materials and supplies to create a piece of jewelry.

Vocabulary

unity *unidad* quality of wholeness or oneness that is achieved through the effective use of the elements and principles of art

FOCUS

Time: About 10 minutes

Activating Prior Knowledge

"Can you take off any part of a bike and still have it work as well as one with all its parts?"

"¿Pueden dejar de colocar una parte de sus bicicletas y aún así hacerla trabajar como una bicicleta que tiene todas sus partes?"

• Discuss the students' answers to the question. Remind them that although all the parts are different, it is necessary to have all of them in order for the bike to work smoothly.

ART Background

About the Artists
Iris Sandkühler (ī′ ris sand′ kū lər, German 1958–   ) was born in Bingen/Rhine, West Germany. She emigrated to the United States in 1964 and became an American citizen five years later. She is on the faculty of Georgia Southern University and holds degrees from Ohio State University and Appalachian State University.

About Subject Matter* Both pieces are functional art and symbolic.

About the Media Iris Sandkühler uses a technique called copper electroforming with the majority of her jewelry pieces. To complement pendants created with that technique, she often uses handmade chains. Making the chains is relaxing to the artist.

Iris Sandkühler. (German). *Pyrite Sun Pendant.* 1992.
7 × 4 inches. Copper, brass, pyrite, sterling, glass, base
metal. Photograph: Sandkühler. Private Collection.

Compare the use of unity in both pieces of jewelry.

✓ What particular shapes do you recognize in each piece
of jewelry?

✓ Are there any unusual objects in either piece? How do
they relate to the work as a whole?

✓ What are some similarities and differences in each
piece?

Lesson 6   **187**

SEEING LIKE
AN ARTIST

How do all the
different parts of a car
work together to
create a whole? What
would happen if one
part were missing?

Cultural Perspectives Sandkühler's ideas come from somewhere inside of her, but they
also come from something in nature, a creative force. Sandkühler states that she has a
"need" to create. Sandkühler learned that after three weeks without art, she misses it.
Even without art supplies, she starts finding objects with which to create artwork.

*See **More About** pages 206–227 for more about art history and subject matter.

Introducing the Art
"Let's look closely at the pieces of jewelry."
"Vamos a observar detalladamente las joyas."

• **Describe:** Have students describe the subject
matter of the artwork. (both: functional art and
symbolic)
• Share and discuss information from **Art
Background** and the **Artist Profiles Book.**
• Have students answer the questions on page
187. (See **Perception Hints** below.)
• **COMPARE AND CONTRAST** Have students make
a list of similarities and differences in the two
works of art. (They are both meant to be worn
around the neck. The *Composition* encircles the neck and
has objects hanging along the whole length. The *Pendant*
has one large piece in the front with smaller pieces
hanging from it.

FOR THE ART SPECIALIST

Use the **Overhead** and the **Large Print**
The Letter or *The Dancing Couple* to
demonstrate how artists create unity by
bringing together different objects or
elements in a work of art so that
everything fits together.

Perception Hints

Shapes *Composition.* Circles and triangles. *Pendant.* Round
shapes.
Unusual objects *Composition.* Recycled earrings and rings
hang from the chain. They relate to the work as a whole
because they are mostly round. They relate to each other
and the round chain that goes around the neck. *Pendant.*
Shards left over from glassblowing. They relate to the
work as a whole in that each piece is uniquely different
from the next, and all are one of a kind. They are unified
with the handmade chain.
Similarities and differences *Both.* Round shapes.
Composition. Recycled jewelry. *Pendant.* Copper
electroforming.

Practice

Materials

• white paper

• pencils

Alternate Materials: magazines

"Let's find an example of unity in a piece of art in this book."

"Vamos a encontrar un ejemplo de unidad en una pieza de arte en este libro."

• Discuss the definition of *unity* on page 188.

• Distribute materials and have students follow the directions on page 188 for observing an example of unity. Have students discuss the answers to the Decide questions.

Create PROBLEM SOLVING

Materials

• found objects such as electrical materials, buttons, wires, beads, or old bits of jewelry

• glue

• string or chain

Alternate Materials: beads

"Let's create a piece of jewelry using found objects."

"Vamos a crear una joya usando objetos."

• Brainstorm ideas to create your necklace or badge. Discuss the definition of *unity*.

• Play a music audiotape from the **Art Manipulative Kit** to stimulate students' activity as they work.

• Distribute materials and have students follow the directions on page 189.

FOR THE ART SPECIALIST

Have students make jewelry by using beads and pendants that are made from clay and paint.

Using Unity

Unity is the quality of wholeness or oneness that is achieved through the effective use of the elements and principles of art.

Unity is oneness. It brings order to the world. It helps you concentrate on a visual image. When an artwork does not have unity, it is very difficult to concentrate on the work as a whole because all the different parts demand separate attention. It is like trying to talk to your friend when someone is playing a loud radio and a dog is barking. To create unity, an artist adjusts all parts of a work so that they relate to each other.

Practice

Observe an example of unity.

1. Find one example of unity in a piece of art in this book. Write the title, the artist, and the location of the artwork.

2. Discuss in a small group why you chose this work of art and how you think unity was created in it.

Decide What art elements are used to create unity in the work of art? What is it about this piece that first drew your attention?

Activities in ART Across the Curriculum Book

Reading/Language Arts Identify sentences that provide unity in a paragraph about jewelry. (page 211)

Math Measure the materials you could use to create your own necklace. (page 212)

Science Learn about different kinds of gems and minerals used in jewelry. (page 213)

Social Studies Design a necklace with the understanding that people wear jewelry for many different reasons. (page 214)

The Arts Plan a play about a missing necklace. Write a brief description of the necklace. (page 215)

Technology Use the *Multimedia Workshop* CD-ROM to design a piece of jewelry using both harmony and variety. (page 216)

How do the student artists maintain a sense of unity in the necklace?
Alia Whitney and **Claire Stanhope**.
Ages 10. *Necklace*. Mixed found objects.

Create

How is unity maintained when making a piece of jewelry with many objects? Create an original piece of jewelry, such as a badge or necklace, using found objects.

1. Think about the things around you that might look good as a piece of jewelry.

2. Arrange the materials to create your badge or necklace. Notice the changes that occur when you rearrange the materials.

3. Select one arrangement. Attach the materials to create one complete and unified piece. Glue a backing onto your badge or add a chain or piece of yarn to complete your necklace.

Describe Describe the materials used to create your jewelry. What colors and shapes are in your piece?

Analyze How did you arrange your materials to create unity? What other art elements created unity in your finished piece?

Interpret Does your ornament remind you of anything you have seen before? If so, what is it?

Decide What part of your completed piece do you like best? Why? Do you feel that you were able to create a feeling of unity in your work?

Lesson 6 189

Change Use the *Composition in Brown and Gold* to open a discussion regarding the change in fashion trends in the United States in the last ten years.

Discovery Use Sandkühler's pendant as a springboard for studying the discovery and value of diamonds.

Some ESL students can benefit from prompting as they discuss their artwork. You can create easier questions related to more difficult ones from the book to engage learners at their level of English proficiency. For example: *Which part do you like the best? The top? The bottom? The middle?*

CLOSE

Time: About 5 minutes

"Were you able to create a piece of jewelry with found objects using unity?"
"¿Pudieron crear una joya con objetos usando unidad?"

 Review
Use the **Large Print** *The Dancing Couple* to have students compare the use of unity to the works of art in this lesson.

Art Criticism
Have students answer the four art criticism questions—Describe, Analyze, Interpret, and Decide—orally or in writing. Discuss the use of unity in their works after their artworks are completed.

Assess
Use the **Assessment Book** pages 71–72 as a formal assessment for this lesson.

Evaluation Criteria
- Can the student identify unity when an artist brings together different objects or elements in a work of art so that everything fits together?
- Can the student create an original piece of jewelry using found objects, maintaining unity?
- Can the student use the four steps of art criticism to evaluate his or her own artwork?
- Can the student demonstrate knowledge of the cultural purpose of each artwork?

Reteaching • • • • • • • • • • • •

Unity Find another artwork in the book that brings together different objects so that everything fits together.

Perception Hints for Student Art

The student artist created unity through the repetition of color and shape in the round disc and star-shaped beads. The wire forms a line adding variety and unity simultaneously.

LESSON PLANNER

Objectives
After completing this lesson, students will be able to:
- write a song demonstrating the basic relationship of lyrics to music. *Aesthetic Perception*
- express emphasis, variety, harmony, and unity in the creation of song lyrics. *Creative Expression*
- use the four steps of art criticism to evaluate the process and product of songwriting. *Art Criticism*
- tell how songwriters like Paul Tracey use personal experiences when writing songs. *Art History and Culture*

FOCUS

Time: About 10 minutes

Activating Prior Knowledge

"Think about songs you have heard. Name some themes that songwriters write about?"

"Piensen en las canciones que han escuchado. Nombren algunos temas que los compositores hayan escrito."

- Discuss students' answers and talk about songs as a way of expressing feelings or relating personal stories or events.

Introducing the Art

"Look at the photograph of Paul Tracey. What type of song do you think he is singing? What can you tell from his expression and posture?"

"Observen la fotografía de Paul Tracey. ¿Qué tipo de canción creen que está cantando? ¿Cómo lo pueden saber de acuerdo a su expresión y postura?"

- Share information about Paul Tracey and composing from **Art Background.** If you have the *Artsource* audiocassette, have students listen to the music by Paul Tracey.

Emphasis, Variety, Harmony, and Unity in Music

Paul Tracey, songwriter.

Paul Tracey is a person who has used his experiences, whether they were sad, happy, frustrating, or funny, as a source for creative ideas. For example, when he got married and had a daughter, his new feelings of love and family closeness inspired him to write songs. His songs express the harmony of music, the variety of his experiences, and the wholeness, or unity, of his life.

190   Unit 6

ART Background

About the Artist

International troubadour Paul Tracey draws upon his cultural heritage and broad personal experience to communicate ideas about life through original songs. Born in South Africa in 1939, he experienced the divorce of his parents when he was seven. He then moved to England to live with his mother, brother, and grandmother. At age 18, he moved back to South Africa to work on his father's farm. He helped create a musical production that took him on a world tour. He got married, ended up in New York, and had a daughter. These new feelings of love and family closeness inspired him to write songs, several of which were sung by The Muppets. Paul Tracey is a prime example of a person who has drawn creative ideas from experiences in his life, whether they are sad, happy, frustrating, or funny.

What To Do

Write a song.

Materials
✓ paper and pencils

1. Choose the method you will use to write a song. You can write both the words and the music. You can put the words of a poem to original music. You can borrow a melody and write your own words.

2. Select a theme or idea for your song. Next, create a word web to identify words that relate to your theme. Then, find words that rhyme with those words.

3. Write words on your theme in rhythmic lines that end with rhyming words.

4. Try singing your song. Change the parts that don't seem to work. Practice and then perform it.

Describe Describe the songwriting method you used.

Analyze Explain how you used emphasis, harmony, variety, and unity in your song.

Interpret What feelings or mood does your song express?

Decide How well do you think you succeeded in writing a song? What would you do differently if you tried again?

Extra Credit

Accompany your song with a musical instrument or with sounds you have tape-recorded from nature. Perform for your class.

Music 191

About Subject Matter Composers create music for many different reasons, such as personal experiences, events, or people. At other times they respond to ideas or things that they see. Compositions are written to commemorate holidays, religious experiences, or specific events. Composers are often hired to write music for musicals, films, and videos. Whatever the motivation, composers respond to their own need to express themselves through music.

About Music A composer works with principles similar to those used by a visual artist when working on a painting or three-dimensional artwork. Emphasis in songwriting is found in the way words are positioned and in their combination with melody. The words establish a framework that is determined by the combination of meter and rhyming patterns. Unity is achieved with the song's successful creation.

TEACH

Time: Two 30-minute periods

Materials
• pencils and paper
• a selection of songs (on audiocassette or CD)

"Let's express ourselves by writing songs of our own."

"Vamos a expresarnos escribiendo canciones de nosostros mismos."

• Let students choose whether to work alone, with a partner, or in a group.

• Have students decide on an idea or theme for a song. Then, list words related to this theme and words that rhyme with the theme words.

• Point out that with an existing melody, students must put words into a set rhythmic pattern. A student who is making up a tune might try whispering the lyrics while cupping his or her hands around the face, as this technique often suggests a melody.

• Encourage students to sing their original songs for the class.

CLOSE

Time: About 5 minutes

"What did you gain from the experience of writing a song?"

"¿Qué obtuvieron de la experiencia de escribir una canción?"

◆ **Assess**
Have students answer the four art criticism questions on page 191—Describe, Analyze, Interpret, and Decide—orally or in writing.

Evaluation Criteria
• Can the student demonstrate the basic relationship of lyrics to music?

• Can the student express emphasis, variety, harmony, and unity in the creation of song lyrics?

• Can the student use the four steps of art criticism to evaluate his or her songwriting experience?

• Can the student demonstrate knowledge of how songwriters like Paul Tracey use personal experiences when writing songs?

UNIT 6

Reviewing Unit Concepts

"Artists use emphasis, variety, harmony, and unity to arrange the elements of art in drawings and paintings."

"Los artistas usan énfasis, variedad, armonía y unidad para ordenar los elementos de arte en dibujos y pinturas."

• Review the use of emphasis, variety, and harmony on page 165.

• Have the students find examples in their books of how artists use emphasis, variety, and harmony.

Examining the Artwork

"How did Hopper use emphasis, variety, harmony, and unity?"

"¿Cómo usó Hopper el énfasis, la variedad, la armonía y la unidad?"

• Ask the students to describe what they see in Hopper's painting using the terms they learned in this unit.

• Discuss the questions on page 193.
(See **Perception Hints** below.)

Student Portfolio

Have students review the artwork they have created during this unit and select the pieces they wish to put into their portfolios.

Art Criticism Activity

Have students select an artwork from another unit and study it using the four steps of art criticism. (See page 206–209 for more information about Art Criticism.)

Perception Hints

Emphasis The first thing that attracts the viewer's attention is the darkened building.

Variety is seen in the difference between the cool, dark-shaded, green ground and the warm, light tones of the sky.

Harmony and unity are used in the horizontal bands of color throughout the painting: the silver of the horizontal railroad tracks; the horizontal bands of orange, yellow, and blue; and the strong, dark bands of the clouds. Vertical and horizontal lines and color tie the painting together.

Wrapping Up Unit 6
Emphasis, Variety, Harmony, and Unity
Reviewing Main Ideas

The lessons and activities in this unit cover the techniques that artists use to create emphasis, variety, harmony, and unity.

• **Emphasis** is the principle of design that stresses one area in a work of art.

• **Focal point** is the first thing in an artwork that attracts the attention of a viewer.

• **Variety** is the principle of design concerned with difference or contrast.

• **Unity** is the feeling of wholeness or oneness.

• **Harmony** is concerned with the similarities of separate but related parts. Similar art elements, such as line and shape, are combined to create visual harmony.

Edward Hopper. (American). *Railroad Sunset.* 1929. Oil on canvas. $28\frac{1}{4} \times 47\frac{3}{4}$ inches. Collection of Whitney Museum of American Art, New York/Josephine N. Hopper bequest/Photography by Bill Jacobson, N.Y.

ART Background

About the Artist

Edward Hopper (ed' wərd häp' ər, American, 1882–1967) was born in Nyack, New York. He was trained as an illustrator at the New York School of Art. He lived and worked in New York and spent most of his summers in New England. Most of his subject matter came from these two places. He often depicted the feelings of isolation and loneliness in his paintings. He wanted to communicate that these feelings existed in urban cities and small towns.

About Subject Matter* *Railroad Sunset* is typical of Hopper's realistic work. His paintings dealt with the loneliness and isolation in cities and towns.

Summing Up

Look at *Railroad Sunset* by Edward Hopper. In this painting, the artist created emphasis, variety, harmony, and unity covered in this unit.

- What is the first thing you see when you look at the painting *Railroad Sunset*?
- How did Edward Hopper use variety in this painting?
- How did Hopper create harmony and unity in his painting?

Emphasis, variety, harmony, and unity are all important art elements in works of art. By creating emphasis, variety, harmony, and unity, artists express what they see and feel to others.

Careers in Art
Jewelry Designer

Iris Sandkühler is a jewelry designer who was born in West Germany. Jewelry designers must have a good understanding of the elements of design. They must also understand the chemicals that make up different metals. The majority of Sandkühler's jewelry is made from a special process using copper. This is a process that uses chemicals and electricity to grow copper on glass. Sandkühler was asked to design an ornament for the White House Christmas tree using this special process. She says that although designing jewelry takes a lot of patience, she loves the challenge of coming up with new ideas.

Iris Sandkühler, jewelry designer

193

Learning About Careers in Art

Jewelry making is one of the oldest of the decorative arts. Iris Sandkühler was born in Germany and became an American citizen five years later. Her reputation and expertise in jewelry making have won her several commissions including one from the White House. She is famous for the jewelry she makes by combining metal and glass. She exhibits in numerous places including the 1996 Summer Olympics in Atlanta.

- Have students look through magazines and newspapers for examples of jewelry. Have them create a list of the materials they see and another list of techniques and styles.

A Final Thought

"Art is not a handicraft; it is the transmission of feeling the artist has experienced."—Leo Tolstoy

---

About the Media *Railroad Sunset* is an oil painting. Hopper used oil paints because he was able to easily blend and rework areas in his paintings to create high contrast in lighting.

About Art History* Hopper was greatly influenced by Robert Henri and the work of the American art movement called the Ashcan School. The Ashcan school began in 1908 when an art critic saw an exhibit by a group of young artists who had realistically painted the scenes of city life. Much of the subject matter was of the city's nightlife, theaters, and alleyways.

Cultural Perspectives In 1908 when Edward Hopper moved to New York, Pablo Picasso and Georges Braque cofounded the art movement known as Cubism. The first Model T automobile was produced by the Ford Motor Company. The NAACP—National Association for the Advancement of Colored People—was founded and *A Wind in the Willows* was published.

*See **More About** pages 206–227 for more about art history and subject matter.

TECHNIQUE TIPS

OVERVIEW

The purpose of the technique tips is to provide additional information, beyond what is on the student pages, about the proper and possible uses for the media. Learning the proper techniques and using materials safely will add to students' confidence and enthusiasm for art. (For more about Safety in the Art Classroom, see page T22.) These pages can help your students combine imagination with media to create art.

Drawing (pages 194–197)

Pencil

Blending is a technique of shading in which the student holds the pencil on its side between the thumb and other fingers and shades with the side of the lead.

- Primary grade pencils with a medium-soft lead are ideal for all shading techniques.
- To create darker values, students should use the side of the pencil lead, press harder, and shade over areas more than once.
- To create lighter values, the students should press lightly and shade over the area less.
- Gradations from dark to light can be created by smearing a shaded area into an area not yet shaded with a paper stump made of a tightly rolled paper towel.

Hatching is a pattern of parallel lines. How closely together the lines are drawn determines the value of that part of the drawing.

In **Crosshatching,** the parallel lines overlap each other. Like with hatching, the distance of the lines from each other determines the value.

Stippling is a series of dots that create value and value change. Careful control of the placement of all shading is important, especially stipple dots. Be sure that students are carefully drawing these dots rather than simply dotting their paper with them.

Colored Pencil

- When blending colors with colored pencils, it is important to color the lighter color before the darker one. A color can be darkened easily, but it is almost impossible to lighten a color.
- To create shadows, blend complementary colors. This will create browns and darker colors.

Technique Tips

Pencil

With the side of your pencil lead, press harder and shade over areas more than once for darker values. With a pencil, you can add form to your objects by shading. You can also use lines or dots for shading. When lines or dots are drawn close together, you get darker values. When dots or lines are drawn farther apart, lighter values are created.

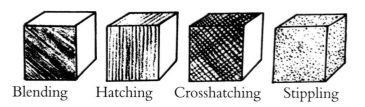

Blending   Hatching   Crosshatching   Stippling

Colored Pencil

You can blend colors with colored pencils. Color with the lighter color first. Gently color over it with the darker color until you have the effect you want.

With colored pencils, you can use the four shading techniques.

Shadows or darker values can be created by blending complementary colors.

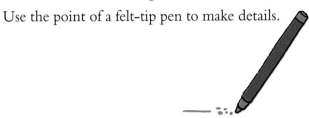

More About...
Technique Tips

Felt-tip Pen

Felt-tip pens can be used to make either sketches or finished drawings. They are ideal for contour drawings.

Use the point of a felt-tip pen to make details.

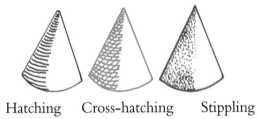

Felt-tip pens can be used for hatching, cross-hatching, and stippling.

Hatching   Cross-hatching   Stippling

Always replace the cap so the felt-tip pen doesn't dry out.

More About...Technique Tips   **195**

Felt-Tip Pen

Felt-tip pens are a practical substitute for pen and ink. Their narrow points make them ideal for drawing details and contour line drawings.

- They can be used to draw over lightly sketched pencil drawings.
- They can be used to draw a picture which can then be painted with watercolors. (The ink is water-soluble and may run when touched by wet paint.)
- Students should avoid pressing too hard when drawing so as not to damage the tip; this is especially true when stippling.
- After use, the cap should always be replaced.

TECHNIQUE TIPS

(continued)

Marker

- To avoid damage and to achieve better control, students should not press hard on the marker tip.
- A conical-tipped marker can be used to make thin lines and dots. The side of the tip can be used to make wider lines and color in areas.
- Remind the students to always replace the cap to prevent drying.

Technique Tips

Marker

Markers can be used to make sketches or finished drawings. Use the point of the marker to make thin lines and small dots.

Use the side of the tip for coloring in areas and for making thick lines.

Always replace the cap so the marker doesn't dry out.

Technique Tips

Colored Chalk

Colored chalks can be used to make colorful, soft designs.

You can use the tip of the colored chalk to create lines, color shapes, and fill spaces. As with pencil, you can also use them for blending to create shadows.

Colored chalk is soft and can break easily. These pieces are still usable. Colors can be mixed or blended by smearing them together with your finger or a tissue.

Oil Pastels

Oil pastels are colors that are mixed with oil and pressed into sticks. When you press down hard with them, your pictures will look painted.

Oil pastels are soft. You can use oil pastels to color over other media, such as tempera or crayon. Then, you can scratch through this covering to create a design.

Charcoal

Charcoal is soft. It can be blended with a piece of rolled paper towel and your finger. Create dark values by coloring over an area several times. Create lighter values by erasing or coloring over the charcoal with white chalk.

Colored Chalk

Colored chalks are used to make colorful, soft designs. The tip of the chalk is used much like an oil pastel to make lines.

- To fill a space or shape with solid color, color over an area more than once.
- Colors can be mixed or blended by smearing them together with a paper towel wrapped around a finger.
- Colored chalks break easily. Reassure students that these pieces can still be used like new ones.
- Colored chalks become dirty from use. Instruct the students to mark with them on a paper towel until the colors are clean.

Oil Pastels

Oil pastels are pigments mixed with oil and compressed into sticks.

- By pressing with gentle force and coloring over an area several times, students can create the effect of paint.
- They can create lines by drawing with the tip.
- They can color large spaces with the tip or side.
- Textures can be created by making marks such as dots and lines. Textures can also be made by layering colors and scratching through with a paper clip straightened at one end.
- Colors can be mixed or blended by smearing with a paper towel wrapped around a finger.
- Oil pastels break easily. Reassure the students that these pieces can still be used like new ones.
- If oil pastels become dirty from use, instruct students to mark with them on a paper towel until the colors are clean again.

Charcoal

Charcoal is a versatile drawing medium.

- Because it is easily erased to create lighter values and blended to create shadows, it is perfect for young artists timid about drawing large or dark marks on their paper.
- While charcoal is messy, it can be cleaned from hands and clothing with soap and water.

TECHNIQUE TIPS

(continued)

Painting (pages 198–199)

Tempera

For best results, it is recommended that quality liquid tempera paint be used.

Emphasize the following with students:

1. To remove excess water from the brush, gently wipe the end of the brush on the inside edge of the container. Discourage the students from tapping brushes on the rim of the can. This will prevent paint splatters.
2. Mix paints on a palette. Paper plates work well and reduce cleanup.
3. Always mix the darker color into the lighter color a little at a time until the desired color is reached. This reduces wasted paint.
4. Use a wide brush for large spaces.
5. Use a thin brush to paint details.

More About...

Technique Tips

Tempera

1. Fill water containers halfway. Dip your brush in water. Wipe your brush on the inside edge of the container. Then, blot it on a paper towel to get rid of extra water. Stir the paints. Add a little water if a color is too thick or dry. Remember to clean your brush before using a new color.

2. Always mix colors on a palette. Put some of each color that you want to mix on the palette. Then, add the darker color a little at a time to the lighter color. Change your water when it gets too muddy.

3. To create lighter values, add white. To darken a value, add a tiny amount of black. If you have painted something too thickly, add water and blot it with a clean paper towel.

4. Use a thin, pointed brush to paint thin lines and details. For thick lines or large areas, press firmly on the tip or use a wide brush.

5. Wash your brushes when you are done. Reshape the bristles. Store brushes with the bristles up.

More About...Technique Tips

More About...
Technique Tips

Watercolor

1. Fill water containers halfway. Dip your brush in water. Wipe your brush on the inside edge of the container. Then, blot it on a paper towel to get rid of extra water. With your brush, add a drop of water to each watercolor cake and stir. Remember to clean your brush whenever you change colors.

2. Always mix colors on a palette. Put some of each color that you want to mix on the palette. Then, add the darker color a little at a time to the lighter color. Change your water when it gets too muddy.

3. To create lighter values, add more water. To darken a value, add a tiny amount of black.

4. Use a thin, pointed brush to paint thin lines and details. For thick lines or large areas, press firmly on the tip or use a wide brush.

5. For a softer look, tape your paper to the table with masking tape. Use a wide brush to add water to the paper, working in rows from top to bottom. This is a **wash.** Let the water soak in a little. Painting on wet paper will create a soft or fuzzy look. For sharper forms or edges, paint on dry paper, using only a little water on your brush.

6. Wash your brushes when you are done. Reshape the bristles. Store brushes with the bristles up.

Watercolors

Below are some tips for using and controlling watercolors.

- Thick lines can be created by gently pressing down on the brush.
- Thin lines can be created by lightly touching the paper's surface with the tip of the brush.
- To create textures such as stipple (dots) or lines, demonstrate these techniques.
  1. Wet a round, soft-bristled watercolor brush.
  2. Carefully squeeze excess water from the bristles.
  3. Gently divide the bristles into spikes.
  4. Carefully touch the moistened paint cake with the bristle tips so that some paint is absorbed by the bristles.
  5. Lightly touch the paper with the separated bristles. Gentle taps create irregular dots. Gentle, upward strokes create irregular lines.
  6. When finished, rinse, clean, and reshape the brush.
- To create lighter values, the hue should be thinned with water using these steps:
  1. Use a watery brush.
  2. Thin the hue on the palette with water.
  3. Brush water over an already painted area.
  4. Blot wet, painted area with a paper towel.
- To create darker values, add drops of black to the hue on the palette, *one at a time,* until the desired value is achieved.

Wash

Painting or sponging water onto the paper prior to painting will create soft lines, soft-edged shapes, and softer colors. The water should be allowed to soak into the paper before painting.

- To create sharp, clear lines and shapes, students should paint on dry paper with a damp brush.
- To create a fuzzy look, students should paint on dry paper with a dry brush and very little paint.

TECHNIQUE TIPS
(continued)

Printmaking (pages 200–201)
Making and Printing Stamps

- The following procedure can be used to make sponge prints:
  1. If students wish to cut a sponge into a specific shape, use thin sponges. Draw the shape on the sponge with a marker and use scissors to cut it out.
  2. Dispense colors onto individual palettes, or spread out on a surface large enough to avoid mixing. Lightly press the sponge into the paint, being careful not to get too much paint on it. Lift the sponge and lightly press it into place on the paper. The sponge should be thoroughly rinsed between colors.

- Oil-based modeling clay can also be used to make a stamp. This is done by drawing or sculpting a design on a flat piece of modeling clay. There are a variety of tools manufactured for carving clay. Some classroom items that will work just as well include plastic eating utensils, craft sticks, and paper clips. The straightened end of a paper clip can be used to draw in the clay. The rounded end can be used as a gouge to carve clay away. To create a raised stamp, simply add pieces of clay to the bottom of the clay stamp.

Printmaking: Making Stamps

Two methods for making stamps for printmaking are listed below. You can cut either a positive or negative shape into most of these objects. Be sure to talk with your teacher or another adult about what kind of tools you can use safely.

- Cut sponges into shapes.

- Draw or sculpt a design on a flat piece of modeling clay using a pencil, clay tool, tip of a paper clip, or other object.

More About...
Technique Tips

Printmaking: Printing Stamps

1. Put a small amount of water-based printing ink or some paint onto a hard, flat surface. Roll a soft roller, called a brayer, back and forth into the ink until there is an even coating of paint on both the surface and the brayer.

2. Brush the ink on with a flat, wide brush also. The ink should cover the stamp evenly without going into the grooves of your design.

3. Or, you can coat the stamp evenly with paint using a brush. Whichever method you use, be careful not to use too much ink or paint.

4. Gently press your stamp carefully to your paper. Then, peel the paper and stamp apart and check your print. If you wish to make several prints of your design, you should ink your stamp again as needed.

5. When you have finished, wash the brayer, surface, and stamp.

More About...Technique Tips   **201**

More About Making Prints

- Below is the procedure for using a brayer, which is a soft roller, to make prints.

  1. Pour a small amount of water-based printing ink or paint onto a flat, solid surface. Roll the brayer in the ink or paint until there is an even coating on the surface and brayer.
  2. Roll the brayer over the top of the stamp. The ink should cover the stamp evenly without getting into the grooves of the design.
  3. Apply the stamp carefully to the paper, rubbing the back of the stamp with the side of the fist.
  4. Peel the paper and stamp apart.
  5. Reink the stamp as needed if you wish to make more than one print.
  6. When finished, wash the brayer, surface, and stamp.

- Another method for making prints calls for a paintbrush to apply the ink or paint. This method works better than the brayer with a raised stamp that the brayer would flatten out. Brush the ink or paint onto the stamping surface. Then follow the steps above, ending with thoroughly cleaning the brush.

TECHNIQUE TIPS

(continued)

Collage
Using Scissors

- It is important to teach the students safety when using scissors. They should always cut away from their bodies. Of course they should never point their scissors at others, spin them on the table, or walk around the room with them.

- There are scissors specially made to spring open for students who are physically challenged. Many scissors on the market today can be used with the right or left hand. If these are not available, keep a supply of "lefty" scissors for students who need them.

- To cut thick yarn or fabric, encourage students to work with a partner. While one cuts, the other can stretch the yarn or fabric. This makes cutting easier and encourages cooperation.

Arranging a Design

A collage is a work of art in which bits and pieces of paper, fabric, and other materials are glued onto a surface to create a **composition.**

- Provide a variety of textured and colored papers, yarns, fabrics, and found objects. Hard-to-cut materials can be precut.

- When using paper, students may choose to tear and/or cut the shapes.

- Encourage them to arrange the design first, paying as much attention to the negative spaces as the positive ones.

- Glue only after the final colors, shapes, and textures have been chosen and arranged.

Colored Tissue Collage

- Review color mixing with students so that they do not overlap colors that do not mix. Otherwise, the colors will appear muddy.

- Store bottles with binder in them separate from the regular glue so that students do not mistake one for the other. An alternative to the binder suggested on page 203 (one part glue to one part water), is full-strength liquid starch.

- Wash brushes thoroughly with soap and water when finished.

More About...
Technique Tips

Collage

In a collage, objects or pieces of paper, fabric, or other materials are pasted onto a surface to create a work of art. When planning your collage, consider such things as:

- Size of shapes and spaces
- Placement of shapes and spaces
- Color schemes
- Textures

Remember that the empty (negative) spaces are also part of your design. Plan a collage as you would plan a painting or drawing. After deciding what shapes and objects you want to use, arrange them on the paper. When you have made an arrangement you like, glue your shapes and objects to the paper.

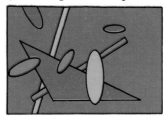

Colored Tissue Collage

When gluing colored tissue, mix a solution of one part glue to one part water.

When gluing the tissue, use an old brush to put a small amount of the glue and water solution onto the drawing paper. Next, put the tissue in place, and brush over the tissue with a small amount of the watered glue. Be careful not to get the color from the tissue on your fingers, which would create a mess. You can mix colors by overlapping different colored tissues.

Be sure to rinse your brush when you change colors. When you finish, wash the brush with soapy water.

More About...
Technique Tips

Papier-Mâché—Strip Method

The strip method of papier-mâché ("mashed paper") uses paper combined with paste. Often, papier-mâché is molded over a form that helps it keep its shape while it's drying.

1. Create a supporting form, if needed. Forms can be made from clay, wadded-up newspaper, cardboard boxes and tubes, balloons, wire, or other materials. Masking tape can be used to hold the form together.

2. Tear paper into strips. Either dip the strips into a thick mixture of paste or rub paste on the strips with your fingers. Use wide strips to cover wide forms and thin strips or small pieces to cover a small shape.

3. To remove the form when the papier-mâché is dry, first cover it with plastic wrap or a layer of wet newspaper strips.

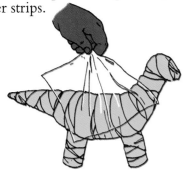

Then, apply five or six layers of strips. Lay each layer in a different direction so you can keep track of the number of strips and layers. For example, lay the first layer vertically and the second horizontally. Smooth over all rough edges with your fingers. If you are going to leave the form in place permanently, two or three layers of strips should be enough.

4. When it is dry, you can paint your sculpture.

More About...Technique Tips **203**

Papier-mâché is a French term that means "mashed paper." It refers to sculpting methods that use paper and liquid paste. The wet paper and paste material is molded over supporting structures such as wadded dry paper or crumpled foil. The molded paper dries to a hard finish.

- Below are three common papier-mâché solutions:
  1. Mix one part white glue to one part water by adding one half the amount of water to a glue bottle that is half full. Close the lid. Shake vigorously. Add second half of the water. Close the lid and shake until mixed.
  2. Make a creamy mixture of wheat paste and water. To mix wheat paste, wear a dust mask and pour dry paste into a large mixing bowl. Add water and stir until the mixture is creamy. Mash lumps with a spoon or your hands.
  3. Use liquid starch.

TECHNIQUE TIPS

(continued)

Sculpting (pages 204–205)

Working with Clay

To help prevent earth clay from drying and cracking, students should not overhandle the clay. Keep damp paper towels nearby for students to keep their hands moist.

- The following steps are for modeling a person or animal from clay:
  1. Roll the piece of clay into an oval-shaped form. Describe this to the students as a "potato" shape.
  2. Pinch a head shape on one end.
  3. Pinch and pull out arms and legs.
  4. Leave some, but not too much, clay for the body.
  5. Squeeze the head, arms, legs, and body into the desired shapes.

Joining Clay

Clay is joined by using **slip,** a creamy mixture of clay and water. Slip can be made by putting a few dry pieces of clay in a container and covering them with water. When the clay dissolves, stir to achieve a creamy consistency. Joining clay also requires a scoring tool such as a straightened paper clip. The steps below are called the four *S's*—score, slip, smooth, and squeeze.

1. **Score** the two pieces to be joined.
2. Apply **slip** to one of the surfaces.
3. **Smooth** the seam.
4. **Squeeze** the two surfaces together.

Carving Clay

There are a variety of tools manufactured for carving clay. Some classroom items that will work just as well are plastic eating utensils, craft sticks, and paper clips. The straightened end of a paper clip can be used to draw in the clay. The rounded end can be used as a gouge to carve clay away.

Technique Tips

Clay

Pinch and pull clay into the desired shape.

Clay Slab Construction

To roll a slab of clay, press a ball of clay into a flat shape on a cloth-covered board. Place one 1/4" slat on each side of the clay. Use a roller to press the slab into an even thickness. With a straightened paper clip, trim the slab into the desired shape.

Wrap unfinished sculptures in plastic to keep them moist until finished.

When you are constructing a form, such as a container or house, with slabs of clay, it may be necessary to stuff the form with wads of newspaper to support the walls. The newspaper will burn out in the kiln.

To join two pieces of clay together:

- *score,* or scratch, both pieces so they will stick together.

- attach the pieces with some *slip,* which is watery clay.

- *squeeze* the two pieces together.

- *smooth* the edges.

More About...Technique Tips

More About...
Technique Tips

Soap and Plaster Sculpture

You can carve sculptures from clay, soap, or plaster forms. Draw the basic shape of your idea onto all sides of the form. Keep your design simple. Carve a little bit at a time, using a spoon, a paper clip, or a plastic knife, while turning your form constantly.

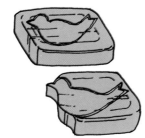

Soft Sculpture Face

Stuff a stocking or other stretchable material with polyester fill. Sew or glue on buttons, beads, sequins, fabric scraps, and other items to create facial features.

Add yarn, string, or raffia for hair. Try some of the stitches on this page to add details, such as eyebrows, wrinkles, or freckles.

You can use fabric paints for details.

Sew on a real hat, scarf, or head band. Use one of the stitches below.

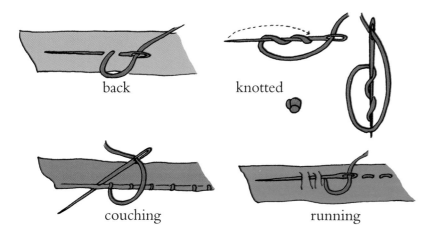

back   knotted

couching   running

Soap Sculpture
Inexpensive bars of white bath soap are recommended for carving.

Plaster Sculpture
- Make plaster carving blocks well ahead of time. Below is a procedure you can use to prepare plaster blocks in preparation for carving by students:
  1. Fill one third of a flexible rubber bucket with water.
  2. Wearing a dust mask, scoop plaster into the water until an "island" peaks and stays above the surface of the water.
  3. Add a couple of handfuls of vermiculite on top of the plaster. (This is added for softness and can be purchased at garden centers.)
  4. Using rubber gloves, mix with your hands, squeezing out any lumps. Do not add more plaster. The mixture will thicken.
  5. Working quickly, pour the plaster into clean, opened half-pint milk cartons, filling them. Plaster will set up in 20–30 minutes.
  6. Leave the excess plaster in the bucket to harden. **Do not pour into the sink.** When the plaster hardens, it can be popped out of the bucket by tapping the bottom and sides.
  7. Remove each carton by tearing it away from the plaster block.
  8. For carving it is best to let the plaster dry completely. Depending on the humidity, this may take a week.

Soft Sculpture Face
- Make a variety of materials available for use in embellishing the soft sculptures. Examples include buttons, sequins, beans, seeds, yarn, raffia, fabrics, ribbons, fabric markers and paints, and articles of clothing such as scarves, ties, socks, shoes, hair bows, hats, and so on.
- Use blunt plastic needles or blunt metal tapestry needles for the stitchery.

OVERVIEW

Art Criticism is an organized system for looking at and talking about art. You can criticize art without being an expert on art. All that is needed are eyes to see and a brain to think about what is seen. The purpose of art criticism is to get the viewer involved in a perception process that delays judgment until all aspects of the visual image have been studied.

Learning art criticism will give each viewer the confidence to discuss a work of art without worrying what other people might think. The more a viewer interacts with a work of art, the better the chances are that the viewer will be involved in an aesthetic experience.

Describe
During this step, the viewer lists all the obvious things in the work. During this step, you must be objective. You do not *know* from looking at *Frieda and Diego Rivera* that this man and woman are related. You must say that you see a man and woman.

Questions to Discuss
Ask the students to list and describe everything they see in the painting.

Perception Hints

- We see the full figures of a man and a woman standing on a plain, brown floor. Behind them is a light, dull green wall. Directly above Frieda's head flies a tan dove with blue-tipped wings.
- Diego almost fills half the painting. He is wearing a plain, dark blue suit, a blue shirt, and heavy looking, brown shoes. He holds a painter's palette with four long brushes. With his other hand, he holds Frieda's hand.
- Frieda looks tiny. She is wearing a floor-length ruffled, dark blue-green skirt, a red Mexican scarf that is trimmed with dark diamond shapes and fringe. Her face has very heavy eyebrows that meet in the center. Her head tilts toward Diego and she rests her right hand on his.

Frida Kahlo. (Mexican). *Frieda and Diego, Wedding Portrait.* 1931. Oil on canvas. 39 × 31 inches. San Francisco Museum of Modern Art, San Francisco, California.

ART Background

About the Artist
Born in Mexico, Frieda Kahlo (1907–1954) lived a short, painful life. As a child, she had polio, which caused one leg to stop growing. When she was eighteen, she was severely injured in a bus accident. Thirty-two operations did not entirely erase her pain and often kept her in bed. Whenever possible, she dressed in elaborate embroidered outfits, wore much jewelry, and tucked flowers in her hair. At age 22, she married the famous painter Diego Rivera, who was 42 at the time and had been married twice before. She and Rivera lived in separate houses, connected by a bridge. Despite their stormy relationship, she wanted to have children and was deeply disappointed by many miscarriages. To deal with her pain, she taught herself to paint. Rivera supported her in this, just as he tried to help her through her illnesses. After winning wide recognition for her painting, the frail Kahlo died at age 47.

More About...
Art Criticism

DESCRIBE

List what you see in this painting. Be sure to describe the people and their clothing. Don't forget to list everything else you see.

ANALYZE

Discuss the way the artist has used line, shape, color, value, space, and texture.

What kind of balance has the artist used?

Can you find examples of rhythm, variety, and harmony?

Has the artist used emphasis to make us notice one thing more than others?

Analyze

Questions to Discuss

Discuss the way the artist has used the elements and principles of art to organize this work.

Perception Hints

Line A horizontal line divides the floor and ceiling. There are diagonal lines in Frieda's skirt and Diego's brushes. All the other lines curve.

Shape The geometric shapes are the rectangular floor, the square wall, and the design on her scarf. Her face looks oval. All the other shapes are free-form. Diego's shape is large, bulky, and has a smooth outline. Frieda's shape is tiny, and the outline is very busy.

Color All the colors are dark or dull except for their skin and Frieda's bright red scarf.

Value The painting is mostly dark. The darkest area is Diego. The lightest area is Frieda's face and scarf.

Space The space is not deep.

Texture All the textures look smooth.

Balance Informal balance. The large, plain shape of Diego is balanced by the small, busy shape and bright color of Frieda. Their hands meet in the center.

Rhythm Repetitions in the design on Frieda's scarf and the folds of her dress.

Variety Strong contrast between Frieda's scarf and face and the rest of the work.

Harmony The green of Frieda's dress relates to the green wall. The warm skin tones are repeated across the work. The brown in Diego's palette, his belt, and his shoes tie him to the ground. All the browns are darker versions of skin color.

Emphasis The bright red scarf leads our eyes to the clasped hands. The hands are in the exact center of the work, and contrast against Diego's dark suit.

The Four Steps of Art Criticism

The process of art criticism is like playing detective. Each viewer must assume that the artist has a secret message inside the work. Art criticism is a four-step system that will help the viewer collect clues to deduce the hidden message. The four steps are **Describe, Analyze, Interpret,** and **Decide** or judgment.

Each step answers a question.

1. "What do I see?" (Describe)
2. "How is the work organized?" (Analyze)
3. "What is the artist saying to me?" (Interpret)
4. "What do I think about this work?" (Decide)

More About...
Art Criticism

Interpret

During interpretation, the student will make inferences about the message in the work of art. This step needs to go beyond narration to a statement about meaning, to a generalization about life. This can be the most difficult step because it requires the viewer to dare to be different.

Each interpretation can be different because each is based upon the feelings and life experiences of the viewer. No person has done or seen exactly the same things as the next person. The viewer may see ideas in a work of art that were never dreamed of by the artist. This is not wrong. It simply means that the work is so powerful that it has special meanings for everybody. Interpretation is a time to guess, but all guesses must be based upon the facts collected during the first two steps.

Questions to Discuss

- What is happening in this work of art?
- What is the artist trying to tell us about these people and their lives?

(These two stand before us holding hands. He looks like a boulder, and she looks as if she could float away. The clasped hands represent the link between them. They are married. This is their wedding portrait. But he turns away from her to the outside world, while she leans toward him. She shows her need for him; he shows his strength and independence. Answers will vary about the success of this marriage.)

More About...
Art Criticism

Frida Kahlo. (Mexican). *Frieda and Diego, Wedding Portrait.* 1931. Oil on canvas. 39 × 31 inches. San Francisco Museum of Modern Art, San Francisco, California.

ART Background

About the Media

Kahlo worked in oils on small canvases, often about the size of a sheet of paper.

About the Technique

Especially in her later work, Kahlo used specific colors to express emotions. Yellow, for example, meant madness, sickness, and fear. Cobalt blue represented love. She painted precisely, carefully controlling her brush strokes.

More About...
Art Criticism

INTERPRET

What is happening? What is the artist telling us about these two people? What can you tell about their relationship?

DECIDE

Have you ever seen another work of art that looks like this painting?

Is this painting successful because it is realistic? Is it successful because it is well-organized? Is it successful because you have strong feelings when you study it?

Aesthetic Theories

There are three common theories about aesthetic perception.

Imitationalism/Realism A work of art is good because the objects in it are realistically portrayed. The subject matter is clear and easily recognized.

Formalism/Composition A work of art is good because the artist has organized the elements using the principles successfully.

Emotionalism/Feelings A work of art is successful because it strongly affects the feelings of the viewer.

Decide

If the viewers were mature adults, knowledgeable about art, they could make a judgment about the quality of the work. Was this the artist's best work? Is this good art? These are the questions a professional critic would answer. The critic may also use aesthetic theories to defend his or her judgment. The students are not ready to make these kinds of decisions. They have not seen enough art to judge the quality of these pieces. On top of that, the works in this book have all been chosen because they are all examples of excellent art. But there are aesthetic decisions they can make.

Questions to Discuss

- Have you seen any works in this book that emphasize hands? (M. C. Escher's *Two Hands Drawing Each Other*)
- Can you find any other double portraits in this book? (Renoir's *Two Young Girls at the Piano*, Ghirlandaio's *Francesco Saesetti and His Son Teodoro*, Nanha the Mughal's *Emperor Jahanan and His Son, Suja*)
- Can you find any works that use informal balance? (Tissot's *Women of Paris, The Circus Lover*, Sofanisba Anguissola's *The Chess Game*, Renoir's *Two Young Girls at the Piano*, Ghirlandaio's *Francesco Saesetti and His Son Teodoro*, Nanha the Mughal's *Emperor Jahanan and His Son, Suja*)
- Which aesthetic theories would you use to judge this work? (*All three.*)

OVERVIEW

Aesthetic perception encourages children to make choices rather than give "right" answers. The perception of works of art happens in a "moment of transaction" in which the viewer/perceiver/learner is totally engaged in the moment. By understanding the process, the perceiver gives the work validity. This encourages students to tap into their own files, to see or hear something with new eyes and ears, and finally, to realize that art is all around them.

Works of art are not created in isolation. The work of art is an expression of the artist who exists in a time and place and who lives within a cultural context. Therefore, insight into a work of art can be heightened by further study of the contextual information which surrounds the work: historical, social, and cultural aspects of the work.

A work of art does not spring complete into the artist's mind, but is created as the result of a deliberate, time-consuming, and at times frustrating process of choice making. An initial vision is worked out by the artist in his/her medium and just as the artist's vision transforms the medium, so too, the medium transforms the artist's vision. The record of the artist's work lies in the medium transformed and is there for perceivers/learners/students to see. The perceivers will be better prepared to see the artist's vision if they themselves have worked to executive their own visions of the work of art.

LOOK

Frida Kahlo. (Mexican). *Frieda and Diego, Wedding Portrait.* 1931. Oil on canvas. 39 × 31 inches. San Francisco Museum of Modern Art, San Francisco, California.

ART Background

About Aesthetic Perception

Aesthetics has been defined as the branch of philosophy that focuses on the nature of beauty, the nature and value of art, and the inquiry processes and human responses associated with those topics. During the mid-1960s, the issue of arts education took on new importance. The shock of Sputnik sparked an educational reform movement, which led to the establishment of the arts and humanities endowments by the U.S. government. As a part of that, a 25-year history in the exploration of aesthetic perception has shown that to give youngsters an understanding of all the arts and the positive values they represent, the feelings and sensibilities of the viewer (perceiver), rather than solely those of the creator of the work of art, become the keystone of current aesthetic perception practice.

More About...
Aesthetics

LOOK AGAIN

Look at the work of art.

What happened just before and just after in this work of art?

What sounds, smells, or feelings are in this work of art?

What kind of music would be playing in this work of art?

If you could take away from or add images or elements to the work of art, what would they be and why?

Is there a relationship between the work of art and your experiences?

Questions to Discuss

There is an unpredictability in the process of learning from aesthetic perception. It is as individual as the participating student. It leads us to new ways of viewing our own experience and clarifies what we have seen in the work of art.

Look

- What do you see?
- What do you hear?
- What do you smell?
- What can you touch?

Look Again

- Does the work of art give you any surprises?
- What do you think is beyond the edge of the painting?
- What did you observe first in the work of art?
- What questions did the work of art pose to you?

More About...
Aesthetic Perception

Questions to Discuss

Look Inside

- What is happening in this work of art?
- What is this work of art about?
- If you were in this work of art, what would you be doing?
- What is your favorite part of this work of art?
- What is most important in this work of art?
- What happened just before and just after in this work of art?

Look Outside

- What have you learned about the work of art?
- How do you feel about the work of art; what does it make you feel?
- What will you remember about this work of art?
- If you could take images or elements away from the work, what would they be and why?
- What are three things that you noticed that you think the artist was trying to tell you in the work of art?
- Tell three things that you changed your mind about after experiencing the work of art.
- What questions do you want to ask about this work of art?

Things to Do

- Draw yourself into this work of art.
- Draw what you can't see in this work of art.
- Act out or show the story in the work of art.
- Collect images that are similar to the qualities, colors, or ideas in this work of art and assemble a collage in response to it.
- Write a journal entry explaining what changes you would make in this work of art to make it more like your own experience.
- Select a single symbol of your own that you think represents your impression of the work of art.

More About...
Aesthetics

LOOK INSIDE

Look at the work of art.

Imagine you are one of these people. Who are you? What are you thinking? How do you feel?

If you could add yourself to the painting, what would you look like? What would you be doing?

Act out or tell the story in the work of art with a beginning, a middle, and an end.

Draw what you can't see in this work of art. Are there hidden images that should be revealed?

Select or create one symbol of your own that you believe represents your impression of this work of art.

Frida Kahlo. (Mexican). *Frieda and Diego, Wedding Portrait.* 1931. Oil on canvas. 39 × 31 inches. San Francisco Museum of Modern Art, San Francisco, California.

ART Background

About Art History

Many of this artist's paintings contain the symbolism that is common in surreal art. A skeleton representing death often appeared in her work. She also created an imaginary friend, her twin. She showed them sitting together in her well-known painting, *The Two Friedas.* An artery joins their exposed hearts.

About the Artwork

Kahlo used her life as the subject matter for much of her work. She painted her own birth, her bus accident, her marriage to Rivera, and even her miscarriages. Kahlo said she painted herself because she was alone so much.

More About...
Aesthetics

LOOK OUTSIDE

Look at the work of art.

How is this like or different from your own world?

How would you change this work of art to be more like your world? What would the changes be? What would the artwork look like?

What does the artist want you to know or think about in this work of art?

Describe your journey about viewing this work of art. Include your thoughts, ideas, and changes in thinking.

If you could ask the work of art questions about itself, what would you ask?

How have you been changed by examining this work of art?

What will you remember about this work?

About Aesthetic Perception

Fifth graders are often fascinated with the intentional aspect of art making—why was it made. They want to know the history, culture, intellect, and relationship that it had to the time or world in which it was made. Fifth graders appreciate synthesizing ideas and concepts into large symbols. They want to know what is true for the artist and why it is true. They gravitate to why they remember certain elements of the work of art, as well as the class's collective experience in viewing the work of art.

There are underlying values that can support the aesthetic perception experience for students.

1. Minimize or simplify structures
2. Use inter-group and interpersonal communication in order to explore structural as well as individual similarities in projects
3. Import bits of the "real world" and keep in mind how things work in "real life"
4. Encourage asking questions
5. Use metaphors to explore interpersonal behavior
6. Always remember that culturally, the past and future are experienced in the present

More About...
Art History

OVERVIEW

Art history is the record of art from the past to the present. Studying it is like looking into a treasure chest of humankind's past. Through close examination of these pages, students will learn more about famous artworks and where they originated.

Understanding Art History

Begin helping your students to learn about the meaning of art history by doing the following:

Art History Is a Story

• Explain that art history is a record of art from past to present—it is the story of art.

TIMELINE Show the students the **Animals Through History Time Line.** Show the visual story of how artists long ago up to the present created images of animals. Have them indicate the oldest image on the time line (the cave art). Explain that by looking at art from the past, we learn what the people who lived before us were like—their feelings and beliefs, clothes, food, houses, and even how the viewed animals.

An Art Historian's Job

• Explain that an art historian investigates who, what, when, where, and how art was created. They are like detectives. They search for clues and evidence so that they can tell the most complete and accurate story about art. Have student name detectives they know about (Sherlock Holmes, Encyclopedia Brown, Colombo,). Tell them that when looking at these images, they need to have a "detective" mind-set.

Artist unknown.
Adena Effigy Figure.
100–300 B.C. United States.

Artist unknown.
Three Cows and One Horse.
15,000–13,000 B.C. France.

Artist unknown.
Statues from Abu Temple.
2700–2000 B.C. Iraq.

Artist unknown.
Tutankhamen Mask (side view).
c. 1340 B.C. Egypt.

Artist unknown.
Kuang.
1100 B.C. China.

214   **More About...Art History**

Artist unknown.
Colossal Head.
1500–300 B.C. Mexico.

Artist unknown.
Woman Playing Harp.
(Detail from vase.) C. 490 B.C.

Artist unknown.
Parthenon.
448–432 B.C. Greece.

Artist unknown.
Stonehenge.
1800–1400 B.C. England.

More About...Art History 215

Art History Coming Alive

- Art history comes alive for students when they role-play the life of an artist or put on a short performance about an artwork. Have students work in pairs to do research on an artist using the **Artist Profiles Book,** the **National Women's Museum of the Arts Collection,** or some computer or library resource materials to find out some facts about an artist's life. (Example: birth and death dates, home country, interests, influences, style of art used, etc.) After researching the topic, have student write a simple story and act it out. A television interview format may be used with one student acting as the host and the other acting as the guest star.

Introducing the Art

- Discuss with students the organization of pages 214-221 (the dates at the top of each two pages, the chronological order of the artwork presented).

Below are some ideas to help you guide your students in using these pages.

- Help students read the artist's name under each artwork. some artists are unknown. Explain to students that the unknown artists' names have been lost over time. Sometimes art historians can discover who created an unknown work.
- Have students read the country label under each artwork. Have students indicate on what continent each artwork is located. Ask students to share interesting facts they know about each country.
- Have students read the date under each artwork. Point out that sometimes there is a span of years rather than one specific year. This is because art historians are not sure exactly when the art was made. Have them indicate the oldest image on each page. Draw a line on the chalkboard and plot some or all of the art.

Questions to Discuss

Based on Bloom's taxonomic categories, guide your students through discussion asking some or all of these questions.

- **Knowledge: What?**
1. Who created this artwork?
2. When was this artwork created?
3. Where was this object found?
4. Have you ever seen an object like this? Where?
5. What is the artwork's title?
6. If you could speak to the artist, what would you ask?

- **Comprehension: What and Why?**
1. Compare the artworks of a similar time period on the page. How are they alike and different?
2. Is this object useful? How is it used?
3. Is this an artwork you would like to own? Explain.
4. What interests you most about this artwork?
5. What is the major theme of this artwork?

- **Application: How, When, and in What Order?**
1. In what countries would this art be used?
2. What type of materials were used to create this art?
3. Explain how this object could have a different use today.
4. Demonstrate how the artwork was created.

- **Synthesis: What, How, and to What Extent?**
1. Create a plan to make this artwork more valued.
2. Devise a marking plan to sell this artwork.
3. How many titles can you think of for this artwork? Name them.
4. Name a person you would like to give this artwork to as a gift? Why?
5. Suppose the self-portrait by Rembrandt have a conversation with the Close self-portrait. What would they say to each other? what would you ask them?

More About...
Art History

Artist unknown.
Ravenna Apse Mosaic. (Detail).
A.D. 100. Italy.

Artist unknown.
Shiva as Lord of the Dance.
1000. India.

Artist unknown.
The Pantheon.
A.D. 118–125. Italy.

Artist unknown.
Hagia Sophia.
A.D. 532–537. Turkey.

Artist unknown.
The Great Stupa (at Sanchi).
200–100 B.C. India.

Artist unknown.
Page from *The Book of Lindisfarne*.
Late 600s. England.

Artist unknown.
*Pagoda of the Temple
of the Six Banyan Trees.*
A.D. 537. China.

Artist unknown.
Stupa (at Borobudu).
800. Indonesia.

Artist unknown.
Great Mosque
(at Samarra).
648–852. Iraq.

More About...Art History   **217**

• **Analysis: What and How?**

1. Name all the paintings on these pages. How are they similar?
2. What are the main elements in this artwork?
3. Name all the architecture on these pages. What do they have in common? How are they different?
4. Name all the sculpture on these pages. How are they alike? How are they different?

• **Perception: Which, Where, and to What Extent?**

1. Name the artist that made a moving sculpture. (Calder)
2. Find an object built by an American President. (Jefferson's Monticello)
3. Find an artwork made out of fabric. (Bayeaux Tapestry)
4. Find a king figure. (King Ife)
5. Find a mysterious artwork from England. (Stonehenge)
6. Find a famous Greek building. (Parthenon)
7. Name the artist that created a dancer. (Degas)
8. Find the most famous painting in the world. (Mona Lisa)
9. Find an artwork with primary colors. (Broadway Boogie Woogie)
10. Find an image with water in it. (The Great Wave)

• **Evaluation: What and Where? How and Why? To What Extent and Why?**

1. What artwork is the most interest to you? How and why did you make your choice?
2. Explain in detail an artwork's unique qualities.
3. If someone were to give you this artwork, what would you do with it?
4. Rank your five favorite artworks from these pages and tell why they are your favorites.
5. How have you learned to see in new ways?

Rembrandt van Rijn.
Self-Portrait.
1660. The Netherlands.

Leonardo da Vinci.
Mona Lisa.
1503–1505. Italy.

Artist unknown.
Bayon Temple Angkor Thom.
1100s–1200s. Cambodia.

Artist unknown.
Shrine Head. (Yorub).
1100–1300. Nigeria.

Torii Kiyotada.
Actor of the Ichikawa Clan.
1710–1740. Japan.

More About...Art History

Artist unknown.
Chartes Cathedral.
1145–1220. France.

Thomas Jefferson.
Monticello.
1770–1784. United States.

Artist unknown.
Bayeux Tapestry. (Detail).
1070–1080. England.

Artist unknown.
Anasazi culture petroglyphs.
United States.

Artist unknown.
Taj Mahal.
1632–1648. India.

More About...Art History

219

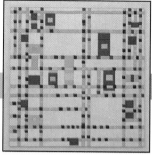

Piet Mondrian.
Broadway Boogie-Woogie.
1941. The Netherlands.

Claude Monet.
Impression, Sunrise.
1872. France.

Edgar Degas.
Little Dancer of Fourteen.
1880–1881. France.

Katsushika Hokusai.
The Great Wave.
1823–1829. Japan.

Pablo Picasso.
Gertrude Stein.
1906. Spain.

Chuck Close.
Self-Portrait.
1987. United States.

Jackson Pollock.
Convergence.
1952. United States.

Maria Martínez.
Black on Black Pot.
1920. United States.

Alexander Calder.
Untitled Mobile.
1959. United States.

More About...Art History

221

OVERVIEW

In art, *subject* means something an artist has depicted or represented in an artwork. For example, the subject matter of Vincent van Gogh's painting of a vase of flowers is called a still life. Some subject matter, like the objects in van Gogh's still life, are easy to identify. Others are more difficult because the artwork may be symbolic or nonobjective. Artists create artworks on a variety of subjects: the natural world, literature, religion, the constructed world, history, and so on. These pages deal with several of the most common subject-matter topics—people, objects, everyday life, stories, things outside, colors and shapes, and things that have a deeper meaning.

How to Use These Pages

Talk with students about each subject-matter topic description below. Encourage them to look for examples of different subject matter in the lessons. By helping them to look at each subject in greater detail and by asking thoughtful questions, your students will begin to develop an understanding for difference among subject matter in art.

Portrait

This category includes portraits, self-portraits, and group portraits. Portraits are one of the oldest subjects in art history. Artists try to present both an accurate depiction and also other aspects of a person's character in a portrait.

Question: This artist painted a self-portrait. What do you think he wanted to tell us about himself?

Artists create art about many topics. *Subject matter* is the artist's term for the content of artwork. For example, the subject of a painting can be a simple portrait. The subject might be an everyday experience like bike riding. These kinds of subject matter are easy to identify. But subject matter becomes more difficult to understand when the artwork stands for something beyond itself. Look at these artworks and become familiar with the different terms used for subject matter.

Portrait

Gerald Dou. (Dutch). *Self-Portrait.* Oil on wood. $19\frac{1}{4} \times 15\frac{3}{8}$ inches. Metropolitan Museum of Art, New York, Bequest of Benjamin Altman, 1913.

More About...Subject Matter

More About...
Subject Matter

Seascape

Winslow Homer. *Gulf Stream.* 1899.
Oil on canvas. $28\frac{1}{8} \times 49\frac{1}{8}$ inches.
Metropolitan Museum of Art, New York,
Catherine Lorillard Wolfe Collection,
Wolfe Fund, 1906.

More About...Subject Matter 223

Things Outside
This area includes the natural world—plants, animals, or a landscape. The suffix "scape" means "a view of . . . ." For example, "cityscape" means buildings and city life seen in an artwork or "seascape," a scene of the sea.

Question: What things in this painting make it a seascape?

Stories

A story is an account of some incident from a real person's life, an historic event, or from a myth, legend, or other symbolic literature.

Question: Tell the story as you see it in this image.

Allegory

Jan van Eyck. (Flemish). *Giovanni Arnolfini and His Bride.* 1434. Tempera and oil on wood. $32 \times 23\frac{1}{2}$ inches. Courtesy of the Trustees of the National Gallery, London, England.

More About...
Subject Matter

Still Life

Vincent van Gogh. (Dutch). *Sunflowers.* 1887. Oil on canvas.
17 × 24 inches. Metropolitan Museum of Art, New York.

Still Life
Artists create artworks that show a variety of
objects. Traditional still lifes are bowls, vases,
bottles, pitchers, fruit, flowers, food on a table,
and/or musical instruments, among other things,
that are artfully arranged.

Question: What are the objects in this still life?

Everyday Activities

In art, the term *genre* is used to indicate subjects that have to do with ordinary people engaged in everyday activities.

Question: What everyday activites are going on in this painting?

Nonobjective

Sometimes artwork is nonobjective. It does not have an identifiable subject matter—no familiar subjects are shown. People respond to the way the artwork has been organized and designed. Nonobjective art focuses specifically on the elements and principles of art: line, shape, color, and so on.

Question: The artwork does not use a subject we can identify. What are some of the lines, shapes, and colors you see in this picture?

More About...
Subject Matter

Genre

Carmen Lomas Garza.
Cakewalk. Acrylics.
36 × 48 inches. Collection of
Paula Maciel-Beneke,
Soquel, California.
Photo by M. Lee Fatherree.

Nonobjective

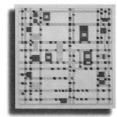

Piet Mondrian. *Broadway Boogie-Woogie.* 1942–43. Oil on canvas. 50 × 50 inches. The Museum of Modern Art, New York. Given anonymously. Photograph © 1998 The Museum of Modern Art.

More About...
Subject Matter

Symbolic

Artist unknown. *Buckskin Ghost Dance Arapaho Dress.*
National Museum of the American Indian, New York, New York.

Symbols

Sometimes artworks contain symbols—visual signs of something invisible. For example, a dove can be a symbol of peace, or an hourglass may represent the passing of time. Symbols represent a broader idea or sometimes have a secret meaning.

Questions: This dress was used for special ceremonies. What do you think the birds, turtle, stars, and moon are symbols for? *(Students may suggest their own interpretations for these objects. In the Arapaho culture, the turtle represents material existence; birds represent the flight of the spirit; stars represent the human spirit's struggle against darkness; and the moon represents change.)*

More About...
Drawing

More About Drawing Still Lifes

OVERVIEW

Objective

After completing this lesson, students recognize that still lifes are made of lines and shapes.

Creative Expression

Set up a still life similar to the one in the photo.

- Find the vertical lines on the red box.
- Find the diagonal lines on the top and bottom edges of the red box. *(The top and bottom side edges are diagonals because they recede into the distance.)*
- During the Practice activity, use a trash can, or other cylinders from the classroom, to point out that the width of the ellipse changes as the viewpoint changes. Stress that true cylinders have vertical sides. Some cylindrical objects may have slanted or slightly curved sides.

More About...
Still-Life Drawing

Everything you see is filled with lines and shapes you already know how to draw.

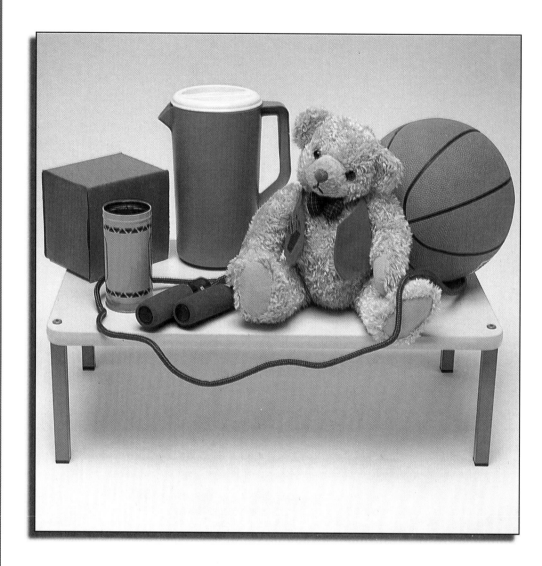

More About...Still-Life Drawing

🎨 ART Background

The objective of these lessons is to improve and increase perception skills. Accompanying each photograph will be a set of statements and questions to help the students observe and perceive specific concepts such as lines, shapes, and forms. Students are given perception readiness activities that involve searching the photograph and classroom for specific shapes and lines. Following this will be a drawing activity in which the students can practice and apply what they have perceived and learned. The students are learning through observing, questioning, thinking, and decision making. By asking questions and guiding the students visually through the photographs and their classroom, the teacher will be an integral part of these lessons. Whenever possible, objects similar to those in the photograph should be set up in the room for the perception activities and drawing practices. Discourage drawing from the photograph.

More About...
Still-Life Drawing

LOOK

Look at the photograph of the still life.

- Find the horizontal lines on the edge of the table.
- Find the vertical lines on the sides of the red box.
- Find the diagonal lines on the top and bottom edges of the red box. Because you see three sides of the box at once, you can tell that it is a form.
- The top of the can is an ellipse, not a circle or a straight line. An ellipse is a flattened circle with rounded ends. The curved line of an ellipse narrows at the ends. It does not have points. Find another ellipse in the photo. Find an ellipse in your room.
- Find the can in the photograph. Its form is a cylinder. Its top is an ellipse. Its sides are vertical lines. Its bottom is a curved line. The curve of the bottom is almost the same as the lower curve of the ellipse at the top.

PRACTICE

Practice drawing cylinders. First draw an ellipse. Next, draw a vertical line down from each end of the ellipse. Draw the bottom of the cylinder by connecting the ends of the vertical lines with a curved line similar to the lower curve in the ellipse.

More About...
Drawing

More About Drawing People
OVERVIEW

Objective

After completing this lesson, students will be able to improve their perception of the shapes and forms of people.

Questions to Discuss

- How are the walking person's arms and legs bending? *(at the elbow and knees)*

- Where does the sitting person's body bend? *(at the waist)*

- How is the shape of the person's head that's facing you different from the profile of the people facing sideways? *(The person's head facing us is like an oval. The profile is a free-form. The back of the head is a curve that curves down and in toward the neck. The edge face is like a line that curves in and out forming the forehead, nose, lips, chin, and jaw. Note that the shape of the eyes in a profile is different from a frontal view. The eyes in a profile are more triangular and are back away from the front edge near the top of the nose. In the frontal view, the eyelids are an ellipse enclosing a sphere.)*

- The standing person's feet are pointing toward you. What shape are they? *(They are like vertical ovals. When drawing feet from a frontal view, children often draw the feet pointing outward. Point out to the students that the feet facing them in the photograph are actually oval-like shapes that are vertical, not horizontal.)*

Practice

Some children may be sensitive about being drawn from observation by peers. Approach the activity carefully.

For the Practice activity, wear a striped shirt similar to the one in the photo, or choose a child wearing one to be a "model." Don't count upon a child wearing a striped shirt, unless you prearrange it. Show the students how the stripes curve around the body to show its form. The students will practice giving their drawings of people form by drawing stripes that curve around the bodies.

230

More About...
Drawing People

People are made of free-form shapes. These shapes change depending upon what position a person is in.

More About...
Drawing People

LOOK

Look at the three people in the photograph. Notice the shape and size of the heads, necks, torsos, arms, legs, hands, and feet. These are free-form shapes.

✓ How is the shape of the person's head that's sitting sideways different from the head of a person who is facing you? The person's head facing you is like an oval. Actually, it is a picture of an oval–shaped form.

✓ The person's head facing sideways is a picture of a free-form form. The bodies are also pictures of free-form forms.

✓ Look at the people in your room. You are looking at free-form forms.

✓ Notice how the form of a person's body changes if he or she is sitting, standing facing you, or standing sideways. When a person is facing you, the body appears wider than when standing sideways.

✓ Look at the horizontal stripes on the shirt of the people in the photograph. Notice how they curve around the body and arms. This shows their form. You can draw curved lines across parts of a person's body to show their rounded thickness.

PRACTICE

Look at the people in your classroom. Practice drawing people. Draw curved lines across parts of their bodies to show their form.

More About Drawing Landscapes

OVERVIEW

Objective

After completing this lesson, students will be able to improve their perception of the lines and shapes in landscape drawing.

Questions to Discuss

If possible, take the students outdoors to compare the photograph with the real outside environment.

- Where is the foreground? *(In art, the foreground is near the bottom of the page. Objects in the foreground appear larger and can extend from the bottom of the page to the top. Objects in the foreground overlap those in the middle ground, and those in the background. To make them appear closer, objects in the foreground are drawn with more detail.)*

- Where is the middle ground? *(The middle ground is in the center of the paper between the foreground and the background. Objects in the middle ground overlap objects in the background. To make them appear farther away than objects in the foreground, objects in the middle ground are drawn smaller than those in the foreground. They are also drawn with less detail than those in the foreground.)*

- Where is the background? *(The background is located near the top. Objects in the background are drawn smaller than those in the middle ground, and than those in the foreground. To make them appear far away, objects in the background are drawn with no detail.)*

- What are two things that overlap in this landscape? *(Overlapping helps create the illusion of depth. Objects in the foreground overlap those in the background.)*

In trying to draw details, the students may become frustrated if their drawings are not realistic enough. Be encouraging, and remind them that they are still learning. Realism is **not** important at this age.

When you look at a landscape, you can see that some things are in front of or behind other things.

More About...
Drawing Landscapes

LOOK

Look at the landscape with the cows.

- ✓ Look at the cow in the **foreground,** the front of the picture.
- ✓ Look at the cow in the **background,** the back of the picture.
- ✓ The area between the foreground and background is the **middle ground.** It is in the center of the paper. Find the cows in the middle ground. They look smaller than the cow in the foreground. They appear larger than the cow in the background.

The difference in the appearance of the cows' sizes gives the picture depth. The cow in the foreground is larger because it is closer.

You can also see more detail in the foreground. Look for the individual blades of grass at the bottom of the picture. Can you see the eyes of the cow in the foreground?

Look at the objects in the middle ground and the background. How have the details changed? Things that are farther away have less detail.

PRACTICE

Practice drawing an object in your classroom such as a pencil, a book, or something you like. Look at the lines that outline the edges and ridges of the object. Draw them.

Now study the lines that make the details on the object. Draw them.

Visual Index

Artist unknown
*Ipuy and his Wife
Receiving Offerings
from Their Children*
1275 B.C.
page 62

**Domenico
Ghirlandaio**
*Francesco Sassetti
and His Son Teodoro*
1480
page 110

Artist unknown
Mask
800–400 B.C.
page 123

Artist unknown
Ardabil Carpet
Sixteenth century
page 144

Artist unknown
*Featherwork
Neckpiece*
1350–1476
page 54

Raphael
Bindo Altoviti
1515
page 114

Artist unknown
*Deep Dish Spain
from Valencia*
1430
page 145

**Sofonisba
Anguissola**
*The Sisters of the
Artist and Their
Governess*
1555
page 141

Visual Index

Nanha the Mughal
Emperor Shah Jahan and His Son, Suja
1605–1628
page 111

Hubert Robert
The Artist Drawing a Young Girl
1738
page 106

Jean Étienne Liotard
A Frankish Woman and her Servant
1750
page 67

Giovanni Pannini
Interior of St. Peters, Rome
1754
page 152

Francisco Goya
Don Manuel Osorlo Manrique de Zuniga
1784
page 107

Artist unknown
Dead-man Mask
Nineteenth century
page 122

Artist unknown
Navajo Loom with Wool Blanket
Nineteenth century
page 170

Artist unknown
Ponca Blouse
Nineteenth century
page 167

Visual Index

Edward Hicks
Cornell Farm
1848
page 153

Vincent van Gogh
A Pair of Boots
1887
page 66

Claude Monet
*The Arrival of the
Normandy Train,
Gare Saint-Lazare*
1877
page 148

William M. Chase
The Park
1888
page 182

**Pierre Auguste
Renoir**
*Marguerite (Margot)
Bérard*
1879
page 115

Artist unknown
*Navajo Blanket,
Eye Dazzler*
c. 1890
page 51

James Tissot
*Women of Paris: The
Circus Lover*
1883–1885
page 140

**Pierre Auguste
Renoir**
*Two Young Girls at
the Piano*
1892
page 33

Visual Index

Artist unknown
Ritual Object
Eighteenth -
nineteenth century
page 123

Artist unknown
Caravan
1915
page 84

Elon Webster
*Iroquois False
Face Mask*
Twentieth century
page 122

Artist unknown
End of Caravan
1915
page 85

Käthe Kollwitz
The Downtrodden
1900
page 29

Amadeo Modigliani
*Portrait of a Polish
Woman*
1918
page 119

Arthur Lismer
*The Guide's Home
Algonquin*
1914
page 149

M. C. Escher
Sky and Water
c. 1920
page 80

Visual Index

M. C. Escher
Reptiles
c. 1920
page 81

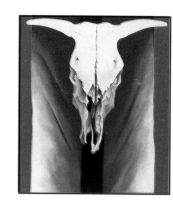

Georgia O'Keeffe
Cow's Skull: Red, White and Blue
1931
page 136

Edward Hopper
House by the Railroad
1925
page 156

Diego Rivera
Detroit Industry, South Wall
1932–1933
page 179

Ralph Steiner
American Rural Baroque
1930
page 37

Charles Sheeler
American Interior
c. 1934
page 157

Frank Lloyd Wright
Fallingwater
c. 1930
page 93

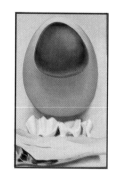

Georgia O'Keeffe
Red and Pink Rocks and Teeth
1938
page 50

Visual Index

Joan Miró
The Beautiful Bird Revealing the Unknown to a Pair of Lovers
1941
page 20

Artist unknown
Maya/Huipil (detail)
plate 263
c. 1950
page 16

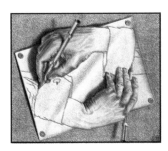

Charles Sheeler
Incantation
1946
page 17

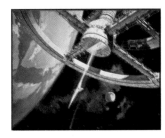

Le Corbusier
Chapelle Notre Dame-du Haut
1950–1955
page 96

M. C. Escher
Drawing Hands
1948
page 24

Robert McCall
Space Station #1
c. 1950
page 88

Jerome Liebling
Boy and Car, New York City
1949
page 36

Jørn Utzon
Sydney Opera House
1957
page 97

Visual Index

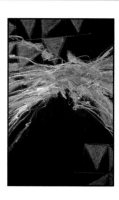

Bing Davis
*Ancestral Spirit
Dance Series*
c. 1960
page 55

Fernando Botero
Ruben's Wife
1963
page 118

Manabu Mabe
*Melancholy
Metropolis*
1961
page 59

Ben Jones
King Family
c. 1965
page 46

Jasper Johns
Map
1962
page 47

Romare Bearden
She Ba
1970
page 175

Visual Index

Elizabeth Catlett
Sharecropper
1970
page 28

George Segal
Walk, Don't Walk
1976
page 126

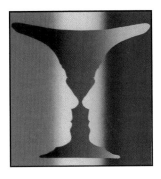

Jaspers Johns
Cups 4 Picasso
1972
page 76

Jesse Treviño
Mis Hermanos
1976
page 32

Jaspers Johns
Cups 4 Picasso
(detail)
1972
page 77

Duane Hanson
Woman with Dog
1977
page 127

Visual Index

Tommye Scanlin
Crow, Crow
c. 1980
page 171

Janet Fish
After Leslie Left
1983–1984
page 174

Elizabeth Plater-Zyberk
Seaside, Florida, a Walkway
1980s
page 92

Robert Lostutter
Baird Trogon
1985
page 58

Wendy Fay Dixon
Deidre
1982
page 25

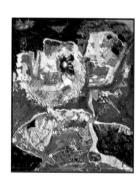

George McNeil
Deliverance Disco
c. 1987
page 62

Paul Wonner
Dutch Still Life with Art Books and Field Guide to Western Birds
1982
page 21

Roger Brown
Homesick Proof Space Station
1987
page 89

Visual Index

Chuck Close
Self-Portrait
1987
page 137

Artist unknown
Playground
1990s
page 183

John Biggers
Tree House
1990–1992
page 178

Iris Sandkühler
Pyrite Sun Pendant
1992
page 187

Anne Beard
Rodeo Jacket
Late twentieth
century
page 166

Iris Sandkühler
*Composition in Brown
and Gold*
1995
page 186

Glossary

Pronunciation Key

at; āpe; fär; câre; end; mē; it; īce; pîerce; hot; ōld; sông, fôrk; oil; out; up; ūse; rüle; pu̇ll; tûrn; chin; sing; shop; thin; <u>th</u>is; hw in white; zh in treasure. The symbol ə stands for the unstressed vowel sound in about, taken, pencil, lemon, and circus.

alternate rhythm
(ôl´ tər nit ri<u>th</u>´ əm), **noun**

When one motif is repeated after a second, different motif.

analogous color scheme
(ə nal´ ə gəs kul´ ər skēm´), **noun**

A color scheme using colors that are side by side on the color wheel.

analogous colors
(ə nal´ ə gəs kul´ ərz), **noun**

Colors that are side by side on the color wheel.

appliqué
(ap´ li kā´), **noun**

Art made by attaching fabric shapes onto a fabric background by gluing or sewing.

architect
(är´ kə tekt), **noun**

A person who plans and designs buildings, cities, and bridges.

architecture
(är´ ki tek´ chər), **noun**

The art of designing and planning the construction of buildings, cities, and bridges.

armature
(är´ mə chər), **noun**

A framework for supporting material used in sculpting.

assemblage
(ä säm bläzh´), **noun**

A work of art in which a variety of objects are assembled to create one complete piece.

asymmetry
(ā sim´ i trē), **noun**

Another name for *informal balance.* Asymmetry is a way of organizing parts of a design so that unlike objects have equal visual weight.

balance
(bal´ əns), **noun**

The principle of design that deals with visual weight in a work of art.

body proportions
(bod´ ē prə pôr shənz), **noun**

Ratios of one part of the body to another.

Glossary

central axis
(sen´ trəl   ak´ sis), **noun**

The central dividing line, sometimes imaginary.

color intensity
(kul´ ər   in ten´ si tē), **noun**

The brightness or dullness of a color.

color scheme
(kul´ ər   skēm´), **noun**

A plan for organizing colors.

complementary colors
(kom´ plə men tə rē   kul´ ərz),
noun

Colors that are opposite each other on the color wheel.

complex geometric shapes
(kom´ pleks   jē´ ə met´ rik
shāps), **noun**

Shapes created from a combination of geometric shapes.

contrast
(kon´ trast), **noun (verb)**

A difference created when elements are placed next to each other in a work of art.

cool color
(kül´   kul´ ər), **noun**

A color that seems to move away from the viewer and suggests coolness. Green, blue, and violet are cool colors.

cross-hatching
(krôs´ hach´ ing), **noun**

A shading technique in which two or more sets of parallel lines cross each other.

curved
(kûrvd), **adj.**

A line that bends and changes direction slowly.

depth
(depth), **noun**

The appearance of distance on a flat surface.

diagonal
(dī ag ə nəl), **noun (adj.)**

A slanted line.

direct observation
(di rekt´ ob zər vā shən), **noun**

The technique of artists studying an object from various viewpoints, looking closely at the important details and recording those details in their drawings.

distortion
(di stôr´ shən), **noun**

Changing an object or figure out of normal shape to communicate ideas or feelings.

emphasis
(em´ fə sis), **noun**

The principle of design that stresses one area in a work of art.

Glossary

exaggeration

(eg zaj´ ə rā´ shən), **noun**

Increasing or enlarging an object or a figure or one of its parts to communicate ideas or feelings.

facial proportions

(fā´ shəl prə pôr shənz), **noun**

The relationship of one feature of a face to another feature.

flowing rhythm

(flō´ ing rith´ əm), **noun**

Rhythm that repeats wavy lines.

focal point

(fo´ kəl point´), **noun**

The area of an artwork that is emphasized.

form

(fôrm), **noun**

Any object that can be measured in three ways: length, width, and depth.

formal balance

(fôr´ məl bal´ əns), **noun**

When equal, or very similar, elements are placed on opposite sides of a central line.

free-form shapes

(frē´ fôrm´ shāps), **noun**

Uneven, irregular shapes made with curved lines, straight lines, or a combination of the two.

geometric shapes

(jē´ ə met´ rik shāps), **noun**

Shapes that can be described by mathematical formulas, such as a circle, a square, a triangle, or a rectangle.

gradation

(grād ā´ shən), **noun**

A gradual change of one value to another.

harmony

(här´ mə nē), **noun**

Concerned with similarities of separate but related parts.

hatching

(hach´ ing), **noun**

A shading technique using a series of fine repeated parallel lines.

highlights

(hī´ līts´), **noun**

Small areas of white or light values.

horizon line

(hə rī´ zən līn´), **noun**

The point at which Earth and sky meet.

horizontal

(hôr´ ə zon´ təl), **adj. (noun)**

A line that moves from side to side.

Glossary

hue
(hū), **noun**

Another word for *color.*

imitated texture
(im´ i tā təd   teks´ chər), **noun**

A two-dimensional texture that imitates or simulates a real texture.

informal balance
(in fôr´ məl   bal´ əns), **noun**

A way of organizing parts of a design so that unlike objects have equal visual weight.

intermediate hues
(in´ tər´ mē dē it   hūz´), **noun**

Made by mixing a primary hue with a secondary hue.

isolation
(ī´ sə lā´ shən), **noun**

When an object is placed alone and away from all the other objects in an artwork.

linear perspective
(lin ē´ ər   pər spek´ tiv), **noun**

A way of using lines to show distance and depth.

line
(līn), **noun**

A mark drawn by a tool such as a pencil, pen, or paintbrush as it moves across a surface.

location
(lō cā´ shən), **noun**

When the eyes are naturally drawn toward the center of an artwork.

mandala
(man´ də lə), **noun**

A radial design divided into sections or wedges, each of which contains an image.

matte
(mat), **adj**.

Textured surfaces that reflect a soft light, with an almost dull look.

monochromatic
(mon´ ə krō mat´ ik), **adj**.

One color plus all the tints and shades of that color.

monochromatic color scheme
(mon´ ə krō mat´ ik   kul´ ər skēm´), **noun**

A color scheme using one color plus all the tints and shades of that color.

motif
(mō tēf´), **noun**

The object or group of objects that is repeated.

negative space
(neg´ ə tiv   spās´), **noun**

The empty space that surrounds objects, shapes, and forms.

Glossary

nonobjective painting
(non´ əb jek´ tiv pān´ ting),
noun

It contains shapes, lines, and colors, not objects or people.

one-point perspective
(wun´ point´ pər spek´ tiv),
noun

One way of using lines to show distance and depth, with all lines that move back into space meeting at one point.

pattern
(pat´ ərn), **noun**

The use of shapes, colors, or lines repeated in a planned way; describes visual rhythm.

perception
(pər sep´ shən), **noun**

The act of looking at something carefully and thinking deeply about what is seen.

perspective
(pər spek´ tiv), **noun**

The method used to create the illusion of depth on a flat surface.

point of view
(point´ əv vū´), **noun**

The position from which the viewer looks at an object.

positive space
(poz´ i tiv spās´), **noun**

Refers to any object, shape, or form in a work of art.

primary hues
(prī´ mer ē hūz´), **noun**

Red, blue, and yellow.

profile proportions
(prō´ fīl prə pôr´ shənz), **noun**

The relationship of one feature of a face to another feature when looking from the side view.

progressive
(prə gres´ iv), **adj.**

Changing or moving forward.

progressive reversal
(prə gres´ iv ri vûr səl), **noun**

When an object starts out as one object or form and slowly changes into another object or form.

progressive rhythm
(prə gres´ iv ri<u>th</u>´ əm), **noun**

When a motif changes each time it is repeated.

proportion
(prə pôr´ shən), **noun**

The principle of art concerned with the size relationships of one part to another.

Glossary

radial balance
(rā´ dē əl bal´ əns), **noun**

When the elements of design (line, shape, color, and form) seem to radiate or come out from a center point.

random rhythm
(ran´ dəm rith´ əm), **noun**

When a motif is repeated in no apparent order.

ratio
(rā´ shē ō´), **noun**

A comparison of size between two things.

realistic scale
(rē´ ə lis´ tik skāl), **noun**

In a work of art where everything seems to fit together and make sense in size relationships.

regular rhythm
(reg´ yə lər rith´ əm), **noun**

Identical motifs repeated with equal amounts of space between them.

relief print
(ri lēf´ print), **noun**

A technique in which the design to be printed is raised from the background.

rough
(ruf), **adj.**

Textured surfaces that reflect the light unevenly.

scale
(skāl), **noun**

Size as measured against a standard reference.

secondary hues
(sek´ ən der´ ē hūz´), **noun**

The result of mixing two primary hues.

shade
(shād), **noun**

Any dark value of a hue.

shading
(shā´ ding), **noun**

A technique for darkening values by adding black or darkening an area by repeating several lines close together.

shadows
(shad´ ōz), **noun**

Shaded, or darker, areas in a drawing or painting.

shape
(shāp), **noun**

Two-dimensional figure that can be measured in two ways: length and height.

Glossary

shape reversal
(shāp´ ri vûr´ səl), **noun**

When a shape or positive space starts out as one image and then in another image becomes the negative space.

shiny
(shī´ nē), **adj.**

Textured surfaces that reflect a bright light.

smooth
(smüth), **adj.**

Textured surfaces that reflect the light evenly.

space
(spās), **noun**

The element of art that refers to the area between, around, above, below, and within objects.

stippling
(stip´ ling), **noun**

A shading technique using dots. The closer the dots, the darker the area.

symmetry
(sim´ i trē), **noun**

A type of formal balance when two sides are mirror images of each other.

tactile texture
(tak´ təl teks´ chər), **noun**

Actual texture that you can touch and feel.

tessellation
(te´ se lā´ shen), **noun**

A type of shape reversal that changes quickly and fits together like a puzzle.

texture
(teks´ chər), **noun**

The element of art that refers to how things feel, or look as if they might feel if touched.

three-dimensional form
(thrē´ di men´ shə nəl fôrm´), **noun**

Anything that can be measured by height, width, and depth.

tint
(tint), **noun**

Any light value of a hue.

two-dimensional shape
(tü´ di men´ shə nəl shāp´), **noun**

Flat figures, measured by length and width.

unity
(ū´ ni tē), **noun**

The quality of wholeness or oneness that is achieved by properly using the elements and principles of art.

unrealistic scale
(un´ rē ə lis´ tik skāl´), **noun**

When size relationships do not make sense in a work of art.

Glossary

value
(val´ ū), **noun**

Lightness or darkness of a color or object.

vanishing point
(van´ i shing   point´), **noun**

The point on the horizon line where all the lines moving back into a space seem to meet.

variety
(və rī´ ə tē), **noun**

The principle of design concerned with difference or contrast. Variety is the opposite of harmony.

vertical line
(vûr´ tə kəl   līn), **noun**

A line that moves up and down.

visual movement
(vizh´ ü əl   müv´ mənt), **noun**

Creating the illusion of movement through visual rhythm.

visual rhythm
(vizh´ ü əl   ri<u>th</u>´ əm), **noun**

Rhythm created by the repetition of shapes, colors, or lines.

visual texture
(vizh´ ü əl   teks´ chər), **noun**

The way something looks like it might feel if you could touch it.

warm color
(wôrm´   kul´ ər), **noun**

Color that seems to move toward the viewer and suggests warmth and energy. Red, orange, and yellow are warm colors.

warp threads
(wôrp´   thredz´), **noun**

Vertical threads attached to a loom.

weft threads
(weft´   thredz´), **noun**

Threads that are woven over and under the warp threads.

zigzag
(zig´ zag´), **noun (adj.)**

Diagonal lines that connect and change direction sharply.

Index

Index

Index

Index

Index

Professional Development for Art Education

Table of Contents

The Elementary Art Curriculum

Rosalind Ragans Ph.D., Associate Professor Emerita, Georgia Southern University

Art education is for all students. It provides learning opportunities for the artistically talented few, as well as the many students who may never produce art outside the classroom.

A strong elementary visual arts curriculum teaches students that they can communicate a variety of ideas and emotions in many different ways. It teaches students to use both verbal and nonverbal methods to express abstract ideas and emotions and to trust their creative intelligence. In art education, students will learn that some problems have many different solutions, and they will not be afraid to use divergent thinking strategies. They will learn concepts and techniques that will give them control of the visual images they produce.

A strong elementary art curriculum will enable students to expand their perceptive, interpretive, and analytical abilities. They will learn to find meaning in visual images, and they will learn to identify aesthetic qualities in a variety of artworks and in the environment. They will learn the language of visual art so that they have a precise vocabulary of visual symbols with which to express their ideas. They will begin to develop the ability to make aesthetic judgments.

In a strong elementary art curriculum, students will become sensitive to and understand the broad cultural foundation upon which their own culture is based. The visual arts have always been an integral component in the history of humanity, and through the study of art history, students will develop a better understanding of beliefs and ideas that are different from their own.

The four components of a quality art program are Aesthetic Perception, Art Criticism, Art History and Culture, and Art Production and Creative Expression.

AESTHETIC PERCEPTION

Aesthetics is a branch of philosophy. In visual art, aesthetics becomes the study of the nature of beauty and art. Aesthetics is concerned with the Big Question: "What is art?" In the past, *aesthetics* was defined as the study of beauty because the creation of beauty was thought to be the purpose of art. Today, in our more complex society, the purpose of art has also become more complicated. Some aestheticians still believe that the purpose of art is to create beauty, or beautifully organized arrangements of the elements of art. Some believe that art must imitate reality. Others think of art as a strong means to communicate ideas and emotions.

Aesthetic concepts are the core of the *Art Connections* curriculum. They are the framework upon which all aspects of art learning are constructed. The **More About Aesthetics** section in the *Student* and *Teacher Editions* offers concrete methods for introducing students to aesthetics.

ART CRITICISM

Works of art are the focus of every lesson. Art criticism is the sequential process used in this text to guide students through the procedures needed to learn from these works. Art criticism enables students to learn from works of art that have been created by artists from many cultures and time periods. Art criticism also provides a procedure that students can use to objectively study their own art products.

The four-step process of art criticism will help students expand their perceptive, analytical, interpretive, and aesthetic valuing abilities. The sequential steps of art criticism are similar to those used in the scientific method. During the first two steps, *Describe* and *Analyze,* students are asked to collect data objectively. During the third step, *Interpret,* students speculate about the

> 66 **Art education is for all students. It provides learning opportunities for the artistically talented few, as well as the many students who may never produce art outside the classroom.** 99

meaning of the work based on the data collected: they make a hypothesis about the idea, emotion, or mood expressed by the artist. During the fourth step, *Decide* or aesthetic judgment, the students offer their conclusions about the work of art.

Art criticism will help students study a work of art noticing subject, composition, and meaning before making an aesthetic judgment. Too often, beginners look at a work of art briefly and immediately make a value judgment. The sequential procedures in art criticism force the students to postpone judgment while becoming immersed in the image. It forces them to have a fully funded visual experience before drawing conclusions about a work.

Detailed lessons in the **More About Art Criticism** sections of *Art Connections* will help teachers and students practice and apply art criticism procedures.

ART HISTORY AND CULTURE

Art Connections is not an art history text, but any study of art should begin with learning something about the history of world art and the people who created it. Information about art history related to the featured work of art in each lesson is provided for the students throughout the text. The **More About Art History Around the World** section provides an overview of the meaning of art history. Additional information is provided for the teacher in each text, and in ancillary materials such as the *Artist Profiles* books, the *Animals Through Time* chart, and on the backs of the *Large Prints.*

ART PRODUCTION AND CREATIVE EXPRESSION

Each lesson includes an art production activity identified as **Practice** and **Create** in the *Student Editions.* This is the place for each student to creatively explore the lesson concept. Hands-on activities are often the most enjoyable aspect of art learning. The student integrates and internalizes the verbal and visual concepts of the lesson during the creative manipulation of art materials. While every component in the art program is equally important, every component does not need equal time. Art Production requires the longest amount of time.

Do not skip the self-assessment section of the lesson. Most students would be embarrassed to offer subjective statements about their own work or the work of classmates. The four steps of art criticism offer an objective procedure for thinking about the concepts and technical procedures used during the creation of art.

CURRICULUM INTEGRATION

Art Connections provides a strong art curriculum that makes connections to all the arts and to all areas of the curriculum. The *Art Across the Curriculum* book at each grade level provides specific activities to connect each lesson to Reading/Language Arts, Mathematics, Science, Social Studies, Technology, and the Arts.

Elementary art programs enrich the entire curriculum in so many ways. In art, unlike so many other subjects, students have a natural opportunity to demonstrate their multiple intelligences every day. In art, students practice problem solving and critical thinking, they learn about history and culture through art, and they learn to more effectively use their senses to explore the world. All of these enrich other areas of the curriculum and help students establish habits of mind that will last a lifetime.

A Sampling of Art Magazines Resources for Teachers	
American Artist	*Arts and Activities*
Art Education	*Arts Education Policy*
Art to Zoo	*Review*
ARTnews	*Crayola Kids*
ARTnews for Students	*Scholastic Art*
	School Arts

Classroom Management and Motivation Strategies for Teaching Elementary Art

Bunyan Morris, Art Teacher, Laboratory School, Georgia Southern University

While motivating students to express themselves visually through creative means, the elementary art teacher is challenged with the task of maintaining proper classroom management. The purpose of this article is to provide some practical methods of motivating creative thought and action under the guidance of successful classroom management. Combine these methods with your own to give students the best learning experience possible.

Be Prepared. Begin the lesson excited and ready. Students will pick up on your mood the moment they walk into the room. If you set the tone at the beginning and grasp immediate control, it will be much easier to keep it throughout the lesson. It is important to have art prints and demonstration materials ready and in place for the initial focus. Practice an activity before demonstrating it if it is the first time that it has been taught. Something might happen that could not be foreseen. Prepare for the best and worst. Also, it might be a good idea to practice if it is a concept or an activity that has not been taught in a long time. Even classroom veterans forget things.

Focus. For the initial focus of the lesson, gather the students into a group on the floor, in chairs, or on benches in an area of the room that is ready for discussion and demonstration. By gathering the students into a compact group, it is easier to make eye contact and to keep the attention of all learners. If there is no room for a separate demonstration and discussion spot, gather the tables or desks into a closer group so that no one is "out of reach."

Introduce the Art. Always introduce a lesson with a work of art that relates to what the students will be learning. Students get excited playing detective. Finding clues and ideas in a painting or sculpture allows them to make their own interpretations and assessments about art. They will in turn learn to apply this to their own work. The students don't have to know that this activity has a lofty term called *art criticism* to gain from its purpose. Encouraging them to ask questions and share ideas about a master work will give the students motivation and fresh ideas to take into the Create portion of the lesson.

Moving to Art Production. Always control the manner in which the students move to the create area from the demonstration/discussion center. Release the students in a manner that will keep order but not quell their enthusiasm about the lesson. Use positive reinforcement by complimenting those who are sitting quietly, and send them first. It will not take long for the others to catch on. After time most of the students will become conditioned to this expectation. Even if they've been involved in a lively discussion, they will automatically become settled as this transitional period approaches.

Classroom Design. Not only should the students be orderly, but the classroom must also be organized and conducive to the movement of the teacher and students. The create stations should have enough space between them for the teacher to reach every student. There should be enough space in traffic areas for student movement. Children need easy access to supply shelves, to sinks, and to move from one create station to another unencumbered. The supplies should be organized on labeled shelves so that the students will return them to their proper places. If the teacher keeps the room and supplies organized, hopefully the students will.

> **❝ Always introduce a lesson with a work of art that relates to what the students will be learning. ❞**

As well as keeping the room and supplies organized, the rest of the room should be visually pleasing. Display student art with master prints. This builds self-esteem. When possible, display every child's work. Make learning centers organized and interesting. Keep interesting objects about the room for visual reference. These objects might include plants, pottery, old bottles, discarded sports equipment, old toys, or anything that might capture the attention and interest of your students. Use these objects in still lifes and as objects of visual reference for lines, shapes, and other elements and principles of art.

When moving about the room assisting students, it is important to keep the senses alive and be aware of what is happening with the other students. See and hear what they think you can't.

Closing the Lesson. Normally one should try to close the class with a review of the lesson's objectives. This should be short and interesting. This is also the time to award the students for good behavior. The art teacher must set the criteria for earning the award. Do not give the award if it is not earned. Of course, the students must be aware of the opportunity to earn an award ahead of time.

One method that works is to award the students with a "Super Behavior Card." This is simply a colorful card that can be given to the class to take back to their classroom teacher for having good behavior during art. This requires the cooperation of the classroom teacher to award the students in some manner for collecting a certain number of Super Behavior Cards. Awards might include a popcorn party or extra time at recess. If the classroom teacher is unwilling, you will have to provide the award in your class. Awarding of the Super Behavior Card can be coordinated with cleanup at the end of the period. Choose one student at the table who cleans up most thoroughly and gets quietest first to carry the Super Behavior Card back to the classroom teacher. The students at each table will work together trying to earn the Super Behavior Card.

Hopefully, these ideas and suggestions will reduce the challenge of maintaining classroom control and motivating students. The individual teacher must decide what works best for each situation. All of the motivation and management techniques here have been tried and have been proven to work. They may not work for everyone, but combined with one's individual strategies, they will increase the probability of success in the art classroom.

A Sampling of Art Games for Home or School

Art Lotto: National Gallery of Art Safari Limited, Miami, FL
ARTDECK Aristoplay, Ann Arbor, MI, 1-800-634-7738
The Fine Art Game Piatnik, Wiener Spielkartenfabrik, Ferd. PIATNIK & Söhne
Where Art Thou? WJ Fantasy, Inc., Bridgeport, CT 1-800-ABC-PLAY

Meeting National and State Standards for Art Education

Nan Yoshida, Former Art Supervisor, Los Angeles Unified School District, California

Art Connections has been carefully designed to help educators meet the standards of state and national art curriculum guidelines.

The *National Standards for Arts Education* are part of Goals 2000, the overarching plan for improving American education, called for by the President. Approved by the United States Congress in 1994, the Standards describe what every young American student should know and be able to do in the arts.

In addition to *National Standards,* individual states have curriculum documents that set forth guidelines and requirements in subject areas. For example, both the *Visual and Performing Arts Framework for California Public Schools, Kindergarten through Grade Twelve* © 1996 and the *Texas Essential Knowledge and Skills for Art* © 1997 discuss four components of visual arts education common to most other state guidelines.

Placing the *National Standards* side by side with the *California Framework* and *Texas Essential Knowledge and Skills,* one can readily see that the documents match in their expectations of what students should know and be able to do in the visual arts.

Art Connections has been developed with these national and state expectations in mind. Every lesson in the program is designed to address the components of art education in Aesthetic Perception, Art History and Culture, Creative Expression, and Art Criticism.

Aesthetic Perception (Artistic Perception)
Each lesson begins with **Activating Prior Knowledge,** which asks students to recall and visualize an image from personal experience that will help them take a purposeful look at the artwork.
Introducing the Art focuses students' attention on specific attributes of the artwork, design elements and principles, underlying structures, and functions. As students answer the questions about the painting or sculpture, they develop critical *looking* skills.
Seeing Like an Artist directs students to extend their artistic perception to their environment and objects in the environment. The transition is made to use keen visual and tactile perception of formal art objects in everyday life (lifelong learning).

Art History and Culture (Cultural Context)
In *Art Connections,* the range of world art is broad as students are exposed to a variety of types and styles of art from many cultures and historical periods. Students study art from Africa; Asia; Australia; Europe; and North, Central, and South America. They learn about the role of the artist in societies. They develop appreciation for paintings, drawings, prints, photographs,

sculptures, textiles, and architecture. They relate to folk, decorative, functional, and formal arts.

While information about the artwork and the artist is necessarily brief in the *Student Edition,* teachers are encouraged to use the **Art Background** section of the *Teacher Edition* and the *Artist Profiles* books to provide students with enriching information about the artist, the period of art history, and cultural perspectives.

Creative Expression (Art Production)
Creative expression is fundamental to every art lesson. The **Practice** activity provides a structure for students to apply lesson concepts in meaningful practice. In the **Create** activity, students refine their new knowledge and skills by producing an original artwork based on their personal vision. The lessons throughout the program introduce a variety of art media and techniques.

Art Criticism (Aesthetic Valuing)
Reflection and self-assessment are inherent in the art-making process. Upon completion of the **Create** activity, students evaluate their own work using the four steps of art criticism: Describe, Analyze, Interpret, Decide. These four steps of art criticism are a method for making an informed critique of others' artwork, as well.

Arts Integration
In addition to the high priority placed on teaching the visual arts as a unique discipline, both the National Standards and the California Framework recommend the appropriate integration or interrelation of the visual arts with the other arts disciplines of music, dance, and theater. Toward this goal, every unit in *Art Connections* culminates with a lesson integrating one of these performing arts.

Curriculum Integration
Furthermore, the *Teacher Edition* has an **Art Across the Curriculum** section that references activities in the *Art Across the Curriculum* books. These activities were developed to relate the visual arts concepts to concepts and experiences in other areas of the curriculum. Every lesson has a connection to reading/language arts, math, science, social studies, technology, and the arts. Thematic connections, technology, and special needs are also addressed.

The lessons in the *Art Connections* program are thoughtfully prepared to assist teachers in meeting the visual arts requirements of the National Standards, the California Framework, the Texas Essential Knowledge and Skills for Art, and most other state guidelines for art education.

National Standards for Arts Education © 1994
1. Understand and apply media, techniques, and processes.
2. Use knowledge of structures and functions.
3. Choose and evaluate a range of subject matter, symbols, and ideas.
4. Understand the visual arts in relation to history and cultures.
5. Reflect upon and assess the characteristics and merits of their work and the work of others.
6. Make connections between the visual arts and other disciplines.

California Framework © 1996
Artistic Perception
Goal 1. Students use their senses to perceive works of art, objects in nature, events, and the environment.
Goal 2. Students identify visual structures and functions of art using the language of the visual arts.
Creative Expression
Goal 3. Students develop knowledge of and artistic skills in a variety of visual arts media and technical processes.
Goal 4. Students create original artworks based on personal experiences or responses.
Goal 5. Students develop skills in the visual arts and appreciation for using the visual arts in lifelong learning.
Historical and Cultural Context
Goal 6. Students explore the role of the visual arts in culture and human history.
Goal 7. Students investigate major themes . . . and styles of the visual arts throughout the world.
Aesthetic Valuing
Goal 8. Students derive meaning from artworks through analysis, interpretation, and judgment.

Texas Essential Knowledge and Skills for Art © 1997
A. Perception: Awareness of and sensitivity to surroundings are important to understanding the structure of natural and human-made objects and to applying that understanding to the creative process. Students recognize this visual information as a source for creating original works of art.
B. Creative Expression/Performance: Visual expression is a unique means of communication which is vitally important throughout the world. Students recognize that visual communication challenges the imagination, fosters reflective thinking, encourages disciplined effort, involves problem-solving, and develops self-confidence.
C. Historical/Cultural Heritage: Art is a visual record of history and diverse cultures. Students understand and appreciate different historical periods, cultures, and artistic styles and develop respect for the traditions and contributions of diverse societies.
D. Response/Evaluation: Evaluation skills are developed by responding to and analyzing the artworks of self and others. Students engage in a critical thinking process while learning to make judicious decisions about art and lifelong consumer choices.

Art and Cross Curricular Connections

Tina Farrell, Associate Director of Visual and Performing Arts,
Clear Creek Independent School District, Texas

The study and production of artwork enhances learning in all areas of the curriculum. When teachers and students connect art to their other subjects, learning occurs in the natural and interrelated way that it exists in the real world. We know from experience that learning is most meaningful when it is interconnected—not isolated. Therefore, making the natural connections that exist within each discipline of study and art enhances total understanding and brings meaning to fragmented information.

Below are just a few of the ways that art education can impact the study of other subjects.

❝ When teachers and students connect art to their other subjects, learning occurs in the natural and interrelated way that it exists in the real world. ❞

Reading/Language Arts. In the viewing and analysis of a work of art, students develop oral and written communication skills. Teachers can enhance the language process by writing art terms and concepts on the board, having students generate lists of adjectives and adverbs to describe artworks, encouraging reflective inquiry into art, having students read about art and artists, and having students use works of art as stimuli for all forms of writing.

Mathematics. Mathematics concepts are enhanced through art. When math concepts are presented or expressed in a visual or manipulative manner, students can more easily grasp them. The comparison and development of shapes and forms, visual-spatial relationships, measurement, proportion, estimation, and grids and graphs, for example, all are best explained through art.

Science. In the art-making process, children learn that multiple ways to solve problems exist. They learn to discover, imagine, try new materials and techniques, experiment, develop and test hypotheses, and observe and record visual data. These are many of the skills, objectives, and habits of mind taught in science.

Social Studies. The history of the world is reflected in the functional and aesthetic works of art produced by the peoples of the world. Children can gain great insights about near and distant cultures through the study of art, artifacts, and architecture.

The Arts. The arts all complement each other in the skills, elements, principles, and beliefs that are emphasized in each discipline. Each area presents a unique way to express ideas and transform emotions into song, dance, interactions, words, and images. Visual artists research, develop rough drafts (sketches), plan, develop ideas, produce completed visual ideas, and sign and title their works. These are the processes that authors, writers, dancers, composers, actors, and poets also employ.

Life Skills. In art, children develop craftsmanship, self-discipline, dedication to a task, skills for working both individually and cooperatively, and pride in one's work. These skills are necessary for success in any area of their lives.

Critical Thinking Skills. Studying the visual arts develops higher-level thinking skills as students analyze, compare, interpret, synthesize, and make inferences and judgments about works of art.

Art is a great integrating subject because art, first and foremost, is a form of human communication. Art is one of the first forms of communication for children. Children often express complex ideas through visual symbols that represent their beginning language system. Art is a vehicle for children to learn about the world around them and to organize the information in a comprehensive format. As young children draw, they take textures, shapes, and colors from a complex world and form them into coherent visual images. This visual cognition, a powerful way for children to process information, is the basis for learning in and through art.

A Sampling of Art Program Resources for Schools

The California Arts Project 415-499-5893 (http://www.ucop.edu/tcap/aeol.html)

Crayola Dream-makers Binney & Smith, Easton, PA 800-CRAYOLA

Getty Education Institute for the Arts Los Angeles, CA 800-223-3431 (http://www.artsednet.getty.edu)

Institute for Arts Education San Diego, CA 619-260-1594

Original Works Yours Stillwater, NY 800-421-0020

Polaroid Education Program Portfolio 2000 Cambridge, MA 800-343-5000

Start with the Arts Very Special Arts John F. Kennedy Center for the Performing Arts, Washington, D.C. 800-933-8721

Safe Use of Art Materials

Mary Ann Boykin, Director, The Art School for Children and Young Adults, University of Houston–Clear Lake, Texas

Elementary art teachers are responsible for the safety of their students. To ensure safety in art class, teachers need to be aware of safety issues that can affect the well-being of the children they teach, as well as themselves. Specific safety standards have been established by the Center for Safety in the Arts, and these guidelines should be diligently followed in order to assure that neither the children nor their teachers are injured by the use of unsafe art materials.

Elementary teachers should do two things to prevent problems. The first is to keep all toxic and hazardous substances out of the classroom. The second is to know how to use the materials safely because any materials can become hazardous when used inappropriately.

TOXIC SUBSTANCES

A toxic substance is defined by the Center for Occupational Hazards as "a poison which can damage your body's organ systems when you are over exposed to it." This harm can be immediate or can be the result of repeated exposure over periods of time. Toxic substances can enter the body in three ways:
1) absorption through the skin;
2) inhalation through the nose or mouth;
3) ingestion through eating or drinking in the area where toxic materials are being used.
It is up to the teacher to make sure toxic substances do not enter the classroom and that all materials are used safely to avoid problems.

Pregnant women and those who are nursing infants must be especially careful to prevent exposure to toxic substances. All of the dangers to the fetus or infant have not been clearly defined, but enough information has been discerned to issue a clear warning to this population. Fumes, sprays, dusts, and powders present a real hazard to the fetus, can be transferred to the infant through the mother's milk, and can be carried home to the infant or young child through dusts and residue picked up by clothing and hair. The safe path is to completely avoid exposure to any toxin by carefully reading labels and applying common sense to the situation. For example, if you plan to mix powdered tempera paint or work with chalks or clay, the safe method would include use of a respirator mask, which would prevent inhalation of these substances.

CHILDREN AND SAFE ART MATERIALS

Preschool and elementary children are particularly vulnerable to unsafe art materials for a variety of reasons. Their lower body weight allows a toxic substance to be more concentrated in their bodies. Recent headlines regarding lead

poisoning in young children point out this fact. In addition, because children have a more rapid metabolism than adults, toxic substances are more quickly absorbed into their bodies.

> **Preschool and elementary children are particularly vulnerable to unsafe art materials for a variety of reasons.**

Children also tend to have more hand-to-mouth contact than adults, which allows accidental as well as purposeful ingestion of toxic materials. Furthermore, children are easily distracted from safety warnings regarding materials as they become involved in the art process. The tendency of children to have cuts and scratches also allows for ready entry of toxins into their bodies.

WHAT THE LABELS MEAN

Since 1990 our government has required the labeling of all hazardous materials. Any product labeled as hazardous is totally inappropriate for the elementary school. Safe art materials carry the statement that the material "Conforms to ASTMD-4236." A simple "nontoxic" statement on a product is not adequate.

The Arts and Crafts Materials Institute developed a voluntary program to provide a safe standard for materials used by children. Products bearing the labels AP (Approved Product) or CP (Certified Product) have actually been tested by toxicologists in major universities and have been deemed safe for children to use. The HL (Health Label) on art products indicates that these products are appropriate to use with children 12 years old or older under the supervision of an art teacher. Products with HL labels are not safe for elementary children.

SAFE ART MATERIALS

The following are guidelines for choosing and using basic art materials in a safe manner.

Drawing Materials
Markers
- Use only water-soluble AP- or CP-designated markers. Permanent markers are extremely dangerous and can cause lung and liver damage if inhaled. Never use permanent markers in the elementary classroom.
- The use of scented markers is also discouraged. This teaches children to sniff or smell materials.

Chalks
Use only dustless chalk. Most chalks are better used outside for sidewalk art. The amount of dust created in a classroom by twenty children wiping and blowing chalk can be irritating to those who suffer from allergies, asthma, and other respiratory problems.

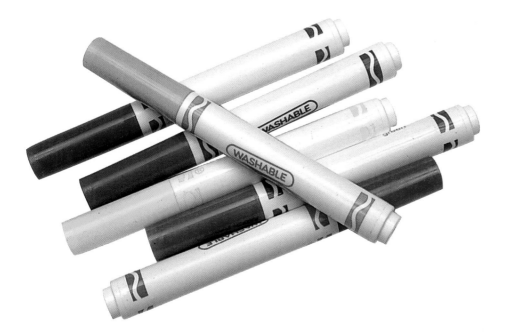

- Use absolutely no permanent markers or solvent-based materials in the art room. If a material stains the clothes or hands and does not clean up with simple soap and water, it is not appropriate or safe for young children to use.
- Use plastic containers for washing brushes; glass is dangerous in the hands of young children.
- Paper cutters should not be used by elementary children. The paper cutter should be kept out of the students' reach, and left in a locked position always with the blade turned to the wall or out of reach.
- Do not use commercial dyes with children; use vegetable or natural dyes (flowers, teas, nut shells, onion skins).
- Do not allow children in the room where a kiln is firing; both the heat and the fumes are dangerous.

Crayons

Use oil pastels; the colors are richer and the satisfaction is greater! Crayons should also bear the AP or CP label to ensure that no lead is present in these materials.

Painting Materials

- Use only liquid tempera and/or watercolor paints. If you must use powdered tempera paints, mix these outside and have the paints ready before children enter the classroom. Avoid inhaling the powders of tempera colors.
- Do not use any spray paints or fixatives. These are extremely dangerous.

Printmaking Materials

- Use only water-soluble printer's inks. Do not use any solvent-based inks.
- Use pencils to carve into unused Styrofoam meat trays for a printing block. Do not use mat knives or other sharp instruments.

Collage Materials

Scissors

Sharp scissors should not be used by young children; blunt points are safe. Fourth and fifth graders may use rounded points with teacher supervision.

Glue and Paste

Use only school paste or white glue for adhering papers. Do not use rubber cement unless it bears the AP or CP label. Do not use any solvent-based glues.

Sculpture and Three-Dimensional Materials

Clay

- Use premixed, moist clay for sculpture and pottery. Do not allow students to take home any unfired clay.
- Remind children to wash their hands thoroughly after using clay. The residual dust can be harmful and irritating if inhaled.
- Paint clay pieces with tempera or watercolor paints.

Glazes

Do not use glazes. Some have the approved labels, but they are not recommended for elementary use.

Carving Tools

Use pencils, craft sticks, or other blunt tools to carve clay. Soapstone should not be used for carving in a closed environment.

Papier-Mâché

Read labels carefully on pastes used for papier-mâché because some pastes contain pesticides or preservatives that are extremely harmful.

Stitchery, Weaving, and Fiber Materials

- Use blunt plastic needles and loosely woven fabrics such as burlap for stitchery. Blunt metal tapestry needles are safe if supervised.
- Young children will have trouble cutting fabric and yarns with their scissors. Precut some lengths of yarn prior to introducing the task.

GENERAL SAFETY PRECAUTIONS FOR ART

- Read the labels on all materials used in the art room. Look carefully for the AP/CP labels. If these are not present, be suspicious. Imported art materials should be looked upon with extreme caution. In this case, "buying American" is the safe path. Other countries have not developed the rigid safety codes adopted by the United States.
- Do not accept or use old art materials that may have been left in the school or donated by some well-meaning adult. If the materials do not bear the current safety codes, toss them out!
- Allow no food or drink in the room where art activities are being created. Dust and even fibers float freely in the air and can readily contaminate food.
- Practice cleanliness. Have children wash their hands thoroughly with soap after using art materials.

References

Babin, A., Editor, *Art Hazards News,* Vol. 17, No. 5, 1994.

Babin, A, Peltz, P.A., Rossol, M. "Children's Art Supplies Can Be Toxic." New York: Center for Safety in the Arts, 1992.

McCann, Michael. *Artist Beware.* New York: Watson-Guptill Publications, 1979.

McCann, Michael, "Hazards in the Arts." New York: Center for Safety in the Arts, 1989.

Qualley, Charles A. *Safety in the Art Room.* Massachusetts: Davis Publications, Inc., 1986.

For further information:

Center for Safety in the Arts
5 Beekman Street, Suite 820
New York, New York 10038
(212) 227-6220

Art Assessments

Assessment in art can be problematic for a variety of reasons. Many educators are reluctant to evaluate a student's creative expression in a work of art as good or bad. Because there are often no right or wrong answers, students and their parents could challenge a teacher's subjective opinion of a work if it were reflected in a letter grade. Furthermore, many teachers without a strong art background do not feel qualified to grade student artwork. In addition, teachers do not want to discourage creative expression by giving a low grade or an undeserved grade. People also often feel that talented students have the advantage in art class and that students should not be evaluated on how talented they are, but rather on how much effort they put into their work and how much progress they make.

All of these assessment troubles stem from a focus on art production in the art classroom, rather than a reflection of art history and culture, aesthetics, or art criticism. A broader focus in the art classroom and a variety of assessment options may help in more effective art assessment.

Assessment of Lesson Objectives

Instead of subjective opinions of whether or not one likes a student's artwork, students can be evaluated on whether or not they met the art lesson objectives or demonstrated the knowledge and skills introduced in the lesson. In a quality art program, there are objectives for aesthetic perception, art history, and art criticism, as well as for demonstrating understanding of the elements and principles of art in art production.

In *Art Connections,* every lesson has four clear, measurable objectives. At the end of each lesson, in the **Evaluation Criteria,** teachers are provided questions to consider for each objective as they evaluate students.

Art Production: Evaluating Student Artwork

Art teachers frequently evaluate student artwork on the basis of how well it reflects the elements and principles of art that are being stressed in the lesson and how well the student met the criteria for the artwork. Some teachers make up rubrics or standards for the artwork beforehand and tell students how their work will be evaluated at the time it is assigned. Some teachers use written or mental checklists of their standards as they look at student artwork. Some teachers use this evaluation as an opportunity to discuss the work with the student and find out whether the student thought he or she met the objectives for artwork.

In *Art Connections,* teachers can also use the **Assessment Masters** in the *Assessment Book* to get an idea of whether a student understands the element or principle of art for the lesson.

Art Criticism and Aesthetic Perception: Self- and Peer-Assessment

The four-step process of art criticism (Describe, Analyze, Interpret, Decide) provides a procedure that students can use to objectively study their own art products, as well as the works of others. The sequential steps of art criticism are similar to those used in the scientific method. During the first two steps, Describe and Analyze, students are asked to collect data objectively. During the third step, Interpret, students speculate about the meaning of the work based on the data collected: they make a hypothesis about the idea, emotion, or mood expressed by the artist. During the fourth step, Decide, the students offer their aesthetic judgment about the work of art. The sequential procedures in art criticism force the students to postpone judgment while becoming immersed in the image. It forces them to have a fully funded visual experience before drawing conclusions about a work.

> **❝ Art educators could claim to have inspired the growing use of portfolio assessment in other subject areas. ❞**

Art Connections includes art criticism questions for every Practice and Create activity. These questions appear in the *Student Edition* in grades 3–5 and in the *Teacher Edition* in grades K–2. Additionally, the **Seeing Like an Artist** feature in every lesson of the *Student Edition* provides students with an opportunity to evaluate their developing aesthetic perception.

Art History and Culture

Art is a visual record of history and diverse cultures. The goals for elementary art education are that students understand and appreciate different historical periods, cultures, and artistic styles and develop respect for the traditions and contributions of diverse societies.

In *Art Connections* every lesson introduces fine art from a particular culture, time, and style. In the **Introducing the Art** strategies, teachers are encouraged to compare, contrast, and share the **Art Background** information as well as the information provided in the *Artist Profiles* to help students develop an understanding of the visual arts in relation to history and cultures. Through discussion and elements in their own artwork, teachers can evaluate students' awareness in this area.

Portfolio Assessment

Art educators could claim to have inspired the growing use of portfolio assessment in other subject areas. Many art teachers collect the best examples of a student's work and look at the progress over time. They display it and discuss it

with students and parents. Student art journals with ideas, drawings, and sketches also provide an opportunity for portfolio assessment.

In *Art Connections,* students are encouraged to keep their best work in a *Student Portfolio* and to maintain an **Art Journal.** Reminders of these types of portfolio assessments appear in the *Teacher Edition.*

Performance Assessment

Unlike other subject areas, art education has a long tradition of performance assessment. In art class students make things to demonstrate what they can do. In quality art programs, teachers use performance descriptions for not only art production, but art criticism, art history and culture, and aesthetic perception to aid them in evaluating student demonstrations of their knowledge and skills in art.

In *Art Connections,* every work of art a student produces can be considered for performance assessment of the lesson concept. Performance assessments can also involve discussions about the artworks to introduce the lesson concept and art criticism questions. The exercises in the *Vocabulary Book* also help teachers to get an idea of how well students understand the art vocabulary of the lesson; they can be using this vocabulary, the language of art, in their discussions about their own and others' artwork.

Art not only enables teachers to evaluate student knowledge and skills in art each year, but it also provides a wonderful opportunity to assess a student's growth and development over time. Students and parents are often reluctant to discard artwork and fondly review it from time to time to see how children's ideas and skills have changed. Schools often keep an example of student artwork in a student's portfolio from year to year. Student artwork can also be evaluated by professionals to assess a student's emotional and mental health.

A thoughtful and fair art assessment program enables teachers to really see how much their students are capable of accomplishing.

References

Armstrong, Carmen. L. *Designing Assessment in Art.* Reston, VA: The National Art Education Association. 1994.

Into the Portfolio Process: A Handbook for Student Assessment. California Art Education Association, Butte County Office of Education. 1995.

Rudner, Lawrence M. and Carol Boston. *A Look at Performance Assessment for Art Education.* Reston, VA: The National Art Education Association. 1994.

Art and Multiple Intelligences

Gloria McCoy, K–12 Art Supervisor, Spring Branch Independent School District, Texas

In the last twenty years, a group of researchers and educators headed by Dr. Howard Gardner, co-director of Project Zero at Harvard Graduate School of Education and Adjunct Professor of Neurology at the Boston University School of Medicine, have come to the conclusion that there are many ways of knowing and solving the same problem. Others such as Thomas Armstrong and David Lazear have written extensively on the subject and have developed practical applications of the theory of multiple intelligences in the classroom. The multiple intelligences theory has direct and indirect connections to art education.

The theory of multiple intelligences addresses the issue of intelligence quotients. At the beginning of the twentieth century, IQ tests were developed and quickly gained popularity as a "radar detector" of genius. These tests, designed on a curved scale, were touted to be able to sort people by their intelligence. Unfortunately, these tests have been shown to be unreliable when measuring *success* in the world outside the classroom. In one study, for example, more than a third of highly successful people scored low on IQ tests. Men and women throughout history, such as Thomas Edison and Albert Einstein, who were not very successful in school have made great contributions to our world. Leonardo da Vinci, one of the finest minds and artists of all time, grieved at the end of his life that he had not lived up to his potential because of his poor spelling, penmanship, and other language skills.

Gardner realized that IQ tests often tested only those skills that were used in schools, such as reading and math. As a consequence, many areas of the human ways of knowing and learning were omitted. Gardner defined intelligence as the *ability to solve problems* or fashion products that are of consequence in a particular cultural setting.

In the development of his theory, Gardner identified at least seven different intelligences. All of us have each of these intelligences to some degree; however, the degree may depend on how fully we have developed them. Some of them such as music develop early in life, while others such as math may develop later. There are indicators that children may repress some intelligences if they are not valued or developed in early childhood. Each of the intelligences can stand on its own, but most of the time they work together with other intelligences to solve problems.

Following are examples of Gardner's intelligences and how they are expressed in the art classroom.

Visual/Spatial intelligence most often comes to mind in the visual arts. It relies on the sense of sight and visualization, as well as creating internal mental images and finding one's way in space. Pilots, artists, and mechanical engineers are a few of those who rely on this intelligence.

In *Art Connections,* the **Create** activity in each lesson includes use of this intelligence. Many students who have a real strength in this area have an opportunity to use it in the art room.

Body/Kinesthetic is related to physical movement, handling objects skillfully, and the wisdom of the body, including the part of the brain that controls motion—the motor cortex. Some of those who use this intelligence are surgeons, craftspeople, athletes, and mechanics.

In *Art Connections* there is a natural link to both the **Practice** and the **Create** activities as students cut, draw, paint, and otherwise manipulate materials and tools. Students will use this intelligence in every lesson.

> **“** Unlike many other subjects that depend on one intelligence, art education provides an opportunity for students to use all of their intelligences to solve problems. **”**

Verbal/Linguistic is the intelligence that relates to words and language, both written and spoken, and dominates most of our educational systems. Lawyers, poets, storytellers, and journalists are a few of the groups who rely heavily on this intelligence.

This intelligence is also a natural part of every art lesson, whether the students are reading, listening to information, expressing opinions, or dialoguing with others.

Interpersonal is the intelligence based on person-to-person relationships and communication, as well as empathy skills. Careers in this area include therapists, social workers, politicians, and pastors.

This intelligence could be used frequently in art lessons as works of art are discussed in groups. Art discussions allow all students an opportunity to participate and often encourage even the most shy student. Structured cooperative learning also supports this intelligence.

Intrapersonal intelligence relates to our understanding of ourselves, reflections on what we've done and why, our inner state of being, thinking about thinking or metacognition, and our awareness of spiritual realities. Counselors, theologians, and even self-employed businesspeople might depend on this intelligence in day-to-day work.

The connection of intrapersonal intelligence to art is a natural as students are asked to express their feelings or thoughts through the creation of artwork or reflect on the process afterward. The **Art Journal** suggestions in *Art Connections* are also intended to support this intelligence.

Logical/Mathematical is the intelligence that is sometimes called "scientific thinking" because it deals with inductive and deductive thinking and reasoning, numbers, and recognition of abstract patterns. Scientists, accountants, and computer programmers are dependent on this intelligence.

In art, students use logical/mathematical intelligence when they look for abstract patterns, use deductive reasoning to determine the meaning of a work of art, use grids and measurements in drawing, or use geometric shapes to create designs.

Musical/Rhythmic intelligence is based on tonal patterns and their recognition. It includes a variety of environmental sounds, as well as the sensitivity to rhythm and beats. Musicians, band directors, and dancers depend on this intelligence.

Rhythm is a principle of art and is part of the artmaking process. In addition, *Art Connections* includes audiotapes of classical music to play during the Create process to enhance creative thinking. **Music Connections** appear in the *Teacher Edition*. In addition, The ARTSOURCE Lessons at the end of each unit focus on connecting visual art to music, dance, and theater.

Unlike many other subjects that depend on one intelligence, art education provides an opportunity for students to use all of their intelligences to solve problems. Often students succeed in art class when they have trouble in other areas.

One of the most profound findings of multiple intelligence is something that art educators have known for years. When students employ a variety of ways to solve a problem, they can all come up with successful solutions. There is no one right answer, but many.

References

Armstrong, Thomas. *Multiple Intelligences in the Classroom*. Virginia: Association for Supervision and Curriculum Development, 1994.

Armstrong, Thomas. *Seven Kinds of Smart: Identifying and Developing Your Many Intelligences*. New York: Plume/Penguin, 1993.

Gardner, Howard. *Multiple Intelligences: The Theory in Practice. A Reader*. Basic Books/Harper Collins, 1993.

Lazear, David. *Seven Ways of Knowing: Teaching for Multiple Intelligences*. Illinois: Skylight Publishing, 1991.

About Aesthetic Perception

Richard W. Burrows, Executive Director, Institute for Arts Education,
San Diego, California

The Association of Institutes for Aesthetic Education promotes and fosters aesthetic education principles and practices through professional and institutional development. The Association provides policy and program leadership to the arts and education field at the national, state, and local levels.

Aesthetics has been defined as the branch of philosophy that focuses on the nature of beauty, the nature and value of art, and the inquiry processes and human responses associated with those topics.

Aesthetic perception can be most simply defined as an educational approach designed to enhance understanding of artistic expression. Aesthetic perception requires two primary elements to exist: the work of art and a viewer to perceive it. An aesthetic perception approach to viewing works of art is predicated on the belief that the arts can be studied in an active, experiential way. The focus is on developing skills of perception by using works of art as a "textbook" or a focus for study. The instruction delivered by the teachers is in partnership with the work of art.

Aesthetic perception provides opportunities to heighten perception and understanding through direct encounters with a broad spectrum of artworks. Students and teachers become actively involved with the artwork: observing, listening to and discussing works of art, and exploring their perceptions of these works through participatory activities. The focus is on developing skills of perception through greater understanding of art forms, of how artists make aesthetic choices, and of how these understandings relate to other aspects of life.

Misconceptions About Aesthetic Perception

As aesthetic perception approaches have become more widely used, a number of misconceptions have developed about the purpose of aesthetic perception education in the understanding of works of art.

Multidisciplinary Versus Interdisciplinary

The purpose of aesthetic perception is not to explore the commonalities among works of art. Each work of art must be studied separately first; connections should be made after an in-depth understanding of that particular work. Every work of art has a separate intention and different meaning. If aesthetic perception is to develop a thinking- or meaning-based understanding of the work of art, then activities must reflect that point of view.

You Cannot Teach What You Do Not Like

A strong "personal" negative reaction to a work of art does not invalidate it as an object for study for students.

Arts Integration

While arts experiences must integrate with all other areas of the curriculum, it is important to understand the separate language that the arts have and acknowledge the connections with other cross-curriculum areas as they arise.

> " Aesthetic perception requires two primary elements to exist: the work of art and a viewer to perceive it. "

The Therapeutic Value of Aesthetic Perception

Very often students and teachers will comment on the therapeutic value of aesthetic perception. . . it seems separate from the actual art-making processes. This is often a side effect of active engagement in artistic creation and perception. It is not the purpose of aesthetic perception, which should be seen as an alternative way of viewing the work of art and the world in which it lives.

Using Aesthetic Perception

Below are some guidelines for using an aesthetic perception approach to education.

Deciding What to Teach

It would not be appropriate to teach the same elements over and over in connection with each work of art. Instead, knowledge of all of the elements within a given art discipline should provide the background knowledge for making a decision about what aesthetic perception experiences to design. These decisions should be based on the most predominant elements in the work of art—the responses and the backgrounds of the students across time.

Creating a Safe Space and Adopting a Critical Stance

It is important to create a working and learning environment with both students and teachers in which they feel comfortable taking risks and trying out new ideas. This does not mean, however, that everything that occurs in aesthetic perception has to be met with uncritical approval. Instead, experiences can be structured so that participants receive feedback on their aesthetic choices and are given an opportunity to revise and improve their solutions to problems.

Documenting the Experience

Various types of documentation serve as a way of recording the aesthetic perception events as they occur or are revisited. This documentation should include written observations, interviews, journals, and student projects. It is important in any case to record this work in order to be able to see the "habits of mind" that reveal themselves in this complex and rich way of thinking and knowing.

Aesthetic perception is a long-term undertaking and requires a patient conviction that the arts and aesthetic perception should be a part of the learning experience of young people. It requires flexibility, stamina, ingenuity, and perseverance. The rewards are astronomical in terms of student response, content understanding, and classroom relationships.

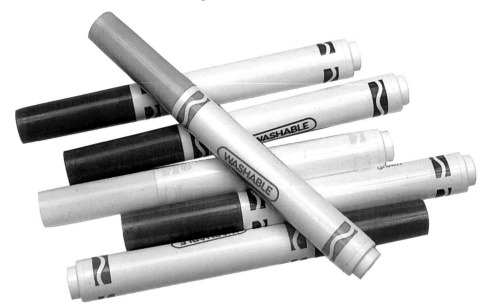

It Takes a Village: The Community as a Resource for Art Materials

Willis Bing Davis, Head of Art Department, Central State University, Ohio

Ingenuity, resourcefulness, and creative survival have always been a close friend to most successful art and classroom teachers when it comes to providing meaningful arts experiences for students. We are known as collectors who never (almost never) throw anything away. Some art and classroom teachers will need to acquire the skill of always being on the lookout for resources, materials, and supplies that can supplement art materials in the classroom. It can be a lot of fun; plus, it stimulates the imagination and creative impulse. This is also a great way to build bridges and advocates for arts education.

Think of all the things you use in the art room. How many can be found locally? Any safe, usable materials or supplies that can be found free or reduced in price leaves more of the art budget to buy the things that have to be purchased. There are different forms of searching for inexpensive to free materials for art activities. The following are a few tried and proven ways to acquire materials, supplies, and resources that can be used for art and other educational activities.

Materials in the School Building
- Leftover wood or metal from a shop class
- Empty milk and food containers from the food-service area
- Cardboard tubes from the food service, rest room, or copy machine
- Scrap paper from copy machines

Annual Open House Night Resources
Open house is a great time to post a small list of hand tools needed for the art program. You would be surprised how many extra hammers, pliers, screwdrivers, bent forks, and so on are lying around garages and basements.

Many parents also work at places that have by-products that could supplement the art materials in the art program.

Local Business Material Sources
- *Wood.* Lumberyards are usually willing to let teachers collect boxes of scrap wood for art production. Some lumberyards will even let you leave a box with your school name on it.
- *Wallpaper.* Ask for discontinued wallpaper design sample books from paint stores.
- *Paper.* Large quantities of damaged paper may be available from local paper or paper distribution companies.

Community Resources
- Many communities participate in the popular "Take-a-Child-to-Work" programs that allow children to see and experience where their parents work. Almost every school also has a Career Day when many professional individuals visit schools to talk to students about potential careers. Both programs put schools, students, or teachers into direct contact with local businesses. Both groups are already open to helping schools and would welcome other, more direct ways to contribute to positive educational experiences.

> **❝ Any safe, usable materials or supplies that can be found free or reduced in price leaves more of the art budget to buy the things that have to be purchased. ❞**

- Teachers may find that companies with national headquarters in their communities often have a strong commitment to those communities and their educational systems. Teachers can assist these companies in reaching their community commitment goals by suggesting ways that they can assist the school art program. Local businesses may want to sponsor the visit of a local artist or donate materials.
- Many local service organizations have an interest and commitment to youth and the arts. They often go begging for art and cultural events and activities to which they can contribute. Find out what they want to contribute and help them reach their goal, be it providing scholarships to talented art students, funding an exhibit, hosting an art reception, donating materials and supplies, framing student artworks for the hallways, sponsoring a local or major art field trip, and so on.

Artist Resources
- Local and regional emerging artists live in every community and can make meaningful contributions to the school art program. Artists from the community or region offer a "realness" to the program from knowing and living in the area.
- Some artists do a good job at demonstrating, some do a good slide-lecture, some are more effective in large groups or small groups, some do great critique sessions, and some may be better mentoring one-on-one. Each individual teacher or school district can develop an annotated artist directory listing the artists' strong points for reference.
- Most communities also have one or more local arts groups or arts organizations that can assist schools in identifying and securing the services of local artists. A local arts group may be willing to do a series of Member Art Demos over the course of the year in your school.
- Another great source of local and regional artists can be found in the colleges and universities in your area. It is a win–win situation because the college and university art program can show your students some of the quality art teachers they may be working with in the future. This a great source of judges for student competitions.

Art Agencies at Local and State Levels: While everyone is aware of the existence of the National Endowment for the Arts in Washington, D.C., many may not be aware that there are state arts agencies and many community-based Arts Councils that can be an important resource for your art program.

Find ways to let everyone in the community help your art program to be the best it can be because remember, **it takes a village.**

A Sampling of Art Supplies Resources
J. L. Hammett Co. Braintree, MA
  800-333-4600
Nasco Arts & Crafts Modesto, CA
  800-558-9595
Sax Arts & Crafts New Berlin, WI
  800-558-6696
United Art and Education Supply Co., Inc. Fort Wayne, IN 800-322-3247

The Importance of Cultural Diversity Through Art in the Elementary Classroom

Jane Rhoades Hudak, Ph.D., Professor of Art Teacher Education, Georgia Southern University

James Banks, noted multicultural expert, says: "By the year 2050 the average United States resident will trace his or her ancestry to Africa, Asia, Latin America, the Pacific Islands, Arabia, and almost anywhere but Europe. Today in New York State 40 percent of the elementary and secondary pupils belong to ethnic minorities. By the year 2000 this figure will be 50 percent." With this in mind, the following is an overview of the benefits of a culturally diverse art program.

Culture is learned. People acquire information about the world and how to deal with it as members of a society. Individuals do not learn about their culture by themselves. Children learn about the art of their own culture and other cultures through family and friends, through the mass media, and through the Internet. The information learned this way is often valuable, but it can not be relied upon to always give adequate and correct information. Schools are often the most effective place for giving students the opportunity to learn about the art of their culture and other cultures.

Our view of the nature of the world and our place in it is expressed and communicated culturally. Every society has institutions that teach culture—family and school are two of the best examples in our society. All societies have religions, which are bodies of cultural knowledge and practices. We also have rituals for birth and death. All cultures have objects that are used for everyday living. We express our world views through dance, drama, music, and art. We decorate our world and our bodies. We paint our faces and the walls of our houses. We make music with instruments and our voices. All this activity is shaped by our participation in a cultural tradition.

A quality elementary art program provides a wonderful opportunity for teachers to expose students to a variety of cultures as well as their own and to help them to become culturally aware. Following are several of the areas such a program can enhance.

Art Promotes Intracultural Understanding

Through a culturally diverse art program, students begin to understand the role and function that art and artists play in society. Through learning about the art of other cultures, they have the opportunity to identify similarities and differences between their culture and others. They learn that art reflects the religion, politics, economics, and other aspects of a culture.

Through a quality art program, students can address issues of ethnocentrism, bias, stereotyping, prejudice, discrimination, and racism. Students can learn that no one racial, cultural, or national group is superior to another and that no one group's art is better than another.

Art Teaches Self-Esteem Through Diversity

Through a quality art program, students learn to recognize, acknowledge, and celebrate racial and cultural diversity through art within their own society. A good program helps promote the enhancement and affirmation of their self-esteem and encourages pride in one's own heritage. Personal expression is encouraged, and the result is often a statement in visual form that is both inventive and filled with personal meaning.

> 66 A quality elementary art program provides a wonderful opportunity for teachers to expose students to a variety of cultures as well as their own and to help them to become culturally aware. 99

Art Teaches Effective Communication

When a quality art program is implemented, students are encouraged to increase their visual literacy skills. Students begin to understand that artists transmit information that cannot be disclosed through other modes of communication. Students learn visual literacy by looking, understanding, talking, writing, and making images. They learn that each society has its own way of communicating through images. Through a culturally sensitive art program, students will be able to discuss and compare art from other societies. Students learn to visually communicate by creating images that convey knowledge, create new knowledge, shape opinions, disclose the depths of human emotion, and impart the most profound values found universally throughout the world.

Art Teaches About the Past

Through a quality art program, students develop a sensitivity and understanding of the history of humankind. For many periods in history, it is only through visual remains or material culture that societies' cultures can be pieced together. A study of art history reveals varied world views, concepts, symbols, styles, feelings, and perceptions. Experiences that students have with these art objects from the past teach them respect for others, challenge their minds, and stimulate not only the intellect but also the imagination.

Art Teaches Critical Thinking

A culturally sensitive art program encourages a variety of critical thinking skills. When students are faced with looking at art from other cultures, they make critical judgments and develop their own opinions. Students are asked to identify and recall information; to organize selected facts and ideas; to use particular facts, rules, and principles; to be able to figure out component parts or to classify; and to combine ideas and form a new whole.

Art Teaches Perceptual Sensitivity and Aesthetic Awareness

As a result of a quality art program, students develop a keen sense of awareness and an appreciation for beauty. They learn that each culture has its own criteria for beauty. Art experiences help cultivate an aesthetic sensitivity and respect for the natural and human-made environment around the world. Art classes are the only place in the school curriculum where students learn about what constitutes quality visual design—about harmony, order, organization, and specific design qualities (such as balance, movement, and unity).

Art Teaches Creativity

When a culturally sensitive art program is implemented, creativity in all students is stimulated and nurtured. Students learn to solve problems creatively. They learn that every society has some form of creative expression. Students learn that artists in other cultures have expressed their creativity in a wide range of ways as a magician, myth maker, teacher, propagandist, shaman, and catalyst of social change. In some societies, no one special person is called an artist—everyone in the culture makes "art" objects.

Teachers can help prevent students from having a simplistic view of other cultures and help them understand the cultural context of how and why artworks are created. *Art Connections* has been carefully constructed so that students will be exposed to artwork that represents a wide variety of cultures. Questions and strategies are designed to help teachers put art in a cultural context for students. The **Art Background** feature in this *Teacher Edition* and the *Artist Profiles* book provides additional information about the artwork and the artists.

As a teacher in the school, you are a cultural transmitter. A quality art education program taught by a culturally sensitive teacher benefits every student. When educators teach in a systematic, meaningful way, students acquire knowledge about art and cultures that will benefit them throughout their lives.

Museum Education

Marilyn JS Goodman, Director of Education, Solomon R. Guggenheim Museum

Museums are truly magnificent places. In recent years, these bastions of culture have taken tremendous strides toward making their collections accessible to a broader audience. Museum educators are usually eager to share new information and ideas and are delighted to assist school educators with programs and materials that can easily be incorporated into the classroom. Museums contain a wealth of treasures that offer extraordinary resources for teachers and their students, and which will undoubtedly enrich the overall classroom experience.

Getting acquainted with museums in your region can be a real eye-opener. Museums collect objects that document human achievement, both in our own and in other cultures. A local historical society or farm museum might contain an array of clothing and tools that can bring history to life. A science museum may offer interactive exhibits about phenomena in the natural or physical sciences, or maybe about sensory perception, new technologies, or space exploration. A children's museum will offer hands-on displays specially designed to motivate young children to learn by doing. And art museums contain a visually stunning smorgasbord of works that reflect the diversity of human thought and experiences.

Museums do not supplant classroom instruction. They enhance and reinforce what is taught by providing honest-to-goodness raw materials in the form of objects, artifacts, and exhibits. They give students the chance to see and sometimes handle the real thing. It's one thing, for example, to talk about Egypt's role in the history of civilization. It's another thing entirely to see the wrappings on a cat mummy, discover hieroglyphs on a sarcophagus, or be overwhelmed by the power and grandeur of large stone sculptures of kings and queens.

When students have the chance to look at portraits, still lifes, landscapes, genre scenes, furniture, clothing, and artifacts, they learn more than by just seeing a picture of a person, place, or thing. They learn how to "read" a culture. But perhaps more importantly, they learn to develop their own processes of investigation and critical inquiry. What was this person's life really like? What can one learn about the class structure of this society? What can we tell about craftspeople, available materials, or the objects this society held dear? How does the clothing tell us about the climate of the region? What can we learn about the geography, topography, and vegetation? What did people eat? How did they spend leisure time? What were their religious beliefs? Is there any evidence of trade and communication with other regions? What scientific inventions were present at the time? Can one tell if they communicated through language or by writing? As children are naturally curious, objects will motivate them to think, research, and learn.

A visit to a museum will make the curriculum come alive as a class begins to explore objects and learn about their meanings. Museum objects give us information in a way that's very different from reading texts. Students must think critically to determine both the questions and answers for themselves. A first-hand, visual investigation of an object's style, material, subject matter, and physical characteristics offers preliminary clues to deciphering its meaning. When the exploration is combined with other knowledge—such as the geography and natural resources of a region; the historical context; the social, political, and economic structure of a culture; or even advances in science and technology—students can be engaged in a type of learning that is truly multidisciplinary, and which may lead them into other areas. Moreover, methods for gathering information go far beyond what one sees.

> ❝ Museums contain a wealth of treasures that offer extraordinary resources for teachers and their students, and which will undoubtedly enrich the overall classroom experience. ❞

Exploring objects and works of art allows students to use a multiplicity of senses combining intellect with intuition. The opportunity for experiential, emotional, and intellectual learning is always present.

Museum objects present different historical and cultural perspectives. One can gather information about a person, a culture, a belief system, values, and the way people lived in the past. Museum visits encourage students to see things from broader global and intellectual points of view, developing respect for the work, lives, and points of view of others. Students are encouraged to respond in a variety of ways and on different levels. Most importantly, students are invited to formulate and express their ideas and then discuss them with others.

To learn about museum resources, teachers can contact the education department of museums in their region. If teachers explain the level of their students, the subjects they are studying, and which specific aspects of the curriculum they would like to supplement, the museum's education department can help to tailor the resources to the classroom. In addition to guided tours and workshops, the museum education department may offer materials for loan including slides, pamphlets, posters, postcards, kits, and other printed materials. Some museums have teacher resource rooms filled with books, films, videos, CD-ROMS, and computer databases geared to educators. There will always be trained staff to answer questions or to help teachers develop a complete learning unit that can integrate museum objects with classroom studies.

Using museums is an excellent way to enrich and enliven the classroom experience. Educators can take the first step by learning all they can about the rich and diverse resources available to them and their students.

A Sampling of Fine Art CD-ROM Resources

A Is for Art, C Is for Cezanne, Philadelphia Museum of Art

Art Gallery, Microscoft

ArtRageous, Softkey

Le Louvre: The Palace and Its Paintings, Montparnasse Multimedia

The Louvre Museum: Museums of the World for Kids, Voyager

Painters Painting, Voyager

A Passion for Art: Renoir, Cezanne, Matisse, and Dr. Barnes Corbis Publishing

With Open Eyes: Images from the Art Institute of Chicago, Voyager

United States Museum Resources

Washington

Montana

Nort
Dako

Oregon

Idaho

South
Dakot

Wyoming

Nevada

Utah

Colorado

Nebrask

California

Arizona

New Mexico

Hawaii

Alaska

• The Minneapolis Institute of Arts
• Walker Art Center (Minneapolis)

• Seattle Art Museum

• Portland Art Museum

• Joslyn Art Museum (Omaha)

• Spencer Museum of
  Art (Lawrence)

• The Denver Art Museum

• San Francisco Museum
  of Modern Art
• The Fine Arts Museums
  of San Francisco

• Norton Simon Museum (Pasadena)

• San Diego Museum of Art

• Los Angeles County
  Museum of Art
• Craft and Folk Art
  Museum (Los Angeles)
• Southwest Museum (Los Angeles)

• Panhandle-Plains
  Historical Museum
  (West Texas A&M
  University)(Canyon)

• Kimbell Art Museum
  (Fort Worth)

• Dallas Museum of Art

• The Heard
  Museum (Phoenix)
• Phoenix Art Museum

• Anchorage Museum of
  History and Art

The Art Institute of Chicago
The David and Alfred Smart Museum of Art (Chicago)

• The Detroit Institute of the Arts

• The Cleveland Museum of Art

• Albright-Knox Art Gallery (Buffalo)

• The Farnsworth Art Museum (Rockland)

• Allen Memorial Art Museum (Oberlin)

• The Butler Institute of American Art (Youngstown)

• Harvard University Art Museums (Cambridge)

• Museum of Fine Arts (Boston)

• Wadsworth Athenum (Hartford)

• The Solomon R. Guggenheim Museum (New York City)

• The Metropolitan Museum of Art (New York City)

• Philadelphia Museum of Art

• The Palmer Museum of Art (Penn State University) (University Park)

Washington, DC
• Smithsonian Museums
• National Gallery of Art
• The National Museum of Women in the Arts
• The White House

• The Andy Warhol Museum (Pittsburgh)

• Michael C. Carlos Museum (Emory University) (Atlanta)
• High Museum of Art (Atlanta) (affiliate: Robert W. Woodruff Arts Center)

• Art Museum, The University of Memphis

• The Nelson–Atkins Museum of Art (Kansas City)

• The Museum of Fine Arts (Houston)

• Florida International Museum (St. Petersburg)

Minnesota
Wisconsin
Iowa
Illinois
Missouri
Michigan
Indiana
Ohio
Kentucky
Tennessee
Arkansas
Mississippi
Alabama
Louisiana
Georgia
South Carolina
North Carolina
Virginia
West Virginia
Pennsylvania
New York
Maine
VT
NH
MA
CT RI
NJ
MD
DE
Florida

UNITED STATES MUSEUM RESOURCES

Allen Memorial Art Museum
Oberlin College
Oberlin, OH 44074
Phone: (216) 775-8665
URL: (WWW address): http://www.oberlin.edu/wwwmap/allen_art.html
Site description: Ohio's Oberlin College is the host of this site. The on-line collection includes ancient to modern, Africa to America.

Andy Warhol Museum, The
117 Sandusky St.
Pittsburgh, PA 15212
Phone: (412) 237-8300
URL: (WWW address): http://www.clpgh.org/warhol/
Site description: The pop art inventer is featured in this Pittsburgh institution. Many of Warhol's most famous images are included, such as Jackie Kennedy. Tour info, calendars, and all other museum offerings.

Boston Museum of Fine Arts
465 Huntington Ave.
Boston, MA 02115
Phone: (617) 267-9300
URL: (WWW address): http://www.mfa.org
Site description: The highlight of the site is the museum's on-line exhibit of 19th century American artist Winslow Homer.

Butler Institute of American Art
524 Wick Ave.
Youngstown, OH 44502
Phone: (330) 743-1711
URL: (WWW address): http://www.butlerart.com
Site description: This museum in Youngstown, Ohio was the first U.S. museum built exclusively for housing American art. Works of Winslow Homer, Mary Cassatt, and Thomas Hart Benton are included.

Cleveland Museum of Art
11150 East Blvd.
Cleveland, OH 44106
Phone: (216) 421-7340
URL: (WWW address): http://www.clemusart.com/
Site description: This site contains images of its collection from ancient Egypt to the present. A selection of education links is accessible.

Farnsworth Art Museum
352 Main Street, Box 466
Rockland, ME 04841
Phone: (207) 596-6457
URL: (WWW address): http://www.midcoast.com/~farnsworth/
Site description: Images from Andrew Wyeth's personal collection in addition to the museum's own can be viewed at this site.

Florida International Museum (Treasures of the Czars)
100 Second St. North
St. Petersburg, FL 33701
Phone: (813) 824-6734
URL: (WWW address): http://www.sptimes.com/treasures/
Site description: A new museum, opened in 1995, the site displays examples from its premier exhibit.

Fine Arts Museums of San Francisco
Golden Gate Park
San Francisco, CA 94118
Phone: (415) 750-3600
URL: (WWW address): http://www.famsf.org/
Site description: This site has the largest searchable art image base in the world. 65,000!

Harvard University Art Museums
32 Quincy St.
Cambridge, MA 02138
Phone: (617) 495-9400
URL: (WWW address): http://www.fas.harvard.edu/~artmuseums/
Site description: The Fogg Art Museum, the Busch-Reisinger Museum, and the Arthur M. Sackler Museum, all located in Cambridge, MA, are accessed at this virtual address.

High Museum (Woodruff Arts Center)
1280 Peachtree St. N. E.
Atlanta, GA 30309
Phone: (404) 848-4711
URL: (WWW address): http://www.high.org/
Site description: Contains information on educational programs, teacher resources, and outreach programs.

Los Angeles Craft and Folk Art Museum
5800 Wilshire Blvd.
Los Angeles, CA
Phone: (213) 937-5544
URL: (WWW address): http://www.lam.mus.ca.us/~cafam/
Site description: This museum celebrates contemporary craft, international folk art, and design from around the world. Includes information on educational outreach, year-round exhibitions, and its permanent collection.

Memphis, University of, Egyptian Artifacts Exhibit
The University of Memphis Campus
Memphis, TN 38152
Phone: (901) 678-2224
URL: (WWW address): http://www.memst.edu/egypt/main.html
Site description: Visitor can take a brief "Tour of Egypt" and view a 4000-year-old loaf of bread from the mortuary temple of Mentuhotep II at Dein al Behari in Western Thebes.

Michael C. Carlos Museum (Emory University)
571 S. King St.
Atlanta, GA 30322
Phone: (404) 727-4282
URL: (WWW address): http://www.emory.edu/CARLOS/
Site description: Described as "the best virtual tour of a museum outside of the Louvre." It includes a video.

Minneapolis Institute of Arts
2400 Third Ave.
S. Minneapolis, MN 55404
Phone: (612) 870-3000
URL: (WWW address): http://www.arts MIA.org
Site description: The museum offers information about its collections, exhibits, and programs. Includes images ranging from African Art to 20th century post-modern.

Norton Simon Museum
411 W. Colorado Blvd.
Pasadena, CA 91105
Phone: (818) 449-6840
URL: (WWW address): http://www.citycent.com/ccc/Pasadena/nsmuseum.html
Site description: Images include works of Rembrandt, Goya, and Picasso, along with some examples of South Asian sculpture and Impressionist art.

Palmer Museum of Art, The (Penn State University)
Curtin Road
University Park, PA 16802-2507
Phone: (814) 865-7672
URL: (WWW address): http://www.cac.psu.edu/~mtd120/palmer/
Site description: This site contains painting images and includes a link to an art class via computer. Considered an example of an excellent Internet site plan and design.

Panhandle-Plains Museum (West Texas A&M University)
2401 Fourth Ave.
Canyon, TX 79015
Phone: (806) 656-2244
URL: (WWW address): http://www.webtex.com/webtex/museum
Site description: Images of cowboys, Indians, gunfighters, and ranchers out of the Old West. The site is dedicated to the preservation of the northwest Texas heritage.

Phoenix Art Museum
1625 N. Central Ave.
Phoenix, AZ 85004
Phone: (602) 257-1880
URL: (WWW address): http://www.azcentral.com/community/phx art/home.html
Site description: Site includes an on-line museum map pointing to areas with art images that can be viewed.

Portland Art Museum
1219 S. W. Park Ave.
Portland, OR 97205
Phone: (503) 226-2811
URL: (WWW address): http://www.pam.org/pam/
Site description: A rotating on-line tour of the collection of this encyclopedic art museum.

San Diego Museum of Art
1450 El Prado-Balboa Park
San Diego, CA 92112
Phone: (619) 232-7931
URL: (WWW address): http://www.sddt.com/sdma.html/
Site description: This site includes works from the Far East, South Asia, Europe, and the U.S. Numerous links to art resources on the Web.

Smart Museum of Art
5550 S. Greenwood Ave.
Chicago, IL 60637
Phone: (773) 702-0200
URL: (WWW address): http://csmaclab-www.uchicago.edu/Smart Museum
Site description: Located at the University of Chicago, this museum has an on-line catalog, a virtual tour, news, and a summary of its collection. Includes a video of kids giving talks about art.

Southwest Museum
234 Museum Dr.
Los Angeles, CA 90065
Phone: (213) 221-2164
URL: (WWW address): http://www.annex.com/southwest/museum.htm
Site description: Site of a collection related to native cultures of the Americas. Includes images of Prehispanic, Spanish Colonial, Latino, and Western American art and artifacts.

Spencer Museum of Arts
University of Kansas
Lawrence, KS 66045
Phone: (913) 864-4710
URL: (WWW address): http://www.ukans.edu/~sma/prints.html
Site description: The University's print collection is available at this site. Contains detailed information about prints.

INTERNET ART RESOURCES

American Memory
URL: (WWW address): http://rsb.loc.gov/amhome.htm
Site description: Hosted by the Library of Congress this site includes collections of art and items relating to American culture and history.

ArtsEdNet
URL: (WWW address): http://www.artsednet.getty.edu/
Site description: Art educators resource sponsored by the Getty Center for Education in the Arts. Contains images, lesson plans, Web gateways, and a search engine.

Native American Fine Arts Movement
URL: (WWW address): http://www.heard.org/EDU/NAFAMRG/full.html
Site description: A resource guide for the Native American Fine Arts Movement.

Eyes on Art
URL: (WWW address): http://www.kn.pacbell.com/wired/art/art.html
Site description: A variety of study guides and art activities for students and teachers.

Art Education Resources
URL: (WWW address): http://www.umass.edu/education/links/art.html
Site description: Well-constructed link to many, many art education resources.

ArtResources (Ferguson-Taylor Group)
URL: (WWW address): http://www.ftgi.com
Site description: A basic art search engine. Gateway to Internet ArtResources.

Crayola
URL: (WWW address): http://www.crayola.com
Site description: Contains education links and art resources.

Kennedy Center for Education In the Arts
URL: (WWW address): http://www.artsedge.kennedy-center.org/
Site description: Lesson plans, curriculum resources, and on-line communication tool for the art teacher. Site contains a catalog of arts education materials and a search capability.

Internet ArtResources
URL: (WWW address): http://www.artresources.com/
Site description: This site is a powerful link to over 1100 museums, galleries, and institutions. It can serve as a starting point for a virtual trip to almost anywhere.

Library of Congress
URL: (WWW address): http://www.loc.gov
Site description: Contains list of databases.

The Incredible Art Department
URL: (WWW address): http://www.in.net/~/kenroar/
Site description: Lesson plans, careers, art news, art images, and more.

Museum Resource Guides
URL: (WWW address): http://www.ucmp.berkeley.edu/subway/musreguide.html
Site description: This site is a valuable navigation aid. A valuable tool to acquire Internet educational resources.

World Wide Arts Resources
URL: (WWW address): http://wwar.com
Site description: A complete listing of arts resources worldwide.

VIRTUAL MUSEUMS (Collections)

Dale Chihuly
URL: (WWW address): http://www.chihuly.com
Site description: The works in glass of America's first National Living Treasure are here.

Diego Rivera Museum, The
URL: (WWW address): http://www.diegorivera.com/diego_home_eng.html
Site description: A virtual museum devoted to the works of Mexican artist Diego Rivera.

Erte Museum – Art Deco
URL: (WWW address): http://www.webcom.com/ajarts/erte.html
Site description: The artist famous for his role in the Art Deco style is represented here. Images of his costume designs are included here.

Mesa Arts Center – Galeria Mesa (Arizona)
URL: (WWW address): http://aztec.asu.edu/AandE/mac5.html
Site description: Images of the most current rotating exhibits are accessible.

Korean American Museum of Art and Cultural Center (KOMA) (CA)
URL: (WWW address): http://koma.org/
Site description: This virtual museum offers information and images of Korean art, including historical background.

Leonardo da Vinci Museum
URL: (WWW address): http://www.leonardo.net/main.html/
Site description: Voted one of the top ten sites on the Web. Images of paintings, drawings, and a historical perspective are included.

New York Museums Home Page
URL: (WWW address): http://www.museumsny.com
Site description: Museums New York provides a tour of various exhibits happening in the city and profiles the work of famous New York artists.

World of Escher
URL: (WWW address): http://www.texas.net/escher/

WebMuseum, Paris
URL: (WWW address): http://sunsite.unc.edu/wm/
Site description: From Paris! A vast collection of images and art resources from museums the world over.

World Art Treasures
URL: (WWW address): http://sgwww.epfl.ch/BERGER/index.html
Site description: Collection of paintings, sculptures and decorative art, representing all movements and periods. A variety of useful links.

Art Connections
Elements and Principles of Art
Scope and Sequence

Elements of Art	Level K						Level 1						Level 2					
	U1	U2	U3	U4	U5	U6	U1	U2	U3	U4	U5	U6	U1	U2	U3	U4	U5	U6
Color			1–6						1–6						1–6			
Form				2–6						1–6				1–3, 6				
Line	1–6						1–6						1–4					
Shape		1–6							1–6				5–6					
Space					1					2, 6					4–5			
Texture					1–6						1–4						4–6	
Value															2–4			

Principles of Art																		
Balance					1–2							3				1–3 6		
Emphasis											1–2					5		
Harmony																		1 4–6
Movement and Rhythm				3–6						5–6					1–6			
Proportion																		
Unity					6						4–6							4–6
Variety																		2–3, 5

★ Numbers indicate lesson numbers within given unit.

Elements of Art	Level 3						Level 4						Level 5					
	U1	U2	U3	U4	U5	U6	U1	U2	U3	U4	U5	U6	U1	U2	U3	U4	U5	U6
Color		1–6							1–6					1–4, 6				
Form			4–6							1–6					4–6			
Line	1–2						1–6						1–4					
Shape	3–6							1–2					2					
Space			1–3								1–4				1–2		4–6	
Texture					1–3						5–6				3–6			
Value		1							2, 5–6				3–6					

Principles of Art	U1	U2	U3	U4	U5	U6	U1	U2	U3	U4	U5	U6	U1	U2	U3	U4	U5	U6
Balance			1–4									1–3					1–3	
Emphasis			5–6									5						1–2
Harmony					1, 3–4							4						4–5
Movement & Rhythm				4–6				3–6						5–6				
Proportion																1–6		
Unity					4–6							6						5–6
Variety					2–4							5						3–5

Art Connections
Media Scope and Sequence

Media	Level K						Level 1						Level 2					
	U1	U2	U3	U4	U5	U6	U1	U2	U3	U4	U5	U6	U1	U2	U3	U4	U5	U6
Collage	4–5	2	2–3	1	1	6		1, 6	2, 5		1	1, 4	5	4		6	1	1–3
Drawing	2, 6	1, 3–5	1, 4–5	3	2	1, 3, 6	1, 4–6	4–6	1, 4–5	6	2, 4	3, 5–6	2–3	4–5	5–6	1–2, 5	2	
Fiber Arts	4				4, 6						5	2					4–5	
Mixed Media			4, 5	5	3			5		5			2–3	5	5	2, 5–6	6	4, 6
Painting	1, 3	3, 6	4–6	5		2, 4–5	2–3	2–3, 5	3, 6	5–6	4, 6	4	2–4	5	1–5	2, 3, 5	2, 3	4, 6
Photography																		
Printmaking					5						6				1	3–4		
Three-Dimensional Forms				2–6	3, 5					1–5	3		1, 6	1–3, 6			3, 6	5–6

★ Numbers indicate lesson numbers within given unit.

Media	Level 3						Level 4						Level 5					
	U1	U2	U3	U4	U5	U6	U1	U2	U3	U4	U5	U6	U1	U2	U3	U4	U5	U6
Collage	4	3, 6		3, 6	1, 5	3		1, 4	2–3				1, 6	3–4	3	2	3	
Drawing	1–2, 5–6	1, 4–6	2–5	1–2, 5–6	2–6	3–4, 6	1–6	1–6	1–6	2–5	1–3	1–4, 6	2–5	1–2, 5–6	1–5	1, 3–4, 6	2, 4–6	2–3, 5
Fiber Arts					2	2					5							1–2
Mixed Media		3, 6	6		1, 3 6	4–5				4, 6	1, 6	1, 4, 6	1			5	3	4, 6
Painting	2–3	2, 5–6	1–2	2, 4	4, 6	4–5	6	2, 3, 5	2 4–6	4	1, 3, 6	1–2, 4	2	1–2 5–6		5	2	4
Photography											4		6					
Printmaking			1		4, 6			3									1	
Three-Dimensional Forms		4	4–6	2–3		1			1–5		4–6				6	5–6		4–6

GLOSSARY

A

Abstract art Twentieth-century art containing shapes that simplify shapes of real objects to emphasize form instead of subject matter.

Abstract Expressionism Painting style developed after World War II in New York City that stressed elements and principles of art as subject matter and emotion rather than planned design. Abstract Expressionism is also called action painting because artists applied paint freely to huge canvases.

active lines Lines that show action and add energy to a work of art. Diagonal, zigzag, and curved lines are active lines.

additive sculpture A type of sculpture to which something is added. The sculpture may be relief or freestanding.

alternate rhythm (alternating rhythm) When one motif is repeated after a second, different motif.

analogous color scheme A color scheme using colors that are side by side on the color wheel.

analogous colors Colors that are side by side on the color wheel.

ant's view Viewers feel they are looking up toward an object or figure.

appliqué Art made by attaching fabric shapes onto a fabric background by gluing or sewing.

approximate symmetry When both sides of a design are almost exactly the same. Approximate symmetry is a type of formal balance.

architect A person who plans and designs buildings, cities, and bridges.

architecture The art of designing and planning the construction of buildings, cities, and bridges.

armature A framework for supporting material used in sculpting.

art form A type of art.

assemblage A technique in which an artist collects found materials and assembles them into a three-dimensional work of art. A work of art in which a variety of objects are assembled to create one complete piece.

asymmetry Another name for informal balance. Asymmetry is a way of organizing parts of a design so that unlike objects have equal visual weight.

B

background The part of the picture plane that seems to be farthest from the viewer.

balance The principle of design that deals with visual weight in a work of art.

Baroque Artistic style that emphasized movement, strong value contrast, and variety. It developed after the Reformation in the seventeenth century. Artists used movement of forms and figures toward the viewer, dramatic lighting effects, contrast between dark and light, ornamentation, and curved lines to express energy and strong emotions.

batik A way to design fabric using wax and dyes.

bird's-eye view Viewers feel they are looking down on a scene.

black ■■■■■

blind contour A type of drawing done by looking at the object being drawn and not at the paper.

blue ■■■■■

body proportions Ratios of one part of the body to another.

bookmaking The art of binding or tying pages together inside a cover.

bright color A pure spectral color.

broken (line) A line interrupted by space.

brown ■■■■■

building Places where we live, work, meet, and play.

Byzantine Artistic style that developed around the city of Constantinople (now Istanbul, Turkey) in the eastern Roman Empire. The style blended Roman, Greek, and Oriental art. It featured very rich colors and figures that were flat and stiff. These works blended Greek, Roman, and Asian styles and usually had a religious theme.

C

carving Cutting away of a hard material like wood or marble to create a three-dimensional work of art.

center of interest Area of an artwork that a viewer immediately looks at first.

central axis An imaginary vertical line that splits a work of art in half. The central axis is used in formal balance.

circle A shape where all points are equidistant from the center.

Classical Referring to the art of ancient Greece and Rome. The Greeks created art based on the ideals of perfect proportion and logic instead of emotion. The Romans adapted Greek art and spread it throughout the civilized world.

close-up Viewers feel they are right next to the object or are a part of the action in a picture.

collage Bits and pieces of things glued onto paper.

Color-Field Painting Twentieth-century style of painting using flat areas of color for the pure sensation of color. Artists creating color-field paintings are not trying to express emotion or use a precise design.

color intensity The brightness or dullness of a color.

color scheme A plan for organizing the colors used in an artwork.

color spectrum Range of colors that come from light.

color wheel A design for organizing colors that shows the spectrum bent into a circle.

complementary color Colors that are opposite each other on the color wheel.

complementary color scheme A color scheme that uses complementary colors.

complex geometric shape A shape made by combining simple geometric shapes such as triangles, squares, and rectangles.

contour The edge or surface ridges of an object or figure.

contour drawing A drawing in which only contour lines are used.

contour lines Lines that show the edges and surface ridges of an object.

contrast A difference created when elements are placed next to each other in a work of art.

cool color A color that seems to move away from the viewer and suggests coolness. Green, blue, and violet are cool colors.

cool hues Blue, green, and violet. Another name for *cool colors*.

cross-hatching A shading technique in which two or more sets of parallel lines cross each other.

Cubism Twentieth-century art movement that emphasizes structure and design. Three-dimensional objects are pictured from many different points of view at the same time.

culture How a group of people thinks, believes, and acts.

curved A line that bends and changes direction slowly.

D

Dadaists Early twentieth-century artists using fantastic and strange objects as subject matter.

darker Having more black in a color.

deckle A framed screen used for papermaking.

depth The appearance of distance on a flat surface.

De Stijl Dutch for "the style." A painting style developed by Mondrian in Holland in the early twentieth century that uses only vertical and horizontal lines; black, white, and gray; and the three primary colors.

diagonal (line) A slanted line.

diamond A four-sided shape made by combining two triangles.

difference The state of being not the same.

dimension Measurement in height, width, or depth.

direct observation Technique when artists study an object from various viewpoints, looking closely at the important details, and recording those details in their drawings.

distortion Stretching an object or figure out of normal shape so that it does not appear real. Distortion is used to communicate ideas or feelings.

dominant element The element that is noticed first in a work of art.

dull color A low-intensity color that has been subdued by the addition of its complement, brown, gray, etc.

E

emphasis The principle of design that makes one part of the artwork stand out more than the other parts.

emphasize To make something look important.

environmental art Art that is created to be part of a landscape.

even balance Both halves are equal. Left side and right side are the same.

exaggerate Make much larger than actual size.

exaggeration Increasing or enlarging an object or a figure or one of its parts to communicate ideas or feelings.

Expressionism Twentieth-century art movement in which artists tried to communicate their strong emotional feelings and which stressed personal feelings rather than composition.

F

fabric Cloth.

facial proportions The relationship of one feature of a face to another feature.

faraway Viewers feel they are standing faraway from the scene.

fiber Thin, thread-like material generally used to make yarn and woven fabrics.

flowing rhythm Rhythm that repeats curved lines or shapes.

focal point The area of an artwork that is emphasized.

foreground The part of the picture plane that appears closest to the viewer.

form Any object that can be measured in three ways: length, width, and depth.

formal balance A way of organizing a design so that equal or very similar elements are placed on opposite sides of an imaginary, central dividing line.

found materials Any items found in your home, school, or outdoor environment that can be used to create new works of art.

free-form (shape) An irregular and uneven shape. Any shape that is not geometric.

freestanding (sculpture) A three-dimensional sculpture that has empty, negative space all around; a type of sculpture that is surrounded by space on all sides.

freestanding assemblage A type of assemblage that has space all around it. Freestanding assemblage is meant to be viewed from all sides.

frozen motion When one action is frozen in time.

functional form Objects created by artists for use in daily life.

Futurists Early twentieth-century Italian artists who arranged angular forms to suggest motion. They called the forces of movement dynamism.

G

geometric A math shape, such as a circle, triangle, rectangle, or square.

geometric form A three-dimensional figure that has precise measurement and can be described in mathematical terms, such as a sphere, a cube, or a pyramid.

geometric shape A figure that has precise measurements and can be described in mathematical terms, such as a circle, a square, a triangle, or a rectangle.

gesture An expressive movement.

gesture lines Lines quickly drawn to capture the movement of a person, animal, or object in a painting or drawing.

gesture sketch A quick sketch to capture movement or action of an object.

Gothic Artistic style developed in western Europe between the twelfth and sixteenth centuries. Gothic cathedrals used pointed arches and flying buttresses to emphasize upward movement and featured stained-glass windows. Sculpture and painting showed humans realistically.

gradation A gradual change of one value to another.

green ▬▬▬

guidelines Lines that help an artist place things in a work of art.

H

harmonious When things seem to go together.

harmony The principle of design that creates unity by stressing similarities of separate but related parts; a pleasing relationship between parts of an artwork.

hatching A shading technique using a series of repeated parallel lines.

height How tall something is.

hexagon A six-sided shape.

highlight Small area of white used to show the very brightest spot on an object.

horizon line The point at which the earth and sky meet.

horizontal A line that moves from side to side.

hue Another word for color.

I

images The things you see in an artwork.

imitated texture A kind of visual texture that imitates real texture by using a two-dimensional pattern to create the illusion of a three-dimensional surface.

implied line A series of points that are connected by the viewer's eyes.

Impressionism Style of painting started in France in the 1860s. It captured everyday subjects and emphasized the momentary effects of sunlight.

informal balance A way of organizing parts of a design so that unlike objects have equal visual weight.

intensity The brightness or dullness of a color.

interior designer An artist who designs the insides of buildings and their furnishings, such as carpeting, furniture, and drapes.

intermediate color One of six colors that are made when a primary color is mixed with a secondary color.

intermediate hue Made by mixing a primary hue with a secondary hue. Another name for *intermediate color.*

invented texture A kind of visual texture that does not represent a real texture, but creates the sensation of one.

isolation When an object is placed alone and away from all the other objects in an artwork.

J

jeweler An artist who designs and makes jewelry.

jewelry Three-dimensional art that is made for people to wear.

L

lighter Having more white in a color.

line A mark drawn by a tool such as a pencil, pen, or paintbrush as it moves across a surface.

line variation Changes in the look of a line.

line variety Lines may be short or long, thick or thin, rough or smooth.

linear perspective A way of using lines to show distance and depth.

location When the eyes are naturally drawn toward the center of an artwork.

M

mandala A radial design divided into sections or wedges, each of which contains an image.

Mannerism European sixteenth-century artistic style featuring highly emotional scenes and distorted figures.

mask Three-dimensional art form of a sculpted face, often made to be worn over the face.

matte Textured surfaces that reflect a soft light, with an almost dull look.

Medieval Related to the *Middle Ages.*

Middle Ages Period of roughly one thousand years from the destruction of the Roman Empire to the *Renaissance.* Culture centered around the Church. The Middle Ages are also called the Dark Ages (because few new ideas developed) and the Age of Faith (because religion was a powerful force).

middle ground Area in a picture between the foreground and background.

minimal detail Very little detail in a drawing.

mola An artwork in reverse appliqué when layers are cut away after stitching, and is sometimes added to clothing.

Glossary   **T39**

monochromatic Using one color plus all the tints and shades of that color.

monochromatic color scheme A color scheme using one color plus all the tints and shades of that color.

mood How an artwork makes you feel.

mosaic A picture made by setting small pieces of colored tile, glass, or stone side by side.

motif Shape or object that is repeated.

movement The look of constant motion in a work of art.

mural A large work of art painted on a wall.

N

negative space The empty space that surrounds objects, shapes, and forms in an artwork.

Neoclassicism New classic. French artistic style developed in the nineteenth century after the *Rococo* style. It used *classical* features and was unemotional and realistic.

neutral color scheme A color scheme using only neutral colors.

neutral colors Black, white and gray.

New Realism Twentieth century artistic style in which artists tried to create the impression of movement on the surface of paintings with hard edges, smooth surfaces, and mathematical planning.

nonobjective painting A painting with no recognizable subject matter.

O

observation brush drawing The first sketch done with brush and watercolors.

observation drawing A drawing made while looking at a person or object.

octagon An eight-sided shape.

one-point perspective One way of using lines to show distance and depth, with all lines that move back into space meeting at one point.

Op Art Optical art. Twentieth century artistic style in which artists tried to create the impression of movement on the surface of paintings with hard edges, smooth surfaces, and mathematical planning.

orange ▬▬▬

outline A line that marks the outside of an object

overlap When one object covers part of a second object.

P

painting A type of art in which paint is applied to a flat surface, such as paper, canvas or silk.

parallelogram A shape with four sides; opposite sides are parallel and equal in length.

pattern The use of shapes, colors, or lines repeated in a planned way.

pentagon A five-sided shape.

perception The act of looking at something carefully and thinking deeply about what is seen.

perspective techniques Techniques used by artists to create the feeling of depth on a flat surface.

photographer Artist who takes pictures with a camera.

picture plane The surface of a drawing or painting.

point of view The position from which the viewer looks at an object.

Pop art Artistic style used in the early 1960s in America featuring subject matter from popular culture (mass media, commercial art, comic strips, and advertising).

portrait A picture of a person.

position Placement of elements in a work of art.

positive space The area in a work of art that shapes and objects fill.

Post-Impressionism French painting style of the late nineteenth century that used basic structures of art to express feelings and ideas. The Post-Impressionism movement, which immediately followed *Impressionism,* was led by Paul Cézanne, Vincent van Gogh, and Paul Gauguin.

Prehistoric Period before history was written down.

primary color One of the three basic colors: red, yellow, and blue.

Primary colors cannot be made by mixing other colors.

primary hue One of the three basic hues: red, yellow, and blue. Primary hues cannot be made by mixing other hues.

printing Pressing a shape from one thing to another many times.

profile proportions The relationship of one feature of a face to another feature when looking from the side view.

progressive To change or move forward.

progressive motion When a scene or motif changes a little each time it is repeated.

progressive reversal When an object starts out as one object or form and slowly changes into another object or form.

progressive rhythm When a motif changes each time it is repeated.

proportion Principle of art concerned with the size relationships of one part to another.

purple ▬▬▬

R

radial balance When the elements in a design come out from a central point.

radiate To come out from a central point.

rainbow Red, orange, yellow, green, blue, and purple curved into a semicircle.

random rhythm Motifs that appear in no apparent order and have irregular spaces between them.

ratio A comparison of size between two things.

real texture Texture you can feel.

Realism Mid-nineteenth-century artistic style in which artists turned away from the style of Romanticism to paint familiar scenes as they actually were.

realistic scale Where everything seems to fit together and make sense in size relation in a work of art.

Realists Artists in the nineteenth century who portrayed political, social, and moral issues.

rectangle A four-sided shape in which opposite sides are parallel and equal in length, and each corner forms a right angle.

red ▬▬▬

Regionalists Artists who painted the farmlands and cities of America realistically.

regular rhythm Visual rhythm that is created by repeating the same motif with equal amounts of space in between.

relief assemblage A type of assemblage where objects stick out from one side only.

relief print A technique in which the design to be printed is raised from the background.

relief sculpture A type of sculpture from which objects stick out of a flat surface.

Renaissance The name given to the period of awakening at the end of the *Middle Ages.* French for "rebirth." Interest in *Classical* art was renewed. Important Renaissance artists are Leonardo da Vinci, Michelangelo, and Raphael.

repeated lines Lines that are repeated give the feeling of movement or motion.

repeated shapes Shapes that are repeated several times give the feeling of motion.

repetition When an artist repeats lines, colors, or textures.

rhythm The repetition of lines, shapes, or colors to create a feeling of movement.

Rococo Eighteenth-century artistic style that began in the luxurious homes of the French aristocracy and spread to the rest of Europe. It stressed free, graceful movement, a playful use of line, and delicate colors.

Romanesque Style of architecture and sculpture developed during the Middle Ages in western Europe that featured massive size; solid, heavy walls; wide use of the rounded Roman arch; and many sculptural decorations.

Romanticism Early nineteenth-century artistic style that was a reaction against *Neoclassicism*. It featured dramatic scenes, bright colors, loose compositions, and exotic settings. It also emphasized the feelings and personality of the artist.

rough Texture that reflects light unevenly.

rough line An uneven, bumpy line.

S

sarcophagus A mummy case.

scale Size as measured against a standard reference.

sculptor An artist who makes sculpture.

sculpture A three-dimensional work of art.

secondary color The mixture of two primary colors. Orange, green, and violet are secondary colors.

secondary hue Orange, green, or violet. Another name for *secondary color*.

shade Any dark value of a color.

shading A technique for darkening values by adding black or darkening an area by repeating several lines close together.

shadows Shaded, or darker, areas in a drawing or painting.

shape A flat, two-dimensional figure.

shape reversal When a shape or positive space starts out as one image and then, in another image, turns into the negative space.

shiny Texture that reflects a bright light.

silhouette The shape of a shadow.

simplicity A method of creating unity by using only one color, shape, or texture in a work of art.

simulated texture A kind of visual texture that imitates tactile texture by using a two-dimensional pattern to create the illusion of a three-dimensional surface.

slanted line A line moving at an angle to the picture plane, not horizontal or vertical.

smooth Texture that reflects light evenly.

smooth line A line that has an even surface, free from irregularities.

solid form A three-dimensional object, having height, width, and depth.

solid (line) An unbroken line.

solid shape A three-dimensional object, having height, width, and depth.

space The element of art that refers to the area between, around, above, below, and within an object.

spectral color One of the six colors of the rainbow. Red, orange, yellow, green, blue, and violet are spectral colors.

spectral color scheme A color scheme using the colors of the spectrum.

square A shape with four equal sides that form right angles.

still life Collection of objects that do not move.

stippling A shading technique using dots. The closer the dots, the darker the area.

stitchery Art made with yarn on cloth.

Stone Age Period of history during which stone tools were used.

straight line A line that does not curve or bend.

subject What the artwork is about.

subtractive sculpture A type of sculpture made from carving a form. The original material is taken away, or subtracted.

Surrealism Twentieth-century artistic style in which dreams, fantasy, and the subconscious served as inspiration for artists.

swirling line A line that curves in a circular motion and creates a sense of movement in a work of art.

symmetry A type of formal balance in which two halves of an object or composition are mirror images of each other.

T

tactile texture The element of art that refers to how things actually feel when you touch it.

tessellation A type of shape reversal that changes quickly and fits together like a puzzle.

texture The element of art that refers to how things feel, or look as if they might feel, if touched.

thick (line) A wide line.

thin (line) A narrow line.

three-dimensional (3-D form) Something that can be measured by height, width, and depth.

tint Any light value of a color.

trapezoid A shape with four sides, only two of which are parallel.

triangle A three-sided shape.

Trompe l'oeil French for "deceive the eye." Style of painting in which painters try to give the viewer the illusion of seeing a three-dimensional object so that the viewer wonders whether he or she is seeing a picture or something real.

two-dimensional (shape) A flat figure that can only be measured by height and width.

U

unity The feeling of wholeness or oneness that is accomplished by properly using the elements and principles of art.

unrealistic scale When size relationships do not make sense in a work of art.

V

value The lightness or darkness of a color or object.

vanishing point The point on the horizon line where all the lines moving back into a space seem to meet.

variety The use of different lines, shapes, and colors in artwork.

vertical (line) A line that moves up and down.

visual movement Visual rhythm that pulls the viewer's eyes through a work of art.

visual pattern Pattern created by the repetition of shapes, colors or lines.

visual rhythm Rhythm created by the repetition of shapes, colors or lines.

visual texture The way something looks like it might feel if you could touch it.

visual weight Weight of elements in a work of art seen with your eyes.

W

warm color Color that seems to move toward the viewer and suggests warmth and energy. Red, orange, and yellow are warm colors.

warm hues Yellow, orange, and red. Another name for *warm colors*.

warp threads Vertical threads attached to a loom.

weaving Creating fabric by criss-crossing.

weft threads Threads that are woven over and under the warp threads.

white ◯

width How wide something is.

Y

yellow ▭

Z

zigzag (line) Diagonal lines that connect and change direction sharply.

PROGRAM INDEX

Items referenced are coded by Grade Level and page number.

T42

ART ACROSS THE CURRICULUM INDEX

Items referenced are coded by Grade Level and page number.

T48